THE JAPANESE FIRM

THE JAPANESE FIRM

The Sources of Competitive Strength

Edited by

MASAHIKO AOKI

AND

RONALD DORE

OXFORD UNIVERSITY PRESS

Oxford University Press, Walton Street, Oxford OX2 6DP

Oxford New York Toronto
Delhi Bombay Calcutta Madras Karachi
Kuala Lumpur Singapore Hong Kong Tokyo
Nairobi Dar es Salaam Cape Town
Melbourne Auckland Madrid

and associated companies in
Berlin Ibadan

Oxford is a trade mark of Oxford University Press

Published in the United States
by Oxford University Press Inc., New York

British Library Cataloguing in Publication Data
Data available

Library of Congress Cataloging in Publication Data
The Japanese firm: the sources of competitive strength / edited
by Masahiko Aoki and Ronald Dore.
p. cm.
Includes bibliographical references.
1. Corporations—Japan. 2. Industrial organization—Japan.
I. Aoki, Masahiko, 1938– . II. Dore, Ronald Philip.
HD2907.J347 1994   93–37583
338.7'0952—dc20
ISBN 0–19–828815–8

3 5 7 9 10 8 6 4

Typeset by Selwood Systems, Midsomer Norton
Printed in Great Britain on acid-free paper by
Bookcraft Ltd., Midsomer Norton, Avon

FOREWORD

With a considerable lag, Japan's importance to the world economy has begun to leave its imprint in the curricula of universities in the West. Most leading US undergraduate and graduate institutions now offer courses on the Japanese economy. Several general textbooks and selections of readings for college students have been published to meet the increasing demand.

This is all valuable, but the next step is more important, and much harder to achieve: to integrate the study of Japan's economy into our core courses of economics and business administration. Students of economics should understand not only the role of the Federal Reserve Bank and the Bundesbank but also that of the Bank of Japan, and they should be familiar not only with the institutions active on Wall Street and in the City of London, but also with those operating in Kabutocho. Business school students should encounter not only cases developed based on the experiences of IBM and Caterpillar but also those taking the perspective of Fujitsu and Komatsu as well as those of Siemens and ABB. Such integration is a prerequisite for the true internationalization of our educational institutions. It is in this process that the present volume will prove its importance.

The contributors to this book clearly demonstrate that the integration of the study of the Japanese economy has proceeded much further in research than in teaching. Only a decade ago the study of Japan's economy was a separate field attracting a small number of specialists. Today much of the academic work on this topic is done in the mainstream of the disciplines of economics and business administration. Studies based on Japanese data now play an important role in the development of both the empirical and the theoretical bases. In the process many Western researchers have spent considerable time in Japan and acquired in-depth knowledge of various aspects of the Japanese economy. Indeed, a number of scholars close to the core of their respective disciplines, but not specialized in the study of Japan, have made significant contributions to our knowledge of Japan in recent years.

In fact, as noted by one of the authors in this volume, the study of the Japanese economy has been a remarkably successful area of research in the last decade. By now we know that what brought Japan economic success was much less of a 'miracle', at least in the supernatural or divine sense of the word, but more a matter of institutional design at all levels from the central administration down to the shop floor. Many of the traits widely perceived as uniquely Japanese were, in fact, imported from the West relatively recently and integrated into existing institutional arrangements. We have also learned that the Japanese economy is much more diverse, and much more competitive, than previously portrayed.

This volume also illustrates how the nature of the academic study of the Japanese economy has changed during this decade. Whereas the research in the 1970s and early 1980s described individual traits of economic and social institutions in Japan, the contributions in this volume focus on the interconnectedness of various institutional arrangements. Most of the authors also explicitly take a comparative perspective including data from the United States and Europe in their analyses. While much of the earlier academic work was static in nature, many of the following chapters emphasize the dynamic properties of the studied institutions — how they adjust to changes in their environment and how they generate and incorporate new knowledge to achieve sustained economic growth. In addition, the various contributions provide ample evidence of the increasingly inter-disciplinary nature of this literature: the authors with economics backgrounds use methods from other disciplines, and those trained in sociology and behavioural sciences frequently rely on concepts from modern economics.

It should be noted, however, that much of the progress in academic research on the Japanese economy and the introduction of this work into the university curricula have taken place in the United States. Until recently there has been a conspicuous lack of academic research on the Japanese economy in Europe. This ignorance is reflected also in policy-related circles, and in the business community. In general, Japanese language skills are very rare, and first-hand experience of Japanese society is confined to a small group of specialists.

There are, nevertheless, encouraging signs that the situation in Europe is improving. As in the United States, the penetration of Japanese products in important market segments has gradually made the European public aware of the importance of Japan in the world economy. In Sweden, we see this interest being reflected in a surge of students wishing to learn Japanese and to devote their university studies to Japan and East Asia. At the Stockholm School of Economics, a number of students are admitted each year partly because of their skills in the Japanese language. Growing numbers of students take courses on Japanese and East Asian economic affairs as part of the requirements for their degrees. We send students to study at leading universities in Japan, and we receive some—albeit few—Japanese students every year as part of our international student exchange programme.

We see the creation of the European Institute of Japanese Studies as a most important and ambitious part of our strategy. The Institute aims to be a centre of excellence in research and education on the Japanese and East Asian economies and enterprises, on their impact on the world economy, and especially in regard to Euro-Japanese relations. As the Euro-Japanese relationship has often, rightly, been described as the weak link in the world economy, a major goal of the Institute is to fill the Euro-Japanese 'knowledge gap'. With the field of Japanese economic and business studies in the West having been dominated by American scholars, the greater insertion of the European dimension should further contribute both to a deeper comparative perspective for the analysis of Japan and to an understanding of the cultural dynamics of the global economic and business environments.

At the Stockholm School of Economics we are deeply honoured by the dedication of this excellent book to our efforts to promote the study of the Japanese economy. However, all credit should really go to the editors of this volume, Professors Masahiko Aoki and Ronald Dore.

Professors Aoki and Dore have played major roles in improving the general understanding of the Japanese economy. Professor Aoki has worked from within the paradigm of modern economics to open it up to incorporate insights from neighbouring disciplines. From his standpoint as a sociologist with deep insights into the workings of economic organizations in Japan, Professor Dore has approached economics from the outside, questioning many of its basic assumptions and methods. When we asked these two pioneers in the study of the Japanese economy to serve as co-chairmen for our conference 'Japan in a Global Economy: A European Perspective', we hoped for a fruitful interaction between their respective fields of research. The high quality and interesting content of the contributions to this volume has proved us right.

We owe deep gratitude to Professors Aoki and Dore for their relentless efforts to bring together such a distinguished group of scholars on the Japanese economy. Without their enthusiasm, the conference, let alone this book, would never have been possible.

Many thanks should also be given to the Prince Bertil Foundation at the Stockholm School of Economics which made it financially possible to organize this important conference.

STØFFAN BURENSTAM LINDER
Stockholm
February 1993

PREFACE

The inspiration for this volume was a most stimulating conference at the Stockholm School of Economics in September 1991, attended by a wide range of leading academic students of Japan from four continents. It was a 'pre-foundation conference' for the European Institute for Japanese Studies and ten of the fourteen papers of this volume were first given there. The Institute was formally opened at the School a year later. We would like to dedicate this volume to that Institute and to its founder Dr Staffan Burenstam Linder. We congratulate them on an important initiative, and look forward to its growth as a centre of excellence and a source of new insights into 'how Japan works'.

We would like to thank the organizers of the Stockholm conference, Dr Thomas Andersson and Dr Erik Berglöf. Acknowledgement is also due to the editors and publishers of those of the papers in this volume which have earlier appeared in journals. The papers are Chapter 9 (Hidetoshi Ito) *Ricerche Economiche* 45, 1991, 345–76, and Chapter 13 (Tetsuji Okazaki) *Journal of the Japanese and International Economies* 7, 1993, 175–203.

LIST OF CONTRIBUTORS

MASAHIKO AOKI, Takahashi Professor of Japanese Studies, Department of Economics, Stanford University.

BANRI ASANUMA, Dean, Faculty of Economics, Kyoto University.

ROBERT COLE, Professor, Haas School of Business Administration, University of California, Berkeley.

RONALD DORE, Research Fellow, Centre for Economic Performance, London School of Economics, and Adjunct Professor, Department of Political Science, Massachusetts Institute of Technology.

TAKEO HOSHI, Assistant Professor, Graduate School of International Relations and Pacific Studies, University of California, San Diego.

HIDESHI ITOH, Associate Professor, Faculty of Economics, Kyoto University.

KAZUO KOIKE, Professor, Faculty of Economics, Hosei University.

YOSHIO NISHI, Silicon Process Laboratory, Hewlett Packard, California.

TETSUJI OKAZAKI, Associate Professor, Faculty of Economics, University of Tokyo.

DANIEL OKIMOTO, Professor, Department of Political Science, Stanford University.

MARI SAKO, Senior Lecturer, Industrial Relations Department, London School of Economics.

PAUL SHEARD, International Cooperation Associate Professor, Faculty of Economics, Osaka University and Lecturer, Department of Economics, Australian National University.

D. ELEANOR WESTNEY, Professor, Department of Political Science, Massachusetts Institute of Technology.

D. HUGH WHITTAKER, Lecturer, Faculty of Oriental Studies, Cambridge University.

CONTENTS

Introduction

MASAHIKO AOKI AND RONALD DORE

The literature on the Japanese firm grows by the day, but this particular collection of papers can claim the reader's attention for at least four reasons.

The first is its interdisciplinarity. Not only are the papers written by specialists in diverse disciplines, ranging from theoretical and institutional economics to economic history, econometrics, sociology, organizational theory, political science, and engineering, but the papers themselves are catholic in their approach. The authors have tried to relate their own interpretations to those deriving from other disciplines, rather than ploughing a lonely furrow of their own. We hope that this interactive multi-disciplinary approach makes for a broader and richer perspective on what is, by any reckoning, a complex phenomenon.

A second dominant characteristic is what one might call a shared 'systemic awareness'. No one here claims to have discovered *the* secret of the Japanese firm, the autonomous factor that explains its competitive strength. Whether their topic be human resource management, the organization of innovation, or *keiretsu* ties, most of our authors see the specific attributes of the Japanese firm with which they deal as elements of a broader system the parts of which are dependent on other parts for their effective functioning. We believe that the range of 'parts' that are treated in these chapters and this recognition of interelatedness add up to a comprehensive survey of the rich complexity of the Japanese firm.

But systems can be systems of systems. If the firm is a system, so is the economy. The third characteristic of the collection is its recognition of *diversity*. While the main emphasis is on the large corporation whose distinctiveness from its competitors in other countries is most marked, two of the papers deal specifically with the small and medium-sized enterprises which still have a prominent share in both employment and output in the Japanese economy, and with their interrelationships with markets and with government as well as with the larger firms.

Systems can be loosely or tightly integrated; their separate elements may *in themselves* be functional or dysfunctional. Even after millennia of competition for surival, human beings still have appendixes which give them nothing but trouble. The economic version of the Darwinian selection story—that only efficient organizations survive in perfect competition—is subject to even stronger caveats. Nevertheless, in so far as systems *are* integrated, piecemeal change in some of their elements—in response to demands from outside the system—may be hard to effect. For example, the Japanese firm, embedded in a structure of mutually complementary institutional arrangements for factor markets, relationships with suppliers, relationships with competitors, relationships with government, etc., may find it difficult to adapt its personnel practices to new 'tastes' on the part of the Japanese population—new demands for more leisure, more job choice.

And for the same systemic reasons, the transfer of certain elements from one system to another may prove problematic. Problematic, but clearly not impossible. 'Systemic awareness' needs to be tempered by a judicious 'system agnosticism', and in these papers it generally is. The *comparative* perspective adopted in nearly all these chapters is the book's fourth characteristic. Some of its chapters, indeed, concentrate specifically on the issue of the transferability and adaptability of Japanese practices, the settings investigated ranging beyond the conventional Anglo-American examples to cover continental European and Nordic economies.

Let us now introduce the individual papers and try to relate them to each other. The book opens with a chapter by Masahiko Aoki entitled 'The Japanese Firm as a System of Attributes', which surveys recent achievements of the economic research programme on the Japanese firm and sets its possible research agenda. The chapter makes a clear manifestation of the 'systematic awareness' referred to above. Instead of merely listing major works on various attributes of the Japanese firm—such as employment systems, internal co-ordination, subcontracting relationships, main bank relationships, corporate governance—in parallel, the chapter attempts to identify their possible mutual dependencies and tries to relate and arrange contributions from different sub-fields of economics from a systematic perspective. Also, the chapter recognizes the roles of institutions, such as norms, regulations, organizations of exclusive membership, that support the reciprocal interactions of agents as equilibrium behaviour. In this regard, the chapter may be regarded as an economist's attempt to bridge a gap between the traditional economic approach and other disciplines (such as sociology, political science, law).

The next three chapters deal with human resource management, specifically, in-house training, of the Japanese firm. Kazuo Koike, the author of Chapter 2, 'Learning and Incentive Systems in Japanese Industry', has been very influential among economists in interpreting the nature of shop-floor efficiency within the Japanese firm. He has stressed the importance of the worker's capacity to adapt to changes in tasks and cope with unforeseen events such as machine breakdown, as distinguished from the operational skills useful for performing routine tasks. On the basis of this distinction, he has identified two types of work organization: the separate system, in which standard operating tasks and problem-solving tasks are entrusted to different specialized workers, and the integrative system, in which two types of tasks are integrated in individual workers. Koike has long argued that the essence of what appears to be teamwork or group-oriented behaviour at the Japanese factory is actually not so much collective as the exercise of the individual's 'intellectual skill' in performing the non-routine element of tasks in the integrative system. In this chapter Koike discusses incentive and monitoring schemes for promoting and rewarding the formation of such skill on the basis of field observation of a Japanese car manufacturing plant. He also finds essentially similar practices at several Swedish factories which he visited.

Chapter 3, 'Different Quality Paradigms and their Implications for Organizational Learning', is by sociologist and organizational theorist Robert Cole. In dealing with a similar subject (learning) to that of Koike, his focus is more on its organizational aspect. To be sure, there cannot be organizational learning which does not presume individual learning; but the organization itself may be said to learn by identifying the best operational practices, standardizing these practices, and diffusing them throughout the organization as routines that guide individual behaviour. These processes may be carried out through traditional hierarchical authority structures or through more peer-to-peer learning activities. The chapter first sets out the traditional Taylor approach to quality as 'controlling' to an acceptable level the (inevitable) occurrence of defects in an authoritarian setting in which management specialists direct organizational learning. Then it analyses the emerged Japanese approach, which seeks ever-increasing 'improvement' of quality and organizes firms on the assumption that workers as well as managers can be induced to share the quality improvement goals. Recognizing that upstream prevention activities, rather than downstream inspection, are keys to quality improvement, and that many quality failures occur at the boundaries between functional specialities, lateral cross-functional interactions are promoted. Cole points out, as do the previous two authors, that the organizational approach to personnel administration provides a proper incentive framework for the Japanese quality control paradigm. This point, however, raises an interesting question of the transferability of the Japanese quality control paradigm to the West, where institutional setups for personnel administration and unionization have been traditionally different from those in Japan. He concludes the chapter with a few interesting theoretical remarks on this factor.

The issue of transferability of the Japanese practices can, of course, be settled ultimately only in practice. By then, however, the systematic accumulation of knowledge regarding how transplants fare in different national economic systems will provide valuable material for analytical thinking on this issue. Chapter 4 by Mari Sako, entitled 'Training, Productivity and Quality Control in Japanese Multinational Companies', is helpful in enriching such knowledge. This chapter is a report of research in eight plants in Britain and six plants in Germany of Japanese multinational firms, making colour television sets, video cassette recorders, and semi-conductor chips. The focus of study is on internal training of workers, shop-floor work organization, and the use of machinery. In each plant, there prevails the Japanese training philosophy that a reliance on on-the-job training, in-house training courses, and internal promotion is the only way to cultivate a worker's capacity for enhancing plant-wide performance. However, actual practices at those transplants were found to be constrained by, and fitted into, the respective national systems, particularly in labour market institutions, regulations on apprenticeships and vocational quali-fications, the accumulated competence of workers, and the quality of general education. Then the productivity and quality performances at those plants are compared with each other as well as with their headquarter-plants in Japan. This study also may be seen as illuminating the workings of the British and German vocational education and training institutions.

Another international comparison, this time between Japanese home and overseas practices and Anglo-American practices, is the theme of Chapter 5, 'Co-ordination between Production and Distribution in a Globalizing Network of Firms', by Banri Asanuma. The author's previous works were directed to subcontracting relationships in the Japanese car industry and have had considerable impact on rethinking the reasons for their widespread existence. Whereas subcontracting relationships had previously been thought of largely as a device enabling large, powerful manufacturers to exploit and utilize small subcontractors as business cycle buffers, Asanuma ascertained, on the basis of detailed field research, that the efficiency of the Japanese car industry owed a great deal to suppliers' own designing capacity. In this chapter Asanuma turns to the downstream side of the core firm, the major assembling firm. He traces the historical development of production scheduling procedures in response to demand situations and the nature of dealer–manufacturer relationships in them. He makes the point that the Japanese core firm has come to realize a faster and more flexible manu-facturing response to actual customers' demand occurring at the dealer's end, but that such capability needs to be supported by greater information-processing responsibilities on the dealer's side combined with more flexible manufacturing capability on the supplier's side. He notes that, although dealers for US manufacturers are allowed greater discretion in sending orders to the manufacturers, accumulated disequilibrium between actual orders and production sometimes has to be restored by a drastic change in production scheduling accompanied by the shutdown of an assembly plant at very short notice.

The next two chapters deal with R&D organizations of Japanese firms. Chapter 6, 'The Evolution of Japan's Industrial Research and Development' by D. Eleanor Westney, is a survey of both the macro data on national trends and the micro data on organizational structures of Japanese R&D. The macro part makes the point that high R&D expenditure by Japanese firms has been a trend that started long before the first Oil Shock. The micro part, on firm organization, starts with useful history concerning changes in the pattern of division of labour between central, divisional, and factory research labs. It then reviews the accumulated body of information— much of it accumulated by the author herself—on research careers, reward structures, professional self-images, the role of Ph.D. research and quali- fications, corporate university links, and the relation of all these to research productivity. She finds a strong isomorphic pattern of career and incentive structure between the Japanese manufacturing and R&D organizations. She also discusses trends for major corporations to hive more and more work off to subsidiaries, one of the purposes of which is to introduce salary and security differentials between different functions, and she examines the nature of the links between R&D workers in core firm and those in subsidiaries. The chapter closes by pointing out that research managers of Japanese firms are concerned increasingly with the challenge of building more creative organizations with greater capabilities in basic research and radical product innovations. For that purpose, they are trying to draw on their Western counterparts for organizational technology.

Chapter 7, 'R&D Organization in Japanese and American Semiconductor Firms', is a collaborative work by political scientist Daniel I. Okimoto and engineer Yoshio Nishi. They deal with the same organizational aspect as Westney, but focus more sharply on the semiconductor industry. They address an interesting question that arises from close observations of this particular industry, but could be of far-reaching relevancy: why the Japanese R&D organization is well adapted for certain kinds of innovation, such as DRAMs (Dynamic Random Access Memories), where the technological trajectories are predictable, but are not well adapted for producing pivotal new products or process technologies, such as MPUs (microprocessing units). The authors observe that the direction and capability of the Japanese R&D organizations is facilitated and, at the same time, constrained by the permanent employment system of engineers. They argue that it is the constant size of its R&D work-force, more than superior corporate planning and strategy, that explains the steady flow of innovation. Close com- munications among engineers and manufacturing, as well as collective learning capacity, made possible through long-term association of engineers, facilitate the transfer of technology from prototype to mass manufacturing. But, they also argue, the practice of permanent employment of engineers constrains the innovative efforts of the Japanese firm in a rather conservative direction. They point out that Japanese firms are trying to break the conservative inertia and make access to leading-edge technology through strategic alliance with foreign companies, particularly American ones. They thus see an important structural interdependence and complementarity of the Japanese and American industries. Whether such interdependency exists only for the semiconductor industry or is potentially a universal phenomenon is an extremely interesting question for predicting the future of the global economy.

Strategic alliances are also the theme of Chapter 8 by D. Hugh Whittaker, 'SMEs, Entry Barriers, and "Strategic Alliances"'. But here the alliances refer to those among Japanese small and medium enterprises (SMEs). The object of study of previous chapters is large established firms or their relationships with smaller firms (dealers or suppliers). But there are many SMEs in the Japanese economy. SMEs in manufacturing, defined as firms having less than 300 employees and capitalized at less than ¥100m, constituted more than 99 per cent of establishments in 1986 and the proportion of employees was about three-quarters. Many of them are not subcontractors. Some have escaped from such relationships by diversifying into new areas, while some others may be established SMEs which acquired the entrepreneurial input and entered the right market at the right time. But those firms also face numerous challenges, ranging from human resources and financing to management, marketing, and succession. The chapter describes 'networking' or strategic alliances among progressive SMEs to meet those challenges collectively, especially in an advanced high-tech area, Ota Ward in Tokyo. Whittaker depicts a mixed picture: such alliances meet the needs of SMEs in certain ways, but do not solve their problems entirely. On the whole, giant and large firms still exert strong influences on SMEs.

The next two chapters are by Hideshi Itoh, who interprets the functioning of various Japanese organizational practices in the light of new theoretical advancements in the agency literature, to which he himself has made substantial contributions. Chapter 9, 'Japanese Human Resource Management from the Viewpoint of Incentive Theory', first summarizes some basic stylized facts about human resource management practices and organizational structure of the Japanese firm as described in previous chapters. The primary purpose of this chapter is to examine how those practices may serve to resolve possible incentive problems arising from the unique organizational structure. In the Japanese organizational structure more decision-making is delegated to lower levels of hierarchy, and co-operation among workers in performing tasks becomes more important because of the greater dependency on lateral interactions. Such organizational structure may make job demarcation more ambiguous and the objective assessment of individual performance extremely difficult. As a result, pay by performance in the short run becomes difficult to administer. This is why promotion based upon the long-term association of the workers with the firm becomes a major incentive device at the Japanese firm. From this perspective, Itoh discusses various agency models of promotion and their relevance to the Japanese practices.

The stylized fact analysed in Chapter 10, 'Co-ordination, Specialization, and Incentive in Product Development Organization', is the growing importance of the so-called 'heavyweight' project managers in the product development organization. These days more authority concerning product concept creation tends to be delegated to product managers by top management. Project managers also control their members' incentives by exerting influence over their next assignments. Thus, they are 'heavyweight'. On the other hand, they allow for more decentralized and lateral engineering co-ordination among their subordinates, who perform broader tasks than in the traditional organization. With the aid of recent contributions of information and incentive economics, Itoh shows how centralization and decentralization are complementary to each other under the emergent technological and marketing requirements of the new product.

The next two chapters bring the financial aspect of Japanese firms into perspective. Chapter 11, on 'The Economic Role of Corporate Grouping and the Main Bank System' by Takeo Hoshi, opens by describing several stylized facts of corporate grouping in general and the firm's relationship with its main bank in particular. It then goes on to summarize main results of a series of the author's econometric studies on the role of the main bank system, carried out jointly with Anil Kashyap and David Sharfstein. Their studies are among the first attempts to subject theoretical propositions regarding the main bank system to serious econometric testing and have been widely quoted among financial specialists. They tested the proposition that the corporate grouping and the main bank system reduce incentive and information problems arising from information asymmetries normally existing between investors and borrowers. Since normally the investor is neither informed of the quality of proposed investment (as is the borrower) nor able directly to control the behaviour of managers, the cost of external funds becomes higher. However, as a result of the main bank's improved monitoring capacity, made possible by its close relationships with borrowing firms, firms in the corporate grouping can borrow from the main bank at easier terms as needs arise. They may also be able to escape from a financially distressed state more easily with the help of the main bank. Results of the author's econometric studies with Kashyap and Sharfstein affirm such predictions. But they also suggest that the decreasing dependence on bank borrowing by large firms which occurred in the 1980s may mean a weakening of bank ties and may create potentially troublesome incentive and information problems for those firms in future.

Chapter 12 by Paul Sheard, entitled 'Stable Shareholdings, Corporate Governance, and the Japanese Firm', discusses the interrelatedness of the financial feature of stable shareholding and the internal feature of permanent employment in the context of corporate governance. Sheard notes that the interlocking stable shareholding arrangement operates as a take-over insulation device for Japanese firms. He explores the idea that some degree of insulation from competition in the market for corporate control is conducive to the operation of the permanent employment system. By making credible an investor's *ex ante* promise not to intervene in the ordinary state of business, stable shareholding provides incentives for managers and workers to invest in firm-specific intangible assets. This chapter also makes an interesting observation regarding the role of securities companies acting as intermediaries for stable reciprocal shareholding arrangements, which does not appear to have been written about before. Insulation from take-over may suggest to neoclassical economists enormous scope for managerial moral hazard. However, Sheard argues that the main bank acts as a kind of delegated monitor, particularly in its intervention role with regard to failing firms, analogous to the take-over mechanism. Also, it is argued that within the context of permanent employment system lower-level managers who have stakes in higher-level managers' decisions may be motivated to do internal monitoring.

The chapter by Sheard captures one aspect of institutional complementarities or systematic effects prevailing in contemporary Japan. The question may then be raised as to how such a system has evolved. Did each institution—e.g. stable shareholding, relationships with the main bank, the permanent employment system, and stable dealer–supplier relationships— emerge independently and spontaneously, or was the cluster of those institutions an outcome of some kind of co-ordinated institutional design? Although it is beyond the scope of this volume to answer these questions fully, Chapter 13 by Tetsuji Okazaki, entitled 'The Japanese Firm under the Wartime Planned Economy', aims to stimulate discussion and research in the future by focusing on institutional changes taking place in a period that has been relatively ignored by researchers. Okazaki points out that in the 1920s the Japanese economy was much more like a classical economy: the labour and capital markets were more competitive, industrial relations were more adversarial, and managers acted as agents for capitalists. The great transformation started to occur in the 1930s and during the Second World War, when government bureaucrats endeavoured to expand Japan's economic capability. To that end, they instituted a quasi-central planning mechanism—called the 'New Economic Order'—by curtailing shareholders' controlling power, promoting workers' indentification of interests with firms, organizing industrial associations, promoting exclusive bank–firm relations, etc. Although the centralized control of the economy was doomed to fail because of the neglect of price incentives, as well as the devastating effects of the war, institutional shake-ups taking place during the 1930s and the Second World War might have had far-reaching impacts on the institutional arrangements that would eventually have emerged after the war and become instrumental in the remarkable economic development that followed.

Ronald Dore's final chapter, entitled 'Equality–Efficiency Trade-Offs: Japanese Perceptions and Choices', is specifically evaluative, and goes beyond the implicit means–end efficiency criteria of most of the other chapters to ask what sort of society—judged by other criteria, in particular the degree and type of inequality it generates—this sort of economy sustains and is sustained by. A 'true-believer' economist may interpret the apparent egalitarian tendency in Japan as a result of a distortion in the proper functioning of the market mechanism. And if there are price distortions, there must be a misallocation of resources, i.e. inefficiency. However, Dore identifies the source of finely graded organizational pay differential, which suppresses gross income inequality in Japan, with 'a valued sense of togetherness' held among the Japanese. Since togetherness may also enhance technical efficiency, he finds that there is no equality–efficiency trade-off.

He points out, however, that there is more than one dimension of inequality of income and wealth, of prestige, and of power. Japan is more egalitarian in the first and third dimensions, but not in the second, and this is probably not accidental. If hierarchies in terms of social prestige are well respected, there is less need for power-asserting behaviour. This theme— the complementary relationship between the egalitarian power structure and the hierarchical structuring of status—is recurrently discussed in preceding chapters with particular reference to the firm level, but its scope and implications are discussed fully only in this chapter, which goes beyond the usual means–end efficiency analysis.

The chapter ends with speculation that togetherness will probably erode, as Japanese society becomes progressively internationalized. But, if the present form of the Japanese firm is built on a cluster of complementary institutions, including coherent work-groups, such erosion will be bound to trigger accommodating changes and modifications in other institutional spheres as well. How will the Japanese firm be transformed then? This book does not directly answer that question, but it is hoped that it provides basic materials for sound discussions of the issue.

1

The Japanese Firm as a System of Attributes: A Survey and Research Agenda

MASAHIKO AOKI

1. INTRODUCTION

An economic literature on the Japanese firm has been rapidly evolving in the past decade or so.[1] It deals with the analysis of various attributes (internal structure as well as external relationships) of the Japanese firm, once regarded as culturally unique and somewhat aberrational compared with the Anglo-American orthodoxy of capitalism. Most works in the literature apply analytical tools developed in game theory, contractual theory, information economics, etc., and make significant progress towards a better understanding of economic rationality latent in apparently unorthodox features of Japanese firm. There remains, however, a wide-ranging difference in the assessments of their uniqueness/universality. Some argue that there is no essential difference between the Western and Japanese systems (e.g. Koike 1988, in the case of labour organization), while others regard the Western and Japanese systems as examples of two different equilibria (e.g. Kanemoto and McLeod 1991).

In making an economic inquiry into the nature of the Japanese firm, researchers normally choose to focus on some particular aspect of its internal structure or external relations—such as employment structure, internal co-ordination mechanisms, supplier relations, or financial *keiretsu* relations. Some writers have drawn an analogy between attributes of separate aspects of the Japanese firm, e.g. between the ranking of workers within the firm and that of suppliers by the core firm in capital *keiretsu*, both operating as incentive devices. A systematic treatise on the inter-connectedness of various attributes in separate aspects is still to be developed, however. As I will argue below, in order to deal with the issue of uniqueness/universality of the Japanese system satisfactorily, it seems desirable to develop a systematic consideration that does not arise when attributes in different aspects of the firm are examined one at a time. (See Williamson (1991) for a similar approach.) Also, the nature of relations between an equilibrium selection of certain attributes of the firm on the one hand and institutional frameworks (implicit and explicit rules of behaviour, enforcement mechanisms) on the other has been little understood by economists, although the significance of an inquiry into the subject is beginning to be recognized.

In this essay I am engaged in a stock-taking of the literature on the Japanese firm from a specific viewpoint. In Section 2, I survey how economists have recently analysed various attributes of the Japanese firm. Then in Section 3 I proceed to examine how those attributes are interconnected and together form a coherent system of the firm. Section 4 deals with the role of institutional frameworks, such as social norms, property right arrangements, and government regulations, in generating the coherent system of the Japanese firm. Section 5 suggests an important research agenda for studying possible consequences of cross-national interactions and competition among firms of different national origins on institutional frameworks.

2.   ASPECTS OF THE JAPANESE FIRM REVISITED

About ten years ago, I wrote an article entitled 'Aspects of the Japanese Firm' (subsequently published as Aoki 1984) in which I summarized succinctly major attributes in various aspects of the Japanese firm and suggested ways to apply neoclassical economic tools for analysing and understanding their economic functions. I believe that the description and analysis in that paper have remained essentially valid until now. However, in the last five years or so there has emerged a substantial body of new works, dealing with various aspects of the Japanese firm with new theoretical insights. In this and the next section, I briefly survery some recent theoretical works which I consider particularly useful for a systematic understanding of the Japanese firm. In this section, the following aspects of the Japanese firm are dealt with: the information system (I); rank hierarchy (R) as an internal incentive device, and the associated employment relationship (E); the subcontracting relationship (S); and the main bank relationship (MB). The next section deals with possible linkages among important attributes of those aspects.

The Information System (I)

Team-theoretic approach   The internal organization of the firm has two mutually interrelated aspects: the information system, and the incentive structure, the latter of which is closely related to the employment relational aspect (relations between the firm and its labour markets). Partly for expository reasons and partly because of the infancy of our state of analytical development, I first deal with the information system separately.

The management structure of the Japanese firm, as well as the work organization of its plant, is organized hierarchically in terms of administrative structure, just as it is in the Western firm. However, if we look at its actual operations from the perspective of how information is processed, communicated, and utilized for organizational decision-making, there is a fair difference between the two. At the Japanese firm there is no clear-cut division of functions between information-processing and decision-making on one hand, and operational implementation on the other. The former function is never limited to management, and operational workers also participate in considerable collective decision-making. Even though the scope of workers' information-processing tend to be limited to the local work environment, there has also been a conscious administrative attempt to broaden the information perspective through job rotation and horizontal communications across job demarcation. Koike regards the essence of work skills on the shop-floor of the modern factory as the integration of operational skills and the ability to cope with various irregularities, such as machine breakdowns, the need to modify tools and programming, the need to adjust task assignments in response to unforeseen circumstances, and so on.

Once a production plan is laid out administratively, actual production scheduling is fine-tuned continually in response to product demand conditions with the aid of the computer-communications network; but necessary co-ordination of operations across workshops is often performed horizontally without managerial intervention (e.g. computer-aided integrative manufacturing, the *kanban* system). Strategic corporate decisions are not made unilaterally by top management on the basis of centralizing relevant information, but rather are formed inductively through intensive vertical exchanges of information and opinions across various levels of administrative hierarchy (Kagono *et al.* 1985).

Those characteristics—the integration of localized information-processing with operational activities, horizontal co-ordination, and inductive strategizing—defy the usual modelling of the internal information system as a hierarchy. Aoki (1986, 1990a) modelled an information system in which the a priori production schedule is continually modified at the operational level on the basis of (Bayesian) learning, as well as horizontal information-sharing, which requires the sacrifice of economies of operational specialization. The informational efficiency of the model is compared with that of the hierarchical information system in which decision-making and operational activities are separated. Itoh (1987) analysed the optimal degree of investment in localized information-processing capacity at the shop-floor level, contingent on the variability of a global variable surrounding the firm organization as a whole.

In both models, when the stochastic process or the variable describing the environmental uncertainty of the internal organization is very stable or extremely volatile, the superiority of traditional hierarchy is suggested. In those cases, economic gains from the integration of learning and operation will not be sufficient for covering the cost of sacrificing economies of specialization between the two. Specifically, in Itoh's model, investment in relatively more specialized skills at the shop-floor level should be made prior to management information-processing at the top in the stable case and posterior to it in the volatile case. However, in the intermediate range of uncertainty, and/or in the production process where economies of scale are limited, the information system relying upon horizontal co-ordination based on decentralized information-processing and relatively wide-ranging skills becomes more efficient. In this regard, it may be worth noting that Japanese firms appear to have competitive strength in such industries as automobiles, steel, and electronic machinery, which are marked by continually changing demand conditions and associated needs for continual adjustments in task co-ordination; whereas they are in less advantageous positions in industries such as chemicals and aerospace, in which large-scale planning across markets is advantageous or where non-repetitive co-ordination needs to be planned *ex ante*.

The model of hierarchies by Bolton and Dewatripont (1992) is highly relevant to this topic, although it does not directly deal with the Japanese organization. Their model suggests that, as communications skills of economic agents develop, a flat organizational mode (the 'assembly line' model), in which operational tasks and co-ordinational tasks are integrated, will become more productive in comparison to traditional hierarchies in which those tasks are rigidly separated, if time constraint for collective information-processing is tight. It may suggest that the Japanese have developed the 'integrated' system earlier partly because of the ethnic homogeneity of organizational participants, but that such a system may reflect an organizational aspect which will become more prevalent elsewhere as well with the development of communication technology and communication skills.

Integrative contractual approach The internal organization in the models of Aoki, Itoh, and Bolton and Dewatripont takes the form of a 'team', in the Marschak–Radner sense that participants are assumed to share the same objective function. This is, needless to say, a simplified assumption adopted for analytical convenience. Obviously, the members of the internal organization of the Japanese firm are not devoid of self-interest, however latent their representations may be. What type of incentive structure is compatible with the information system as described above? When and how are workers to be motivated to co-operate in decentralized problem-solving as well as horizontal communications/co-ordination? Horizontal co-ordination may make individual contributions ambiguous specifically in terms of output (team production in the sense of Alchian–Demsetz-

Holmstrom). How can free-riding problems be avoided under such circumstances? Why is Japanese middle management willing to delegate responsibilities to workers?

In economics, the integrative approach to the information system and incentive structure of the organization is still at a very primitive stage. In recent times, economists seem to have been more preoccupied with incentive issues. An underlying presumption seems to have been that information can be transmitted among the members of an organization if appropriate incentives for revealing true information are provided. If that is the case, the choice of information system may become almost irrelevant.[2] But obviously, such an assumption is as heroic as the assumption of the identity of objectives among team members. Recently, motivated by the USA–Japan comparison, a few interesting works emerged, which deal with information–motivation interactions within the contractual framework. One type of such work is concerned with the conditions under which 'side-contracting' among workers (horizontal co-ordination) is more productive, and the other is concerned with the conditions under which non-hierarchical/non-specialized job assignments may be induced among participants in the organization.

Itoh's work (1991a) represents the first type. If workers (agents) can observe only the output of each other, which the management (the principal) can also observe, then co-operation among workers will not add any value to the organization (Holmstrom and Milgrom 1990; Varian 1990). But if workers can mutually monitor 'actions' of others, the horizontal co-ordination of efforts ('side-contracting', in contractual terminology) among workers may improve the collective workers' performance, provided that vertical communications are costly.[3] Itoh identified some conditions under which the co-ordination of efforts at the operational level is desirable from the organizational (principal's) point of view: (1) weak systematic risk among work processes (the degree of stochastic correlation among work processes is low); and/or (2) workers are relatively homogeneous in their attitudes towards risk and cost evaluation of own efforts.

I mentioned that in the Japanese firm more responsibilities are delegated to workers and less specialized, overlapping responsibilities are assigned to workers. The former aspect is analysed by Prendergast (1991), who claims that, under the condition of an imperfect labour market and slow internal promotion, middle management is less threatened by the delegation of responsibilities to workers. The latter aspect is studied by Itoh (1992). He showed that, if help (co-operative effort) can be provided by workers without a large sacrifice of effort in own tasks (if the marginal cost of help is zero at zero help), then co-operation and joint responsibility of workers over a range of risk-independent tasks are desirable from the organizational point of view and should be induced by relating compensations of workers to the outcome of joint efforts (team contracts). It is important to note that, when workers co-operate under such a scheme, they are acting in their own self-interest rather than out of loyalty to the group.

Internal Rank Hierarchy (R) and the Employment Relationship (E)

The primary incentive device of the Japanese firm is an internal rank hierarchy along which employees compete for faster promotion. Rank hierarchy is status–wage differentiation which is not based on job classification. In order to be promoted to a certain rank, the employee must satisfy multi-dimensional requirements, including a certain degree of depth and width of skill, experience (seniority), co-ordination skills, attitude towards co-operation, etc. It is usually the case that the speed of promotion is slow at the early stages of internal career development and that wider differentials among employees become evident at the later stages.

Another important characteristic of the employment relationship is that workers who are separated from the rank hierarchy of a large firm at mid-career at the firm's discretion (or by their own will) have a relatively low probability of finding alternative jobs of comparable rank elsewhere. As I will discuss later, we observe a social ranking of firms based on their financial positions and history; and, with high probability, separated employees are re-employed by firms of lower rank. Upward mobility or horizontal mobility across firms is relatively difficult except at the very early stages of career development or among skilled workers of a general type (e.g. editorial work). Recruitment of core workers who are employed as candidates for internal career promotion is done directly out of school, and such employees are placed at the lowest rank initially.

The workings of rank hierarchy as an incentive device have been analysed theoretically with two types of modelling: hierarchy of termination contracts (MacLeod and Malcomson 1988) and rank-order tournaments. MacLeod and Malcomson are concerned with the (adverse selection) problem of the unobservability of workers' abilities by employers. They constructed a model of a repeated game between the firm and the employee in which a strategy of the firm is rank assignment of worker and a strategy of the employee is effort choice. For each rank, a required minimum performance level and promotion performance level are associated. The following constitute the best strategies for the worker and the firm. Every worker is initially placed at the lowest level of rank hierarchy. If a worker's performance exceeds the promotion performance level in a contractual period, the firm will promote him/her to the next higher rank in the next period; if the worker's performance falls short of the required minimum performance level, the firm will terminate his/her employment contract at the end of the contractual period. Other firms believe that separated workers were mistakenly placed one rank too high; possible shirking of the worker is thus penalized by demotion to one rank below at a new firm. (Allowing the possibility of demotion within the firm may generate moral hazard behaviour by the firm.) The worker expends effort at the promotion performance level as far as he/she can expect net gain.

There exists an equilibrium hierarchy in which workers self-select ranks matching their abilities and the firm makes zero profit. Workers' shirking will not occur, in spite of hidden information regarding workers' ability. This model does not directly address an important aspect of Japanese promotion sheme, i.e. incentives for learning on the job. It may be conjectured, however, that threat of termination of the employment contract may also stimulate continual efforts of workers to learn (realization of potential capacity). Another model combining the features of contract termination and consequential social demotion is presented by Okuno-Fujihara (1989); I will discuss this model later.

A rank-order tournament is based on an assessment of the relative performance of workers. A fixed proportion of workers exhibiting relatively better performance will be promoted and will receive a preset prize. This model has several nice features. Since promotion is based on relative assessment, the information requirement is low. Further, if errors in measuring individual performances are correlated, randomness can be filtered out by relative performance comparison and relatively precise information regarding individuals' actions may be obtained (Holmstrom 1982). Moreover, if prizes are set ahead of time and the firm can commit itself beforehand to the aggregate wage bill, there will be no morally hazardous behaviour on the side of the firm not to promote qualified agents, so that contracts become self-enforcing (Malcomson 1984). As a model of the rank-order tournament as an incentive device for learning (firm-specific investment) in the Japanese context, Kanemoto and MacLeod (1989) may be mentioned.

If there are production externalities among individual tasks, relative performance assessment may invite sabotage of workers to disrupt others tasks (Lazear 1989). Itoh (1992) has shown that, if positive production externalities (such as help, teaching) are possible, and if systematic risk among tasks is low, team contracts in which workers are paid according to team performance provide better incentives than relative assessment. Garvey and Swan (1992) showed, however, that if the prize is not fixed beforehand but is made contingent *ex post* on total output, relative performance measures may provide incentives for help, although wage differentials between the promoted and the not-promoted should be compressed. Such a reward scheme contingent on unverifiable output will require credible commitment on the side of management, to be discussed later.

Which model, hierarchical termination contracting or rank-order tournament, reflects the essential attribute of the Japanese promotion scheme? Kanemoto and Macleod (1991) argue, and Itoh (Chapter 9 below) seems to concur, that the latter is better modelling, because it captures the essence of 'permanent employment' by the Japanese firm. They argue that the

Japanese firm does not use discharge as an enforcement mechanism. It is to be remembered, however, that in the termination contracting model separation of workers will not be observed at equilibrium. The essential difference between the two types of modelling is that the absence of mid-career discharge is explained as an equilibrium outcome of a game or is excluded from the strategy domain of the firm by rules of the game. I would maintain that the possibility of mid-career separation of employees can never be dismissed as an unlikely event, even in the Japanese context. Although I am not aware of any reliable data, casual empiricism suggests that a considerable number of employees, particularly white-collar employees (e.g. in banking), have their employment contracts with their original employer terminated at a relatively late stage of their career, at the latter's discretion. The termination is often disguised by the arrangements of new jobs by the original employers (the so-called *shukko* and *tenseki*— Brunello 1988). As I will discuss later, there is a ranking of firms based on financial position, size, and history; and the securement of new jobs for workers separated from their original employers is normally with firms of lower rank (e.g. subsidiaries, subcontractors of original employers).

Subcontracting Relationships (S)

The Japanese firm tends to rely upon subcontractors and/or spin-off subsidiaries to externalize activities heterogeneous to those performed at the core of its internal organization. As a result, the size of Japanese firms in terms of employees relative to sales tends to be smaller. The subcontracting structure of the automobile industry and the electric and electronics machinery industry has been clarified by a series of important works by Asanuma (see Asanuma 1989; Asanuma and Kikutani 1992; also see Sako 1992). The prime manufacturing firm—the P-firm—systematizes its direct and indirect relationships with subcontracting firms—S-firms—on the basis of hierarchical transactional structuring (e.g. the first-tier subcontractor, the second-tier subcontractors, and so on). The direct linkage of operational units of the P-firm with the first-tier S-firms and the successive linkage among lower-tier S-firms in production co-ordination economize on information flows and transaction costs: market information regarding final demands collected through the dealers network of the P-firm is fed into the production site of the P-firm for output adjustment of final products and then is decomposed successively as demands for parts and half-processed products of upstream S-firms (see Asanuma, Chapter 5 below). The delivery of supplies is made directly to the downstream production site (shop) in response to the demand information with only short time lag. The chain-linked information–commodity exchange is realized without the superimposition of a large-scale administrative structure, specialized in expediting in-house supply, inventory storage, and monitoring. The simplified information system which is interwoven with the multi-layered subcontracting relationships appears to be conducive to a more efficient use of on-site information and to contribute to the generation of information value which may not be realizable in the large integrated firm. The model of Aoki (1986) and Bolton and Dewatripont (1992) mentioned above may be relevant here.

In order for continual co-ordination of manufacturing operation between the P-firm and its satellite of S-firms to be effective, co-ordination at the design and development stage appears to be essential; this in turn requires mutual long-term association. In the locked-in situation, two-way morally hazardous behaviour may become a possibility, however. The P-firm and S-firms may try to exploit their monopsony–monopoly positions respectively in the absence of an appropriate contractual governance structure to safeguard such opportunistic behaviour.

According to a recent econometric study by Asanuma and Kikutani (1992) based on the linear contracting model of Holmstrom and Milgrom (1987), the P-firm (and upper-tier S-firm) actually assumes the role of insuring (lower-tier) S-firms against income fluctuations in the long-term S-relationship, and this tendency becomes stronger as the financial and technological position of the S-firm become weaker. In order to counteract the disincentive effect of income insurance, the P-firm adopts the so-called multi-vendor system in which the same type of parts are supplied by multiple S-firms. Relative performance assessment of S-firms filtering the effect of a common risk among them may curtail morally hazardous behavior of S-firms. Riordan (1991) argues that, on the other hand, cost-sharing associated with the partial ownership by the P-firm of the S-firm's equity curtails the incentives of the P-firm to act monopsonistically, while it leaves room for incentives for the S-firm to reduce production cost.

While the hierarchically systematized subcontracting relationships in the assembly industry appear to contribute to the generation of information value, the spinning-off tendency of Japanese industry may also become detrimental to efficiency, depending upon the technological and market conditions of an industry. For example, in the petroleum refining and chemical industries, too many small downstream firms across markets, each specialized in limited product variety, are connected to a large upstream firm, some of them even through a single-pipeline complex. As hinted before, in such industrial organization production scheduling by the upstream firm tends to lag behind changes in final market conditions facing the many small firms because of information lags and the lack of integrative planning. The adoption of a rule of thumb for price-setting for the purpose of avoiding price haggling with many small buyers does not induce efficient production scheduling, either. Also, the presence of too many small downstream firms is said to be not conducive to information feedback from user firms to the upstream supply firm, and opportunity for 'learning by using' appears to be limited. These problems are discussed in a comprehensive manner by Itami (1991).

The Main Bank (MB) Relationship

It is widely known that the primary financial relationship of the Japanese firm is with its main bank (MB). The relationship is not limited to credit dealings, however. In fact, even firms that do not borrow from banks normally have their MBs. The MB relationships are manifold, and which aspects of the relationship dominate depends upon the financial position of the firm.

Aspects of the main bank relationship with the firm are as follows: (1) the MB carries major payment settlement accounts; (2) the MB is a major stockholder; (3) the MB acts as the bondholders' trustee in the case of domestic bond issues and the co-lead manager in the case of overseas issues; (4) the MB is the major creditor and the *de facto* lead manager of an 'informal' loan syndication in the case of borrowing; (5) the MB may supply information regarding opportunities for new businesses, acquisitions, etc., as well as managerial human resources.

The actual combination of these possible aspects in particular relationships between a firm and its MB is contingent upon the wealth position of the former, described in detail in the matrix representation of the MB relationships by Aoki *et al.* (1994). Firms enjoying the highest wealth position have only aspects (1) and (2) activated. Firms with favourable wealth condition may add aspect (3) but not (4), because of its reputation in capital markets (Hoshi *et al.* 1991). A large number of firms with a normal wealth position may still rely upon bank loans for investment financing (4). But an important point to be noted is that, when firms of this category borrow, they are not financed exclusively by their MB (a MB's loan share is normally around 20 per cent of total long-term borrowing), but by other banks as well, banks that are themselves MBs to other firms. Banks, however, reciprocally delegate monitoring of borrowing firms to their MBs through implicit agreements (Sheard 1994). I will discuss this interbank relationship later, but it may be noted here that, because of the non-exclusive lending relations, the MB relationship should be conceptually distinguished from the so-called 'relational banking', often observed in financially immature developing economies (including Japan up to the 1930s), in which particular banks and firms are engaged in close relationships in which either the bank or the firm is *de facto* captured by the other.

When a firm goes from the normal to the critical wealth state, a mechanism is triggered for control to shift from the incumbent management to the MB, the strongest form of aspect (5) above. Because of the role played in aspects (1), (2), and (4), the MB may be able to acquire information indicating possible financial trouble of the firm at a relatively early stage; and the shift of control may be relatively swift, as well as legally and financially less costly, in comparison with the case of dispersed stock ownership and arm's-length debt holdings. The MB is then in a position of deciding whether a failing firm is to be rescued or liquidated. On the possible role of the MB as a 'rescuer' of financially depressed firms, an econometric study by Hoshi *et al.* (1990) may be mentioned.

One aspect of the MB's role in the financially depressed firm may be conceptualized as *ex post* monitoring, referring to the verification of the financial state of the firm combined with disciplinary action applied to failed management based on that information. We may also consider the role of *ex ante* monitoring by the MB (i.e. assessment and approval/rejection of proposed investment projects) as well as its interim monitoring role (i.e. assessment of true value of ongoing projects. It is a distinct feature of the MB relationship that the MB combines all these roles, while in a market-oriented financial system those functions may be dispersed among many different agents—for example, *ex ante* monitoring by investment banks, venture capitalists, and bond rating firms; interim monitoring by market arbitrageurs, security analysts; *ex post* monitoring by an auditing firm, bankruptcy court, or a corporate raider; etc.

Because of the decreasing reliance on bank borrowing for investment financing by firms of better financial positions, *ex ante* monitoring capability of the MB is declining. However, those firms that are now able to finance investments through bond markets are the ones that have established reputations through the MB credit relation (4) (Hoshi *et al.* 1991). In that sense, the MB relation functions as a screening device. The MB may maintain superior ability of interim monitoring because of the combined roles (1), (2), and (5).

Cross-Stockholding (CS)

Cross-Stockholding among firms constitutes another important financial aspect of the Japanese firm. On the average, 40 per cent of equity of non-financial corporate firms listed on the Tokyo exchange is owned by financial institutions, such as city banks, trustee banks, and insurance companies, and about 30 per cent is owned by other non-financial corporate firms. Such extensive cross-holdings lead to the higher valuation of individual equity. But, from the viewpoint of ultimate investors, the over-valuation effect is of no consequence. The investors supply the same level of capital and face the same random returns under both the cross-holding regime and the no-cross-holding regime. But Shreard (1991) argues that the over-valuation creates a form of insurance against financial failures to the firms involved. Over-valuation creates a pool of financial reserves upon which firms can 'draw' when their profit state becomes critically low. In fact, the

ability to realize capital gains in times of financial distress is a typical
feature of the Japanese firm.

3. INTERCONNECTEDNESS OF ATTRIBUTES

In the last section, we identified some important attributes of the Japanese
firm and surveyed recent theoretical contributions dealing with them. For
the most part, they have been treated separately, one at a time. But those

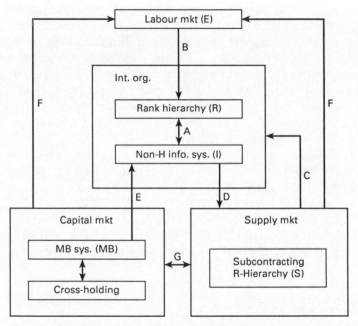

FIG. 1   The Interconnectedness of Attributes of the Japanese Firm

attributes may be in fact interrelated and linked. In this section, I discuss
possible interrelations and linkages among them (see Fig. 1). By this, I
mean the relationship in which an attribute of one characteristic enhances
the effectiveness (productivity) of attributes of other characteristics and vice
versa. For example, the effectiveness of internal rank hierarchy in the R-
aspect and that of rank-ordering of subcontractors in the S-aspect may be
not only parallel but also mutually reinforcing. In what follows, I denote
such relationships by $(R) \Rightarrow (S)$ and $(S) \Rightarrow (R)$, or by $(R) \Leftrightarrow (S)$.

A similar 'system effect' analysis of the Japanese firm has been recently
attempted by O. E. Williamson (1991). Also, it is to be noted that a new
technique for the (qualitative) analysis of complementarity relationships,

called the 'super-modularity analysis', is being developed by Milgrom, Roberts, and Shanon (Milgrom and Roberts 1990; Milgrom and Shannon 1994). See Holmström and Milgrom (1991) and Meyer *et al.* (1992) for its application to the analysis of the firm as clusters of attributes.

$(R) \Leftrightarrow (I)$

It is easy to recognize that the rank-hierarchy attribute of the Japanese firm is conducive to the effectiveness of the decentralized, horizontal information system by providing incentives for wide-ranging learning among a relatively large body of employees and facilitating the accumulation of information-processing capacity specific to the information network. Conversely, the administration of rank hierarchy, constructed as a status differentiation of workers, will be redundant (and possibly ineffective, by hurting the sense of fairness among agents) if job assignments are vertically and horizontally specialized so that the objective market evaluation of skills needed for each task is well developed.

$(E) \Leftrightarrow (R) + (I)$

There are several factors to make the effectiveness of rank hierarchy dependent upon the imperfection of labour markets. Investment in information-processing capacity specific to the internal information network is presumably observable to the firm and the worker but is not verifiable to a third party (such as the court), so that any reward scheme contingent on firm-specific human investment must be self-enforcing; otherwise there may incentives for the firm to default on the promise of promotion after workers have invested. Kanemoto and MacLeod (1989) maintain that the promotional scheme for permanent workers becomes self-enforcing if the firm commits to the total wage bill for senior workers. In their model, the firm promotes all permanent workers who have invested in firm-specific human capital, while the creation of the status of temporary workers, who are not given incentives to invest in network-specific skills, provides flexibility for employment adjustment under changing demand conditions.

Interconnectedness between the imperfect labour market and the R-attribute of the Japanese firm is analysed by Prendergast (1993). He is concerned with the case in which only the employer has information about the value of the employees' potential capability for improving skills (learning). If the employer signals this information at the early stage by promoting the high-learning type, it may discourage the learning efforts of others. If returns to learning are generally high, it is better for the firm to conceal this information by slow promotion of the high type. But if the labour market is competitive, an outside offer may signal this information. Conversely, in order not to discourage learning among junior workers, the firm may refrain from recruiting trained mid-career workers from outside.

As already mentioned in connection with another work by Prendergast, a possible reason why Japanese middle management is willing to delegate more responsibility to workers at the operational level is that they are not threatened by doing so, since their status is protected by rank hierarchy in which the promotion of junior workers is slow. American middle managers face keener competition from junior workers, internal as well as external, and in a milieu of egalitarian social values. Their authority needs to be reasserted and assured by the more rigorous hierarchical structuring of task assignments within the organization (Aoki 1988, 1990*b*).

Thus, we have an interesting symmetry: centralized hierarchical structuring in the I-aspect is complementary to decentralized market competition in the E-aspect (as in the American firm), while the centralized (organizational) administration of rank hierarchy insulated from the external labour market competition in the E–R aspect is complementary to the decentralized information structuring in the I-aspect (as in the Japanese firm). I have called such symmetric relations the *Duality Principle*, as a dualistic combination of centralization and decentralization is necessary for the effectiveness of the internal organization (Aoki 1988, 1990*b*).

$(S) \Rightarrow (I)$

One possible motive for the Japanese firm to externalize a relatively large proportion of operational activities is to make the body of employees relatively homogeneous and to make personnel administration relatively easier (Aoki 1984; Williamson 1991). As workers become homogeneous in their attitude towards risk and cost evaluation of effort, co-operation (mutual help) becomes incentive-compatible with team contracts, and horizontal co-ordination of efforts among workers will be promoted (Itoh 1992, 1993). Also, by making the work process of each firm in a subcontracting relationship relatively homogeneous, the delegation of operational decision-making to the place where on-site information is available becomes facilitated. 'The system as a whole supports variety, but each of the parts is homogeneous' (Williamson 1991).

$(I) \Rightarrow (S)$

The long-term S-relationship may be conducive to the dissemination of technological knowledge from the advanced P-firm to technologically less sophisticated S-firms. In fact, the systematization of S-relationships was initially promoted by the government in the 1930s and 1940s exactly for that purpose. In the early part of the twentieth century, large engineering firms were much more integrated, and S-relationships, when they took place, were often mediated by non-specialist brokers who charged high fees. During the period of rapid expansion of military-related production, increasing reliance upon subcontracting became inevitable because of the limited productive capacities of established engineering firms. The military government, alarmed by low-quality standards of subcontractors, outlawed the use of brokers by decree and enforced the stable S-relationships of established P-firms with government-designated S-firms which were to receive technological transfer from the former. For this historical development, there is a pioneering work by Tasugi (Tasugi 1941).

$(MB) + (CS) \Rightarrow (I)$

The MB system and cross stockholding enhances the effectiveness of the described information system of the Japanese firm. Under the regime of cross stockholding in which the MB actively participates, monitoring of management is delegated to the MB. The MB does not interfere with the strategic and operational decision-making of a monitored firm, however, as long as the latter's financial condition is not depressed. Vertically interactive strategizing within the framework of the internal organization is thus assured from external interference. Also, the contingent assurance of management autonomy allows management to recoup returns from investment in firm-specific information-processing capacity (Sheard 1991). It is analogous to the commitment by management to assure the promotion of senior workers invested in non-contractible firm-specific capital. Some authors (e.g. Mayer 1988) attribute the ability of the MB to commit to a long-term relationship, made possible through the superior ability of interim monitoring, as a source of the 'long-term' horizon of management.

As noted already, only when a portfolio firm is financially depressed do the control rights shift to the MB. It is normally the case that the incumbent management of a failing firm is expelled by the MB, often only after a fierce fight for control, but the job security of permanent workers is kept intact as much as possible and normal wages, if not bonuses and perquisites, are guaranteed in the process of restructuring. Also, bank management dispatched to a financially distressed firm is normally called back to the MB after the recuperation of the firm, and management is handed over then to a new team recruited from within. This contrasts with the case of hostile take-over through the stock markets, where drastic restructuring is often performed at the expense of employees. The 'breach of trust' (implicit contracts) issue that Shleifer and Summers (1988) associated with hostile take-over is thus mitigated, contributing to the preservation of potentially useful firm-specific human capital (Williamson 1991).

(MB) (S) ⇒ (E)

If we make a reasonable assumption that the management of a firm prefers the higher wealth state partly because of the increased managerial discretion free from the MB's monitoring and partly because managers and their employees can enjoy a higher payment scale, bonuses, and perquisites, then we may derive an interesting analogy between the MB relations and the internal organization. Just as rank hierarchies within the Japanese firm can serve as an incentive device for workers under a long-term tenure arrangement, the wealth contingent aspect of the MB relationship may be viewed as an analogous incentive device for the firm as a team of insiders— managers and employees—by providing a ranking of firms in the capital market along which successful firms can successively move up (failed firms are forced to successively move down).

The corporate ranking implicit in the MB relationships (and hierarchically layered S-relationships) as described above is not only analogous to the R-attribute of the Japanese firm, but also complements the latter as an incentive device for internal members—managers and permanent employees—of the firm participating in the decentralized information system. It does so through conditioning the imperfection of labour markets.

If a firm that has enjoyed a certain respectable rank is caught by financial distress and its MB is forced to resort to discharge in the process of liquidation/restructuring, it is normally obligated to arrange new jobs for discharged employees.[4] In that case, discharged workers normally get jobs at firms of lower ranks and/or jobs of lower ranks at equivalently ranked firms. This implies that employees of financially failed firms will be penalized by the loss of a certain amount of employment value owing to 'demotion' across firms.

Aoki (1994) conjoined the MB's dual roles of insurance cum *ex post* monitoring (discipline of employees in the event of financial distress) with the team nature of production within the firm, and analysed the incentive impact on 'team' members (managers and permanent employees of the firm) of MB contracts which specify *ex ante* the transfer of control from internal management to the MB in the event of the former's poor performance. It clarifies conditions under which MB contracts dominate normal debt contracts as an incentive device coping with moral hazard in team-oriented production. Using the supermodularity technique, the model also analyses mutually enhancing incentive effects of MB contracts and the imperfection of the labour market.

The work by Garvey and Swan (1993), already mentioned, discusses interconnectedness between the MB relationship and the R-attributes of internal organization. In their model, management strikes a balance of interests between stockholders, the debtholders (the MB), and the workers. The management provides bonuses *ex post* to workers if output not verifiable by the third party is large, while it is subject to bankruptcy discipline if the output is low. Under this institutional setup, workers are motivated to provide positive mutual help in spite of relative performance evaluation (tournament) because by doing so they can expect a higher reward. Garvey and Swan showed that this institutional setup Pareto-dominates the institutional arrangement of stockholders' sovereignty, although in the former workers may provide super-optimal efforts.

$(MB) \Leftrightarrow (S)$

City banks in Japan compete for the MB status for highly ranked firms, although those firms may not rely upon bank borrowing for investment financing because of sufficient internal funds or good reputations in bond market. A major benefit of being the MB for those firms comes from possible extensions of MB relationships to the latter's subcontracting (and dealers') networks. On the other hand, a membership in the S-network of an highly ranked P-firm signals the creditworthiness of lower-ranked S-firms, which would help reduce their capital costs. Thus, the profitabilities of the MB and S-firms in the S-network are mutually reinforcing.

4. INSTITUTIONAL FRAMEWORKS AND DESIGNING

In the previous section, we saw that various attributes of the Japanese firm complement each other and thus appear to form a consistent system conjointly. This system operates on somewhat different principles from those envisaged in hard-boiled neoclassical thinking. Instead of facing perfectly competitive markets for factors of production—labour, capital, and intermediate products—the firm is related to other agents—the worker, the investor, and the supplier—through long-term relational contracting, and agents on both sides of various relationships reciprocate economic benefits on a long-term basis. This does not mean that they are insulated from outside competition, but rather, that the results of competition emerge in the form of a ranking among a fairly stable group of agents instead of on the basis of continual re-evaluation through perfect markets.

It is probably not fruitful for a better understanding of economic systems to draw too stark a contrast between the Japanese practice as presented above and the stylized Western practice. Nor is it constructive for drawing implications about policy. One may tentatively hypothesize, however, that the stylized Japanese firm and the stylized Western firm may be on different equilibrium paths in their relationship with factor market environments and in internal structuring, setting aside for a while the problem of whether those paths are convergent or distinct. Why are there different equilibrium paths; i.e., why are there different systematic sets of attributes of the firm?

Economists have recently paid increasing attention to institutional factors, such as implicit and explicit rules of the game and their enforcement characteristics (North 1990; Hurwicz 1991), as well as historical initial conditions (Arthur 1989; David 1985), as determinants of equilibrium paths. In this section I take up some recent economists' discussions of institutional factors, such as social norms of reciprocity at various levels, and the role of government as an institutional builder, which I believe have played very important roles in shaping the system characteristics of the Japanese firm. This section is far from complete, but it is illustrative, and is added only as a necessary route to setting an important research agenda in the next section.

The Collective Norm

The work organization at the shop-floor level involves a high degree of reciprocal interactions such as mutual help, teaching–learning among overlapping generations, and horizontal co-ordination of efforts and tasks. In the contract-theoretical framework, these interworker interactions may be captured as side-contracting among workers (Itoh 1992, 1993). But side-contracting can be only implicit, because it is likely to be costly for workers to write explicit contracts. Then the problem is how such implicit contracting can be enforced. The internalization of a collective norm of effort and behaviour required for each rank and position may play an important role here. In personnel assessment and promotion/transfer decisions based on it, the supervisor and/or the personnel department rely upon the reputation of workers held among their peer group on the basis of conformity to the collective norm.

Okuno-Fujihara (Okuno 1984; Okuno-Fujihara 1989) makes a contribution in modelling this important aspect of the Japanese firm. He starts with the presumption that the effort levels of workers are mutually observable, but not to the firm. He also assumes that a high collective standard of behaviour (effort level) is established at high-ranking firms ('prestigious' firms). In the 1984 model he simply assumed that those workers who failed to meet the norm are ostracized. In the 1989 model he contrived a mechanism in which the firm can elicit truthful reports from all workers on their evaluation of other workers. If a worker is evaluated as not meeting the norm by more than two fellow-workers, or if a worker deviates from truthful report, he/she is dismissed and ends up in the next period working for a firm of lower rank where a lower standard of behaviour prevails. Okuno-Fujihara showed that the standard of efficient co-operative behaviour emerges as perfect 'norm equilibrium' at prestigious firms.

Enterprise Unionism

The employee's welfare derived from career association with the firm clearly depends upon various decisions taken by management, such as the rate of expansion of the firm, which affects the probability of promotion within the rank hierarchy. Suppose that the level of payment is fixed for the period of one year. Suppose that in the interim period management makes various managerial decisions unilaterally only to maximize stock value subject to the bargained wage rate, and that the worker chooses his effort level only to maximize labour surplus subject to the same constraint. The resulting situation is a two-sided prisoners' dilemma. By reciprocating faster growth or fewer layoffs at the sacrifice of short-term value maximization and higher effort (aimed at maximizing value added net of effort cost), the management and the worker could Pareto-improve the situation and approximate the efficient Nash bargaining solution (Aoki 1988).

Considering that the prisoners' dilemma situation constitutes the Nash equilibrium of a one-shot bilateral trading game within the period of payment fixation, and thus could form another perfect equilibrium, how can the high equilibrium based on reciprocity become viable? Repeated games between the enterprise-based union, composed exclusively of permanent employees, and the management team, recruited from within the rank of permanent employees, may provide institutional frameworks which promote mutual commitments to the standard of behaviour conducive to the high equilibrium. Morishima (1991) found in his empirical work that information-sharing between the enterprise union and the management contributes to a Pareto-improving trade-off between the wage rate and other managerial decision variables contributing to the employees' welfare: a finding that is not observed in the US economy.

Capital Keiretsu

We have seen that there is a multitude of reciprocal relations between the P-firm and its S-firms. The P-firm furnishes business security as well as technological know-how to S-firms, while S-firms reciprocate higher effort in cost reduction, timely delivery co-ordination, quality improvement, and information feedback necessary for the P-firm's 'learning by using'. Such exchange of reciprocity may be institutionally supported by the P-firm's stockholding in S-firms and the S-firms' membership in the association of P-related S-firms. These institutional arrangements are conventionally referred to as *capital keiretsu*.

The Government as an Institutional Designer

I have emphasized the role of reciprocity operating within various aspects
of the firm. Although the norm of reciprocity is enforced by membership
control, stock ownerships, etc., the norm itself is implicit. Since implicit
norms are generally considered as culturally conditioned, one may think
that those attributes of the Japanese firms are also culturally conditioned
and that their development has been continual and incremental since the
beginning of the birth of capitalism in Japan. But that is not necessarily
the case!

Take the 1920s. In that decade, advanced Japanese firms were patterned
more on the classical type, although some aspects were marked by clear
backwardness. The internal organization of the firm was much more
hierarchical, functionally as well as in terms of status differentiation. The
workers were more mobile across firms and industrial relations were more
adversarial (Gordon 1985). Relatively advanced firms were more integrated
and less reliant upon backward subcontracting relations. The banking
sector was much more decentralized and deregulated. (There was no entry
restriction except for a minimum capital requirement, and there were more
than 2,000 banks competing in the mid 1920s: Teranishi 1990). Banks did
not extend long-term investment credits to firms. The stock market was
much more actively utilized for investment financing and the transfer of
corporate control, as expansive conglomerate operations of new Zaibatsu
symbolized. Japanese firms, then, operated in the milieu of classical market
competition and hierarchical authority. Commitment to reciprocity was
evident only within political cliques, village life, etc., but it did not play any
substantial role in the 'modern' economic sphere.

When and how did decisive changes occur? Undoubtedly, the post-war
reforms played a very important role in shaping the foundation for the
present-day economic system, and there have already been many reliable
works written on this subject. However, institutional changes that took
place during the war period (1941–5), and in particular their possible
impacts on the formation of the post-war economic system, is a relatively
unexplored subject. The post-war generation of economic historians in
Japan tended to regard the period of the military regime as aberrational
(although important exceptions by T. Nakamura and A. Hara should not
be overlooked). Recently there emerged a revisionist view, advanced by a
new generation of economic historians who pay more attention to the role
of authoritarian administration under the military control in shaping new
institutional frameworks. For example, Okazaki (1987: chapter 13) documented and analysed the process through which the government pursued
its objective of controlling the war economy through the removal of
stockholders' control and the introduction of its own planning apparatus.
The government, or at least one division of it (*Kikakuin*—the Planning

Agency), at first tried to implement a direct quantity-guided planning mechanism through the organization of industry-based 'controlling associations' (*Toseikai*) as an intermediary for information-processing and commands. The attempt to introduce this 'Economic New System' turned out to be abortive because of the lack of profit incentives, and soon had to be modified with the introduction of profit incentives based on the administrative manipulation of price parameters. However, these incentives were directed towards managers and workers. While dividend pay-out ratio was capped at a fixed percentage rate of the initial issue value of the stock, the managers and workers were given the limited status of residual claimant by the law. Stockholders' rights at the general meeting were curtailed, however, and the stock market was closed in 1945. Although all these laws and institutional setups were abolished in the post-war reform, Okazaki argues that the changes in the structure of the firm and the use of industry-based organizations provided a basis for the post-war formation of the 'Japanese management' and industrial policy.

Regarding the formation of the MB relationship, too, the role of the inter-war period government appears to be important. After the 1927 financial crisis, the Banking Act enforced the merger of small banks whose paid-in capital was below the new standard. In the 1930s, merger and acquisition was further promoted through administrative guidance and, after 1937, through military coercion. The number of commercial banks was reduced to 625 in 1932 and further to 65 in 1945. Particularly interesting for the evolution of the MB relationships was the so-called 'designated banking system', enforced by the Ministry of Military Supply created in 1943. This Ministry planned the production of military supplies as well as the supply of funds necessary for the implementation of the plan. For each firm receiving military procurement orders a single bank was designated, and the actual supply of funds to the firm was made through its designated bank. Firms were allowed to hold deposit and loan accounts only with their designated bank. At the end of the war there were 2,240 firms to which the designated banking system was applied, and among them 1,582 firms were designated to one of five major *zaibatsu* (conglomerate) banks (Cohen 1948). There is no doubt that those relationships provided a foundation for the formation of post-war MB relationships through institutional inertia, although in the post-war period the government has administratively guided banks to diversify their portfolios and avoid an exclusive lending relationship with any particular firms.

The impact of institutional changes that took place during the military administration on the formation of the post-war economic system has only recently become an active research topic, and we expect that important contributions are yet to come.

Reciprocal Monitoring of MBs and Entry Regulation

It was already pointed out that, although almost every firm has a particularly close relationship with one bank (normally, one of eleven city banks for large firms or a regional bank in the case of small and medium firms), when it borrows, it does so from many banks. This multiple credit relationship has arisen partly because of the administrative guidance mentioned above and partly because the firm has tried not to be locked into an exclusive relationship with a single bank so that it would not lose bargaining power *vis-à-vis* the M B. But the monitoring of borrowing firms has been exclusively delegated to their M Bs. As pointed out, the M B must bear a great deal of the cost of rescuing failing firms and it loses the priority of claims over seized assets of liquidation firms. Such cost-bearing may be interpreted as a penalty for the M B's failure of *ex ante* monitoring.

The M B is in a position to detect a possible financial problem of a monitored firm through its superior interim monitoring role earlier than any other firm, so that it could have, if it wished, withdrawn credits to the failing firm and abandoned the position of M B before other banks had become aware of the problem. Such opportunistic behaviour of M Bs is actually not unheard of (Horiuchi *et al.* 1988), but the question remains why it does not happen more frequently when the delegation of monitoring to the M B is only an implicit agreement. Further, depending on the potential value of the information system internalized within the firm and the magnitude of the financial failure, a financially failing firm may be either in a state where it should be rescued or in one where it should be liquidated. Since investors and banks other than the M B may not be able to distinguish between the two states, it may be hard for them to judge whether or not the M B has shirked its responsibility when it liquidates a failing firm. If the M B is not penalized for shirking the responsibility of rescuing a potentially valuable firm, its best strategy may be for it to shirk even *ex ante* monitoring in the future. On the other hand, if the M B expects always to be penalized harshly for a liquidation, its best strategy may be always to rescue failing firms. As a result, inefficiency somewhat similar to the 'soft-budgeting' problem (Kornai 1980) that has plagued the former centrally planned economies may occur: the M B is never able to commit itself to liquidating inefficient firms.

Aoki (1994) suggested two possible mechanisms for coping with the above double-edged moral hazard problem involving the M B. First, the strong 'voice' of the permanent employees endowed with strong employment rights may deter the M B from failing to rescue, although it may very well induce the opposite problem of soft-budgeting. The second mechanism is reciprocal *ex post* monitoring among banks that act as M Bs for major firms (Sheard 1994). Suppose that banks co-operate in penalizing liquidating banks, for example by refusing to participate in a certain number of loan consortia organized by these liquidating banks in the future, without knowing whether the firms should in fact have been liquidated or rescued from the efficiency point of view. There is a certain range of penalties, proportional to the magnitude of defaulted values, whereby the MB is deterred from both illegitimate liquidation and soft rescuing.

How can the mechanism of reciprocal monitoring among MBs be implemented? It is suggested that the reciprocal monitoring mechanism is effective if the number of MBs is limited so that the imposition of collective sanctions can be effectively implemented without being eroded by non-cooperative behaviour of (uninformed) outsiders. On the other hand, it may also be necessary that the number of MBs is not so small that a low equilibrium, characterized by collusion among them never to penalize, will result.

It is noteworthy that the crux of banking regulation by the Ministry of Finance in the post-war period has been to regulate severely the entries of commercial banks into the exclusive club of city banks qualified as MBs for major firms. It has also consistently punished liquidating banks while rewarding rescuing banks by fine adjustments of the number of annual awards of branch licensing to city banks. It may be an interesting empirical research agenda to look into whether such a regulatory framework has not contributed to a 'soft-budgeting' tendency.

5. A RESEARCH AGENDA: THE INTERNATIONAL COMPATIBILITY OF THE J-SYSTEM

I have argued that attributes characterizing various aspects of the Japanese firm—which may be referred to as the 'corporate system'—are mutually interconnected, that they are supported by a distinct institutional mix, and that their evolution was not spontaneous and continual, but that the government as an institutional designer may have played a certain role. It may be considered that the Japanese corporate system (the J-system) more or less contrasts with the corporate system found in the West (the W-system), whose essence may be encapsulated, as a first approximation, as the hierarchy of functions surrounded by relatively more competitive factor markets.

I have emphasized that the J-system, even if unique to some extent, is not entirely culturally conditioned. Conscious institutional design by the government was just one of the decisive factors in promoting its emergence and development, although any governmental design that is either out of alignment with the fundamental evolutionary trend in Japan or incompatible with the economic incentives of the agents involved has been abortive or ineffective. The J-system in its indigenous form will not be universally viable, either, because it has operated within the institutional mix that regulates membership of players in economic games, although one cannot deny that similar or identical attributes of internal organizational structure of firms are found in or are transplantable into other systems.

The partially designed nature of the J-system, as well as the relative closedness of its supporting institutional framework, raises an interesting question concerning its future dynamic path. Will the J-system and the W-system converge in the future, or are they already not so distinct in spite of differences in the institutional frameworks in which they have evolved? Although the institutional mix of Japan may have provided a useful developmental framework in the past, has it fulfilled its historical mission by now, and is it to be modified to be more compatible with the norm of free competition? Will the J-system remain viable, or will it transform itself? Answers to the above questions may be very intricate. We economists do not yet seem to have understood the nature of interactions between the equilibrium selection of dynamic path, institutional change, and historical initial conditions.

From the efficiency point of view, the relative advantage of one corporate system over the other is likely to depend upon the market and technological conditions under which the firm is placed. If only efficiency matters in the determination of an outcome of competition among different corporate systems, one may be inclined to expect that a different type of corporate system will eventually evolve for each industry the world over. But the matter may not be so simple. A certain attribute which is presumably favoured in certain industries (e.g. the J-type information system for the car assembly industry, and the W-type information system for the chemical industry) may be most effective or viable only if it is complemented with certain other attributes (e.g. subcontracting network *v.* a tendency towards integration) and is placed in appropriate institutional frameworks of social norms and enforcement mechanisms (e.g. *keiretsu* reciprocity, or an anti-monopoly regulatory framework).

A factor that complicates the matter more is the increasing inter-penetration of organizations of diverse national origins into foreign institutional and market milieu. Globalizing organizations sometimes act as carriers of a set of behavioural rules originating at home, while they sometimes learn and adapt to market environments and institutional frameworks abroad. The future of the dynamic paths of corporate systems may thus have rather intricate interactions with institutional mixes in each economy.

Instead of speculating on definitive answers to the above questions at a very primitive stage of research in the field of comparative institutional analysis, I shall simply suggest some plausible scenarios below; this brief survey is made open-ended to entice further research among economists.

Scenario A   Actual differences in corporate systems in the West and Japan are not so great. In the W-system, too, high commitment plays an important role in employment relations, supplier relations, etc. Ranking competition in the J-system is not so different from market competition or rank tournaments in the W-system except for a longer time-horizon in which the outcome of competition is worked out. The increasing autonomy of Japanese firms from MBs for investment financing on the one hand, and the decreasing likelihood of take-over raids, combined with increasing activism of some of large institutional stockholders in the Western corporate governance structure (Grundfest 1993; Jensen 1989) on the other, will lead to a convergence of financial attributes of the two corporate systems. This is the most optimistic scenario.

Scenario B   All important attributes of a corporate system are viable only as an integrated set and with the support of the corresponding institutional frameworks. However, the compatibility of the institutional framework of the J-system, which has regulated the number and qualifications of players in economic games, with that of the W-system, which has enforced free competition, are problematical. The inter-penetration of globalized organizations across the two systems, then, may have destabilizing effects on both systems. In order to control such destabilizing effects and protect respective corporate systems from malfunctioning, cross-border corporate activities will need to be regulated. This is the scenario advanced by isolationists on both sides.

Scenario C   In each aspect of the firm, either an attribute of the W-system or one of the J-system will eventually dominate when the two interact in ever-greater frequency. One possibility is that when J-firms permeate the W-system they will gain the competitive edge by taking short-term advantage of free entry, while securing and limiting benefits available from reciprocal contracting to their own number. The opposite scenario is that the W-system, based on the universalistic norm, will dominate the J-system, because the latter is supported by a 'closed' institutional framework essentially inconsistent with globalization. The historical mission of the closed developmental statist framework will be laid to rest. In this scenario, it is the institutional framework, rather than the efficiency properties of the corporate system, that will be decisive in an outcome of organizational competition.

Scenario D   The two corporate systems will eventually converge to a hybrid form of higher order; or else they will be able to coexist by the design of an integrative institutional framework. However, as the two existing systems have so far constituted two different equilibria supported by their own institutional frameworks, it may be difficult to change them by piecemeal social engineering. In any event, an integrative institutional framework on an international scale may need to be sought through reconciliation among different value systems, the conscious design of international regulations administered and enforced by international agencies and/or the harmonization of laws (in the area of anti-trust, intellectual property rights, corporate taxes, finance and banking), etc. Although the path to such a scenario may be very painstaking, it may be most conducive to efficiency on a global scale.

It is difficult to say at present which of the above scenarios is most likely to evolve in the near future. It seems clear, however, that the present 'trade disputes' among nations pose a very fundamental question of the compatibility of different institutional frameworks, and an urgent task for economists is to face up to the issue. It is not sufficient for the Westerner to preach the universal value of free competition, because dynamic efficiency gained from 'classical' competition may not be ubiquitous. It is not effective for the Japanese to defend the rationality inherent in the J-system, since the closed nature of its institutional framework needs to be modified to enable it to become enmeshed in the global system in a more consistent way. It is important for both sides to understand the nature of the two systems more deeply in a comparative perspective and to seek a reasonable choice of a scenario, which may have profound significance for the future of market economies, as well as for that of transforming economies and developing economies.

NOTES TO CHAPTER 1

1. As useful surveys of the literature, see Aoki (1990*b*), Itoh (chapter 9), and Kanemoto and MacLeod (1991).
2. An important implication of the 'revelation principle' developed in the mechanism-design literature (e.g. Myerson 1985) is that information structure is irrelevant: any non-cooperative equilibrium outcome of an arbitrary organization can be replicated by a centralized two-tier information structure, wherein agents communicate their entire private information to the principal (the centre). But this principle assumes that information transmission from agents to the centre is technologically (not motivationally) costless.
3. Ma (1988) proved that, if actions of agents are mutually observable, the principal can design a multi-stage mechanism to implement any desired actions as a unique perfect equilibrium with first-best outcome. But this possibility depends upon the assumption that the principal can motivate truthful revelation of observed action of others from each agent at no communication cost.

4. The Reorganization Law (*Kaisha Koseiho*) explicitly stipulates that the court must hear the opinion of the employees before it decides on the reorganization plan submitted by the custodian of a bankrupt firm.

REFERENCES

Aoki, M. (1984), 'Aspects of the Japanese Firm', in M. Aoki (ed.), *The Economic Analysis of the Japanese Firm*, North-Holland, Amsterdam 3–43.

—— (1986), 'Horizontal vs. Vertical Information Structure of the Firm', *American Economic Review*, 76: 971–83.

—— (1988), *Information, Incentives and Bargaining in the Japanese Economy*, Cambridge University Press.

—— (1990a), 'The Participatory Generation of Information Rents and the Theory of the Firm', in M. Aoki, B. Gustafsson, and O. E. Williamson, *The Firm as a Nexus of Treaties*, Sage, London, 26–52.

—— (1990b), 'Towards an Economic Model of the Japanese Firm', *Journal of Economic Literature*, 28: 1–27.

—— (1994), 'Contingent Governance of Team Production: Analysis of Institutional Complementarity', *International Economic Review*, forthcoming.

—— Sheard, P., and H. Patrick (1994), 'The Japanese Main Bank System: An Overview', in M. Aoki and H. Patrick (eds.), *The Japanese Main Bank System*, Oxford University Press, forthcoming.

Arthur, B. (1989), 'Positive Feedbacks in the Economy', *Scientific American*, no. 262: 92–9.

Asanuma, B. (1989), 'Manufacturer–Supplier Relationships in Japan and the Concept of Relationship-Specific Skill', *Journal of the Japanese and International Economies*, 3: 1–30.

—— and Kikutani, T. (1992), 'Risk Absorption in Japanese Subcontracting: A Microeconometric Study of the Automobile Industry', *Journal of the Japanese and International Economies*, 6: 1–29.

Bolton, P., and Dewatripont, M. (1992), 'The Firm as a Communication Network', mimeo, Brussels.

Brunello, G. (1988), 'Transfers of Employees between Japanese Manufacturing Enterprises: Some Results from an Enquiry on a Small Sample of Large Firms', *British Journal of Industrial Relations*, 26: 119–32.

Cohen, J. B. (1948), *Japan's Economy in War and Reconstruction*, Institute of Pacific Relations, New York.

David, P. (1985), 'Clio and the Economics of QWERTY', *American Economic Review*, 75: 332–7.

Garvey, G. T., and Swan, P. L. (1992), 'The Interaction between Financial and Employment Contracts: A Formal Model of Japanese Corporate Governance', *Journal of the Japanese and International Economies*, 6: 247–74.

Geanakoplos, J., and Milgrom, P. (1991), 'A Theory of Hierarchies Based on Limited Managerial Attention', *Journal of the Japanese and International Economies*, 5: 205–25.

Gordon, A. (1985), *The Evolution of Labor Relations in Japan: Heavy Industry, 1853–1955*, Harvard University Press, Cambridge, Mass.

Grundfest, J. (1993), 'Just Vote No: Minimalist Strategies for Dealing with Barbarians *inside* the Gate', *Stanford Law Review*, 45: 857–937.

Hellwig, M. (1991), 'Banking, Financial Intermediation and Corporate Finance', in Alberto Giovannini and Colin Meyer (eds.). *European Financial Integration*, Cambridge University Press, 35–63.

Holmoström, B. (1982), 'Moral Hazard in Teams', *Bell Journal of Economics*, 13: 324–40.

—— and Milgrom, P. (1987), 'Aggregation and Linearity in the Intertemporal Provision of Incentives', *Econometrica*, 55: 303–28.

—— —— (1990), 'Regulating Trade among Agents', *Journal of Institutional and Theoretical Economics*, 146: 85–105.

—— —— (1991), 'Multi-Task Principal–Agent Analyses: Incentive Contracts, Asset Ownership and Job Design', *Journal of Law, Economics, and Organization*, 7 (Special Issue): 24–52.

—— —— (1994), 'The Firm as Incentive Systems', *American Economic Review*, forthcoming.

Horiuchi, A., Fukuda, S., and Packer, F. (1988), 'What Role has the "Main Bank" played in Japan?' *Journal of the Japanese and International Economies*, 2: 159–80.

Hoshi, T., Kashyap, A., and Sharfstein, D. (1990), 'The Role of Banks in Reducing the Costs of Financial Distress in Japan', *Journal of Financial Economics*, 27: 67–88.

—— —— —— (1991), 'On the Choice between Public and Private Debt: An Examination of Post-Deregulation Corporate Financing in Japan', paper presented to the conference on 'Japan in a Global Economy', Stockholm School of Economics.

Hurwicz, L. (1991), 'Implementation and Enforcement in Institutional Modelling', mimeo, University of Minnesota.

Itami, H. (1991), *Nihon no Kagaku Sangyo: Naze Sekai ni Tachiokuretanoka*? (The Japanese Chemical Industry: Why has it Lagged behind the World?), NTT Shuppan, Tokyo.

Itoh, H. (1987), 'Information Processing Capacity of the Firm', *Journal of the Japanese and International Economies*, 1: 299–326.

—— (1992), 'Cooperation in Hierarchical Organizations: An Incentive Perspective', *Journal of Law, Economics, and Organization*, 8: 321–45.

—— (1993), 'Coalitions, Incentives, and Risk Sharing', *Journal of Economic Theory*, 60: 410–27.

Jensen, M. (1989), 'The Eclipse of Public Corporation', *Harvard Business Review*, 67(5): 61–74.

Kagono, T. *et al.* (1985), *Strategic vs. Evolutionary Management: A US–Japan Comparison of Strategy and Organization*, North-Holland, Amsterdam.

Kanemoto, Y. and MacLeod, W. B. (1989), 'Optimal Labor Contracts with Non-contractible Human Capital', *Journal of the Japanese and International Economies*, 4: 385–402.

—— —— (1991), 'The Theory of Contracts and Labor Practices in Japan and the United States', *Managerial and Decision Economics*, 12: 159–70.

Koike, K. (1988), *Understanding Industrial Relations in Modern Japan*, Macmillan, London.

Kornai, J. (1980), *The Economics of Shortage*, North-Holland, Amsterdam.

Lazear, E. P. (1989), 'Pay Equality and Industrial Politics', *Journal of Political Economy*, 97: 561–80.

Ma, C. (1988), 'Unique Implementation of Incentive Contracts with Many Agents', *Review of Economic Studies*, 55: 555–71.

MacLeod, W. B. and Malcomson, J. M. (1988), 'Reputation and Hierarchy in Dynamic Models of Employment', *Journal of Political Economy*, 96: 832–54.

Malcomson, J. E. (1984), 'Work Incentives, Hierarchy, and Internal Labor Market', *Journal of Political Economy*, 92: 486–507.

Mayer, C. (1988), 'New Issues in Corporate Finance', *European Economic Review*, 32: 1167–88.

Meyer, M., Milgrom, P., and Roberts, J. (1992), 'Organizational Prospects, Influence Costs, and Ownership Changes', *Journal of Economics and Management Strategy*, 1: 9–35.

Milgrom, P., and Roberts, J. (1990), 'Rationalizability, Learning, and Equilibrium in Games with Strategic Complementarities', *Econometrica*, 58: 1255–77.

—— and Shannon, C. (1994), 'Monotone Comparative Statics', *Econometrica*, forthcoming.

Morishima, M. (1991), 'Information Sharing and Collective Bargaining in Japan: Effects on Wage Negotiation', *Industrial and Labor Relations Review*, 44: 469–85.

Myerson, R. (1985), 'Bayesian Equilibrium and Incentive Compatibility: An Introduction', in L. Hurwicz, D. Schmeidler, and H. Sonnenschein (eds.), *Social Goals and Social Organization*, Cambridge University Press.

North, D. (1990), *Institutions, Institutional Change and Economic Performance*, Cambridge University Press.

Okazaki, T. (1987), 'Senji Keikaku Taisei to Kakaku Tosei' (The War Period Planning System and Price Control), *Kindai Nihon Kenkyu*, 9: 175–98.

Okuno, M. (1984), 'Corporate Loyalty and Bonus Payments: An Analysis of Work Incentive in Japan', in M. Aoki (ed.), *The Economic Analysis of the Japanese Firm*, North-Holland, Amsterdam, 387–412.

Okuno-Fujihara, M. (1989), 'On Labor Incentives and Work Norm in Japanese Firms', *Journal of the Japanese and International Economies*, 4: 367–84.

Prendergast, C. (1991), 'A Theory of Worker Responsibility', mimeo, University of Chicago.

—— (1992), 'Career Development and Specific Human Capital Collection', *Journal of the Japanese and International Economies*, 6: 207–27.

Riordan, M. (1991), 'Ownership without Control: Toward a Theory of Backward Integration', *Journal of the Japanese and International Economies*, 5: 101–19.

Sako, M. (1992), *Prices, Quality and Trust: How Japanese and British Companies Manage Buyer–Supplier Relations*, Cambridge University Press.

Sheard, P. (1991), 'The Economics of Interlocking Shareholding in Japan', *Richerche Economiche*, 45: 421–48.

—— (1994), 'Reciprocal Delegated Monitoring the Japanese Main Bank System', *Journal of the Japanese and International Economies*, 8: forthcoming.

Shleifer, A. and Summers, L. (1988), 'Breach of Trust in Hostile Takeovers', in A. Auerbach (ed.), *Corporate Takeovers: Causes and Consequences*, University of Chicago Press.

Tasugi, K. (1941), *Shitauke Kogyo Ron* (A Treatise on Subcontracting Manufacturing), Yuhikaku, Tokyo.

Teranishi, J. (1990), 'Financial System and the Industrialization of Japan, 1900–1970', *Banca Nazionale del Lavoro Quarterly Review*, no. 174: 309–41.

Varian, H. (1990), 'Monitoring Agents with Other Agents', *Journal of Institutional and Theoretical Economics*, 146: 153–74.

Williamson, O. E. (1985), *The Economic Institutions of Capitalism*, Free Press, New York.

—— (1991), 'Strategizing, Economizing, and Economic Organization', *Strategic Management Journal*, 12: 75–94.

2

Learning and Incentive Systems in Japanese Industry

KAZUO KOIKE

1. INTRODUCTION

This chapter aims to elucidate, first, the learning systems with which workers acquire skills and, second, the incentive systems which promote skill acquisition in contemporary Japan. A comparison with Swedish cases will also be developed, but only tentatively, owing to insufficient data.

These two themes are extremely important for dispelling the myths concerning Japanese efficiency on the shop-floor, particularly the myth concerning teamwork or group-oriented behaviour. According to a popular view which strongly emphasizes teamwork as the major source of efficiency, jobs are rarely defined clearly in Japanese industry, contrary to ordinary workshops in the West. For most workers such ambiguity would usually result in inefficiency; difficult parts of the work would be left untouched. On the other hand, in Japan, workers pay close attention to their fellow-workers' jobs, and this tremendous teamwork, which extends to the instruction of junior workers, clearly produces high efficiency. According to the popular view, however, it is difficult to transfer such team spirit to other countries, because of the peculiar culture of group-oriented behaviour among Japanese workers.

This myth raises a question of incentives: how to promote such teamwork. According to the prevailing view, payments based on results or pay for the job are uncommon, and salaries are mainly dependent on length of service. If so, how can each member of the group be induced to work efficiently? Since the group consists of individual workers, once again, a peculiar group-oriented character seems to be central, and this strengthens the myth.

Two theses are presented here. First, it is the character of the workers' skills that produces high efficiency on the shop-floor, and what appears at a glance to be teamwork is the operation of these skills. The workers deal skilfully with those problems on the shop-floor that cannot be predicted beforehand and hence cannot be fully defined. Consequently, if we include problem-handling, individual jobs naturally become difficult to define entirely because they contain an ambiguous element. Through examining the process by which the workers' skills were learned, the critical character of skill should emerge. This constitutes the first half of the paper.

Second, without proper incentive systems, obviously, few workers are willing to acquire necessary skills. The actual incentive systems in contemporary Japanese industry are basically individual, and promote intensive competition among individual workers over the long term. This analysis constitutes the second half of the paper.

Emphasis is put on the second part, because analysis of workers' skills has been fully written about elsewhere (Koike and Inoki 1990: ch. 2). However, we cannot wholly skip a discussion of workers' skills, because that is the very foundation of this paper. Here, incentive systems are examined mainly as an analysis of a case, supplemented by examining relevant statistical data. Since few reliable, detailed statistics on payment methods are available, an insight into the case of a major car manufacturer comprises the main body of the second part. This paper concerns mainly the blue-collar workers, only peripherally referring to white-collar workers.

The following section examines the character and content of workers' skills on the shop-floor in production workshops. Section 3 makes clear the learning process in which the skills are formed. Section 4 examines the incentive systems, which need to be different from ordinary ones. Section 5 analyses the incentive system of a major car manufacturer. Section 6 develops a comparative study with several Swedish cases. The final section sums up the discussion.

2. INTELLECTUAL SKILLS

Dealing with Changes

The most vital kind of skill that contributes to efficiency in contemporary Japanese industry is undoubtedly intellectual skill, i.e. the ability to deal skilfully with those problems and changes that are called 'unusual operations' in this paper.[1] What, then, are unusual operations?

When you observe operations on mass-production assembly lines for longer than a couple of hours, you can clearly identify two types of operation: usual operations and unusual ones. Usual operations are routine, repetitive, and monotonous; little skill is necessary to carry them out.

But even in the most repetitive mass-production workshops, changes in production and unforeseen problems of a minor scale frequently occur, and actions to deal with them are repeatedly called for to maintain the steady flow of production. It is this kind of work that we call 'unusual operations'.

There are two kinds of unusual operation: those dealing with changes, and those treating problems, often of an unexpected nature. Changes may be classified as variations in (1) product mix, (2) amount of production, (3) production methods, (4) products, and (5) labour mix. To save space, I give examples of only three of these types of change: those occurring in the product mix, in the labour mix, and in products or the appearance of new products. I feel that these three types capture most of the distinctive features.

Even in one line of production, it is not uncommon for several minor variations of the product to flow through in the course of just one day. Naturally, this implies a change of jigs and tools, which in turn requires further small adjustments after the change has been made. In terms of both quality and quantity, not only the speed with which such changes are made, but also the skill of the subsequent adjustments are crucial to productive efficiency. The ability to deal with these changes and adjustments is indispensable for a worker on the shop-floor.

Another skill needed to deal with changes is the ability to carry out many jobs in a single workshop, whereby the cost of dealing with changes in product mix is greatly reduced. Consider for example an assembly line for a car of fixed size with some small variation, say, from a two-door to a four-door sedan. Suppose that the less experienced workers can maintain a given line speed with the two-door type, but will not be able to keep up this speed if a number of four-door cars flow into the line. If there are veteran workers who can take over the jobs that were performed by inexperienced workers when two-door cars were being made with no decrease in line speed, and inexperienced workers can be transferred to easier jobs, then normal operations will not be disrupted. Given the diversity of consumer demand, this system of accommodating various product mixes is more efficient. Being able to run several jobs in the same production line is a great advantage.

Although this is frequently cited as an illustration of teamwork, it is not as simple as that. It is evident that each individual worker is allotted a particular job for a short run, and only over the long term will he cover many jobs, which are, again, distinctly identified. This is quite different from the situation in which all the members of the group handle all the jobs by helping each other in the workshop, which is what is often conjured up by the word 'teamwork'. This skill is basically an individual one.

Another example is a change in the labour mix, which can occur in one of two ways. In the first place, absenteeism naturally causes changes in the allocation of workers within a workshop. Secondly, there can be changes in the proportion of workers who are experienced in a particular workshop; the more veteran workers there are who can fill many different positions, the less costly any changes in their deployment will be.

It is crucial to the level of efficiency that the proper production procedures and the right jigs and tools are selected when new products are about to be produced. Naturally, there will be production engineers and designers in charge of designing these. But if there are also production workers who can point out some part of the process that should be modified according to their own experience, then efficiency can be greatly improved. In order to do this, such workers must know both the structure of the machines and the logic of the production process, and this is precisely the intellectual element of the skill. When it comes to dealing with unplanned problems in production, it is then that intellectual skills become all the more necessary.

Dealing with Problems

The second part of unusual operations concerns handling any problems that may arise. If we consider all problems, even those of a minor scale, then there can hardly be a production line that is free from them. The ability to deal with problems efficiently is an essential part of the skills needed. Actions taken to cope with problems can be divided into three steps:

1. Detect the smallest problem in goods or production equipment as soon as possible. This requires long experience to acquire knowledge of a variety of patterns or symptoms in unusual operations.
2. Diagnose the sources of the problem. This step is crucial to prevent recurrence of problems.
3. Rectify or mend the process to eliminate the problem. If the source of the problem lies in the machinery, then repairs are obviously called for. A complete overhaul of the equipment will normally be outside the job definition of its operators, but some repair and maintenance can be entrusted to the worker.

Being able to diagnose and rectify such problems implies a knowledge of the structure, functions, and mechanisms of the equipment, the products, and the production process itself, since most problems are due to troubles in some part of the machinery or to a part of the production process. This ability can be called the intellectual skills, because it is shared at least partly with engineers or technicians whose formal role is to know the mechanics of the equipment and product and to make efficiency-improving changes. Or perhaps it would be more appropriate to call production workers in Japanese workshops 'technicians'.

Integrated Systems v. Separate Systems

A question of crucial importance will often be raised: is it always necessary for production workers to conduct difficult and unusual operations which require intellectual skills? This question is divided into two different parts: one concerns the possibility of standardizing unusual operations, and the other, the allocation of unusual operations to engineers or technicians, rather than production workers. Let me begin with the first of these.

Some might argue that a careful study of problem-solving would reveal consistent patterns, and that the standard ways of dealing with such problems could be described in a manual, so that not much time or skill would be required to deal with such situations. According to veteran workers, however, potential problems are so varied that standardization is not feasible. Even if it were possible to compile such a manual by analysing problems in terms of standard patterns, the number of patterns to be consulted would be too large to enumerate clearly and would hinder a quick response.

This characteristic of problem-solving is a source of the so-called ambiguity of job definition. Since problems are not easy to predict, nor is it easy to standardize the operations necessary to handle them, it is not feasible to describe the job span distinctly, once it includes dealing with problems as a part of the job. In other words, if we clearly and fully define the job, there is always a danger of missing the treatment of some problems, and as a result many defects may be overlooked.

The second point about intellectual skills is by and large more crucial. Why cannot unusual operations be allotted to engineers or technicians rather than burdening to production workers with such difficult work? Clearly, two strategies for division of labour are conceivable, which we will call an integrated system and a separate system. A separated system divides operations between two worker-groups: 'usual' operations for the production workers, and 'unusual' operations for the higher grades of workers such as engineers or technicians. In the case of integrated systems, both operations are mainly in the hands of production workers.

These are two distinct systems in their division of labour. We might be able to reason which system allows a more efficient allocation of labour, subject to an important constraint: the condition that production workers must have the aptitude to acquire intellectual skills without much cost. To the degree that this condition is met, then, an integrated system is definitely superior to a separated system in terms of efficiency, for three reasons.

First, an integrated system has more workers available to deal with unusual operations. At a glance, this statement seems to ignore the benefits due to specialization under a separated system in which engineers or technicians are specialized in handling problems. So far as the surveyed cases are concerned, however, problems tend to be specific to individual types of machine as well as to individual types of product; different problems occur by for each type of machine and product. So, an operator under an integrated system can be considered to be specialized in handling problems specific to certain machines or products in his/her control span. Although in one sense engineers or technicians are specialized in handling problems, in another sense they are less specialized than an operator, in that they are required to deal with a wider range of machines as well as more types of product, each of which produces specific problems. Therefore, it seems hard to say that an operator working under an integrated system is less specialized in handling problems than the engineers or technicians. Without this specialized knowledge, few operators could be expected to devise new tools or measures to lessen the troubles in production that are often recognized on the Japanese shop-floor.

Moreover, a certain level of knowledge concerning problems and, accordingly, the structure of machines would undoubtedly contribute to the efficiency even under a separated system; unless an operator along the production line can feel there is something wrong with the machine, and unless he or she calls in engineers or technicians, how could they immediately handle the problem? If the above statement were valid, then the number of workers dealing with problems becomes critical, and, almost self-evidently, the number is larger under integrated systems than under separated systems.

Secondly, in an integrated system there are workers on the spot, i.e. beside the machinery, to perform unusual operations; when there is any sign of unusual trouble, these workers can handle it immediately. Compare this with the scenario where production workers have to call technicians or engineers from their offices every time they feel that something unusual is occurring. It is very likely that more than a few defective parts might pass without detection unless the operators themselves are able to identify what is wrong. If, on the other hand, engineers or technicians walk around the production line regularly enough to give a similar benefit, then the number of engineers tends to be quite large. This becomes extremely costly, particularly as engineers' salaries are relatively high.

Thirdly, an integrated system can encourage higher morale among production workers. If production workers are confined to routine jobs for long periods without any hope of encountering more advanced work, it is only natural that their morale should deteriorate.

A Fully Electronic Production Workshop

To understand the above statement, it is useful to consider a fully electronic production workshop as an illustration. This is also important in deciding whether or not fully electronification or computerization would make intellectual skills unnecessary.

The production workshop to be studied here belongs to a very large car-parts producer with nearly 10,000 employees.[2] This can be considered a typical mass-production workshop machining car parts of small size. Fifteen workers were working under one foreman at the time of study, the summer of 1986. The workshop consisted mainly of several machining lines, each of which had 10–20 machines, fully connected continuously, in the form of a letter U. One worker per shift was in charge of operating the line.

At a glance, all the production was perfectly automated, under the direction of computers attached to the machinery, with no operation being left to the workers. Materials were automatically supplied from one end of the line, machined, transferred to the following machines, and finally finished. No room for intellectual skills would seem to remain.

An in-depth observation clearly revealed the reverse. The major content of a worker's job now solely concerned unusual operations. True, most of the usual operations were transferred to the fully electronified, automated machines; cutting, drilling, and any other machining was performed by machines far better than workers could have done it. But this is not to imply that workers' skill has become unnecessary. Now it is in order to examine the 'unusual' operations one by one.

Unusual operations, even those simply dealing with changes in production, had become more difficult in terms of the growing extent of demanding components. Less difficult operations, such as treating changes in the product mix, accounted for a small part of daily operations. Normally, only four kinds of part were machined in this line in one day, instead of the several dozen that was more common. As a result, time for changing tools and jigs occupied only a small part of each day's work. Taking over for an absent employee was none the less important. There was a table for each line, in which were listed the names of those persons who could fill in at each position. Needless to say, those who could take over more positions tended to be assessed more highly.

The major components of dealing with changes pertains to the more difficult operations, that is, handling changes in the production line itself or to do with new products. Owing to model changes in car production, major changes in the production line occur about every four years, with minor changes in between. Old lines need to be replaced with new ones, which require new tools and jigs. Engineers cannot always design the most appropriate jigs and tools first time. During the trial period of operating new lines, veteran workers may find something inappropriate in the new tools and jigs. They then recommend improvements via their foremen to the engineers, which contributes greatly to increased productivity.

Along with their suggestions for improving production, dealing with problems constituted the main part of the workers' job content. Here, problems causing 'short stops' need to be noted. These occurred rather frequently. On the production line described above, the rate of production would be 120 pieces per an hour if there were no stops. In practice, ordinary output was around 85–100 pieces, and this was achieved when the operators were able to handle problems skilfully; if not, the output level would be far lower. Only with the help of workers with intellectual skills could most problems be remedied within 5–10 minutes. Yet, these 'short stops' occurred about once every hour. It is now evident that, as electronification proceeds, devising operations to treat problems and changes is crucial in maintaining efficiency, and intellectual skills are becoming increasingly important to this end.

Once we presume a world of uncertainty, as described by Frank Knight (1921), the above statement, that as computerization proceeds intellectual skills become more crucial, can be applied generally. The assumption of uncertainty never requires unrealistic presumptions; but just suppose that there are many potential problems whose occurrence cannot be easily predicted, and that their proper handling cannot be efficiently standardized. In order to standardize operations to deal with such problems, we need to know the exact patterns of their appearance as well as the best ways to handle them. Rationally, this is extremely unlikely to happen.

3. DEVELOPING INTELLECTUAL SKILLS

Broad OJT

Shop-floor workers acquire intellectual skills by one major and two supplementary methods. The major way is broad on-the-job training (OJT). One supplementary measure is other OJT by participating in maintenance work, while the second is short off-the-job training (OffJT) inserted between OJT. Let me explain these in turn.

Broad OJT implies that a worker experiences not only the major jobs in his own workshop but also, over a long term, the many jobs in a couple of other workshops which are closely related in technology. The extension of his job career should be within those workshops between which skill development is reasonable. In other words, the skill acquired in the original workshop can be fully utilized in the next workshop; in addition, that skill can be enlarged through the experience in the second workshop; movement from a workshop assembling a certain type of product of small size to another shop assembling products of a similar type but larger size would be an example.

This broad OJT takes a variety of forms. One is to make a job career, beginning with the easiest job in a workshop, promoting the worker to more difficult jobs in that shop, and eventually extending to the adjoining shop. In contemporary Japanese industry, rotation systems seem more common in production workshops. This is perhaps because nowadays most of the members of the workshop are veterans with long work experience. Rotation between major positions in one workshop and an exchange of one or two members with the adjoining shop every year is an ordinary form of OJT. (Examples are described in Koike 1988; Koike and Inoki 1990.)

One simple question might be raised: how can a new entrant acquire the necessary skill under such egalitarian rotation systems? Usually, a veteran worker is in charge of instructing him; he occupies the position next to that of the recent entrant in the rotation. In other words, the veteran has to play a dual role: he must do his own job, and he must also instruct the young worker. As the trainee's skill increases, the veteran's role as instructor becomes less. This is one of the most frequently cited examples involving teamwork. Whether or not this *is* teamwork depends on whether there is any remuneration system to reward an experienced individual for instructing the junior workers; this will be examined later.

One of the most important parts of OJT is to study problems on the shop-floor. It is common practice for each worker to write short reports on significant problems he has recently encountered: on what they were, how he dealt with them, and what problems still remain. These reports are filed, and are discussed in workshop meetings. Only important problems are filed, because many workers are familiar with the ordinary ones.

Broad OJT lets workers experience a wide range of functioning of machinery. This is the best opportunity for them to acquire knowledge of the structure and mechanism of machinery and the production process, which is the very core of the intellectual skills. This is conventionally cited as evidence of teamwork.

Supplementary OJT

One of the two supplementary forms of OJT is 'other OJT', in which workers participate in the maintenance workers' jobs. Originally, mending machinery was solely the work of maintenance men. Now, production workers first watch the maintenance workers at work, then proceed to take part in the work, and finally do it largely by themselves, although extremely difficult problems still require the maintenance workers' expertize. This again is an example usually cited as evidence of teamwork.

To give one instance, a food chemicals fermentation process workshop consists of ten workers, divided into five small teams with two operators each.[3] Five teams rotate the following roles: (1) shift work around the clock in operating fermentation tanks; (2) day work in charge of maintenance of equipment; and (3) holidays and vacation time. The type (2) work is the part described above. The workers inspect all the equipment every half-day to check for any problems, say a pinhole leak; if there are any, they mend them if they can. As shown above, this is not a part of so-called quality control (QC) circle activities, contrary to what is often assumed.

Short Inserted OffJT

Another supplementary way of developing intellectual skills is short inserted OffJT. The word 'short' implies a period lasting from two days to one week, and being 'inserted' means that short OffJT courses are sandwiched between OJT—say, every half-year or few years. The main role of this short inserted OffJT is to theorize and systematize the experience that workers have acquired. Without systematizing or theorizing the experience, intellectual skills cannot be established at the level that enables workers to deal with problems effectively.

Thus, the topics handled in the courses are naturally inclined towards theory, rather than practice. For example, in the workshop of the fully automated and electronified car parts manufacturer described above, courses on the theory of machining, of electrical sequence, of electronics, of hydraulic pressure, and of air pressure are arranged at both elementary and advanced levels.

The necessity of setting up a course on machining theory is that defective parts are often due to inappropriate adoption of cutting methods. If the cutting angle is not correct, for example, machining cannot be exact. Appropriate cutting methods depends on not only the cutting angle but also on the cutting speed, the character of the materials, and many other variables. This is taught in the theory of machining.

Similarly, a continuous line of automated machinery is directed by electronics and is driven either by hydraulic pressure or by air pressure. Troubles in either of these definitely cause problems in the assembly line. In order to understand the causes of such problems, it is indispensable to acquire theoretical knowledge in the above fields. One of the defects in contemporary Japanese training systems is that these short inserted OffJT courses are not provided in sufficient numbers.

4. INCENTIVE SYSTEMS FOR INTELLECTUAL SKILL DEVELOPMENT

Payment by Job

Without appropriate incentives, few workers are willing to acquire intellectual skills. There is no particular way to encourage them to do so other than by orthodox measures, that is, fair assessment and fair compensation for skill development. The practical methods for assessment and compensation, however, will be complicated because of the nature of intellectual skills.

The central features of intellectual skill attainment that need to be measured are two: broad experience, and the ability to handle problems. These features are not compatible with ordinary methods of payment. One such method is to assess workers simply by the jobs on which the individual workers are currently deployed; those performing difficult jobs are paid more. Another is payments by results: among those workers deployed on the same job, those who produce more are paid more. Neither method works well in creating intellectual skills, for the following reasons.

It is almost self-evident that the first feature of intellectual skill, broad experience, cannot be assessed simply by the current job the worker holds. Suppose there are two workers deployed on the same position, but one is able to work at many other positions in the workshop while the other is not. The former distinctly contributes far more to efficiency than the latter, by adjusting to changes such as covering for absent workers, or instructing newcomers. Unless the former is paid a higher wage, however, he will certainly become reluctant to perform these tasks. Under payment-by-results systems, workers are naturally eager to raise their skills to perform only the job on which they are currently deployed, but no effort would be made to elevate their skill level to cover broader experience, simply because this may even decrease their earnings. Similarly, workers are reluctant to substitute for or instruct fellow-workers for the same reason.

The second feature of intellectual skill attainment that needs to be assessed—handling and mending problems—is again hardly measured by simply looking at the current job. Even though workers are deployed in the same positions, the efficiency can vary enormously between those who can deal with problems well and those who cannot. And such problems are likely to be overlooked under payment-by-results systems.

Three Measures: Grade, Yearly Increments, and Merit Rating

In order to promote the development of intellectual skills, three measures in incentive systems are vitally important: job grade systems, yearly increments, and individual performance appraisal.

First, the size of remuneration needs to reflect individual differences in skill development both horizontally and vertically. If the same amount of remuneration is applied to all members, irrespective of skill development, no incentives will work. Payment-for-skill is needed, to be implemented by the payment by job grade with a range of rates. This plan can reward skill development in two ways. First, through the progression in the job grade, this can pay more for higher skill development. Secondly, the range rate for each job grade makes it feasible to reward skill development while the worker is staying on the same job, and hence to pay more to workers with a broader job experience than those with less experience among those currently deployed on the same job.

Second, workers must be encouraged to adopt a long-term perspective, without which the formation of intellectual skills cannot be expected. *Yearly increments of payments* naturally make a long-term commitment more favourable. A word of caution: the extent of increments varies with job grade, and there is a ceiling of increments for each grade.

Third, *merit assessment* is necessary. Even in the short run, and among the workers in the same job grade, the extent of skill development can differ, and this needs to be assessed. The practical method of assessment has to depend on the judgement of a person who is capable of measuring exactly the level of intellectual skill attainment. For complicated work such as 'unusual' operations, it is the foremen who are able to make such assessments, since most foremen have been promoted from the rank-and-file in the workshop and, accordingly, know the workshop well. Not even the foreman, however, can be entirely free from the pitfall of favouritism, under which few are willing to make a serious effort to elevate their skills. Devices to mitigate such favouritism are required. As will be described later, 'job matrix' is a measure of mitigation.

Interestingly, these three measures—job grade systems, yearly increments, and individual performance appraisal—are the favourites not only of Japanese industry, but also for white-collar workers in the West. The US Bureau of Labor Statistics survey on white-collar compensation clearly indicates that all the above components are common in the US medium-size and large firms. Range rate systems (where the pay rate for each job grade is not a single rate, but a range of rates) prevail, with about 50 per cent of ranges, accompanied by yearly increments under merit rating.[4] Even the number of job classes is, according to another survey, not much different from that of Japanese firms: 9 is the medium for non-managerial white-collar workers, and the Japanese figure is 8 (TPF & C 1979). Thus, the compensation systems in present-day Japanese industry can be said to be the same one, extended to cover blue-collar workers, that was originally developed for white-collar workers in the West.

Any conclusive remarks are to be reserved, however, since no intensive comparative study can be made here. An insight into a specific case would shed more light, with relevant statistical evidence based on government surveys of payment systems.

5. THE CASE OF A MAJOR CAR MANUFACTURER

The Job Grade System

Let us start with a short look into the Japanese Government Survey on Payment Methods, which reveals that few workers are subject to payment-by-results in Japan today. Table 1 shows that the proportion of payment-by-results to monthly wages is extremely small: as little as 0.5 per cent for manufacturing industries. Even for steel, which has the largest percentage, it is merely 2.0 per cent. (A word of caution: this is not the Japanese tradition, since payment-by-results was common in the period before the Second World War.)

TABLE 1   The Diffusion of Payment-by-Results
The ratio of the extent of payment-by-results to the average amount of monthly wages per worker, by size of firm and by industry: manufacturing industries, 1986

Industry	Monthly wages	Payment by results		
		Total	Individual	Group
Manufacturing industrial total	100	0.5	0.3	0.2
1000– employees	100	0.5	0.4	0.1
100–999 employees	100	0.4	0.2	0.2
30–99 employees	100	0.8	0.4	0.4
Food	100	0.9	0.9	0.0
Apparel	100	0.6	0.5	0.1
Wood	100	0.9	0.2	0.7
Furniture	100	0.7	0.3	0.4
Leather	100	0.8	0.1	0.7
Cement, pottery	100	0.7	0.4	0.3
Iron and steel	100	2.0	1.7	0.3
Metal products	100	0.7	0.4	0.3
Transportation and communication	100	2.5	2.4	0.1
Retail trades	100	2.5	2.1	0.4
Real estates	100	2.0	1.8	0.2
Service	100	1.1	1.1	0.0

Notes
Only those industries with more than 0.5% are listed above except for manufacturing industries as a whole. Monthly wages do not include overtime pay.

Source: Ministry of Labour, *Chingin Rodo Jikan Seido Chosa* (Survey on Payment Systems and Working Hour Systems) for 1986.

It is job grade systems that prevail in Japanese industry today. To have an insight into the job grade system, a case of a major car manufacturer is examined in detail. The job grade system consists of three categories: blue-collar workers, office workers, and managerial staff. There are eight job grades for production workers (P1–P8 in Table 2), seven for office workers, and five for managerial staff excluding senior management. These numbers coincide almost exactly with the prevailing systems in the government statistics, as shown in Table 3.

A newly recruited production worker starts at P1, and proceeds to the upper classes as skills develop. The criteria for proceeding are clearly stipulated in the 'job class assessment table', which is well known by the workers. The detailed criteria for promotion vary with the area—assembly

TABLE 2   Job Grade System: A Major Car Manufacturer

Job grade	Qualification
P8 Foremen	Foremen
P7 Foremen	Foremen
P6 Subforemen	Subforemen
P5 Group leaders	(1) Capable of performing all positions in the subforeman's unit at the third level
	(2) Able, as a leader, to promote quality and productivity in the unit
'Highly skilled'	(1) Capable of performing many of the positions in the foreman's unit
	(2) Capable of advising effectively during new production line starts
P4 Team leaders	(1) Capable of performing all positions in the subforeman's unit at the second level, and a part of the positions at the third level
	(2) Capable of dealing with problems
P3 Senior workers	(1) Capable of performing nearly two-thirds of the positions at the second level
	(2) Capable of being a leader of small group activities
	(3) Capable of dealing with slightly difficult problems
P2 Grade 2 workers	(1) Capable of performing about one-third of the positions in the subforeman's unit at the second level
P1 Junior workers	

Notes
The 'third level' means that the worker can perform the job skilfully enough to be able to instruct other workers.
The 'second level' means that the worker can perform the job without any help from others.

TABLE 3   Number of Job Grades, by Size of Firm: Manufacturing Industries, 1987

Size of firm	Number of job grades	
	Non-managerial staff including supervisory positions	Managerial staff
Total	8.2	5.5
1000–	8.1	6.1
100–999	7.9	4.8
30–99	8.4	6.2

Source: Ministry of Labour, *Chingin Rodo Jikan Seido Chosa* (Survey on Payment Systems and Working Hour Systems) for the year 1987.

line, painting, body welding, stamping, and machining. Table 2 indicates those for assembly line shops. The criterion for promotion to P2 is to be 'capable of performing about one-third of the positions in the subforeman's unit at the second level'; 'the second level' means that a worker can do the job without the help of any of the others.

To understand this criterion, we need to know the organization of the shop-floor. In assembly lines a subforeman's unit consists of 15–20 workers, while smaller units in machining shops have 10. Consequently, a worker has to be able to fill five or six positions for promotion to P2. This suggests that the Japanese workers are likely to be able to fill more positions than their US counterparts; even the most lowly ranked Japanese worker would be almost identical to the US workers who are working under team systems, in terms of breadth of experience. It is dangerous, however, to overestimate the difference between the two, since the careers of most Japanese workers remain within a subforeman's unit, so they do not differ much from those of the utility men or relief men in the US car assembly lines in terms of the breadth of experience.

The subforeman works partly on the line, filling in at times for absentees; he is also in charge of some administrative work as well as instructing newcomers. Therefore, subforemen are ranked in between foremen and group leaders in US industry. Four or five subforemen's units constitute one foreman's unit, having 70–100 workers. And three or four foremen's units make a section, supervised by a section chief. Both subforemen and foremen come from the shop-floor and are union members, while most section chiefs are BSc degree engineers, though a few are ex-foremen.

It should be stressed that two factors indicating the extent of skills development—breadth and depth of experience—are stipulated as the main criteria in the assessment table. For promotion to P3, a worker should be able to fill two-thirds of the positions in the subforeman's unit without any help from others. For promotion to P4, he is required to fill all positions in the unit independently and some of them skilfully enough to be able to instruct fellow-workers. And for promotion to P5, he must be able to handle all the jobs in the unit skilfully enough to instruct fellow-workers, or to handle the jobs in the next subforeman's units.

The depth of experience, that is, the ability to deal with problems, is also emphasized. The criteria for promotion to P3 require workers to be able to treat problems that are not too difficult, and those for P4 are to handle most unusual operations in the work of the unit. Since there is no limit to the number of posts in each class under P6, there is no reason why a worker cannot proceed to the upper classes, provided his capability meets the relevant criteria. Therefore, job grade is clearly connected with the extent of skill development.

For grade P6 and over, the story becomes different. Here, the job class is directly connected with the functional posts of subforemen and foremen, so that without a vacancy in these posts no one can be promoted to these classes.

Concentrating on the situation under P6, where job grade roughly coincides with the extent of skill development, the measurement of such skill attainment becomes critical. Because this assessment can be made only by those who know the work well, it falls on the subforemen in the workshop.

'Job Matrix'

This implies, however, a danger of favouritism, which might cause demoralization on the shop-floor. To lessen this risk, some constraints on the foreman's discretion are needed. The major constraint adopted in this case is to make a 'job matrix' and to post it on the bulletin board at the shop-floor.[5] This consists of two tables: one for breadth of experience and another for depth of experience.

The practical style of the tables varies from workshop to workshop even within a single factory, though a sample is shown as Tables 4 and 5. The first column of the breadth table lists the names of workers in the workshop, while the row indicates the titles of all positions in the workshop. The table not only marks those positions that individual workers have experienced so far, but also indicates the level of skill with which they can conduct the job; the highest level, being able to instruct fellow-workers, is indicated in red ink, the next level, being able to conduct the jobs on his own, in pink,

TABLE 4 Job Matrix 1: Breadth of Experience

Name	Usual operations			
	Job 1	Job 2	Job 3	Job 4 ...
Mr A	c	c	b	b
Mr B	c	b	a	b
Mr C	a	a	b	b
.
.
.

Notes
a: Having received instructions on the job
b: Able to perform functions alone
c: Able to teach fellow workers how to perform functions

and the lowest level, having just finished training, in white. The depth table is of similar style, with one difference: the major units of unusual operations make up the column headings.

These two tables are revised about every three months, depending on each workshop's practice, to reflect the skill development of individual

TABLE 5   Job Matrix 2: Depth of Experience

Name	Usual operations			
	Problem 1	Problem 2	Change 1	Change 2 ...
Mr A	—	c	c	—
Mr B	c	b	b	c
Mr C	a	a	b	b
.				
.				
.				

Notes
See Table 4.

workers. It is the subforeman in the workshop who makes and revises these tables, and consequently they are not perfectly free from his subjective judgement. In many workshops, however, the tables are posted on the bulletin board in the workshop. This means that the subforeman's assessment is examined by the workers, who work together every day in the workshop and accordingly have keen critical eyes. In this case the personnel department encourages the posting of tables, and in practice many workshops post them, though it is at the discretion of each subforeman's unit whether to post or not. Moreover, identification of the breadth and depth of individual experience is basically clear-cut, so that not much room remains for subjective judgement, quite unlike the case of simple merit assessment.

Remuneration

It is this job class system that largely affects the levels of wages and salaries. Apart from some benefits such as family allowance or housing benefits, the main part of remuneration consists of the four components:

(a) 'Basic rates', occupying nearly 30 per cent of the main part of remuneration
(b) 'Age rates', occupying about 25 per cent
(c) 'Job grade rates', occupying slightly less than 40 per cent
(d) 'Merit rates', occupying 7 per cent

Job grade exclusively determines job grade rates, the largest component, and heavily affects merit rates and basic rates. Thus, more than three-quarters of remuneration is basically influenced by the job grade system.

Job grade rates are, as described in Table 6, composed of a single rate for each job grade. Table 6 was obtained from the *Labour Union News*, which clearly states that the union negotiates this table at every spring 'labour offensive'. Tables for managerial staff are not available because they are not union members.

TABLE 6   Job Grade Rates, 1991

Job grade for production workers	Job grade rate		Job grade for office workers	Job grade rate	
	¥en	Index		¥en	Index
P1	82,200	100	O1	82,200	100
P2	85,900	105	O2	85,900	105
P3	89,900	109	O3	97,100	105
P4	94,200	115	O4	102,800	118
P5	99,200	121	O5	108,000	131
P6	103,700	126	O6	112,500	137
P7	124,100	151	O7	117,900	143
P8	132,400	161			

Source: *Labour Union News*.

There is intense competition among workers under the job class system. Demotion may occur when capability declines, and this is not confined to language, but is actually implemented, though infrequently, when workers become old. This implies extremely intensive pressure for workers to maintain their skills even towards the end of their career.

Although job grade rates consist of a single rate for each grade, this does not mean that the same pay is applied to those in the same job grade. There is variance in payments between workers on the same job grade, due to merit rates, and basic rates. Merit rates are determined, again, mainly by job grade, varying according to individual performance appraisal. For each job grade, the extents of merit rates are divided into five grades, say, A, B, C, D, and E, the difference between grades being quite small. No rules are stipulated for the proportion of each grade, but the average of those on the same job class in each foreman's unit must be grade C.

This individual assessment similarly affects the level of basic rates, which consist of (1) entry wages and (2) yearly increments. Entry wages are determined by the grade of education and by the previous experience a worker has. One of the prevailing misunderstandings of Japanese payment systems is that no consideration is paid for any experience in firms other than the current one. In practice, however, it is customary for previous experience to be assessed: almost fully rewarded in the case of a similar occupation, and even in other occupations 60–80 per cent of the period worked is credited as length of service. Interestingly, the difference by grade of schooling is small: the number of school years is given almost equivalent weight to the length of service.

Yearly increments in basic rates, again, depend on individual assessment by supervisors. The standard amount of increment is determined by job grade, around which the individual extent of increments is set according to individual performance appraisal. Moreover, each job grade has its standard level of basic rate, and when a worker's basic rate is below this level the amount of increment is large, whereas it becomes smaller when the basic rate exceeds the standard. This mechanism again strengthens the influence of the job grade on the level of basic rates. Unlike job grade rates, no deduction occurs in basic rates.

The only part of remuneration free from job grade and performance appraisal is the age rate. As shown in Table 7, a single rate for each age is stipulated, irrespective of occupation. Interestingly, remuneration systems that depend largely on age were recognized in the salary tables for British banking employees in the 1960s.[6] A difference was that those for British banking employees constituted the main part of their remuneration, whereas here they account for only a quarter of the worker's main remuneration. As the table shows, it increases most for workers in their twenties and thirties, less for those in their forties, and even decreases in for those in their fifties.

University Graduates

The remuneration system for the white-collar workers, including university graduates, is basically similar to that for the production workers described above. A noted divergence is the speed with which white-collar workers are promoted along the job grade ladder. At first glance, even this speed does not seem to vary much. The usual age to arrive at the position of subforeman, P6, is thought to be less than 40, since one of the qualifications for promotion is for the worker to be less than 40 years old. On the other hand, the university graduates arrive at 07, which is equivalent to P6 in the status, by the latter half of their thirties at the latest.

However, the probability of promotion differs greatly. Only a part of the production workers reach the level of P6, while almost all university graduates proceed to 07. Moreover, managerial classes are available for the majority of university graduates, whereas only a very small part of all production workers can progress to even the lowest grade of managerial class. Nevertheless, the extent of the gap between these two groups is one of the smallest among developed economies.

K. Koike

TABLE 7   Age Rates, 1991

Age	Age rate	Difference
18	43,150	0
19	43,650	500
20	44,150	500
21	44,900	750
22	45,650	750
23	47,400	1,750
.		
.		
.		
30	59,650	1,750
31	60,950	1,300
.		
.		
.		
35	66,150	1,300
36	67,150	1,000
.		
.		
.		
40	71,150	1,000
41	71,850	700
.		
.		
.		
45	74,650	700
46	75,150	500
.		
.		
.		
50	77,150	500
51	77,150	0
52	77,150	0
53	75,650	− 1,500
.		
.		
.		
59	63,650	− 2,100

Notes
See Table 1.

6.   A TENTATIVE COMPARISON WITH SWEDISH CASES

Differences in Blue-Collar Workers

In 1990 six businesses in Sweden were visited. Two were studied for the blue-collar workers: a car assembly workshop and a numerically controlled (NC) machine shop. Four were visited for the study of the white-collar workers: two banks and two large manufacturers. Since all visits were of short duration, and each blue-collar site was visited only once, I present here merely a preliminary analysis.

For the production workshops, similarities as well as differences with Japanese cases were identified. First, a broadening of experience of workers is not uncommon in the two Swedish cases. The car assembly workshop employed regular rotation of the positions every two hours within a group leader unit. Even in the NC machine shop, where exchange of positions is more difficult because the operator conducts various operations while staying in the same station, 5 operators out of 21 could command two machines, and it was a distinct policy of the foreman as well as the engineer in charge of the workshop to encourage workers to broaden their experience. It was thought that the workers' experience might be slightly broader in Japan, though decisive evidence is lacking.

Second, it is common in the two countries for shop-floor workers to be encouraged to deal with troubles and problems arising on the line. The operators on the assembly line in the Swedish car manufacturer handled problems that were not too difficult, and those on NC machines adjusted and mended programming when there was any problem.

The greatest difference lay in the remuneration systems. Whereas payment for Japanese production workers increases as their skills improve, wages hardly increased in the Swedish cases after the initial few years. Apart from the revision by collective bargaining, the basic rates for the operators on the assembly line in this Swedish car manufacturer never increased after one-and-a-half years of service, and no merit rating existed. Accordingly, there were no incentives for any improvement in workers' skills, in contrast to the Japanese car assembly line.

However, another Swedish case of machinists would seem to share some common features with Japanese, having both yearly increments and merit assessment. Yet, the extent of wage increases due to skill development is far smaller in the Swedish case: only two grades of payment for machinists were established. It should be noted, however, that most engineers who wrote computer programs were promoted from machinists, though not all machinists could be promoted. The machinist's career, then, was extended at least in part to include the engineers, which might lessen the difference between two countries under the same trend, termed 'white-collarization'.[7] This could be regarded as a new tendency, as the remuneration system in question had been in operation for only two years, transformed from the ordinary payment-by-results methods, and no statistical data are available to indicate how widely this new system is being practised.

Similarity in White-Collar Workers

A different story emerges when comparing the white-collar workers in the two countries: greater similarity with less variance.

First, remuneration is according to job grade, whose numbers in two large Swedish banks did not vary much from those of the Japanese; at one bank there are seven grades for the branch manager level and below, and at another seven for all employees including the director level. These small numbers of job grades imply that a job grade does not exactly coincide with a particular job, unlike a firm having several dozen job grades. In a large Swedish bank, for example, assistant branch managers can be graded to job class 3, 4, or 5; branch managers are ranked 5, 6, or 7, over which they can progress even while they stay at the same post in the same branch.

Second, yearly increments with merit rating were common and the ceiling of age–salary profiles is reached very slowly in the four large firms visited. This again is similar to the Japanese white-collar workers.[8]

Yet, differences cannot be overlooked so far as aggregate statistical figures are concerned. Both countries similarly afford national statistics of high quality on age–salary profiles, in which two points of difference are evident. The one is the peak age in the payments, which comes slightly later in Japan: 45–49 for all salaried male employees in Sweden, and 50–54 for those in the Japanese manufacturing industry. The other is less steep profiles for Sweden: the peak level is around 165–70 in Sweden but 255 in Japan, the salary level for the age 20–25 being set at 100.[9]

Alongside these differences, three basic features—pay for job grade, yearly increments for a long period, and merit rating—are wholly shared with Japanese white-collar and blue-collar workers.

7. SUMMING UP

I can now sum up the conclusions to be drawn from the above discussion.

1. Workers' skills on the shop-floor as characterized by their intellectual skills play a key role in promoting efficiency. Efficiency depends heavily on workers' skills to deal with the problems and changes that frequently arise. To deal with such problems and changes skilfully, knowledge of the structure and workings of the machinery as well as the production process is essential, and this is exactly what comprises the content of intellectual skills. Moreover, this type of skill will become increasingly important in areas where a high degree of computerization prevails; computerization tends to relegate more of the usual and routine operations to machines, leaving the more unusual operations—operating problems and changes—in the hands of workers. It

is mainly broad OJT on the shop-floor that serves to develop intellectual skills.

2. The popular argument concerning group-oriented behaviour seems to be based on a misunderstanding of the character of workers' skills. It has long been emphasized that, in spite of the ambiguity of job definition, Japanese workers work efficiently because of their group-oriented behaviour. An insight into work on the shop-floor, however, reveals a different story. The above assumption of ambiguity does not tie in with the work-handling routine and monotonous operations of the workshop. These are clearly defined and allotted to individuals; if not, no assembly line could work well. But another crucially important part of work, 'unusual operations', cannot by its nature be clearly defined. The unexpected problems that arise are difficult to predict with any accuracy, and it is extremely costly to standardize operations to deal with them effectively. If we try to define them in a clear-cut way and forcibly standardize the operations beforehand to allow for all such problems and changes, then many defective products are frequently apt to be overlooked. This coincides with the assumption described by Frank Knight, pioneer of the economics of uncertainty.

3. In order to develop intellectual skills, appropriate incentive systems are indispensable. No magic wand exists for developing such skills, but only orthodox methods such as fair assessment and fair compensation. Because of the complicated character of intellectual skills, however, these fair measures are not simple to implement. This implies that incentive systems must not be of a group character, but rather of an individual one, since individual skill development is essential.

Ordinary methods of assessment simply by the current job position or payment-by-results system are not effective for developing intellectual skills. If we assess a worker's skill merely by his current job, any experience that has been accumulated so far is wholly neglected, and it is this broad experience that enables the worker to handle problems. Payment-by-results promotes skill only in conducting the current job, but not in developing broader experience.

Fair assessment of skill development must take into account any previous experience, including the handling of problems. A popular practice on the Japanese shop-floor is to detail a job matrix, whose revisions indicate the enhancement of skills among the workers.

Fair compensation for skill development consists of three major components: job grade systems, yearly increments, and performance appraisal. Job grade systems are effective for rewarding skill development for a middle range of term, by appreciating the development in breadth and depth of skill. Yearly increments of remuneration make long-term service favourable, one of the major conditions for forming intellectual skills that need a long time to be acquired. Merit rating by supervisors is also necessary. Skill development includes the capability of handling problems, which is difficult to identify accurately without the keen observation of those who know the work well. To mitigate possible favouritism, a job matrix should be utilized.

4. These three major components are not peculiar to Japanese workers, but also apply to the white-collar workers in Sweden, and possibly elsewhere in the West. Since these are already in place, the remuneration systems can be transferred to the production workers there, if considered necessary and desirable. One of the possible, and most persuasive, reasonings for extending them to the blue-collar workers is the question: why shouldn't those practices be applied to the production workers, that already exist for white-collar workers in the same industry and in the same country?

This does not imply that the incentive systems for production workers in present-day large Japanese firms are identical to those of the white-collar workers in the West. Whether this is the case is left for further comparative investigation. If tentative remarks could be made, however, the Japanese system seems to promote intensive competition in the long term, even among production workers.

NOTES TO CHAPTER 2

1. The following statements are founded on two series of case studies. One deals with six workshops in five Japanese plants (Koike and Inoki 1990; Inoki 1991); the other analyses 10 workshops in 8 plants in Aichi-Prefecture (Aichi-Prefecture 1987). The concept of intellectual skills is fully developed in Koike and Inoki (1990).
2. This case is described in detail in ch.1 of Aichi-Prefecture (1987).
3. This case is described in Inoki (1991).
4. Personick (1984) and Roomkin (1989: esp. ch. 1) indicate typical remuneration methods for the white-collar workers in the contemporary UK.
5. Examples of job matrix are described in a series of articles in a journal, *Kojo Kanri* (Factory Administration), 34 (7): 25–65 (in Japanese), on various types of workshops, ranging from machine shops and assembly shops to process shops.
6. Blackburn (1967) explains the salary systems of British banking employees for that date; see pp. 71–5. The salary tables are shown in Koike (1966; only in Japanese).
7. The explanation of the word 'white-collarization' is fully developed in Koike (1988).
8. There is one exception on the Japanese side. The Japanese workers are paid less after their mid-fifties in many large firms (see Koike 1988: ch. 1).
9. For Sweden, figures are obtained and calculated from: Swedish Employers Confederation *et al.* (1989: 27, table 8). For Japan, figures are obtained from the Ministry of Labour, *Chingin Kozo Kihon Chosa* (Basic Survey of Wage Structure)

for the year 1988. For the Japanese data, the classification by salaried and non-salaried employees is not available for all industry but only for the manufacturing mining and building industries. This is why the figure does not stand for all industry but only for the manufacturing industry.

REFERENCES

Aichi-Prefecture, Department of Labour (1987), *Chiteki Jukuren no Keisei—Aichi-Ken no Kigyo* (Intellectual Skill Formation in the Firms in Aichi-Prefecture), Aichi-Prefecture, Department of Labour (in Japanese).

Aoki, Masahiko (1988), *Information, Incentives, and Bargaining in the Japanese Economy*, Cambridge University Press.

Blackburn, R. M. (1967), *Union Character and Social Class: A Study of White-Collar Unionism*, Batsford, London.

Inoki, Takenori (1991), 'Skill Formation Systems in the Food Processing Industry: A Comparison between Thailand and Japan', *Economic Papers*, 41(1): 1–19.

Itoh, Hideshi (1991), 'Japanese Human Resource Management from the Viewpoint of Incentive Theory', *Ricerche Economiche*, Special Issue.

Knight, Frank H. (1921), *Risk, Uncertainty and Profit*, University of Chicago Press, 1971.

Koike, Kazue (1966), *Chingin* (Wages), Daimond, Tokyo (in Japanese).

——(1988), *Understanding Industrial Relations in Modern Japan*, Macmillan, London.

——and Inoki, Takenori (1990), *Skill Formation in Japan and Southeast Asia*, Tokyo University Press.

Personick, Martin E. (1984), 'White-Collar Pay Determination under Range-of-Rate-Systems', *Monthly Labor Review*, December: 25–30.

Roomkin, Myron (1989), *Managers as Employees*, Oxford University Press.

Swedish Employers Confederation *et al.* (1989), *Salaries of Salaried Employees* [for the year 1988], SEC, Stockholm.

TPF&C (Towers, Perrin, Forster, and Crosby) (1979), *Survey of Salary Administration, Policy and Practices*, TPF&C.

3

Different Quality Paradigms and their Implications for Organizational Learning

ROBERT E. COLE

1. INTRODUCTION

Our subject is organizational learning in the context of alternative quality paradigms. The traditional quality control paradigm that has evolved in Western industry over the last seventy years will be elaborated primarily through the ideas of Frederick Taylor. The new paradigm is the quality improvement paradigm that has emerged over the past few decades in Japan and is now diffusing to Western industry.

Implicit in both paradigms is a distinctive approach to organizational learning. The argument presented here is that a great deal of the strengths and weaknesses of the two paradigms can be understood in terms of their approach to learning. The focus of this paper is on organizational learning. To be sure, organizational learning presumes individual learning. However, there can be a great deal of individual learning without that being translated into organizational learning. The power of the new quality improvement paradigm rests very much on its implications for organizational learning, and it is this theme that I will seek to explicate.

Following the work of Cyert and March (1963) Nelson and Winter (1982), and Levitt and March (1988), I treat organizational learning as routine-based, history-dependent, and target-oriented. Organizations learn by encoding inferences from history into routines that guide behaviour. Routines are the basis for organizational memory, with routinization of an activity the most important form of storage of the organization's specific operational knowledge. Organizational routines include the forms, rules, procedures, conventions, strategies, and technology around which the organization is constructed and through which it operates. They also include the structures of beliefs and cultural codes that reinforce, elaborate, and sometimes contradict the formally prescribed routines. The routines are independent of the individual actors who enact them, although individuals contribute to their formation and sustenance. Organizational routines are transmitted, evolve, and displace one another through socialization, education, problem-solving, imitation, professionalization, personnel movement, mergers, and acquisitions (cf. Levitt and March 1988: 320). These activities may be carried out through traditional hierarchical authority structures or through more horizontal peer-to-peer learning activities.

This process of transmission and evolution is what we mean by organizational learning. Identifying and creating best-practice organizational routines, standardizing these standards, and diffusing them throughout the organization is a central issue determining the quality of an organization's products or services. Quality itself is defined, following Joseph Juran's classic definition, as fitness for use as defined by the final user (Juran 1988).

Figure 1 identifies the major organizational tasks involved in quality improvement. The first of these is to create the organizational routines that correctly identify potential customers and help you grasp what these customers want. The second is to create the organizational routines that translate those wants into design criteria and specifications for elements of the planned service or product. The third task is to create the organizational routines that ensure that design criteria and specifications are retained throughout the stages of organizational processing through the actual delivery of the product or service to the customer. As is suggested by the figure, during the execution of each of these three large tasks, final quality will be enhanced though a process of standardization and diffusion of best practices associated with the respective routines and their myriad subroutines. Even the very act of innovation can be enhanced by routinization of problem-solving routines (cf. Nelson and Winter 1982). In short, the final results will be enhanced by a process of continual improvement of the major routines and subroutines. It is this picture of the organizational tasks involved in quality improvement that guide our analysis. The organizational tasks associated with quality improvement can be done well or badly. Our theme will be that large Japanese manufacturing firms have learned to do them very well indeed.

2. THE TRADITIONAL PARADIGM

Frederick Winslow Taylor was a remarkable man with remarkable ideas that helped shape the modern organization of work. Whether they be his observations about shop-floor organization that so heavily influenced American management, or the application of his ideas to the administrative level in Europe, his ideas received a wide audience. He is perhaps best remembered for his advocacy of the separation of planning from execution, the benefits of specialization, and his contributions to detailed job analysis. Above all, he helped bring order to the rather chaotic and inefficient practices that existed prior to the application of his ideas.

Taylor also had definite ideas about quality which, while not particularly

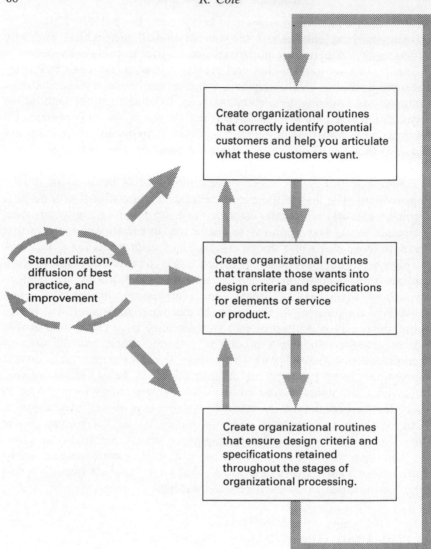

FIG. 1   Discrete Organizational Tasks Involved in Quality Improvement

original, captured the dominant quality paradigm in Western industry, a paradigm that remained unchallenged in the West until the 1980s. Hereafter this paradigm will be referred to as the 'traditional quality paradigm'. Even when he didn't directly discuss the implications of his ideas for quality improvement, Western managers for the next seventy years commonly applied his managerial ideas to the quality sphere. In this sense, Taylor contributed directly and indirectly to the dominant quality paradigm.

Taylor's approach to quality improvement must be understood, of course, in the context of the motivation and reward systems of the day. He describes his approach in his treatise, *The Principle's of Scientific Management*, published in 1911 (Taylor 1967: 87–97). Taylor was given the task of systematizing work at the largest bicycle ball factory in the United States. He was particularly concerned about quality, and the 120 inspectors responsible for visually picking out defective ball bearings. There were four kinds of defects: dents, bearings too soft, scratched, and fire-cracked. It took a trained eye to detect these defects. Taylor made a number of changes that resulted in shorter working hours, greater efficiency, and higher wages. But here the focus is on how he handled the quality problem. The first step, he says, was to make it impossible for the inspectors to neglect their work or perform it carelessly without being found out. This was accomplished by over-inspection. Each day, four of the most trusted inspectors was given a lot of balls to inspect which had been examined the day before by one of the regular inspectors; the number identifying the lot to be over-inspected having been changed by the foreman so that none of the over-inspectors knew whose work they were examining. In addition, one of the lots inspected by the four over-inspectors was examined on the following day by the chief inspector, selected on the basis of her accuracy and integrity.

You might think that was enough, but that was not the case. Fred Taylor took no chances. In addition to the above-mentioned steps, every two or three days, a *lot* of balls was especially prepared by the foreman, who counted out a definite number of perfect balls and added a recorded number of defective balls of each of the four kinds. Neither the inspectors nor the over-inspectors had any means of distinguishing this prepared lot from the regular commercial lots. In this way, concludes Taylor, 'all temptation to slight their work or make false returns was removed' (Taylor 1967: 86–95).

A number of observations can be made about Taylor's approach to quality improvement. Above all, it represents an inspection-oriented rather than a prevention-oriented approach. Until the 1980s, this was the dominant approach to quality improvement in Western industry; defect detection through inspection, rather than upstream problem-solving to eliminate the cause of problems, has been the characteristic approach to quality control. Defect detection—the search for error—pushes management towards a coercive approach to learning. It encourages the 'policing of quality' to ferret out the culprits, fostering a blame-oriented culture. Employees respond to such an environment by withholding information, thereby minimizing learning opportunities.

For all of Taylor's emphasis in his writings on the importance of co-operation, he never could really understand why workers resisted his ideas when they were given the clearly specified tasks called for in his design. But the policeman's mentality, and the lack of trust implicit in his dealings with workers, speak volumes on the subject. Despite Taylor's remarkable insights into the organization of work, he had a remarkably oversimplified view of human motivation (Fox 1982: 1091).[1]

Central to Taylor's ideas was the importance of identifying the best method of organizing work tasks and then making that method the standard—in other words, the need to modify the existing work routine through standardizing on the best process in order to reach high levels of efficiency and quality. His understanding of how this organizational learning should take place is described in the following extract:

This one new method, involving that series of motions which can be made quickest and best, is then substituted in place of the ten or fifteen inferior series which were formerly in use. This best method becomes standard, and remains standard, to be taught first to the teachers (or functional foreman) and by them to every workman in the establishment until it is superseded by a quicker and better series of movements. (Taylor 1967: 118)

Unlike many contemporary Western managers, Taylor understood well the importance of standardization and diffusion of best practice, not only for efficiency but also for continuous quality improvement. As we can see from the above, however, his understanding of the mechanism by which one routine replaced another took place (organizational learning) was more limited.

Taylor assumed a rather simplistic process of diffusion, relying on the hierarchical control of superiors to see that the proper knowledge was transferred and implemented. His description makes it appear to be a rather unproblematic set of events. Since Taylor's time, Western industry has developed expert systems for organizational learning. That is to say, management specialists relying on the authority system analyse, propose, and introduce changes in work procedures and organization.

Borrowing and adapting DiMaggio and Powell's terminology (1983) to intra-company transfers of organizational practices, I may say that Taylor and those who followed him relied on coercive isomorphism to bring about uniform organizational practices. That is to say, managerial confidence that best practice will be diffused and standardized rests on using the authority structure of the firm. This approach ignores the costs (both in time and in distortion of information) that may occur from involving third parties (i.e. managerial levels not directly involved in the work process) in the learning process. Generally speaking, replication of work routines through imitation, even within the same firm, is a lot more problematic than the traditional additivity models of economists would suggest (cf. Nelson and Winter 1982; Levitt and March 1988:331).

An additional characteristic of the traditional approach to quality which has strong implications for learning is the specialization of the quality function. True to Taylor's ideas, the quality function evolved in Western firms as a specialized staff responsibility. In principle, this meant that a highly focused resource was made available to support quality initiatives in the organization. In practice, it meant that other departments and employees in those departments felt little responsibility for quality. Consequently, it is not surprising that their motivation for learning and applying the essentials of quality control, much less quality improvement, were quite low. Similarly, there was little incentive for those with line responsibility to build quality improvement considerations into performance routines. In short, organizational learning was limited to a small group of organizational eunuchs.

Managerial understanding of employee motivational considerations has become remarkably more sophisticated since the days of Frederick Taylor. Yet, the structural constraints imposed by the traditional quality paradigm have greatly limited the utilization of these more sophisticated approaches.

Finally, under the traditional model, the objective has been quality control rather than continuous quality improvement. The implications for organizational and individual learning are profound. In saying that the objective for the traditional model was quality control, we mean that the target was a quite limited one: to control quality problems. The implicit assumption grounded in a very constrained cost–benefit equation was that there were limits beyond which quality improvement could not be justified on an economic basis.

The practical implications of this view were that, once modest quality objectives were achieved, attention could be turned to higher-priority objectives. More often than not, quality results would then deteriorate, thereby requiring renewed attention to quality and imposition of the usual 'firefighting fixes'. From an organizational learning perspective, this meant that there was set in motion a rather limited repetitive cycle of detect and repair requiring only modest rotation of existing organizational routines as modest improvements were followed by regression. The amount of organizational learning needed to sustain this cycle was limited indeed. Limited targets meant limited organizational learning. Individual motivation for learning was correspondingly limited.

3. THE MODERN QUALITY PARADIGM

The following list describes the characteristics of the modern quality movement as reflected in the approach taken by its leading practitioners in Japan:[2]

1. 'Market-in' approach, which provides strong external customers orientation and uses internal customer chain as connection to final user
2. Quality as umbrella theme for organizing work
3. Improved quality as strong competitive strategy

4. All-employee, all-department involvement pivotal strategy for improving quality of every business process
5. Upstream prevention activities key to quality improvement
6. Well defined problem-solving methodology and training activities tied to continuous quality improvement
7. Integration of quality into control system of goals, plans, and actions
8. Focus on cross-functional co-operation

This is not to say that every firm equally manifests these characteristics, or pursues them with equal robustness: only that together they characterize a model of the modern quality movement. We can pursue this discussion by examining the implications of each characteristic for learning. The discussion is premissed on the assumption that, for organizational learning to take place, the organization needs: willingness (motivation), capacity (tools), and opportunity (structure). Absent any one of these elements, and organizational learning will be minimized. I argue that, taken as a whole, the modern quality paradigm provides all three elements in reinforcing fashion.

1. 'Market-in' has evolved in the post-war period as a major focus of Japanese quality-improvement activities. This means deploying information on customer needs as widely as possible in the organization and defining those with a need to know as broadly as possible. It means bringing customer needs into every possible part of the organization. In principle, every work process in every department is seen as linked in an internal customer chain which extends to the most important customer, the end-user. By infusing the organization with market considerations, additional sources of uncertainty—and motivation to cope with that uncertainty—are introduced. To respond effectively to these pressures, training and flexibility through decentralized employee responsibility are required. Such training (reflected in characteristic 6) and flexibility (reflected in characteristic 4) ensures that rapid changes in organizational routines can take place. Both individual and organizational learning are inevitably part of this process.

2. Quality improvement has emerged increasingly as an umbrella theme for managing Japanese firms. This means that a great many organizational objectives traditionally presented as cost-reduction and productivity-improvement initiatives are reoriented towards and packaged as quality-improvement objectives with the focus on decisions that enhance customer satisfaction.

This is not simply a matter of cosmetics. To be sure, quality improvement is much more saleable to employees, and therefore more motivating and less threatening, than traditional cost-reduction and productivity-improvement programs.

A quality-improvement focus, however, does turn targeted objectives towards customer satisfaction. This leads to a different set of management decisions than would be the case if management were by guided by cost-reduction objectives alone. Cost-reduction targets typically lead to managers making arbitrary decisions (e.g. across-the-board cuts) which more often than not detract from quality. In short, the quality-improvement theme focuses the opportunities for organizational learning.

By making quality an umbrella theme, a common language of quality improvement develops through all functional specialities and organizational levels, thereby enhancing communication, understanding, and acceptance of common objectives. Individual learning capacities are enhanced. The upshot of these various considerations is that quality as an umbrella theme greatly increases individual motivation to learn, enhances individual capacity to co-operate through a common organizational language, and focuses learning activities on the customer satisfaction axis. In this fashion, the probability is increased that individual learning will be reflected in revised organizational routines.

3. A major characteristic of the modern quality paradigm involves seeing improved quality as a strong competitive strategy. Effectively pursued, it means larger market share, lower costs (through reduced rework, scrap, etc.), and larger profits, with corresponding benefits for employees in terms of wages and employment security. With stretch targets and ample benefits to spread around to all stakeholders if successfully pursued, this characteristic provided strong motivational incentives for individual learning and for individuals to embody their learning in new best-practice routines.

4. All-employee, all-department involvement in quality improvement is the pivotal characteristic of the modern quality paradigm that relates to learning. It means that all employees, individually and in work-teams, are expected to participate in improving the quality of their work processes so that they more efficiently and effectively serve internal and external customer needs. The implications for learning are profound. It reflects and reinforces Ronald Dore's observations (not made with specific reference to the quality movement) that everyone is presumed to be a learner (Dore *et al.* 1989:52). This assumption, combined with enhanced motivational incentives for employees to engage in learning, combines to make possible the organizational learning that underlies Japanese efforts.

We have seen that motivation is a necessary but not sufficient cause of organizational learning. Opportunities need to be created for employees to make continual changes in organizational routines and to communicate best practices so that they are spread throughout the firm. This is certainly the key contrast with the traditional Taylor model. Japanese firms have laboured hard to create opportunities for exactly such participation. Most widely known in the West are the quality circles, in which workers design and continually redesign their own jobs and work processes. But these efforts go far beyond quality circles. Kazuo Koike, in his study of production workers, remarks:

One of the most important parts of OJT is the study of problems on the shop-floor. It is common practice for each worker to write short reports on significant problem he has recently encountered, on what they were, how he dealt with them, and what problems still remain. These reports are ... discussed in workshop meetings. Only important problems are filed, because many workers are familiar with the ordinary ones. (Koike, Chapter 2 above)

We see here that public presentations in the workshop of problem-solving methods and solutions is the norm. In so doing, of course, broad-scale diffusion of best practice (organizational learning) takes place. However, these practices are used not only by production workers.

In my interviews with the twenty manufacturing firms noted for their quality achievements, I found public presentation (*happyō*) of best practices (both problem-solving methods and solutions) to one's peers (with some management superiors typically present) to be a pervasive management practice. For engineers, the development and presentation of case studies is often the primary method of training. Larry Sullivan, president of the American Supplier Institute (an organization devoted to diffusing Japanese manufacturing methods to the US manufacturing sector), describes his interviews with managers at Nippon Densō, the leading electronic auto-motive supplier in the world. They report that Nippon Densō engineers and managers spend (on average) eight hours per week in education and training, four hours on company time and four hours in their own time. This includes the development and presentation of case studies, which is the primary method of training—one 'must apply in order to learn'.[3]

Expressing these practices in analytic terms, we see an example of controlled normative isomorphism taking place under the new quality paradigm. This contrasts sharply with the coercive isomorphism fostered by using management experts to improve organizational learning, as typified by the old paradigm; DiMaggio and Powell see normative isomorphism as being driven largely by professionalization and the need to establish a base for occupational autonomy (DiMaggio and Powell 1983: 152). In large Japanese firms, however, these activities are organized by the firm to promote organizational interests, i.e. the creation of best-practice solutions to organizational problems and their rapid diffusion within the firm.

The firm also provides incentives for the employees to engage in problem-solving activities and to present them publicly to peers and for peers to absorb and apply such knowledge. In particular, the personal assessment (*satei*) system in force in most large firms operates to evaluate both objective performance in such activities and subjective elements of effort and commitment. This assessment in turn indirectly affects promotion opportunities and pay. Thus, underlying the process of normative isomorphism is a kind of 'soft' coercive isomorphism. It is for this reason that we may label the Japanese approach 'controlled normative isomorphism'.

The Japanese approach is characterized by a broadcasting of problem-solving methods, failures, and solutions through presentations to the relevant plant-wide/speciality-wide/corporate-wide network of potential adopters. In this fashion, the diffusion of best practices is enhanced (cf. Dimaggio and Powell 1983: 148; Levitt and March 1988: 329). At Honda Motor Company they call it 'horizontal development' (*suihei tenkai*). By facilitating direct learning from one employee to another through a broadcast technique, the time and inefficiency of diffusing knowledge through hierarchical inter mediaries can be minimized. By relying on normative learning through peer-group activities, significant barriers to the individual learning process associated with hierarchical intervention are avoided. This approach dove-tails well with Aoki's observations (1988) that decentralization of decision-making involving operational decisions can be more efficient than the practices of a more centralized organization. The hierarchical approach, by contrast, is associated with Tayloristic thinking (separate planning from execution partly in the belief that engineers are the source of new improved ideas). Those managers operating in this tradition are expected to pull information out of the heads of employees, reorganize it, retain planning elements, and then feed back operational information to employees.

Witnessing the steady stream of such presentations gets one to thinking about the factory as a school and laboratory, and not just a producer of goods and services. Indeed, some firms, such as Aishin AW, a leading auto parts supplier in the Toyota group, have consciously sought to model themselves as schools. Presentational activities of the kind described above help ensure that the same mistakes are not made twice, and they both reflect and reinforce broad employee participation in corporate activities.

Typically, these problem-solving presentations follow the 'Quality Improvement Story' format. Fig. 2 provides a description of the seven steps used in such presentations. Note that they model the problem-solving process itself. The presentations typically include a history of the problem-solving activity pursued by the individual or group, including a discussion of the blind alleys and failure modes that were pursued. In so doing, they document a process by which failure and errors are overcome to produce success. In that fashion, errors and failures are treated as positive learning experiences. Top management officials attending such sessions associate themselves and the firm with events in which learning from failure is a key theme.

To give readers a better sense of what is actually involved, consider the observations of Mr Takagi, the head of the quality department at Honda Motor Company. He was responding to a question on 'What was the company's approach to special training activities to improve quality?' His

QC story step	Function	Tools
1. Select theme	Decide theme for improvement Make clear why the theme is selected	'Next processes are our customers' Standardization Education Immediate remedy v. recurrence prevention
2. Grasp the current situation	Collect data Find the key characteristics of the theme Narrow down the problem area Establish priorities: serious problems first	Check-sheet Histogram Pareto diagram
3. Analysis	List all the possible causes of the most serious problem Study the relations between possible causes and between causes and problem Select some causes and establish hyopotheses about possible relations Collect data and study cause–effect relation	Fishbone diagram Check-sheet Scatter diagram Stratification
4. Countermeasures	Devise countermeasures to eliminate the cause(s) of a problem Implement countermeasures (experiment)	Intrinsic technology of the firm Experience
5. Confirm the effect of countermeasure	Collect data on the effects of the countermeasure Before–after comparison	All 7 of the tools
6. Standardize the countermeasure	Amend existing standards according to the countermeasures whose effects are confirmed	
7. Identify the remaining problems and evaluate the whole procedure		

FIG. 2   The QC Story
   Source: Lillrank and Kano (1989: 26).

answer highlights the difference between experience learning and a narrow view of science as a source of improvements.

One of our principles is that we must not make the same mistake twice. This was taught by our founder Soichiro. Once is okay. The automobile industry consists of experience engineering—how to make the most of failure and then how to reflect this thinking in all our tens of thousands of employees. It is a Herculean problem. We use many different methods for this—making failure example reports, using these for design know-how, entering it into computers, etc. It is hard to perfect, but we continue to aim for improvement in this area; it is important and necessary.

   For example, I am head of the product technology field for all of Honda. What I do is receive blueprints from the lab and check by different tests such as standardization whether the ideas for new car models can actually withstand mass production. In connection with this activity, at each factory all different problem cases are collected and arranged in a specific form to demonstrate what types of failure can and must be avoided. Once a month the people at the respective workshops gather and bring their various problems and, typically using an overhead projector, report on what they have learned in front of everyone. There the factory officers and I listen and judge the manner of the analysis and explanation and we make suggestions and praise the best presentation. The best reports will be bound as books and passed out or used in newcomer education. This is only one example, but we do many things of this type. Our management officials and engineers also go to visit and sit in on similar presentations among our suppliers. ...

The good part about Honda is that one tends to be praised for admitting failure. Our system is such that everyone tries to keep an open mind and discuss problems, failures, without having to fear reproach. The philosophy of our top people is that failure is itself wealth (*zaisan*). The thinking here is that a problem can get trapped in a container with the lid welded shut. We have to try and wrench open this lid, to get our people to do it. We do not want a situation in which top management are the only ones aware of critical problems relating to the company's survival. It is a fundamental of quality control to ensure that this is not the case.

This quote makes clear that Honda officials do not believe they have solved the problems of encouraging employees to take risks that might lead to failure while at the same time avoiding making the same mistake twice. Yet, what is impressive here is the tremendous organizational attention devoted to the problem and the continued efforts to improve on their performance. Remarkably, from a Western perspective all this focus on learning from failure takes place in an industry that is not launching rockets but is in the seemingly routine business of producing cars. We also see that 'presentations' of problem-solving cases are a central part of their strategy for learning (horizontal development) in ways that diffuse best problem-solving methods and solutions. In so doing, organizational learning receives a powerful boost.

5. A major element of the post-war quality movement in Japan has been the recognition that solving problems at each stage 'upstream' yields important savings to the firm. As one uncovers quality problems downstream, the costs multiply. This recognition has directed organizational efforts at quality improvement to the design stage where opportunities for prevention strategies can be most effectively applied. At the same time, it has encouraged problem-solving activities in which root-cause analysis is stressed at all levels of the firm. Many of the formal problem-solving methods in use are designed to get employees to engage in root-cause analysis. Root-cause problem-solving activity increases the probability of organizational learning because of its greater potential to create opportunities for significant change in performance routines. By contrast, traditional problem-solving often addresses the symptoms of problems and leads to few changes in organizational routines.

6. Well defined problem-solving methodologies characterize the modern quality movement in Japan. Many of the corporate training activities are oriented towards teaching and applying problem-solving behaviour. Such training is not limited to management personnel but is broadly diffused to

all employees. Presentations of case studies are just as oriented towards diffusing the best problem-solving methods as they are towards diffusing the solutions to particular problems. Problem-solving tools such as 'value engineering' and 'failure mode effect analysis' (FMEA), which are used by a limited number of engineers in Western manufacturing firms, are widely diffused among employees in large Japanese manufacturing firms. At Honda, in 1986 the card that every production worker was expected to carry in his pocket that year described how to engage in a simplified form of FMEA. Of course, not every employee is capable of sophisticated execution of FMEA, but it is impressive that many are able to make modest use of this tool.

Japanese off-the-job training is oriented towards improvement training, not teaching employees how to do their jobs; the latter tends to be taught through on-the-job training. Improvement training involves more than teaching specific problem-solving methods. As we saw in the steps of the quality improvement story shown in Fig. 2, the generic steps of problem-solving activities are emphasized. Note especially step 6, which stresses the importance of standardizing the solutions through diffusing best practices. When one mentions the concept of standardization to Western managers, their eyes tend to glaze over as they conjure up images of dusty unused manuals. Yet standardization of best practices lies at the heart of the organizational learning required for quality improvement. The critical difference in attitudes towards standardization is explained by who has responsibility for it. In Western firms it is often the managers who impose the standards on employees who must use them; in Japanese firms employees are more likely to have responsibility for devising and revising standards as well as implementing them.

What the Japanese have done is to evolve and diffuse some very well defined routines for problem-solving activities. The implications for increasing the capacity for individuals to engage in individual and organizational learning are profound.

7. The post-war quality movement in Japan has developed in tandem with the management control system (policy deployment). The deployment of quality improvement efforts is carefully cascaded down through the organization starting from assessing customer needs, constructing a long-term plan, moving to the annual plan, and then having each level (from managers down through worker quality circles) formulate quality-improvement objectives that tie into these plans. Progress towards these plans is checked regularly through personal audits by top executives. By integrating quality into the control system in this way, middle manager as well as workers are made central to the execution of quality improvement and implicitly are told that what they are doing is important. There is a clear structure provided for individual and organizational learning associated with specified targets appropriate to one's level in the organization. Con-

tinuous quality improvement is the official corporate principle, with its assumption that organizational learning will lead to continuous improvement. One can hardly imagine a Western factory with a large banner over the assembly line that reads 'Fear Established Concepts' (*kyofu kisei gainen*). Yet that was the sign I saw at the Mazda Hiroshima transmission plant in 1988. The invitation to apply one's problem-solving skills to create a better performance routine is clear. We see here that management, through a structured control system applied to quality improvement, provides the motivation, capacity, and opportunity for individual and organizational learning. What we see here is not maverick creativity, but a highly disciplined approach to improvement.

8. Cross-functional co-operation is a hallmark of the modern quality movement. It developed through the recognition that many quality failures occur at the boundaries between functional specialities—the white spaces in the organization chart—and result from the functional specialities' lack of co-operation with one another. Managers of departmental hierarchies are often rewarded for optimizing their functions (e.g. marketing, engineering) in ways that tend to lead to sub-optimization for the whole organization. The modern approach to quality seeks to manage and improve processes that cross functional boundaries. Career development strategies are designed and executed to ensure a great deal of cross-functional experience. In pursuing this course, individuals are compelled to learn about more than just one functional speciality. Organizational learning comes through the opportunities provided for process-improvement activities that incorporate this broad-based knowledge. These process-improvement activities are carried out not by outside experts, but by those involved in the process itself.

4. CONCLUSION

In my observations of American and Swedish industry, I have been struck that the renewed emphasis on learning is seen primarily as an individual phenomenon, with scant attention being given to organizational learning. It is assumed that individual learning will lead to organizational learning. Consider the document *Towards a Learning Organization*, which reflects many of the findings of the Swedish Work Environment Fund's Development Programme for New Technology, Working Life, and Management (Swedish Work Environment Fund 1988). Despite its title, the contents of this document are focused almost entirely on individual learning issues. Yet, individual learning does not automatically lead to organizational learning! As we have seen, it requires an organizational framework and consistently targeted action to bring about this more demanding result. Volvo's innovative Uddevalla factory is another case in point. The focus is heavily on having workers learn broad skills to expand their individual cycle time. Yet, scant attention is paid to workers' systematically learning from others in their work-group, much less from those outside the work-group, in such a way that best practices are broadly diffused and continuous improvement of performance routines are achieved. Moreover, the emphasis on work-group autonomy and, indeed, competition among work-groups often prevents issues of broader co-operation from being raised. From an organizational point of view, all this is waste; individual learning or work-group autonomy cannot be seen as ends in be themselves or be assumed to lead in magical fashion to organizational learning. The process must be managed.

Can this quality paradigm with its strong implications for organizational learning work outside Japan? Although Japan's cultural experiences undoubtedly contributed to the creation of this paradigm there, my evaluation is that basically it represents good management practice. The strongest objections to this view that I have encountered rest on notions that non-Japanese nations lack the lifetime employment system that underlies normative learning among peers, and lack the *satei* personal assessment system which provides strong incentives for employees to learn from one another. Let us consider these claims in turn.

The argument about lifetime employment rests on the sound notion that turnover is the enemy of quality because it involves the loss of organizational memory. However, this argument is often presented in simplistic terms, as if all Japanese male employees in large firms have it and want it and no employees in America either act as though they are expected to stay with their firm for any length of time or actually do stay. Lynn *et al.* (1989) recently studied a large sample of American and Japanese engineers from Carnegie Mellon University and Tohoku University (each with a median age of roughly 41 years). They found that 74 per cent of the Japanese engineers were still with their first firms, meaning that a not trivial 26 per cent had changed jobs at least once; this compared with some 43 per cent of the American engineers who were still with their first firm—a not unsubstantial number, given the stereotypes of job-hopping American workers. These results are consistent with earlier results reported by Cole (1979) using a representative sample of employees in Detroit and Yokohama. These latter results also showed that as employees age there is a rapid reduction of job-changing in both economies. In short, there is ample time for employees to build networks for sharing information and learning from one another. The issue is not length of service, but rather, the task of building organizational structures that support such learning processes. This is a difficult but not unsurmountable obstacle.

The second objection to the idea that normative learning of the kind I have described in large Japanese firms is transferable to non-Japanese firms rests on the incentives employees have to support these new organizational structures. Western firms in particular tend not to have well developed personal assessment systems similar to *satei* for production workers, because of union and worker objections to its subjective elements. In the case of white-collar employees, individual merit reward systems are customary, but they tend to downplay the assessment of subjective elements such as attitudes, seeing these elements as unacceptable intrusions into an individual's rights of privacy.

Unions are declining in Western societies; those that survive are learning to co-operate with management, building on their joint interest in job security and firm prosperity. As a consequence of both these developments, unions have become less of an obstacle to the introduction of merit reward systems and the peer-to-peer learning activities that I have described. One does not need to rely on intrusive measures of personal effort and proper attitudes (in the manner of the Japanese model) to evaluate whether an employee has carried out and presented an effective problem-solving activity, or whether another employee has applied to his or her own work the lessons of that presentation. In summary, there is no guarantee that non-Japanese firms will rapidly absorb the ability to advance organizational learning as contained in the new Japanese quality paradigm. Nor is there, however, any reason to assume a priori that such learning is impossible.

I have described the ingredients of the modern quality movement and how it embodies the idea of individual and organizational learning. It is most plausible to believe that these underpinnings account for a significant part of the success of the Japanese quality movement and to the competitive advantage high quality products have bestowed on Japanese firms more generally.

It must be pointed out that the process by which the modern quality paradigm developed in Japan was itself a process of organizational learning. Individual firms collaborated with one another under the framework of the Japanese Union of Scientists and Engineers to develop and diffuse best practices. I have traced these developments elsewhere (Cole 1989), but let it be said that it was a highly creative process that went far beyond the initial inspiration provided by American quality leaders. Indeed, Japanese success in this area can be seen as part of a broader patterned approach to organizational learning. Imai *et al.* (1985) have characterized this in terms of a sequential learning systems, with information-sharing, information exchange, and information linkages producing continuous interactive innovation.

NOTES TO CHAPTER 3

1. Notwithstanding, in the above-mentioned example Taylor claims to have raised both productivity and quality, thereby, in this respect at least, putting him in the company of those committed to the modern approach to quality.
2. These characteristics are drawn from the literature (Ishikawa 1985; Mizuno 1988; Scherkenbach 1986), as well as from my own first-hand research on the subject in 1989. This research involved interviewing officials at 20 leading Japanese manufacturing firms noted for their quality achievements. The standardized format used in these interviews included questions on learning strategies employed by these firms.
3. Interview with Larry Sullivan, February 1987, Ann Arbor, Mich.

REFERENCES

Aoki, Masahiko (1988), *Information, Incentives and Bargaining in the Japanese Economy*, Cambridge University Press.

Cole, Robert (1979), *Work, Mobility, and Participation*, University of California Press, Berkeley, Calif.

——(1989), *Strategies for Learning*, University of California Press, Berkeley, Calif.

Cyert, Richard, and March, James (1963), *A Behavioral Theory of the Firm*, Prentice-Hall, Englewood Cliffs, NJ.

DiMaggio, Paul, and Powell, Walter (1983), 'The Iron Cage Revisited: Institutional Isomorphism and Collective Rationality in Organizational Fields', *American Sociological Review*, 48: 147–60.

Dore, Ronald *et al.* (1989), 'Review of Flexibility in Japanese Labor Markets', Working Paper, Manpower and Social Affairs Committee, OECD, Paris.

Fox, William (1982), 'Scientific Management: "Taylorism"', in Carl Heyel (ed.), *The Encyclopedia of Management*, 3rd edn., Van Nostrand Reinold, New York, 1087–94.

Imai, Ken-ichi, Nonaka Ikujiro, and Takeuchi, Hirotaka (1985), 'Managing the New Product Development Process: How Japanese Companies Learn and Unlearn', in Kim Clark, Robert Hayes and C. Lorenz (eds.), *The Uneasy Alliance*, Harvard Business School, Cambridge, Mass.

Ishikawa, Kaoru (1985), *What is Total Quality Control?* Prentice-Hall, Englewood Cliffs, NJ.

Juran, Joseph (1988), *Juran's Quality Control Handbook*, 4th edn., McGraw-Hill, New York.

Levitt, Barbara, and March, James (1988), 'Organizational Learning', in Richard

Scott and Judith Blake (eds.), *Annual Review of Sociology*, xiv, Annual Reviews Inc., Palo Alto, Calif., 319–340.

Lillrank, Paul, and Kano, Noriaki (1989), *Continuous Improvement: Quality Control Circles in Japanese Industry*, Center for Japanese Studies, University of Michigan, Ann Arbor, Mich.

Lynn, Leonard, Piehler, Henry, and Zahray, W. (1993), 'Engineering Careers, Job Rotation and Gatekeepers in Japan and the United States', *Journal of Engineering and Technology Management*, 10: 53–72.

Mizuno, Shigeru (1988), *Company-wide Quality Control*, Asian Productivity Center, Hong Kong.

Nelson, Richard, and Winter, Sidney (1982), *An Evolutionary Theory of Economic Change*. Belknap Press, Cambridge, Mass.

Scherkenbach, William (1986), *The Deming Route to Quality and Productivity*. CEEP Press, Washington, DC.

Swedish Work Environment Fund (1988), *Towards a Learning Organization*. The Development Programme, Stockholm.

Taylor, Frederick (1967), *The Principles of Scientific Management*, W. W. Norton, New York (first published in 1911).

4

Training, Productivity, and Quality Control in Japanese Multinational Companies

MARI SAKO

1. INTRODUCTION

Comparative research on vocational education and training has often been conducted in order to outline another country's practices with a view to highlighting, and prescribing for, the shortcomings in one's own country. This paper sustains that tradition by providing a Japanese perspective on training in Britain and Germany. In particular, it reports on interim results of a systematic investigation of training practices and their effects on performance in Japanese manufacturing plants in Britain and Germany.

Much interest has been focused recently on education and training (ET) and its contribution to industrial competitiveness in public policy as well as in corporate strategy in most advanced industrial countries (e.g. OTA 1990, NEDC/MSC 1984). In Britain, for example, a low quality of available manpower as compared with Germany is said to be responsible for a large productivity gap, of up to 60 per cent in Germany's favour (Prais *et al.* 1989).[1] In particular, Britain is deficient in the supply for intermediate skills, i.e. those above routine skills but below professional ones (Ryan 1991). A reform of the education system may be necessary to rectify this supply deficiency, but it is not in itself a sufficient condition to bring about improved performance. For, without creating an effective demand for such skills, there are no incentives to acquire such skills. And, without the reform of the production system and the accompanying work organization at the corporate initiative, such skills would be mis- or under-utilized (MacDuffie and Kochan 1991). Hence the possibility of getting stuck in a difficult-to-break vicious skill-denying circle (Finegold and Soskice 1988), and the difficulty of breaking into a virtuous circle of skill promotion, which Finegold (1991) calls a 'high skill equilibrium'.

To date, Japanese multinational companies (MNCs) in Europe have been studied intensively, but often from a broad angle of 'Japanization' or the transferability of so-called Japanese techniques (e.g. Oliver and Wilkinson 1988, Takamiya and Thurley 1985, White and Trevor 1983). None of these studies concentrates on training and the process of skill formation on the shop-floor. In the present research, the Japanese MNC is also used as a vehicle to tackle some puzzles that remain unanswered in the above line of concern. One issue concerns the nagging doubt that differences in skills and training in themselves are perhaps not so important in accounting for the observed performance gaps. In fact, Pratten (1990) cautions against an over-emphasis on ET at the exclusion of many other factors affecting industrial performance. A study of Japanese multinational plants provides a potentially ideal setting for separating out multiple factors. In particular, the quality of management (at least at the top) can be controlled to a certain extent as management in Japanese plants in Europe has not yet been greatly localized. Moreover, given that the product development and design function has not been greatly decentralized by most Japanese MNCs to date, British-based and German-based plants are producing goods similar to those manufactured at their headquarter (HQ) plants in Japan. Their process technology may also be alike, because large investment decisions are taken not autonomously at the plant level, but with the approval of the corporate HQ in Japan. These facts undoubtedly make it easier to conduct a study of the link between training and its performance outcome, which is infested with a multiplicity of explanatory variables. Here, uniform product design and process technology, combined with common management principles within a MNC across locations, enable the researcher, albeit imperfectly, to control for the demand side of the skills equation.

A related issue is the extent to which the vicious circle of low skills or the virtuous high-skill equilibrium is difficult to break. Japanese MNCs again offer a testing ground, because, as greenfield sites, they may have an advantage over indigenous firms when setting up a training system totally different from the established practice in a particular country. Within Japan, major manufacturing plants have perfected a flexible production system characterized by high quality, low inventory holding, and flexible product mix. Automation embodying the most recent microelectronic technology helps such plants achieve consistent quality. But ultimately, shop-floor workers themselves must be oriented towards self-inspection of quality, problem-solving, and 'continuous improvement' of the production process to make the hardware operate at their high efficiency. The resulting dynamic interaction between machinery and labour—which Shimada and Macduffie (1986) appropriately call 'humanware'—facilitates .learning, as problems exposed must be dealt with at decentralized levels. A written record is commonly kept, of how new machinery was installed, of breakdowns and problems encountered, and of how they were resolved (Koike 1991: 161). Every solution worked out then becomes part of the accumulated know-how not only of individuals, but also of work-teams and the organization as a whole. The recent US–Japan bilateral SII talks, in identifying ET as one of the 'structural impediments' to international trade, was referring to the difficult-to-break nature of the virtuous circle of learning, enhanced worker capability, technical innovation, and corporate performance.

If a similar production system is to be implemented in Europe, Japanese MNCs would also require a particular type of worker who is capable of engaging in team-work, problem-solving, and mutual teaching and learning. A core issue is the extent to which the training practices of Japanese MNC plants are constrained by, and fitted into, the national systems of the countries in which they are located. It takes time to set up a training system within any organization. Since European-based Japanese plants do not as yet have a very long history, we may not find a fully established system. But it should be possible to gauge the extent to which they are attempting to blend into the existing national systems, or else to build an island in a sea of unfamiliar practices.

The following questions summarize the issues to be addressed in this paper:
1. What modifications, if any, are being made to the philosophy and type of training that Japanese companies provide in Japan when training non-Japanese workers at their European plants? Does the nature of modifications differ from country to country in Europe, and if so what are the reasons for this?
2. Is there a systematic difference in performance (as measured by productivity and quality levels) between Japanese plants located in Britain and those located in Germany? If so, how much of the difference appears to be explained by differences in the approach to training?

The rest of the paper is structured as follows. A framework for analysing training is outlined in Section 2. This framework is used to generate some hypotheses about training practices and their performance outcomes at Japanese plants in Britain and Germany. Section 3 then provides an overview of Japanese direct investment in Europe and the electronics plants that were studied. Section 4 describes the work organization and training practices at these plants in detail. Section 5 discusses the performance gap between British-based and German-based plants, and partially accounts for it by factors other than machinery and human resources. Section 6 focuses on the interaction between machinery and labour. Section 7 provides a summary and conclusions.

2. AN ANALYTICAL FRAMEWORK: TRAINING SYSTEMS IN BRITAIN, GERMANY, AND JAPAN

This section concentrates on setting up a framework for analysing variations in training practices and their consequences for performance across firms. Variations are to be explained in terms of (1) the firm-level strategic choice over the nature of production system to be set up and sustained, and (2) the influence of national-level institutions and regulations.

Corporate and Plant Levels

In a manufacturing setting, the level and type of training that firms provide are essentially dictated by the demands of the production system to be set up. The production system is here defined in a broad sense, to include not only the hardware (i.e. the nature of product and process technology) but also the 'humanware' (i.e. the interface between technology as embodied in machinery and human resources) (Shimada 1988: 104).

Japanese manufacturing firms have pursued high quality and high productivity as mutually compatible goals. The underlying production system relies on eliminating buffers of inventory to expose quality and other problems immediately when they occur. These problems are solved with the full involvement of shop-floor workers, so that quality and machine maintenance responsibilites can be decentralized to the level closest to the source of potential problems. Productivity is enhanced by reducing the need for inspection and repair, by good preventative maintenance of machinery, and through the 'continuous improvement' of process technology. Machinery is therefore regarded as dependent on, and complementary to, workers. Added to this, small-batch production of a large variety of products is managed by job rotation and transfers within and between work-teams.

This type of production system has the following implications for training of shop-floor workers. First, workers must be trained to be multi-skilled, so that they can do different tasks as and when required to cope with a change in product mix. Second, workers must come to possess a fairly high level of technical knowledge about the production system, so as to be able to engage in routine preventative maintenance and to make suggestions for process improvement. Third, a good basic education is a necessary prerequisite, because numeracy, literacy, logical reasoning, and communication skills are required in order for workers to take part in problem-solving activities, such as quality control circles and total productive maintenance. Koike calls the set of engineering knowledge and problem-solving skills possessed by shop-floor workers 'intellectual skills' (Koike 1991). Fourth, on-the-job training (OJT) is the preferred mode because it facilitates imparting plant-specific know-how accumulated through problem-solving and continuous improvement activities. Lastly, workers' incentives to learn and to stay on in the company are enhanced by a clear promotion track, accompanied by pay increases and individual performance appraisal.

Turning now to the specific context of Japanese MNCs, their European-based plants are likely to be investing heavily in training their own workers in order to set up and sustain their production system. This is because the need to implement identical product design and process technology in

Europe partially dictates the work organization and hence training needs. Also, each corporation has its own management philosophy and principles, which in turn influence the type of training provided, and the HQ control over subsidiaries is likely to be strong in the early stages of subsidiary operation. Moreover, Japanese corporations' preference for OJT means that the HQ factories provide the initial training ground for European supervisors, who learn not only requisite technical skills but also work habits and supervision patterns directly from their Japanese counterparts.

At the same time, Japanese subsidiary operations have to take account of locally available manpower. Both young recruits straight out of education and experienced workers may, to a certain extent, be carefully selected for suitable characteristics. But they bring with them elements of the national education and training system which Japanese subsidiaries must accommodate. It is to this aspect that we will turn next.

Impact of National Training Systems

This subsection does not provide a general description of how education and training systems function in Britain, Germany, and Japan. Instead, it will compare and contrast the main features of the three countries' systems so as to gauge the options available to Japanese MNCs in modifying, or not modifying, their training philosophy and practices when setting up plants in Britain and Germany. A certain degree of stereotyping—or 'stylization'—is inevitable at this level of generalization. The comparisons focus on dominant practices in dominant sectors in each economy. This focus is considered not so inappropriate to the present context, which is confined to the internationally traded sectors in which Japanese MNCs invest overseas.

The first aspect to be compared is the general educational attainments of school-leavers. Partly because of differences in the respective education system, there is evidence that the mathematical attainments of British secondary school-children are lower on average than those of corresponding children in Germany and Japan (Prais 1987). The gap is accounted for not so much by attainments of the most able students but by a wide dispersion in attainments among those in the lower half of the ability range. The accumulated effect of this wide dispersion implies that employers cannot put too much faith in educational qualifications alone to screen workers of all ages for adequate literacy and numeracy. One expected outcome, therefore, is that Japanese MNC plants may need to engage in a more lengthy and rigorous selection process in Britain than in Germany. Another related possible outcome is that not enough workers in Britain will be found to have the required competence in reading, mathematics, and communication skills in order to learn how to engage in problem-solving. Attempts to train shop-floor workers in 'intellectual skills' may therefore encounter more problems in Britain than in Germany, which may result in the need to modify the work organization to suit the level of available worker skills.

TABLE 1 Education and Training Enrolment Rates for Young People, 1988 (%)

	16-year-olds			17-year-olds		
	Full-time	Part-time	Total	Full-time	Part-time	Total
Germany	69	31	100	43	49	92
Japan	92	3	95	89	2	91
UK	47	37	84	32	34	66

Source: reproduced from Training Agency (1989: Table 8.1).

The gap in general educational attainments between Britain and Germany is accentuated by the fact that more young people stay on in education beyond compulsory schooling in Germany. As Table 1 shows, only 47 per cent of 16-year-olds in the UK, as compared with 69 per cent in Germany and 92 per cent in Japan, were in full-time education in 1988. This means that there is a viable youth labour market for 16- and 17-year-olds in the UK, whereas there is none in Germany because of the legal requirement that employers provide some form of education for workers up to the age of 18, and none in Japan because of the majority's individual choice to stay on in full-time education. Japanese plants have the opportunity to tap into this youth market to train and internally promote very young workers. The idea of moulding young people with no previous work experience tallies with Japanese personnel practices.

A second aspect for comparison is the mode of vocational education and training for young people. Both of the host countries to be studied have had, as a central mode, the apprenticeship system, which is absent in Japan. A contrasting trend is evident in the two countries, however. In Germany, the sole route to skilled status remains the 'Dual [apprentice] System', which incorporates around two-thirds of young people (aged 16–19), spread across all sectors of the German economy. Apprentices receive a formalized programme of training, which combines in service training at the employer's premises and part-time attendance at vocational schools for a three-year duration. A relatively low apprentice allowance has been maintained by the 'social partners' (i.e. employers' associations and trade unions), which jointly regulate training standards as well as pay levels. High pay differentials by skill status ensure that returns to apprenticeship are high for individuals, and that employers' incentives to provide training are also enhanced. Moreover, a strict linking of qualifications to pay levels in industry-wide collective agreements contributes towards the elimination of 'poaching' as a viable alternative to in-house training for most employers.

Thus, the German training system is sustained by external regulation, which requires much co-ordination among employers, unions, and the public sector. Although such coordination may be prone to rigidities and inertia, the tripartite actors in Germany have worked towards adapting the Dual System to meet new needs, e.g. in technology, rather than attempting to transform the existing regulatory framework in any fundamental way.

In Britain, by contrast, apprenticeships were eroded particularly in the 1980s, with the number dwindling from 150,000 in 1979 to 55,000 in 1988 in the manufacturing sector (Training Agency 1989: 15). Youth Training (YT), or the Youth Training Scheme (YTS) in the past, has not earned its currency in the eyes of employers and young people as a viable alternative to traditional apprenticeships. Consequently, by 1988 only 16 per cent of 16–17-year-olds were on YTS, while 32 per cent were in full-time education. The rest were either employed (42 per cent) or unemployed (10 per cent). Outside YTS and declining apprenticeships, long-duration training given by employers is the exception rather than the rule; three-quarters of the school-leavers going into employment outside YTS in 1985 received either no training or training lasting less than a year (Training Agency 1989). Marsden and Ryan (1990) attribute the erosion of apprenticeship-based training, and the degeneration of British labour markets into more internal forms, to the absence of an appropriate regulatory framework as in Germany. In particular, as part of deregulation policies in the 1980s, Industrial Training Boards and Wage Councils were abolished. This led to the widening of youth-adult pay differentials in sectors requiring relatively little training, while relative youth pay crept upwards in sectors such as engineering requiring expensive training. The latter was an outcome of collective bargaining, in which unions feared 'low-pay, low-quality' apprenticeships in the absence of a regulatory safeguard against the substitution of apprentices for adult workers. The perverse incentives, created for employers as well as for individuals, not to train are evident. Moreover, the recently created TECs (Training and Enterprises Councils) have not yet proven to regenerate employers' commitment to train through local-level co-ordination.

A third aspect of comparison is the volume of technically qualified manpower available as a result not only of initial but also of further training. In Germany, skilled workers with technical apprenticeship qualifications may, after a stipulated number of years of work experience, study for and obtain the Meister certificate, a widely held supervisory qualification, or the Techniker certificate to become technicians. The Meister course involves learning a breadth of technical knowledge, as well as receiving formal training in instructional skills and management techniques. A corresponding course in Britain is the NEBSS (National Examinations Board for Supervisory Studies), which is more narrowly about the management of people. The British technician qualification is called the Higher National Certificate (HNC) or Higher National Diploma (HND). Most students entering courses for HNC or HND have previously taken an Ordinary National Certificate or Diploma (ONC/OND) in the same area. These Ordinary and Higher National qualifications are commonly taken at the end of apprenticeship-type arrangements with employers. As shown in Table 2, people who are qualified with these certificates are more than twice as numerous in Germany than in Britain, after adjustments are made for the size of labour force. At a higher level, by contrast, technical manpower is more abundant in Britain than in Germany: there were 270 people with first-degree-level engineering qualifications per million of population in Britain, as compared with only 110 in Germany (and 630 in Japan), according to one calculation (NEDO/MSC 1984: 83).

TABLE 2 Numbers obtaining Technical Qualifications at Intermediate Levels, 1986 ('000)
Standardized for size of total labour force in each
country

	UK	Germany
Higher intermediate		
Higher technicians[a]	23	13
Meister-qualified	—	31
Lower intermediate		
Lower technicians[b]	14	—
Craftsmen[c]	27	107
Total	64	151

[a] HNC/HND in Britain; Techniker qualification in Germany.
[b] ONC/OND in Britain.
[c] City and Guilds Part II passes in a relevant subject in Britain; Berufsabschluss (after the 3-year apprenticeship) in a relevant area in Germany.

Source: Steedman *et al.* (1991).

From the above description, one likely outcome is that Japanese plants located in Germany are more likely to have apprenticeships that conform to the national regulatory framework than in Britain, where lack of regulation allows them to apply company-specific training methods. From the viewpoint of Japanese MNCs, British and German labour markets offer different trade-offs of opportunities and constraints. On the one hand, Germany might be chosen as a location because of the availability of good-quality technical manpower. But the statutory regulation concerning training would bind Japanese MNCs to conform to the German way if they wished to establish a reputation for being good corporate citizens. On the other hand, Britain might be selected for its lack of regulations in training and other areas, because this would allow Japanese MNCs to adopt the same well tried and tested methods there as in Japan; but they would face a labour market with workers whose levels of general educational attainment are lower on average than in Japan.

Deregulation in Britain, however, only creates a scope for applying 'Japanese-style' training philosophy and methods. Training in large Japanese companies is characterized by broad-based initial training of young recruits with high general education attainments. This becomes a basis for recurrent training and retraining, both on-the-job and off-the-job, in life-long careers with one firm. Conditions may be created by Japanese MNCs to 'Japanize' their British work-places—by choosing a greenfield site unaffected by past experience, by signing a single-union agreement which would enable flexible working and the de-linking of pay from skill status, by engaging in rigorous selection for attitudes as much as for technical skills, and by offering employment security and internal promotion prospects. However, Japanese plants cannot be totally insulated from external labour markets, particularly because of their small and medium size. The lack of lifetime employment orientation is likely to militate against the wholesale adoption of Japanese training philosophy and methods.

The exact way in which the absence of a lifetime employment norm affects training is not straightforward. For instance, German labour markets are often portrayed as occupational, in stark contrast to internal labour markets of large Japanese companies (Marsden 1986). The apprenticeship enshrines the principle of individual freedom inherent in training contracts; no skilled worker is obliged to remain loyal to the firm that trained him/her, and no training firm is obligated to employ those young people to whom it provided training. Qualifications attained through training are perfect passports to future job mobility. This, however, is too simplistic a picture to portray. In reality, large prestigious German enterprises prefer to train apprentices in-house and retain them after training. This is because externally available apprentice-qualified workers are second-best to the best pick they have had among a cohort of school-leavers. Thus in Germany, as in Japan, labour markets for core skilled workers are internalized to an extent.

Despite seemingly different labour market structures, other common features also exist in the training area in Germany and Japan, as follows (Sako 1991):

1. Both German and Japanese employers provide a broad-based foundation training of technical knowledge and skills for young workers as a basis for further learning.
2. The individual motivation to acquire skills is enhanced by employers

who provide a clear progression route for promotion and the reaching of higher skill levels (via the Meister qualification in Germany, and via more finely graded promotion to group leaders and supervisors in Japan).

3. Employers' incentives to provide general as well as specific training are enhanced by lower relative youth pay, although the steep earnings profile corresponds to skill differentials in Germany and to seniority-plus-merit in Japan.

4. Much responsibility for training young workers falls upon supervisors and foremen who themselves receive sufficient training in pedagogical as well as technical skills.

In fact, this last feature points to a German–Japanese similarity in shop-floor work organization: much discretion is given to supervisors, leading hands and operators who are entrusted to solve problems and to engage in mutual learning as well as to carry out routine tasks. Sengenberger makes a related point as follows:

Jobs in Great Britain are defined in terms of a set of tasks or a job territory and viewed as a property right by the job holder, whereas in Germany, jobs tend to be defined more as a range and level of technical and organizational competency. So, the difference is really between a rather exclusive job territory and a non-exclusive territory of skill or competence. And it is in this respect where I consider the Japanese system of work-place relations despite the absence of vocational training to be much closer to the German than to the Anglo-Saxon pattern. (Sengenberger 1987: 256–7)

Thus, apprenticeship-based training does not necessarily encourage a sense of job demarcation. What it does reinforce in Germany, however, is a clear link between qualifications and job status.

To summarize from the discussion above, the following hypotheses may be put forward. First, Japanese MNC plants are expected to conform more to the German training methods when located in Germany than to the British mode when located in Britain because of a greater degree of regulation and co-ordination among 'social partners' necessary in Germany than in Britain. However, the German training principles are not so different from the Japanese ones, making assmilation by Japanese plants easier than is often thought. Second, because of the lower level of education and technical knowledge on the part of British relative to German workers, Japanese plants are more likely to engage in rigorous selection processes and to modify the work organization to match available worker capability in Britain than in Germany. Third, many of the features of training—e.g. systematic OJT—at the Japanese HQ plants are likely to be retained in European-based plants because of the transposition of the identical hardware technology, if not the whole 'humanware' system.

3. THE CASE STUDY COMPANIES

The rest of the paper reports on interim findings from an ongoing research project on Japanese MNCs in Europe. The sample consists of Japanese manufacturing plants in Britain and Germany. These two countries were chosen, as explained earlier, so as (*a*) to directly compare how Japanese training practices are constrained by, and fitted into, different national settings, and (*b*) to examine if the performance gap between British and German plants persists in the case of Japanese MNCs. It so happens, also, that Britain is the most popular, and Germany the fourth most popular (after the Netherlands and France), locations for Japanese direct investment within Europe.

Japan's direct overseas investment (on an accumulated value basis) in Europe as of 31 March 1990 was worth $45 billion, which constituted 18 per cent of Japan's worldwide overseas investment. Of the $45 billion, $8 billion was in the manufacturing sector (Anglo-Japanese Economic Institute 1991: 16). Within the manufacturing sector, a regular JETRO survey identified 676 Japanese subsidiaries and affiliates in Europe as of the end of January 1991 (JETRO 1991). Japanese manufacturing companies' participation in Europe has accelerated particularly since the latter half of the 1980s in response to stricter anti-dumping and local content regulations.[2] Of the 676 firms, the greatest concentration is seen in Britain (with 187 firms), and the third highest concentration after France is in Germany (with 109 firms). By sector, electronic and electrical machinery is most common, accounting for 178 firms, of which 58 are located in Britain and 41 in Germany.

The electronic and electrical machinery industry is a sector that in Japan is enjoying relatively high productivity, together with the car industry, compared with the rest of the economy (such as retail and distribution) (Abbeglen and Stalker 1985: 61–2). In these sectors, the assembly processes involve a large number of interdependent steps which must be co-ordinated, implying a potentially large loss in productivity arising from machine breakdowns and line stoppages. In fact, labour accounts for a small percentage of the total cost of operation, and therefore enhancing efficiency depends much on increasing machine-processing time. Thus, workers' instant judgement and ability to deal quickly with unusual situations are of utmost importance. The electronics plants therefore offer a good opportunity to examine the nature of interdependence between machinery and workers.

While offering this benefit, one drawback of this sector is that it contains a variety of products, each requiring different process steps. Products produced by Japanese companies in Europe now range from colour television sets (CTVs), video cassette recorders (VCRs), and CD players to paper copiers, printers, facsimile machines, portable telephones, computer monitors, electronic typewriters, microwave ovens, air conditioners, and components including printed circuit board (PCB) assemblies and semi-conductor chips. In order to enable comparisons to be made between plants, the present research attempted to control for different process steps by concentrating mainly on the automatic and manual assembly processes.

Of the 58 electronics plants in Britain and 41 in Germany, 14 plants were chosen for study, 8 in Britain and 6 in Germany. In Table 3, plants with pseudonyms of the same alphabet letter belong to the same corporation.

TABLE 3 Summary of Case-Study Firms in the UK and Germany

Company name[a]	Date established[b]	Capital	No. of employees[c]	Union recognition
A_T Electronics Ltd	1981	£10m	1062 (7)	Single union (EETPU)
B_T Electronics Ltd	1981	£ 9m	900 (15)	Single union (EETPU)
C_T Electronics Ltd	1982	£ 5m	600 (12)	Single union (EETPU)
D_T Electronics Ltd	1976	£15m	2100 (44)	Single union (GMB)
E_T Electronics Ltd	1979	£ 8m	550 (6)	No union
E_V Electronics Ltd	1983	£ 8m	690 (11)	No union
F_V Electronics Ltd	1985	£26m	1100 (26)	Single union (EETPU)
A_V Electronics GmbH	1987	DM 13m	220 (5)	IG Metall
B_V Electronics GmbH	1982	DM 20m	570 (6)	IG Metall
C_V Electronics GmbH	1984	DM 14m	410 (8)	IG Metall
D_V Electronics GmbH	1982	DM 25m	1100 (12)	IG Metall
G_S Electronics Ltd	1982	£170m	840 (24)	No union
A_S Electronics GmbH	1984	DM 15m	200 (6)	IG Metall
B_S Electronics GmbH	1980	DM 66m	360 (10)	No union

[a] The subscripts indicate: T = television sets; V = video recorders; S = semiconductor chips.
[b] When production started.
[c] The figure in brackets is the number of Japanese employees at the plant.

Some of the plants made more than one product type on one site, but interviews focused on operations for manufacturing either CTVs (T), VCRs (V), or semiconductor chips (S); the product type is indicated by a subscript following the company alphabet. Only those plants that have been established for some time were chosen, so that their operations involve more than mere 'screwdriver' assembly, and their in-house training system has had time to take shape. The sample to date is too small to make broad generalizations, but details on variation between, as well as within, Britain and Germany are of interest and will be the basis for further investigation.

The plants were visited during May 1991 and February 1992, for a factory tour and semi-structured interviews. Interviews lasted between two hours and a day and a half. At a minimum, one Japanese manager and one local top manager were interviewed at each plant. Usually, the local manager was in the personnel function, while the Japanese manager was knowledgeable about industrial engineering, and could make explicit comparisons of performance at the British-based or German-based plant and at its HQ plant in Japan. According to circumstances, specific questions were also addressed to other Japanese and local managers in quality control and purchasing, and to supervisors.

4. TRAINING, SKILLS, AND WORK ORGANIZATION

This section concentrates on examining differences in the amount, mode, quality, and breath of training provided in the British-based and German-based plants, while making implicit comparisons with their HQ plants in Japan where appropriate. As discussed in Section 2, this section explores the extent to which skill formation has been affected by external regulation in each country, and by the level of general and technical education attainments of local workers. The latter interacts with shop-floor work organization, resulting in varying degrees to which decision-making power is devolved to lower levels of the shop-floor hierarchy, placing a greater or lesser need for problem-solving 'intellectual skills' on the part of operators and supervisors (Koike and Inoki 1987; 1990). Limits must be noted to gauging this aspect of work organization in the present research, which relies solely on interviews with managers.

The findings will be analysed in detail below, starting with the job grading system and promotion tracks and followed by training provided to semi-skilled operators, apprentices, technicians, and supervisors.

Job-Grading Systems and Internal Promotion Tracks

The job-grading systems at the case-study plants differ from those at their HQ plants in Japan, but to varying degrees. This is partly because the scope for subsidiary plants to adapt to local ways to suit the respective national labour markets differs according to the tightness of HQ control over the subsidiary. The tightest control was found at C_T Electronics Ltd, which adopted wholesale the Japanese HQ grading systems with its finely graded length-of-service and job-responsibility-related rungs in the payment system. C_T Electronics Ltd is the least localized of all the plants, with Japanese advisors shadowing various job functions including personnel. In other plants in both Britain and Germany, the personnel function is very much left to local managers, particularly when it concerns shop-floor workers. In Germany, this was said to be a necessity, because Japanese managers lack the knowledge of German labour law.

In general terms, the job-grading system in Japan may be characterized as follows. First, because opportunities for internal promotion are used as a means to motivate workers, many finely graded ranks are created for workers to climb up from the shop-floor to lower and middle management. Second, opportunities for horizontal job transfers are also abundant, facilitated partly by the relative absence of occupational consciousness guarding task demarcation. Third, a combination of vertical and horizontal movements facilitates good communication among workers, engineers, and managers on the shop-floor. Here, a pivotal role is played by the supervisor, who takes on a dual role: on the one hand a human relations manager who motivates, oversees and trains subordinates; and on the other a technical trouble-shooter, being the first to identify, and if possible solve, any production and quality control problems. The deviations from this norm at Japanese-based plants will be analysed below by picking up one VCR plant in Britain (E_V Electronics Ltd) and another VCR plant in Germany (B_V Electronics GmbH), and describing intra-country variations based on each national case study.

Germany   In Germany, B_V Electronics GmbH had the most undiluted German-qualification-based system which conforms with the tariff agreement with the IG Metall union. This involves the company evaluating each job in terms of its technical knowledge and organizational responsibility requirements, and working out a one-to-one correspondence between the job, the job grade, and its wage rate. There is therefore no scope for introducing length-of-service-related pay in Germany. At B_V Electronics GmbH, there are 48 jobs to be evaluated by a committee for blue-collar workers alone. However, this is said not to hinder job rotation, as (*a*) jobs are defined not in terms of demarcated tasks but in terms of technical and organizational competence and responsibility (a point made by Sengenberger (1987), as noted in Section 2); and (*b*) there is a tacit understanding that the main job is what a worker spends at least 50 per cent of his time doing. All the other German plants had a similar system to conform to the union agreement, even in the case of B_S Electronics GmbH, which does not recognize a union.

Next, B_V Electronics GmbH's work organization and promotion tracks are as follows (see Fig. 1). Each assembly line is headed by a supervisor (known as a 'line leader'), who oversees an assistant supervisor (known as a 'foreman' or 'forewoman'), several 'jumpers' who can undertake part or all of the tasks on the line, and a few dozen operators. The line leader is responsible for administration, for thinking of improvements to be made, visiting suppliers at times to ensure materials scheduling, and coping with normal technical and engineering problems. Forepersons are responsible for managing the line flow and taking interest in operators' personal well-being so as to create a good social environment to work in. Operators, who are nearly all female, can be internally promoted up to the foreperson level, but their initial semi-skilled entry status forecloses any chance of their rising higher, as line leaders must have a *Meister* qualification which in turn

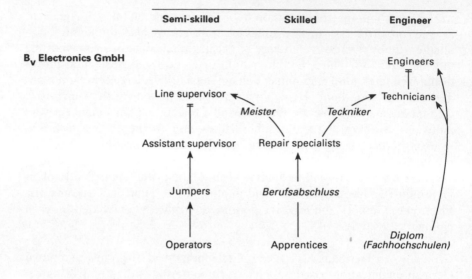

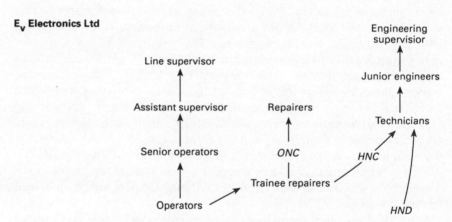

FIG. 1   Illustrations of Job-Grading Systems and Promotion Routes
↑ = promotion possible; ‡ = promotion blocked. Qualifications are in italics.

requires prior technical dual apprenticeship qualification. Commonly, those with a technical apprenticeship qualification become repair specialists. Some of them work towards gaining a Meister qualification, and are then promoted to line leaders. Thus, B$_V$ Electronics GmbH maintains the most rigid distinction between semi-skilled and skilled career tracks, as is the norm in Germany, with one-to-one correspondence between qualification and job status. Qualifications are cumulative, so that a prior choice in one occupational track forecloses one's option to switch to another skill status.

The other German-based plants have made modifications to the 'pure' qualification-based system, as follows. For example, C_V Electronics GmbH has not insisted on a Meister qualification for the job of line leader, so that the four line leaders are qualified, respectively, as an engineer, a technician, a Meister, and a skilled worker. Also, the 18 assistant supervisors (known as 'group leaders') consist of a minority of apprentice-qualified repair specialists on job rotation, who work alongside a majority who have been promoted from the rank of operators.

A more drastic modification has been made at A_V Electronics GmbH to break through the barriers to both vertical and horizontal transfers of operators. First, five women who were recruited as operators and promoted to jumpers were trained in-house-on-the-job in quality assurance, repair, and leadership, and were conferred in-house Meister qualifications upon satisfactory continuous assessment. This has opened a way for them to be promoted to assistant supervisors and line supervisors, who must all have Meister qualifications at this plant. Second, three women who were also recruited as operators received three months' training by in-house engineers in repairing; upon passing written and oral examinations and a practical test sct by A_V Electronics GmbH, they were promoted to become repair helpers, working alongside ex-apprentices in radio, TV, and communication electronics. The skill and knowledge base of this in-house training programme was said to be much narrower than the Dual System curriculum; moreover, the in-house qualifications have no currency outside A_V Electronics GmbH in the German occupational labour market. But they have given the women, who might otherwise have been stuck in a semi-skilled status for life, an opportunity to acquire higher technical skills and to be promoted internally.

Britain In Britain, Japanese plants have placed an enormous emphasis on flexibility of labour deployment in a belief that this would promote efficiency. The plants studied have secured this goal either by signing a single-union agreement, which spells out a commitment to worker flexibility, or by not recognizing a union. An attempt at reforming what was considered bad old British industrial relations led to establishing a flat organization with little job demarcations. One extreme case is C_T Electronics Ltd, which is said to have 70 per cent of all workers on one grade. But the inability to motivate workers by pooling all operators and 'jumpers' in one grade has elicited the following recent modifications. One is the introduction of length-of-service pay, as practised at A_T Electronics Ltd and B_T Electronics Ltd, so as to retain and motivate good workers. Another is the use of more finely graded ranks reflecting length of service. For example, at D_T Electronics Ltd there are eight ranks on the shop-floor, whereas in reality four would suffice to distinguish among workers according to their skill levels. These are both Japanese-inspired adaptations.

In most British assembly plants, operators have been internally promoted up to the level of supervisors heading assembly lines. C_T Electronics Ltd is most conspicuous in actively encouraging internal promotion, so that two employees who had started out as ordinary operators were promoted to supervisors and then further to production controllers. While internal promotion is considered good for motivating workers and eliciting loyalty from them, an increase in the technical knowledge requirements of most jobs on the shop-floor was pointed out by several plants including D_T Electronics Ltd as placing an invisible ceiling to promoting operators much beyond the assistant supervisor level.

A separate track exists for trainee technicians who, together with fully qualified technicians, engage in on-line repair. Repairers are therefore people with at least a City and Guilds qualification, and more typically have an Ordinary National qualification. Once qualified with HNC/HND, however, these technicians apparently prefer to become fully fledged technicians, away from the production area. Consequently, they rarely become line supervisors. D_T Electronics Ltd notes that it is harder to train supervisors in technical matters than to train technicians in supervision, but it has succeeded in turning only one or two technicians into supervisors. F_V Electronics Ltd does not expect its line supervisors to have much technical knowledge; their responsibility is to spot a problem and to know whom to contact in the technical department.

The case of E_V Electronics Ltd illustrates the difficulty in deciding whether or not to have technically trained supervisors present on the shop-floor. E_V's job-grading system with progression routes is described in Fig. 1. As with B_V GmbH, there are four layers of hierarchy: operators, senior operators, one assistant supervisor, and one supervisor per assembly line. The similarity stops there, however. There are two major differences from the German plant. First, 16-year-old operators are screened for two years, before good ones are chosen to undergo a three-year part-time training course (tailor-made for the plant) leading to an ONC qualification while working as trainee repairers. There are therefore no separate entry routes for semi-skilled and skilled workers as in Germany. Second, there is no established route for repair specialists to become line supervisors, as noted earlier. E_V Electronics Ltd is unusual in having insisted in the past that all line supervisors and assistant supervisors have a technical qualification (i.e. HNC/HND or a time-served apprenticeship): 'we looked for technical knowledge first, but also preferably supervision experience.' This proved to be too ambitious, as not all could cope well with satisfying both technical and supervisory roles. E_V Ltd currently has an interim measure for (*a*) internal promotion of operators up to the assistant supervisor level, and (*b*) a clear division of labour between supervisors, who control people, and engineers, who take care of technical aspects. In the meantime, the plant hopes to establish a stable core of technicians, who are currently sent to

Japan where they are learning both technical and supervisory functions, and who are expected to become supervisors on their return.

Semi-skilled Operators

The great bulk of recruits at the case-study plants are for semi-skilled assembly jobs. By far the clearest difference between Britain and Germany lies in educational attainments of operators prior to recruitment. In Germany, operators had gone through a three-year Dual System training, typically in sales assistantship, garment making, or hairdressing. They were therefore receiving some form of education at least until the age of 18.

In Britain, by contrast, operators had typically left school at the age of 16, some with CSE or O-level qualifications, but others with fewer, if any, qualifications. The British plants laid down no minimum educational requirement for the job, but G_S Electronics Ltd's operators typically had three O-levels, while only 10 per cent of direct workers at A_T Electronics Ltd were said to have some educational qualifications of any worth (i.e. at least one CSE with grade 3 or above). Similarly, four or five CSEs of any grade were said to be a typical educational qualification of recruits at C_T Electronics Ltd. At one extreme, the British manager at C_T Electronics Ltd was so appalled by some operators' inability to spell and add up that he started registering a simple literacy and numeracy test as part of the initial selection process, while providing remedial education to a few operators at the company's expense.

In both Britain and Germany, the selection method was similar, involving the use of references, school reports and qualifications, and interviews with the personnel and the production departments. But more British plants relied also on aptitude tests (involving simple maths, letter recognition, etc.) and practical dexterity tests than German plants (see Table 4). Several German personnel managers interviewed thought neither type of test necessary as they trusted the school system. This supports one hypothesis in this research: that British-based plants use direct tests of aptitudes to compensate for the unreliability of school qualifications.

The initial induction training, involving explanations of health and safety regulations and practising some basic tasks (such as component recognition and soldering), lasts from one day up to five days. Explaining about the company worldwide and company history was an exception rather than the norm. If anything, German-based plants tended to rush operators on to the shop-floor with little induction, compared with British-based plants (see Table 4). Thereafter, newly recruited operators are looked after by team leaders and supervisors who provide training on-the-job and whose discretion it is to rotate in a few different tasks during the probationary period of up to one year. A_T Electronics Ltd has the most formalized system of

M. Sako

training every new operator in at least three tasks, which are commonly manual insertion, soldering, and mechanical assembly.

TABLE 4   Training Practices at the Case-Study Firms

Company	Semi-skilled operators		Number of apprentices and long-term trainees[c]	Performance appraisal	Labour turnover (%)
	Selection methods[a]	Induction training (days)[b]			
A$_T$ Electronics Ltd	A, D, I	1.5	None now	All employees	15–20
B$_T$ Electronics Ltd	D, I	5	18	All employees	3–4
C$_T$ Electronics Ltd	A, D, I	5	20	All employees	9
D$_T$ Electronics Ltd	D, I	2	19	All employees	18
E$_T$ Electronics Ltd	A, I	5	None now	Ungraded workers only	20
E$_V$ Electronics Ltd	A, D, I	0.5	20	All employees	12–14
F$_V$ Electronics Ltd	A, D, I	3–5	18–20	All employees	14–15
A$_V$ Electronics GmbH	D, I	1	0	All employees	Near 0
B$_V$ Electronics GmbH	I	1	12	Skilled workers only	18%
C$_V$ Electronics GmbH	D, I	2	11	All employees	14–15
D$_V$ Electronics GmbH	I	0	15	All employees	5 or less
G$_S$ Electronics Ltd	A, I	3	24	All employees	13
A$_S$ Electronics GmbH	I	0–0.5	0	None	10
B$_S$ Electronics GmbH	I	0	0	All employees	5 or less

[a]A = aptitude test (simple maths, logical reasoning, letter and pattern recognition).
 D = dexterity test (timed practical tests).
 I = interview(s).
[b]Induction training is the duration spent off the shop-floor, before a supervisor is assigned.
[c]Only technical apprenticeships are recorded.

The personnel managers interviewed both in Britain and Germany showed a preference for a good age mix, so that some recruits were school-leavers while others were mature women in their thirties with children. Partly for this reason, recruitment takes place all the year round, though concentrated in the spring and summer. This makes it costly to conduct a proper induction training course for new recruits who also enter the shop-floor in dribs and drabs. This was said to be in contrast to a more cost-effective concerted annual recruitment and induction drive in the spring in Japan.

Apprentices and Long-Term Trainees

The majority of the Japanese plants have adapted to the respective national training regulation when it comes to the training of apprentices in the technical field. In Germany, three out of the six plants had technical apprentices, numbering between 12 and 15 (see Table 4). Of the three that do not have any, A$_V$ Electronics GmbH and B$_S$ Electronics GmbH had apprentices in the field of office administration only. All three indicated a plan to start training apprentices in the near future, as soon as enough in-house processes and facilities (including a workshop) are installed.

The technical fields for which the Japanese plants provide apprenticeship training are 'radio, TV and communication electronics' and maintenance. The apprentices typically spend four days at the plant and one day at school. Not much work contribution is expected from them, however, as much off-the-job training takes place in the plant's education room, and because they must study for the school and pass the examinations. At C_V Electronics GmbH, one engineer with a supplementary trainer qualification from the Chamber of Industry is responsible for educating the technical apprentices. Such a person used to be a Meister, but was changed to an engineer, reflecting the rapid technological change in the electronics field. Training by in-house engineers is also quite common in Japan (Dore and Sako 1989: 89). At B_V Electronics GmbH, there is, besides six in-house qualified trainers of apprentices, one full-time additional outside trainer, who is a teacher paid by the plant to provide supplementary instruction, for example by explaining to apprentices what they did not understand at vocational school classes. Training was provided on the expectation that around half would leave upon completion. This the plants' personnel managers considered acceptable, as 'education is always also for the common society, not only for the company'.

In Britain, six out of the eight plants visited had a programme of long-term training for young people in the technical field. One plant with no apprentices is A_T Electronics Ltd, which had two former apprentices who had successfully completed the programme in the past, but all subsequent recruits had left before completion. The six plants each have around 20 long-term trainees, who may be studying for electronics or maintenance qualifications. The exact arrangement varies from course to course and from company to company, owing to changes that are taking place after the abolition of the Engineering Industry Training Board and in the system of validating qualifications. On the one hand, general off-the-job courses on offer are used by some. As an example, D_T Electronics Ltd's apprentices are recruited as apprentices, first to study full-time over two to three years at further education (FE) colleges in order to obtain an OND in electronics, and then to study part-time over two years on block release at a college, while working at the plant to qualify for HNC. On the other hand, company-specific tailor-made courses are developed by Japanese plants in collaboration with local FE colleges and are validated externally. E_V Electronics Ltd has one such course, for two evenings per week over three years, leading up to an ONC in repairing. It is attended by trainee repairers selected from among well performing operators. They work full-time, and are paid above the average operator salary. This is in stark contrast to German apprentices, whose allowances are no more than a third of the operator pay.

Supervisors

Production supervisors, as mentioned earlier, tend to be internally promoted from among operators more commonly in Britain than in Germany. In those British plants where supervisors are not expected to have technical expertise, training has focused more on leadership and inter-personal relations skills than on engineering skills. For example, both A_T and B_T Electronics Ltd have recently started training supervisors and team leaders in supervisory skills, as part of a one-year NEBSS (National Examinations Board for Supervisory Studies) course taught by instructors from local further education colleges. C_T Electronics Ltd prefers to use a training programme adopted from its HQ plant in Japan. This training course—TWI (Training within Industry)—is totally in-house, and uses an English translation of the manuals used at the Japanese plant. The course is offered also to supervisors and foremen at other local companies in the area.

Only a few British-based plants have made a concerted effort to educate supervisors in technical knowledge, although many managers recognize its growing importance with the greater technical sophistication of most shop-floor jobs. E_T Electronics Ltd is exceptional in having adopted, again from the HQ in Japan, a six-week in-house production engineering course to be attended by all supervisors and leading hands. Another approach pursued by E_V Ltd is to send technicians to the Japanese HQ plant for training in supervisory as well as technical skills, to turn them into effective supervisors on their return.

In Germany, as noted before, the plants appoint mainly Meister-qualified workers to the position of supervisors. None of the plants has as yet had its employees study for and pass the Meister examination after recruitment, although A_S and B_S Electronics GmbH have accommodated a small number currently working towards the qualification. The Meisters already possess broad-based technical knowledge in the relevant area, and pedagogical skills to train apprentices. Because technical knowledge is taken for granted when supervisors are hired, D_V Electronics GmbH, like other companies, concentrates on in-house OJT in leadership and organizational skills. Short off-the-job courses on leadership offered by consultants and the local Chamber were also used to supplement the OJT.

Summary

The British-based plants generally have a system of internal promotion up to a higher level of shop-floor organization than the German-based plants. The latter adopted the German qualification-centred job-grading system, with clear career tracking determined by entry-level qualifications. In Britain, technicians may emerge from among operators, but technician-qualified

people rarely became line supervisors. By contrast, in Germany, the operators' choice to pursue a repair-technician route is clearly foreclosed, but
technically qualified people, Meisters in the main but also technicians, can
become supervisors. It is this difference that makes technically qualified
workers more directly part of the shop-floor organization in Germany,
while British technicians stand apart from the shop-floor, a contrast also
found by Daly *et al.* (1985).

Japanese companies' responses vary. But in Germany, main modifications
focused on getting around the rigid qualification system so as to provide
more flexible learning and promotion opportunities for semi-skilled workers.
In Britain, the major problem lies in the unavailability of Meister-like
people who can take on both supervisory and technical roles. The dilemma
presented to Japanese plants in Britain lies in a choice between training
supervisors in technical skills and making supervisors out of reluctant
technicians on the one hand, and being content with the British norm of a
more centralized technical department supporting the shop-floor on the
other. For the moment, only a few (E_T Electronics Ltd and E_V Electronics
Ltd) were making a concerted effort to transpose the Japanese shop-floor
work organization with a long-term view.

Lastly, although external courses were used as part of training, preference
was shown by some Japanese plants also to develop tailor-made off-the-job
training courses, or to adopt in-house courses developed at the HQ plant
in Japan. Another mode of firm-specific training is sending supervisory and
technician workers for short-term training to Japan; this is regarded as a
means of communicating to them, through direct experience, not only
technical skills but also how to train, and relate to, subordinates.

5. PRODUCTIVITY AND QUALITY LEVELS

How has the difference in training practices, as analysed above, affected the
performance of Japanese plants in Britain and Germany? This section first
considers evidence on shop-floor labour productivity and quality levels at
the 14 plants. Table 5 shows the average productivity and quality differentials
between each British-based or German-based plant and its corresponding
HQ plant in Japan. The limited size of the sample ought to be kept in
mind. Plant-by-plant variations rule out making generalizations about
whether British-based or German-based plants are performing better.

The measure of productivity most commonly used in the sample plants
is the ratio of standard time to actual time taken to process and assemble
final products. Standard time is calculated in Japan and adjusted locally,
for example for the degree of automation. But the same formula is used to
calculate standard time at each European-based plant as at its corresponding

TABLE 5 Productivity and Quality Differentials, UK and Germany

Company name	Productivity[a]	Quality defect rate[a]
A_T Electronics Ltd	90–95	200–1,000
B_T Electronics Ltd	95	200 +
C_T Electronics Ltd	90	250
D_T Electronics Ltd	95	slightly worse in UK
E_T Electronics Ltd	100	100
E_V Electronics Ltd	100	120
F_V Electronics Ltd	90	slightly worse in UK
A_V Electronics GmbH	80–90	100–150
B_V Electronics GmbH	85–100	300–400
C_V Electronics GmbH	95	200
D_V Electronics GmbH	n.a.	200

[a]Indexed at productivity in Japan = 100; quality defect rate in Japan = 100.

HQ plant in Japan by virtue of its belonging to the same corporation. Thus, comparability of measure is preserved, even if the measuring formula may differ from company to company. Each plant was asked to make its best judgement on what productivity level it is achieving if hypothetically the same conditions (degree of automation, capacity utilization, batch size, etc.) were assumed at the corresponding HQ plant in Japan. If the Japanese productivity level is indexed at 100, the productivity is said to range from 90 to 100 in Britain, and from 80 to 95 in Germany.

In reality, however, various conditions differ between the European-based plant and the Japanese HQ plant, affecting the standard time itself. In particular, the degree of automation is lower in Europe because of smaller scales and batches, and much lower at British-based plants because of lower wage rates. This means that, for example, although E_V Electronics Ltd has achieved the same degree of efficiency (as measured by the ratio of standard time to actual time) as its HQ plant in Japan, the standard time itself is 50–60 per cent longer in Britain than in Japan. The actual British labour productivity is therefore around 60–70 per cent of that at the Japanese plant.

The measure of quality varied more greatly from plant to plant. Some companies used the end-of-line reject rate (or the corresponding pass rate), while some others counted the number of defective points discovered at any point in process. The rates were typically a few percentage points up to 15 or 20 per cent in some cases which counted all minor defectives. Whatever measure was used, however, the consistency of measure between each European-based plant and its Japanese-based counterpart again ensures comparability. The British defect rates range from twice to ten times as high as in Japan, while the German defect rates from roughly the same to four times as high as in Japan.

The sources of productivity and quality differentials are various. The rest of this section concentrates on factors other than human resources, namely (1) the nature of product markets and (2) the quality of raw materials and components.

The Nature of Product Markets

The fierce competition that exists in the Japanese domestic consumer electronics markets has been transposed to Europe through direct overseas investment by all major Japanese manufacturers. The competition is based as much on new product development and shorter product cycles of existing goods incorporating new features, as on competitive prices. In Japan, the model cycle for such goods as colour television sets and VCRs which the case-study plants manufacture have shortened to one year. The cycles within Europe, according to some plants, are apparently slightly longer, up to two years. However, the same pressure to shorten model cycles exists because of the competition among Japanese manufacturers, and because the design and development of the chassis in the case of TVs and the mechanism in the case of VCRs are undertaken at the HQ plants in Japan.

While there might be respite for some European-based plants as a result of the longer model cycles, the plants must also cope with a smaller target market than their Japanese HQ counterparts or subsidiary plants in the USA. The target market for the case-study plants in most cases is the EC region, which consists of twelve countries requiring different specifications. Consequently, British- and German-based plants produce a greater number of models in smaller batches than their HQ plants in Japan. For example, in Germany, A_V Electronics GmbH makes 60–70 models in a year, B_V Electronic GmbH 40, and C_V Electronics GmbH 55. In Britain, A_T Electronics Ltd makes 110–120 models and B_T Electronics Ltd, 30 models. At C_T Electronics Ltd the number of models, 80, was smaller than the 200 models produced at the HQ plant in Japan for export and domestic purposes, and the average batch size, ranging from 500 to 1,000, was considerably smaller than the Japanese plant average of 3,000–5,000. Smaller batch sizes make it more difficult to exploit economies of scale and to control for quality, because they add to the difficulty in automating processes.

The Quality of Raw Materials and Components

Next, plant-level performance is affected by the quality of raw materials and components. There is evidence that, although improvements have been made, poor quality of local supplies and subcontracting work remains a source of concern for Japanese companies (JETRO 1991: 50–8). Moreover, with the exception of a few European supplier companies such as Philips, local suppliers do not generally contribute to the product development and design process of European-based Japanese plants. This lack of supplier involvement in the design stage hinders local suppliers' willingness to pursue continuous cost reduction and quality improvements for Japanese plants in Europe (Sako 1992).

The case-study plants all had local content ratios well above the EC guideline. The modal ratio was in the range of 60–65 per cent, with B_T Electronics Ltd achieving a maximum of 90 per cent. At the time of the interviews, none of the plants was simply assembling from SKD (semi-knock-down) kits; the nature of the assembly and processing was therefore more than mere screwdriver operations. In this context, the inferior quality of locally purchased components was mentioned as one of several reasons why British- and German-based plants had lower productivity and quality than their Japanese HQ plants. B_T Electronics Ltd also mentioned the lack of service of some suppliers; for instance, some non-standard components were said to be not automatically inserted on to printed circuit boards because the local supplier of those components refused to undertake special packaging so as to enable them to be fed directly onto the insertion machines.

Loss of efficiency also derives from the higher level of inventory-holding at European-based plants. This results in part from longer lead-times for ordering from the Far East, and in part from the need to insure against late delivery from local European suppliers.

6.   MACHINERY AND PRODUCTION ORGANIZATION

This section considers evidence on differences in the use of machinery among the plants with respect to the following aspects: (1) the number of machines per employee (or manning levels per machine); (2) rates and causes of machine breakdowns; (3) ages and technical sophistication of machinery and equipment; (4) relationships with equipment suppliers; and (5) the process of installing new equipment. All these aspects concern the 'humanware' (Shimada and MacDuffie 1986), which highlights the complementarity between capital equipment and labour.

Manning levels

Direct comparisons among all plants proved impossible, because not all plants had a single common process in which machinery played a major part. But there is strong evidence that manning levels at the British-based plants are higher than at their HQ plants in Japan, and weak evidence that the German–Japanese gap in manning levels is small. This tallies with the relative wage rates in the three countries.

The comparison of plants focuses on the automatic insertion machine workshop. At A_T and F_V Electronics Ltd, one operator attends one machine, whereas their plants in Japan have an operator looking after up to five machines. Both B_T and E_T Electronics Ltd had a manning ratio of one operator to two machines, compared with one to four in Japan. D_T Electronics Ltd also had a manning level that was double that at the Japanese HQ plant. The only German-based plant with an automatic insertion machine shop, A_V Electronics GmbH, had a normal manning level of one operator per line, with three to four machines per line, which was said to be the same as in Japan.

Manning levels are affected by capacity utilization to an extent. For example, C_T Electronics Ltd had a manning ratio of 1 : 1 at the time of the interview, although up to four machines per operator were considered possible at busy times. They also change over-time. For example, E_T Electronics Ltd achieved a gradual transition from one-to-one manning to two machines to one operator by sending maintenance and programming technicians to Japan for OJT for a three- to four-month period at a time.

What is different from Japan in all the cases is that in Europe, each machine is self-contained and standalone, while in Japan insertion or surface mount machines along a line are all interconnected. A lack of skills in preventative maintenance among British and German machine operators was cited as a major reason for this difference.

Machine Breakdowns

Interconnected machines tend to make it difficult to achieve a high machine utilization rate, because a breakdown of one machine affects all other machines in the line. Even without such a problem, machine breakdowns were said to be higher at the British-based plants than at their HQ plants in Japan. At B_T Electronics Ltd, for example, the mean time between failure (MTBF), which is the average time between stoppages, was said to be three times longer in Japan than in Britain. Low maintenance skills and inferior components quality were said to cause more frequent stoppages. Both B_T and C_T Electronics Ltd pointed out the absence of machine operators and technicians with long lengths of service as in Japan, who have accumulated a better expertise than the machine manufacturers in how to maintain, repair, and improve the machines. At A_V Electronics GmbH, by contrast, the machine utilization rate was judged to be the same as at its HQ plant in Japan, if smaller batch sizes in Germany were taken into account. Interconnecting machine installation was said to be just a matter of time and experience. However, small-batch production contributes to a slower pace of learning.

Age and Technical Sophistication

Older machines and newly installed machines are more difficult to maintain. There was, however, said to be no major differences in the age, size, running speed, or technical sophistication of machines used at the European-based and Japanese-based plants. In the case of automatic insertion and surface mount machines, the same Japanese brand of machinery was installed at the British-based and German-based plants as at their HQ plants in Japan. These machines are relatively standardized, and have already been tried and tested at the Japanese plants by the time they are installed in Britain or Germany.

At B_V and C_V Electronics GmbH, where PCB insertion was subcontracted out in the Far East, questions were asked about the video cylinder machining shop. The machines were all Japanese-made, except for a few Swiss-made ones. In fact, some of the machines at C_V Electronics GmbH had been used, and were handed down, by its HQ plant in Japan. However, both German-based plants showed a strong preference for in-house innovation and joint development with German equipment suppliers. In the case of C_V Electronics GmbH, a Japanese manager proudly pointed out testing jigs and equipment that had been developed by German technicians at their own initiative; the ease of maintenance and the accumulation of in-house know-how were said to be two important reasons for encouraging such innovation. The B_V Electronics GmbH German production manager, during one of his regular visits to the HQ plant in Japan saw that two assembly processes that were difficult to control manually were automated; on his return to Germany, he asked a German equipment supplier nearby to develop two customized machines jointly to automate the processes. They are now up and running, attended by one operator.

Equipment Suppliers

It is common for users of machinery to prefer to buy locally whenever possible, for ease of repair and service. As pointed out above, the British-based and German-based plants are using predominantly Japanese brand machinery and equipment, mainly because the investment decision is taken by Japanese managers in Europe and Japan. There is an advantage in using Japanese brands of machinery, as it is well tried and tested in Japan, and the good relationship with equipment suppliers which the plants in Japan have developed over the years can be extended to their European subsidiaries. However, it also has its disadvantages, as Japanese equipment suppliers tend not to have the resources to post too many service personnel at their European sales offices. This means that a major machine breakdown is not serviced immediately, and a high level of inventory must be carried in order to insure against a long period of stoppage. Moreover, C_V Electronics GmbH pointed out that Japanese equipment suppliers tend not to be experienced in installing machinery in Germany, where the health and safety regulations require various unfamiliar modifications to be made, adding 20 per cent to the equipment price. German equipment suppliers are therefore preferred, as they are located nearby, have more service personnel, and are familiar with German requirements.

None of the British-based plants mentioned the possibility of sourcing equipment from British suppliers. Moreover, in both Germany and Britain, the three semiconductor plants studied had sourced practically all the equipment from the suppliers, mostly Japanese, with whom their HQ plant in Japan has worked closely. Localizing equipment supply therefore appears more difficult in the semiconductor industry than in the electronic equipment assembly industry.

The Process of Installing New Equipment

Equipment suppliers typically send their own personnel to help install new machinery, and leave behind manuals and operating instructions. Initial teething problems may be solved jointly with the equipment supplier, but subsequent maintenance and operation depend much on in-house know-how. Here, close links with the HQ plant in Japan become crucially important for improving the learning curve. Common practices include (*a*) sending technicians and supervisors to the equipment manufacturer and the HQ plant in Japan to work with the machinery before it is installed in the European-based plant, and (*b*) sending Japanese engineers to Europe to instruct workers at the European-based plant. They both place an emphasis on on-the-job training and experience. An even more hands-on manner of training was found at G_S Electronics Ltd, which started to bring over ten or so Japanese shopfloor workers with seven to eight years of work experience from the HQ plant in Japan on a three-monthly basis to work alongside, and assist, British workers.

Summary: Attitudes, Feedback, and Experience

A number of the plants studied had achieved a significant improvement over time in both productivity and quality. Some, such as E_T Electronics Ltd, have managed to match the level of efficiency at the HQ plant. But it remains a fact that most of the European-based plants lag behind their HQ plants. What accounts for this gap?

The respondents' answers are not straightforward, but may be summarized as follows. First, European-based plants have to deal with tougher conditions for product and quality control, owing to product variety and small batches, lack of subcontractors taking on difficult-to-automate tasks, and higher defect rates and inventory holding of components. Second, even without these problems, there are some aspects of the 'humanware' that are in need of reforming: they are (*a*) attitudes towards quality, and (*b*) an orientation towards feedback and problem-solving.

Reforming workers attitudes towards quality involves instructing them on what is an acceptable level of cleanliness or concentration, but also developing a sense of teamwork. For example, A_T Electronics Ltd mentioned British operators' inability to work in a team, referring specifically to their tendency to pass on defective items to the next operator if defects are due not to oneself but to previous operators. The Japanese manager at C_T Electronics Ltd also implied that attitudes, in particular a sense of responsibility, are more important than technical skills in improving quality. According to him, 'In Japan, there are overlaps in tasks between workers, so that mistakes are avoided by several people following up the same task or issue from different angles. This overlap is perhaps what responsibility is all about.'

At A_T Electronics Ltd, a Japanese industrial engineer referred to the tendency of British inspection operators to reject faulty assembled products summarily, thus raising the defect rate and repairing costs. At the firm's HQ plant in Japan, by contrast, inspection operators tend to adjust and repair minor faults there and then, without rejecting. Moreover, a repair operator is likely to tell the inspection operator what was wrong and what to do next time he or she comes across similar faults. Such informal communication across functions was said to be relatively absent at the British-based plant. A Japanese manager at B_V Electronics GmbH also thought that, apart from the daily five-minute meeting which takes place among the line leader, quality assurance personnel, and a production technician, more informal, yet essential, communication about quality and other matters tended to happen less in Germany than in Japan because there is less overtime and socializing after work in Germany.

Thus, managers at European-based plants attributed their inferior performance to work attitudes affecting how production is co-ordinated in the plant as a whole. And while attitudes have some cultural basis, they are treated as something that can be selected for and changed through training and participation in problem-solving activities. One indication of this is the existence of performance appraisal for individual workers at all levels at most of the plants in the sample (see Table 4). The format of the appraisal differs slightly from plant to plant, but what is common is the assessment of various aspects of the job, including such things as flexibility, co-operativeness, attention to detail, initiative-taking, problem-solving, and communication skills. Performance appraisal, then, is a means for Japanese plants to promote in individual workers the attitudes that they believe lie at the core of improving plant performance. The technical and cognitive skills of British and German workers are therefore seen to affect the plant-wide performance, but only as part of a broader definition of capability which includes work attitudes.

7. SUMMARY AND CONCLUSIONS

Since the research reported in this paper is not yet completed, any con-clusions that may be drawn from a small sample can be no more than tentative. With this proviso, the main findings may be summarized.

First, training practices at the Japanese plants were found to be modified to suit local national situations, particularly in their use of apprenticeships and vocational qualifications. However, they were utilized in such a way as not to undermine the essence of a widely held training philosophy. This rests on a belief that a reliance on OJT, in-house training courses, and internal promotion is the only way to cultivate and retain workers capable of enhancing plant-wide performance.

Second, the productivity and quality performance at Japanese plants in both Britain and Germany was found on average to be not as good as at their HQ plants in Japan. Inferior quality in Europe is due to a combination of reasons, including small scale and batch production, inferior component quality, and the lack of awareness and accumulated know-how in main-taining and improving quality.

Third, no significant gap was found in the productivity and quality performance between British-based and German-based Japanese plants. This is despite the fact that the work-force at German-based plants is better qualified in general than those at British-based plants. Not only are semi-skilled operators better educated and qualified vocationally in Germany, but lower-level supervisors are also better trained and qualified in technological matters, thus enabling them to deal with technical as well as managerial problems at source quickly. This pattern, in which supervisors and some blue-collar workers possess sufficient engineering knowledge to solve prob-lems, approximates the situation in a typical shop-floor in large Japanese firms. The advantage in productive efficiency of this work organization, as compared with an organization in which the technically qualified staff is more scarce and centralized, appears obvious.

If that is the case, why are the German-based plants not out-performing the British-based plants? The solution to this puzzle seems to lie in the nature of decisions over location and localization by Japanese MNCs. It can be argued that, thus far, what has mattered for plant performance is the quality of management decisions rather than shop-floor skills. The fact that product design and process technology are largely fixed by Japanese engineers and managers in Japan might have pre-empted a major source of variability in performance between British-based and German-based plants.

At the same time, it may be that, at least in the electrical and electronics industry, the quality of British manpower has been sufficient, and that of German manpower more than adequate, to carry out standardized assembly tasks. Besides, relatively low labour costs in Britain give it a large comparative advantage in undertaking semi-skilled operations. In fact, Britain has gained a disproportionate share of Japanese plants manufacturing electronics goods (58 out of 178 plants in Europe in 1991), while Germany has attracted Japanese operations in a more dispersed range of industries, including rubber and plastics, chemicals and machinery (see also Yamawaki 1990).

Looking to the future, there are grounds for thinking that the British comparative advantage for Japanese MNCs might be eroded. As more companies localize the design and development of products for the European market, they may face constraints in recruiting adequate numbers of engineers and technicians. Moreover, localizing process technology development may also lead more Japanese companies to tap into the network of local equipment and machinery suppliers; as noted earlier, such a network is more readily available in Germany than in Britain. The ease of maintenance and the speed of response in repairing in Germany would enable a lower holding of inventories at German-based than at British-based plants.

These are some of the reasons that may reinforce the location decisions of Japanese multinational companies in the future, with Britain being chosen mainly for its low semi-skilled labour costs and Germany for the availability of technical manpower for design and development as well as for process innovation.

NOTES TO CHAPTER 4

1. Prais *et al.* (1989) conducted a series of studies which compared productivity in indigenous British and German companies in a range of carefully chosen sectors, i.e. metalworking, woodworking, clothing, hotels, and retail sectors. Earlier, Pratten (1976) also found, in his study of multinational companies with plants in Europe and North America, that productivity was up to 35 per cent higher in Germany than in Britain.
2. The same JETRO survey identified 157 companies in 1983, 188 in 1984, 242 in 1986, 282 in 1987, 411 in 1988, and 529 in 1989.

REFERENCES

Abbeglen, J. C., and Stalker, G. (1985), *Kaisha*. Basic Books, New York.

Anglo-Japanese Economic Institute (1991), *Britain and Japan 1991: An Economics Briefing*, Anglo-Japanese Economic Institute, London.

Campbell, A., Sorge, A., and Warner, M. (1989), *Microelectronics Product Applications in Great Britain and West Germany*, Avebury Press, Aldershot.

Cole, Robert (1989), *Strategies for Learning*, University of California Press, Berkeley, Calif.

Daly, A., Hitchens, D. M. W., and Wagner, K. (1985), 'Productivity, Machinery and Skills in a Sample of British and German Manufacturing Plants', *National Institute Economic Review*, February.

Dore, R. P., and Sako, M. (1989), *How the Japanese Learn to Work*, Routledge, London.

Finegold, D. (1991), 'Institutional Incentives and Skill Creation: Understanding the Decisions that Lead to a High Skill Equilibrium', in Ryan (1991).

——and Soskice, D. (1988), 'The Failure of Training in Britain: Analysis and Prescription', *Oxford Review of Economic Policy*, 4(3): 21–53.

JETRO (1991), *Zaiou nikkeikigyo (seizogyo) no keiei jittai: dai nanakai jittai chosa hokoku* (Report of the Sixth Survey on the State of Management of Japanese Manufacturing Affiliates in Europe), JETRO, Tokyo.

Koike, K. (1991), *Shigoto no Keizaigaku* (Economics of Work), Toyo Keizai Shinpo sha, Tokyo.

——and Inoki, T. (1987), *Jinzai keisei no kokusai hikaku: tonan ajia to nihon* (An International Comparison of Human Capital Formation: South East Asia and Japan), Toyo Keizai Shimposha, Tokyo.

————(eds.) (1990), *Skill Formation in Japan and Southeast Asia*, University or Tokyo Press.

MacDuffie, John-Paul, and Kochan, T. A. (1991), 'Does the US Under invest in Human Resources? Determinants of Training in the World Auto Industry, mimeo.

Marsden, David (1986), *The End of Economic Man? Custom and Competition in Labour Markets*, Wheatsheaf Books, Brighton.

——and Ryan, Paul (1990), 'Institutional Aspects of Youth Employment and Training Policy in Britain', *British Journal of Industrial Relations*, 28(3): 352–69.

NEDC/MSC (1984), *Competence and Competition: Training and Education in the Federal Republic of Germany, the United States and Japan*, NEDO, London.

Oliver, Nick, and Wilkinson, Barry (1988), *The Japanization of British Industry*, Basil Blackwell, Oxford.

OTA (US Congress, Office of Technology Assessment) (1990), *Worker Training: Competing for the New International Economy*, US Government Printing Office, Washington DC.

Prais, S. J. (1987), 'Qualified Manpower in Engineering: Britain and Other Industrially Advanced Countries', *National Institute Economic Review*, February.

——et al. (1989), *Productivity, Education and Training: Britain and Other Countries Compared*, NIESR, London.

Pratten, C. F. (1976), *Labour Productivity Differentials Within International Companies*, Cambridge University Press.

—— (1990), 'The Limits to Training', *Financial Times*, 3 April.

Ryan, P. (ed.) (1991), *International Comparisons of Vocational Education and Training in Intermediate Skills*, Falmer Press, Brighton.

Sako, Mari (1990), 'Enterprise Training in a Comparative Perspective: West Germany, Japan and Britain, report prepared for the World Bank, mimeo, London School of Economics.

—— (1991), 'Institutional Aspects of Youth Employment and Training Policy: A Comment on Marsden and Ryan', *British Journal of Industrial Relations*, 29(3): 485–90.

—— (1992), *Prices, Quality and Trust: Inter-firm Relations in Britain and Japan*, Cambridge University Press.

Sengenberger, W. (1987), 'Vocational Worker Training, Labour Market Structure, and Industrial Relations in West Germany', in J. Bergmann and S. Tokunaga (eds.), *Economic and Social Aspects of Industrial Relations*, Campus Verlag, Frankfurt.

Shimada, H. (1988), *Hyuman Wuea no Keizaigaku* (The Economics of Humanware), Iwanami shoten, Tokyo.

—— and Macduffie, J. P., (1986), 'Industrial Relations and "Humanware"', Alfred Sloan School of Management Working Paper.

Steedman, H., Mason, G., and Wagner, K. (1991), 'Intermediate Skills in the Workplace: Deployment, Standards and Supply in Britain, France and Germany', *National Institute Economic Review* May: 60–76.

Takamiya, S., and Thurley, K. (eds.) (1985), *Japans Emerging Multinationals*, University of Tokyo Press.

Training Agency (1989), *Training in Britain: A Study of Funding Activities and Attitudes*, HMSO, London.

White, Michael, and Trevor, Malcolm (1983), *Under Japanese Management*, Policy Studies Institute, London.

Whittaker, D. H. (1990), *Managing Innovation: A Study of British and Japanese Factories*, Cambridge University Press.

Yamawaki, Hideki (1990), 'Location Decisions of Japanese Multinational Firms in European Manufacturing Industries', Discussion Paper FS IV 90–21, Wissenschaftszentrum Berlin für Sozialforschung.

5

Co-ordination between Production and Distribution in a Globalizing Network of Firms: Assessing Flexibility Achieved in the Japanese Automobile Industry

BANRI ASANUMA

1. INTRODUCTION

Take any of those products of assembly type industries that we use in our daily life and are characteristic to the contemporary society. Be it a personal computer, a copier, or a car, each unit bears the brand of some company which has produced and supplied it. However, if we trace back the route through which a given unit came down to its user, all the way back from the retail outlet to the final assembly plant, and therefrom further upstream to the sources of parts and components, we are bound to find that, of all of these vertically related stages of production and distribution, only a limited number of them is carried out by the company that has given its brand name to that product.

In other words, a typical manufactured good today is neither completely made by one single producer nor sold directly by that producer to the final consumer, as is presumed in usual microeconomics textbooks. It is produced and distributed by a network of firms, which a firm responsible for a specific brand (or a set of several specific brands) creates by initiating business relations with other firms. For future reference, let us call this organizing firm the *core firm* of that network. The core firm typically contrives the key concept for the design of each model of its products, develops and determines the basic design, and provides quality assurance for its products. In addition,

This paper was written originally from research supported by a grant from the Telecommunications Advancement Foundation in the academic years of 1989 and 1990. The interview study conducted in 1989 in the United Kingdom was financed partly by the British Council in Japan and benefited from the help provided by several faculty members of the University of Manchester Institute of Science and Technology (UMIST), especially by Dr Nigel J. Holden. This final revision was made based on the data collected in 1991 and 1992 under a grant from the Kikawada Foundation.

it frequently operates in-house final assembly plants for its most important products, as well as in-house manufacturing plants for some key components. However, a substantial portion of the parts and components assembled into the final products is generally manufactured by and procured from other firms. At times, the assembly or part of the designing of some of the final products is carried out by other firms based on contractual arrangements. Further, most of the retail outlets are run by other firms. Regarding the sales activities in foreign countries, planning and co-ordination of sales and marketing in a relatively large national market are in many cases exercised by an overseas subsidiary created by the core firm as its direct extension in this market. But here again, sales activities themselves are largely carried out by independently owned franchised dealers.

Thus, competition in the manufacture and sale of mass-marketed durable goods characteristic of today's economy inevitably becomes competition between networks of firms. This fact is partly reflected when, in the discussion of trade and industrial policies, several writers refer to the close and cohesive type of relationship that core firms in Japan frequently develop with their respective suppliers and dealers. But, unfortunately, most of the writers stop here, associating that kind of relationship with *keiretsu*, a Japanese word meaning a group of firms linked by some special relations, assuming implicitly that such a close and cohesive relationship is in every respect to be ascribed to Japan-specific factors. An underlying presumption is that, to give description of, or prescription for, inter-firm relations in other countries, the ordinary notion of 'market' would suffice.

It is worthwhile noting here the following threefold tendencies in contemporary manufacturing, recognized by Milgrom and Roberts (1990). First, manufacturing today is undergoing a fundamental transition, from mass production of a standardized product to flexible production of diversified products. Second, extensive complementarities between the product, production, and marketing strategies involved in flexible production requires that, as production becomes more flexible, greater co-ordination becomes necessary between the traditionally separate functions of design, engineering, manufacturing, and marketing. Third, to the degree to which use of flexible, general-purpose equipment increases, the necessity of vertical integration decreases. Combining these tendencies, Milgrom and Roberts predict that, in place of vertically integrated manufacturing of final products and their parts, 'extensive use of independently owned suppliers linked with the buying firm by close communications and joint planning' will increasingly appear. This prediction suggests that the network point of view will become increasingly more important in analysing production and distribution in any country, regardless of the country-origin of each individual core firm. The same prediction also suggests that, to conduct such analysis of production and distribution, it will become vitally important to develop a conceptual framework with the following features. First, unlike the term *keiretsu*, the concepts therein should be applicable universally to every network in a given product area, regardless of the country-origin of its core firm. Second, the concepts should have the power to distinguish systematically various types and facets of intra- and inter-firm relations, which the traditional concepts of the firm and the market have failed to capture.

To develop a framework with such features, it seems of utmost importance to conduct focused empirical studies first, and then to make generalizations based on the findings. Such efforts have already been made, to a considerable degree, regarding the upstream side of the network of firms. For instance, Asanuma (1984*a*, 1984*b*, 1988, 1989) has reported the findings from a series of field research projects on manufacturer–supplier relationships in the automobile and electronics industries. Based on these findings, Asanuma (1989) has presented a scheme to classify parts and suppliers, and a related concept of *relation-specific skill*, which can be interpreted as an enrichment of the concept of bilateral governance submitted by Williamson (1979, 1985). Kawasaki and McMillan (1987) have shown econometrically that core firms in Japan absorb risks to a considerable degree in their transactions with suppliers. Asanuma and Kikutani (1991) have extended this work for the automobile industry, interpreting the observed behaviour of core firms as a means to promote development of the relation-specific skill by suppliers. This interpretation implies that the attitude taken by Japanese core firms may have some applicability in other countries as well, especially in developing countries, where conscious promotion of an accumulation of organizational skill seems to be an urgent task for industrial development. Further, recent empirical studies by Clark and Fujimoto (1991) and other scholars will certainly contribute to a refinement of the conceptual framework to analyse the manufacturer–supplier interface.

In comparison, relatively more work remains to be done concerning the downstream side. To analyse the structure and workings of a network with symmetrical precision on both sides, we need to know, among other things, the following points. How does the core firm co-ordinate the sales activities with the manufacturing activities? What kind of contractual devices are used by the core firm to govern the transaction with its dealers? What dealers incentives are built into the contractual devices, and how is the risk involved in the transaction shared between the core firm and its dealers? What kinds of capabilities or skills are required on the part of dealers to enable the network to adapt efficiently to the changes in the network's environment? What kinds of capabilities or skills are required on the part of the core firm? How does the tendency towards more flexible production affect the intra- and inter-firms interactions within the network?

To promote the development of research in this direction, this paper reports findings from the field research that I made on the automobile industry during the period April 1989–July 1992. Setting aside discussions on relatively longer-term aspects of the manufacturer–dealer interface for later occasions, in this paper I spotlight intra- and inter-firm interactions involved in the ongoing, daily operation of the network. Although this may seem to be focusing on a more humdrum aspect of the network, it serves to illuminate how the transition towards more flexible production has been affecting interactions in the network, prompting different kinds of organizational skills to develop. In this regard, the paper provides a natural starting-point from which one can proceed to longer-term aspects.

Regarding the issue of flexibility, it has recently come to be widely perceived that one of the competitive edges of Japanese car manufacturers must lie in the degree of flexibility they have achieved.[1] Their practices in Japan therefore constitute an important object of observation in this paper. However, to distinguish universal elements from country-specific ones, I try to retain a comparative viewpoint throughout, using the data that I collected in the United Kingdom in 1989 and the United States in 1991 and 1992 on the operations of some Japan-based globalizing companies, a British firm, and a US-based global enterprise.

Section 2 explains how product diversity proceeds in today's automobile industry, and the new challenge this creates for manufacturers. Section 3 expounds the general pattern of the solution that major automobile manufacturers throughout the world have found to meet this challenge, focusing on methods of drawing up the monthly production plan. According to the three stages recognizable in the evolution of the methods, I submit a measure of flexibility of a production system in this section. Further, using this measure, I present a rough picture of the current status of flexibility achieved by several firms. This suggests that one or two of the Japanese core firms have indeed achieved a relatively high degree of flexibility, as widely perceived; but the achievement has been limited to their domestic operation. To determine the critical factors that have enabled flexible operation in Japan, Sections 4 and 5 analyse how co-ordination is made in the network developed by a representative Japanese core firm, comparing it with the mode of co-ordination used in a network spanned by a US core firm in its domestic market. Section 4 deals with the co-ordination between the distribution side and vehicle assembly plants regarding the formation and execution of the monthly production plan. The discussion sheds some light on the sharing of risks between the core firm and its dealers. Section 5 turns to how co-ordination is achieved between the vehicle assembly plants and the parts manufacturing plants, including those of outside suppliers. The argument identifies two kinds of organizational skill that seem to be of critical importance for core firms to achieve a flexible production system. Section 6 briefly discusses the overseas operation of Japanese firms. Section 7 concludes the paper.

2. THE CHALLENGE FACED BY AUTOMOBILE MANUFACTURERS

The Nature of Product Diversity in the Automobile Industry

Production of the Model T car by Henry Ford is always quoted as a classical example of mass production of a single standardized product. Although Ford achieved dramatic success in the 1910s with his introduction of modern mass production lines, his company's position in the industry was superseded by GM in the 1920s. Chandler (1962) has ascribed this victory by GM to the multi-divisional structure introduced by Alfred P. Sloan, which enabled conscious implementation of the product diversification strategy; with different car-lines—Chevrolet, Pontiac, Buick, Oldsmobile, and Cadillac—GM was able to tap a wider market than Ford, addressing a spectrum of different market segments simultaneously.

Let us look in this subsection at how the product diversification strategy is pursued by major car manufacturers today. Certainly these companies have followed GM's strategy in the 1920s, in that they typically offer a number of different car-lines simultaneously. However, proliferation at the car-line level does not constitute the main facet of product diversification at present.

In January 1991, GM was offering the following ten car-lines to the US passenger-car market under the Chevrolet name, or through the Chevrolet channel of dealers: Astro/GMC Safari, Beretta, Camaro, Caprice, Cavalier, Corsica, Corvetta, Lumina, Lumina APV, S-10 Blazer/GMC S-15 Jimmy. In addition, it offered eight other car-lines under the Pontiac name, eight under the Buick name, nine under the Oldsmobile name, six under the Cadillac name, and one under the Saturn name, totalling forty-two for the corporation as a whole.[2] In Japan, in April 1990 Toyota was offering twenty-two car-lines to the Japanese passenger-car market. If we include light-duty trucks, mini-buses, and so-called 'wagons' sold through the same channels, the total number comes closer to the GM's figure.[3] Forty car-lines may be considered a considerable degree of product diversification, but we will miss the point if we stop here.

Today, a far greater proportion of product diversity in the car industry is brought forth at the level of variations within each car-line. Let us look at Table 1. This table shows how many variations were offered by Toyota within the single car-line of Crown, at two different times in the past. We see there that, over the twelve years from April 1966 to April 1978, the number of variations orderable within this particular car-line underwent an explosive growth and reached the order of 100,000. Interviews that I conducted at large US automobile manufacturers revealed that the figure of 100,000 as the size of orderable variations within a single car-line does not constitute any surprise; managers of these companies testified that they frequently have even more variations. Thus, proliferation of orderable variations can be taken as a fairly universal phenomenon, at least among large automobile manufacturers.[4]

Table 1 provides a clue as to the way in which such a large number of orderable variations emerges. For each of the items, such as the body type, the engine, the transmission, and so on, the collection of which is used to determine the specification of a given unit of vehicle, the manufacturer

TABLE 1   Increase in the Number of Orderable Variations of Toyota Crown, 1966–1978

Name of item	No. of different kinds available, April 1966	No. of different kinds available, April 1978
Body type	2	4
Engine	2	4
Carburetor	2	2
Fuel to use	2	3
Transmission	3	7
Grade of luxury	4	8
Seat shape	2	5
Option	1	20
Colour	14	13
Final specification of the vehicle	322	101,088

Note
The number of orderable different final specifications of the vehicle is not equal to the number of all possible combinations of selectable items calculated by simple multiplication. This is because some combinations are not offered by the company.

Source: Jidosha Kogaku Zensho Henshu Iinkai (1980): 186.

comes to offer a multiple number of choices. Although this number itself is typically not very large, the number of possible combinations of choices can become enormous, since the number of the items is substantial.

The number of variations that are actually produced in a given period of, say, one month or three months is typically much less than the total number of orderable variations. Nevertheless, it can become sizeable, causing the average number of units of vehicles produced and sold per variation to be quite small. Table 2, which shows, for each of four car-lines selected from those offered by Toyota, the numbers of variations and units of the vehicles actually produced in a certain three-month period in the past, gives a good illustration of this point.

Further, going beyond the averaged figures, Fukuoka and Iwatsuki (1989) has conveyed the following facts. In one of the months in 1985, Toyota sold 153,569 units of vehicles in the domestic market, which units consisted

TABLE 2   The Numbers of Different Final Specifications and of Units of Vehicles, by Car-Line, Produced by Toyota in a Three-Month Period

Code name of car-line	No. of different final specifications of the vehicles produced	No. of units of vehicles produced	No. of units per final specification of the vehicle
A	3,700	63,000	17
B	16,400	204,000	12
C	4,500	53,000	12
D	7,700	44,000	6
Total of the sample	32,100	364,000	11

Source: Ohno and Monden (1983: 15).

of 19,349 different specifications of vehicles. Of these specifications, 9,544 or 49.3 per cent, registered only 1 unit of vehicle sold per specification. The 9,544 units sold thus occupied only 6.2 per cent of the total units sold. Further, 19.9 (14.9, 7.5, 1.9) per cent of the 19,349 specifications registered, respectively, 2–3 (4–10, 11–30, 31–50) units of vehicles sold per specification. Finally, the remaining 1,289 specifications, or 6.6 per cent of the total variations, registered more than 50 units sold per specification. The 76,745 units that belonged to this category occupied 50.0 per cent of the total units sold in that month.

For good or ill, this is the way in which large automobile manufacturers in today's world have been pursuing product diversification, in order to tap the demand of consumers with very individualized needs and tastes.

A Dilemma Posed by Product Diversity

With such proliferation of product variations, it becomes increasingly more difficult and more complex for car manufacturers to achieve adjustment between their production and the market demand for their products. More specifically, car manufacturers come to face the following kind of dilemma.

In the case of the Model T production, any unit in the product inventory could be sold to any consumer, as far as he or she wanted to purchase a Model T car. Thus, the company was able to base its production plan solely on the anticipated aggregate demand for the Model T cars. In other words, the problem of matching supply to demand could be reduced to one single dimension of the total quantity. The same can be said of multiple car-line production, if the number of variations per car-line is small. But, once such enormous number of variations as described in the beginning of this Section is introduced, matching supply to demand comes to require, in addition to matching at the total quantity level, precise matching to be made in kind. For instance, the data we saw in the previous subsection shows that, for nearly half of the entire set of different specifications of the products supplied by the company in a month, there appeared just one consumer in that month who wanted the vehicle with that particular specification. This suggests that it becomes quite risky for the company to build such cars without receiving orders from those who actually want to buy that particular version of the vehicle.

On the other hand, as was true in the Model T era, production still requires considerable lead time. Therefore, at least some part of the manufacturing activities necessary to produce a vehicle has to be started prior to the receipt of an order from the consumer who will finally purchase and use that particular vehicle. Otherwise, the consumer would have to wait too long, which, except for the cars of an especially luxurious kind, consumers today are not willing to do.

How do the manufacturers solve this dilemma? There seems to be a fairly general pattern of solution that major automobile manufacturers in the world have come to find in their respective searches for the solution. I outline this pattern in the next section.

3. HOW MANUFACTURERS HAVE BEEN COPING WITH THIS CHALLENGE

Three Methods for Monthly Production Planning

Method 1 Let us first look back at Table 1 and think about how the full specification of a vehicle can be expressed in a general abstract way. The general form can be given as follows: $X = (X_0, X_1, \ldots, X_m, \ldots X_s)$. Here X_0 denotes a set $\{x_{01}, x_{02}, \ldots, x_{0k}\}$ of different car-lines that this firm offers to the public; X_1 denotes a set $\{x_{11}, x_{12}, \ldots, x_{1d}\}$ of body-types from which choice can be made when this firm is going to build a vehicle; X_2 denotes a set of available engines to be mounted to a vehicle produced by this firm; X_3 a set of available transmissions; and so on. If one completes all of the possible choices and fully specifies the components of the vector X, for instance as $(x_{05}, x_{13}, \ldots x_{m6}, \ldots, x_{s9})$, the full specification of a concrete unit of vehicle is determined. Let us therefore call X the *specification vector*.

Suppose now that a given automobile manufacturer is to make the monthly production plan for the month M. The most primitive way to do this is to fix, by some target date, based on a signal received by the company from downstream prior to this date and on the company's own judgement, all of the units to be produced during the month M, with all of the components of the specification vector determined firmly for each unit in this list. Upon completion of this list of fully specified monthly requirements, the company proceeds to draw up a production schedule. Scheduling can proceed gradually, begining with the allotment of units in the monthly requirements list to each of the four to five weeks or three ten-day periods of the month, ending with completion of the assembly-sequence plan for each working day. This method is the most rigid (or least flexible) way of making the montly production plan, as will become clear in the course of the following discussion.

If all of the items from X_0 to X_s require the same length of lead time prior to the assembly of a specific unit of vehicle, then there would be no other choice than to use method 1 to make the monthly production plan. In reality, however, some of the items require a longer lead time, while others can be prepared relatively more quickly. Taking this difference into consideration, the monthly production plan can be made up stepwise as time proceeds. This is the way to introduce elements of flexibility into the process of making and executing the monthly production plan.

The item that has to be fixed first is X_0. More exactly, any given automobile manufacturer should first determine, by each car-line, how many units are going to be built during the month in question (M). This is because the management of each of the vehicle assembly plants uses the planned monthly volume of each car-line assigned to its plant as the signal according to which monthly determination of the speed of their assembly-lines and montly adjustment of the size and deployment of their work-force are to be made before the beginning of month M. After the number of the units to be built during month M has been determined by each car-line, the planned units are allotted to each of the working days of the month. This provides the basic frame of the monthly production plan, and for each of the units in this frame plan the specification items from X_1 to X_s can be filled later, since they need less time for preparation than X_0.

Method 2 A second method of drawing up the monthly production plan consists of two stages. At the first stage, by some target date the number of the units to be built during month M is determined by each car-line, and then the allotment of these units to each of the working days is made. The second stage is exercised repeatedly, either for each of the weeks of the month or for each of the ten-day periods of the month, depending on the practice of individual companies. (Note here that in Japan it is more customary in business practice to divide one month into three ten-day periods, while in the United States and Europe it has been more common in business scheduling to rely on the concept of a week.) Suppose for the moment that the manufacturer in question has chosen to use the ten-day system. Then the second stage proceeds as follows. Upon completion of the first stage, the company allocates the planned units of vehicles to dealers, and asks them to send orders for the allocated vehicles with some time sequence, each order of which should specify, for each unit of vehicle, the items X_1 to X_s based on the dealer's expectation and plan of sales. Based on the orders sent from the dealers by some date, the manufacturer makes the production schedule for the first ten-day period of the month. The same process is repeated for the second and third ten-day periods. The logic is unchanged under the system where a week is used instead of a ten-day period.

Let us compare the two methods at this point with the aid of Fig. 1. Under method 1, all of the units to be built during month M have to be

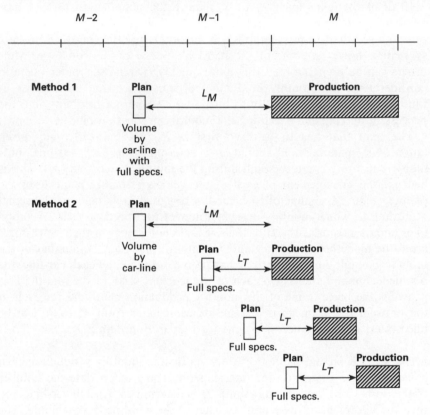

FIG. 1   Two Methods of Monthly Production Planning

determined in every detail by some target date. Denote the lead time between this date and the first day of month M by L_M. Assume for the moment that L_M is 1 month, as shown in Fig. 1. This means that the monthly plan determined at the end of month (M-2) has to be based entirely on a forecast demand which is to be finalized somewhat earlier than this date. It is easy to see generally that, the longer L_M is, the greater the probability of error will be, and vice versa.

On the other hand, under method 2, even if the length of L_M is kept the same as in method 1, the plan that includes specifications of the vehicles to be built can now be made three times a month for each ten-day period of production, each time with the lead time L_T measured backwards from the first day of the ten-day period. The merit is not solely that L_T is generally smaller than L_M. In addition, the production during the second and third ten-day periods of month M can now be based on demand forecasts made much later than under method 1. For instance, in the situation depicted in Fig. 1, the plan relating to the final specifications of vehicles to be built in the last ten-day period of month M can now be made at the beginnig of month M, more than one month later than with method 1. This means that the plan can be based on the demand forecasts and judgements formed more than one month later than for method 1. Consequently, in comparison with method 1, method 2 can substantially reduce the risk of the car manufacturer and its dealers misjudging which specifications of vehicles are easier to sell than others.

Method 3 Upon completion of the vehicles-to-be-built list and the production schedule for a given ten-day period, the manufacturer lets each dealer know, of the vehicles that he has ordered, which one has been scheduled to be built on which day of that production period. Method 2 ends its planning cycle with this feed-back of information to the dealers. However, further flexibility can be introduced by adding some steps to method 2, as follows.

As previously noted, under method 2, the items X_1 to X_s for individual vehicles to be built are all specified at the stage in which the manufacturer makes the ten-day (or weekly) production plan. However, there are differences between these items as to the necessary lead times for production. Typically, items like the body type, the engine type, the transmission type, and the grade of luxury have to be fixed at this time or earlier; let us call that part of specification of a vehicle determined by these items the *basic specification*. However, other items, such as options and colour, need not be finalized at this time; let us call the part of specification that complements the basic specification the *secondary specification*. This third way of making the monthly production plan admits later changes to orders concerning the items that belong to the secondary specification. Under this method, dealers are allowed, after the receipt of the feed-back information mentioned above, to send in orders daily regarding the changes that they may come to want regarding the secondary specification of the vehicles they have on order. Each of these daily change-orders has to be made with a lead time L_D before the scheduled production date of the vehicle concerned. Fig. 2 illustrates how method 3 works.

In practice, the original orders from dealers are based almost entirely on the expectations and forecasts of these dealers; it is very rare that a dealer's order has, from the begining, an order actually placed by a final consumer

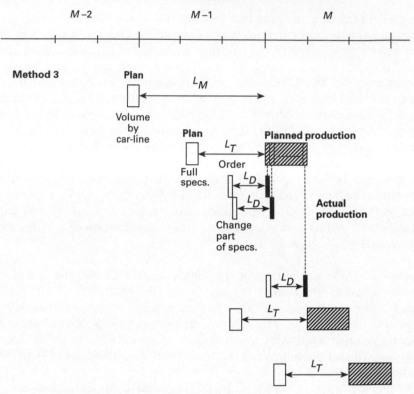

FIG. 2   Method 3 of Monthly Production Planning

as its origin. On the other hand, the daily orders issued by a dealer concerning changes to items on the secondary specification are in most cases traceable to a final consumer, who either has visited the dealer's store or has been visited by one of the dealer's salespersons, but has not been able to find in the dealer's inventory, or in the list of vehicles scheduled to be delivered to the dealer's store, a car that has precisely the specification that he or she wants. For these reasons method 3 serves to reduce the dealer's risk significantly.

Comparison of Production Systems in Terms of Flexibility

As should already be clear, a production system consisting of an automobile manufacturer and its dealers can be said to have achived an evolution to a higher stage with more flexibility when the system is operating under method 2 instead of method 1. When the same system comes to operate under method 3, it can be said to have achieved a further evolution. Noting this, let us say that a production system is in *stage 1 (2, 3)* of evolution when it operates under method 1 (2, 3) of making the monthly production plan.

We should also note that, within stage 1, a production system can be said to have achieved a higher degree of flexibility if the system comes to operate constantly with smaller L_M than previously. Likewise, within stage 2, a system can be said to be more flexible than another if the former has achieved smaller (L_M, L_T) or (L_M, L_W) in the sense of vector ordering than the later. Similarly, within stage 3, two systems or two different states of a system can be ranked in terms of flexibility by comparing (L_M, L_T, L_D) or (L_M, L_W, L_D).

Combining these observations, I measure the degree of flexibility of a production system by a three-dimensional vector (L_M, L_T, L_D) or (L_M, L_W, L_D). When the system is in the stage 1, we can denote L_T (or $L_W) = L_D = \infty$. Similarly, when the system is in stage 2, it can be expressed by denoting $L_D = \infty$. Let us concentrate on these measures for the moment in our discussion of flexibility.

Historical Developments Observable in Japan

The evolution from stage 1 to stage 3 via stage 2 can clearly be traceable in the history of the Japanese car industry. According to Jidosha Kogaku Zensho Henshu Iinkai (1980), Toyota introduced method 2 in 1966 as a reform linked with the commencement of the 'wide-selection' strategy in the car-line Crown. Note that, as Table 1 shows, the number of orderable variations was still quite modest at this time. By 1974, however, an explosive proliferation of variations in several car-lines had prompted the company to invent a new method that would enable greater production flexibility combined with quicker delivery of completed vehicles to customers. Thus, in 1974 the company introduced method 3.

Although published material reveals little on this point, from interviews we can infer that Toyota must have been the first firm to introduce both method 2 and method 3. Nissan introduced its version of method 2 in 1971 and of method 3 in 1983. Other automobile manufacturers seem to have followed with longer lags.[5]

Ever since they introduced method 3, both Toyota and Nissan have continually strive to improve further the operation of their respective networks; this has resulted in a gradual decrease in the values of the components of their (L_M, L_T, L_D). Thus, in 1989, one of the two companies achieved a lead time of $L_D = 3$ days. This means that, if a vehicle has been scheduled to roll off the final assembly line on the day D (in other words, the building of this vehicle has been scheduled to begin on the day $D - 1$), the order to change its secondary specification is acceptable from the dealer as late as the end of the $D - 4$. For the other company, $L_D = 4$.

It should be noted here that, with such a short notice, the companies may not be able to accommodate all of the changes in the specification of the vehicle that the dealer may want. First, as already remarked, the companies normally admit changes only in the secondary specification. Second, for a great majority of options, changes are normally admissible for each item *up to* 10 per cent of the scheduled volume. Third, depending on the situation surrounding the supply of each kind of part, the ceiling might be set lower than 10 per cent. Fourth, these admissible ceilings may vary depending on the environmental changes and life-cycle of the models. When the supply of some item is especially tight, the ceiling must be set quite low; when the end of production of a given model is drawing near, the daily change-order system has to be suspended for that model. All of these constraints are set in the computerized system of order files held by the manufacturers; as a dealer accesses this file and tries to put in a change-order, he can see whether this order has been accepted, or rejected because of such constraints.

With all of these constraints, however, admissibility of changes with such a short notice gives the production system a remarkable degree of flexibility, and at the same time reduces the risk assumed by the dealers to a considerable degree. In 1989, according to the managers of these two companies whom I met on separate interviews, 35 per cent of the car sold in the domestic market by these firms were being produced on daily change-orders.[6] This in turn means that, on average, 35 per cent of the orders from each dealer come to have, by the deadline for daily change-orders, the backing of orders from specific consumers. Each of the consumers who have placed such an order at a dealer's store can receive the car with the exact specification requested, without much waiting,[7] while the dealer can concentrate his efforts on selling the remaining 65 per cent, which have been ordered from the core firm at the dealer's own risk.

The observations made in this subsection may evoke the following question: What kind of situation is projected to emerge as the development along this line proceeds? Is it very likely in the near future that 100 per cent of the vehicles produced by a manufacturer will come to be built to fill orders entered by consumers at some electronic terminal, eliminating thereby the risk borne by dealers? Before tackling this question, let us see how car manufacturers in other countries have been responding to the same challenge met by these Japanese core firms.

A Tentative International Comparison of Production Systems

In October 1989, in order to conduct interviews with managers engaged in sales planning, order processing, and production control, I visited in the United Kingdom a production subsidiary of a Japanese company, a UK-based firm, and the headquarters of a European corporation of a US-based global enterprise, all three of which were automobile manufacturers. In January 1991 and July 1992, with a view to developing these studies, I visited in the United States the headquarters of North American sales subsidiaries of four Japanese automobile manufacturers, North American production subsidiaries of these manufacturers, and a US automobile manufacturer the European subsidiary of which I visited in 1989. In this subsection I briefly compare the degree of flexibility of the production systems developed by these companies, based on material collected in the course of these interviews.

The order-bank system   First, I should note a difference in business practice between Anglo-American and Japanese car manufacturers, to provide a proper framework for comparison. The difference is in the way in which Japanese manufacturers collect orders from their dealers compared with the method used by US and UK manufacturers for the same purpose. As I already mentioned, taking orders from dealers for each individual unit of vehicle to be delivered begins after the monthly allocation of the planned units to dealers has been made. This applies to all of the car companies that I visited, regardless the country-origin of the firm. However, US and UK manufacturers commonly use a system called the *order-bank system*, a notion that is not used in Japan.

Each of the Anglo-American manufacturers has a two-stage order-bank, or information-file, to receive and store orders from its dealers for some time before the production of the vehicles commences. The first-stage order-bank is provided typically in the sales planning department. To this bank, each of the dealers throws in, through the district office of the sales organization of the manufacturer, the orders for individual units bit by bit (in many cases daily) as time proceeds. This order-bank is a pool of orders yet to be scheduled for production by the car company. Considering both the relative priority given to individual dealers and the current situations of production capacities, the sales planning department at some intervals gives rank priority to the orders in this order-bank, and transmits the scheduled orders to the second-stage order-bank, which each of the vehicle assembly plants has. Then, pursuing 'levelled' production (the meaning of which will be clarified in Section 5) and, at the same time, checking availability of parts, the manager of the assembly plant makes actual production schedules for these orders, readjusting where necessary the original priority given by the sales planning department.

In Japan, on the other hand, each dealer is required to send in orders in a more controlled manner, as follows. Suppose that the system is already in stage 2 or stage 3 of evolution, in the sense defined earlier, and that the ten-day system is used instead of the weekly system. Then, as described in the beginning of this Section, the ten-day production plan has to be made three times a month. Japanese manufacturers ask their dealers to send in their orders according to the ten-day cycle of production. Thus, each dealer sends orders three times a month in a package called the *ten-day order* (a package of orders for individual units that the dealer in question wants the car company to build during a given ten-day period—say, the period that begins twelve days after the deadline for that ten-day order).

Recall that such strict deadlines do not exist for the dealers of Anglo-American car manufacturers. Moreover, these dealers need not achieve exact matching between the number of units by car-line that each of them had been allocated for a given month and the number of the vehicles for which the dealer can throw in orders after the allocation. Even after the latter number has passed the allocated level, each dealer can continue to throw orders into the manufacturer's order-bank, because, depending on contingencies, it may turn out that the factory is capable, during the production month for which the allocation applies, of building additional cars that correspond to the extra orders taken in. At least, it can be hoped that the car company will give high priority to such backlog of orders in the production schedule for the following month. Thus, in the Anglo-American system, the size of order-bank (the quantity of orders in the order-bank) typically swells up during the period when the demand is larger than the supply, and shrinks when the demand slackens. In the Japanese system, on the other hand, although the information on emerging excess demand or excess supply is compiled and exerts influence on production decisions in the car manufacturer's organization, more strict quantitative matching is made each time a ten-day order is submitted, between the number of the units in this order package and the number of the units allocated to this dealer for the given period.

Thus, in the Japanese system dealers seem to be doing somewhat more information-processing work with a tighter time constraint than in the systems developed by US or UK car manufacturers. The other side of the coin is that Japanese dealers can expect to receive the cars they have ordered with more uniform time lags, more on 'First ordered, first built' basis.

The situation in the United Kingdom With due care to this difference regarding the order-bank system, let us apply the framework introduced in this Section for a comparison of the production systems developed by different companies of different country-origins. I first describe the situation in the United Kingdom in 1989, using the present tense.

Each month $M-3$, the production subsidiary of a Japanese car company in the sample receives, both from the company's sole sales agent in the United Kingdom and from the manufacturer's main office for sales activities on the Continent, a list of vehicles, with full specifications from the beginning, that the subsidiary is required to build and ship to them during month M. Thus, this subsidiary is operating according to method 1, with L_M = about 3 months.

The British firm, on the other hand, operates on a method in which elements of method 1 and method 2 are combined in the following way.

Unlike the US-based enterprise taken up later, this firm begins the sale of vehicles to be manufactured by asking its dealers to send in orders with full specifications right from start. In other words, this firm does not operate the process of so-called 'wholesaling', which means allocating the units to be manufactured to individual dealers without asking them to give a specification of each unit apart from car-line. Normally, an order from a given dealer stays in the company's order-bank for 11 weeks; picking up suitable orders from this bank, the company makes a weekly production schedule, advising dealers of the status of their orders from time to time. And, up to 3.5 weeks before the beginning of the week during which the vehicle corresponding to a given order has been scheduled to be assembled, any dealer can change the priority of the orders it has already thrown into the order-bank. Thus, this company's system is to some extent more flexible than that of the Japanese subsidiary.

The US-based enterprise is using method 2, which was introduced in 1973 for all of the car-lines offered by the company. Currently, the wholesaling of the units planned to be built during month M is done during month $M–3$ based on the monthly production plan made immediately before the beginning of this process. Then, at a later stage, dealers send in orders for these units specifying all of the specification items. They do not have to send in orders at an even rate; half of the total orders are sent in in three batches a month, and the remaining half can be thrown into the company's order-bank through daily transmission. But in any event, dealers are required to submit orders no less than 20 days before the planned production date of the corresponding vehicle. It takes about 5 working days (one week) for offices in the sales organization of the company to process the submitted orders and transmit them to a suitable one of the company's vehicle assembly plants. To keep production undisturbed and stable, it is regarded in this company as a norm to have each vehicle assembly plant always maintain orders for cars corresponding to 15 working days' (three weeks') production. In other words, the normal size of the order-bank is 5 days for order-processing and 15 days in the plant order-bank, making 20 working days (four weeks) in total.

This company cannot currently give its dealers opportunities to amend the orders already thrown into the order-bank. The managers of the company regard it as one of their most urgent tasks to find ways to reform the current system into one that not only allows dealers to change the orders already thrown into the order-bank, but also enables such changes even after the orders have been scheduled for assembly at the vehicle assembly plants.

The situation of Japanese-based firms in the United States I shall next describe the situation in the United States in 1991 and 1992, again in the present tense. All of the sales subsidiaries of Japanese automobile manufacturers visited submit each month to the corporate headquarters, for the monthly production meeting of the corporation, a list of vehicles, with full specifications, that they want to sell through their dealers in North America. At the meeting, it is decided that some of the vehicles in the list will be built in Japan, and others in the company's North American transplants. For those cars that are to be produced in Japan during month M, the monthly production plan is made some time during month $M-1$. Of these cars, some are for the domestic market; for such cars, as seen from historical development in Japan, method 3 is used, hence only the number of units by car-line has to be determined at this time. For the cars to be built in Japan for overseas markets, specifications have to be determined at this time. In other words, the system, consisting of the vehicle assembly plants in Japan and the sales subsidiary in the United States, is operated along the lines of method 1. Thus, this part of the corporation's global network is significantly less flexible than the domestic part. Further, the vehicles that are determined at the monthly production meeting of the corporation in month M to be built at the North American transplants can be built only in month $M + 1$. In this regard, the system consisting of the sales and production subsidiaries in North America is even less flexible than the system for producing cars to export.

The situation of a US-based firm in the United States The US-based corporation that I visited uses a method in which elements of method 2 and method 3 are mixed in their operation in North America. I shall describe the operation of this company in some detail in order to explain how the system constitutes such a variant.

Each of the dealers of this car firm can daily make changes to the orders already thrown into the manufacturer's order-bank, using the electronic terminal of a computerized telecommunication network; this message has to be checked and processed by the district office of the sales organization to the sales planning department of the company. Dealers can make such changes both before and after the sequencing of orders by the sales planning department. Further, dealers are even allowed to make changes daily, via the district office and the sales planning department, to the orders already transferred to the plant order-bank. Thus, from the point of the individual dealers, there is little differnce between this system and method 3 as described in the beginning of this Section. The difference resides in the fact that, in this company's system, daily change-orders from dealers are acceptable only in so far as the order in question remains unscheduled for assembly, whereas the description given in the beginning of this Section is based on the practice of some Japanese firms which allow daily change-orders up to some deadline *after* the establishment of the ten-day (or weekly) production plan that determines the date of assembly of each vehicle corresponding to each order in the plan. In the practice of this US-based firm, once the order has been given to schedule for assembly, it is normally regarded as firm, and dealers are no longer allowed to make changes to it. In business parlance, such orders are in the 'lock', or 'frozen'.[8] As is the case for the European subsidiary of this company, in order to maintain undisturbed and stable production, it is regarded as a norm to maintain in the plant order-bank orders corresponding to three weeks' (or fifteen working days') production. And, of these orders, those that correspond to two weeks' (or ten working days') production have to be firm in the sense just mentioned. In other words, once made, every ten-day production schedule has to be frozen. Thus, from the viewpoint of production, this company's system is not different from method 2 with L_W = 11 depending on which day of the week is assigned to a given order as its production date although, from the viewpoint of dealers, the system appears the same as method 3, with L_D = 11 to 15.

To get a fuller picture of this company's system, we need to check one more aspect. Of the total number of vehicles sold by this US-based firm in the domestic market, how large a proportion is occupied by the cars built at the domestic plants based on the daily change-orders sent from the dealers? According to an interview given in 1992 at the sales planning department of this company, 92–93 per cent of all cars are being sold from the inventory at the dealers' stores. This means that, at least at that time, the company was relying much less on the daily change-order system than the two Japanese car companies, which, as mentioned before build 35 per cent of the cars sold in their domestic market responding to daily change-orders. Regarding this point, however, the following two factors should be taken into account. First, because of the scarcity and high price of land, Japanese dealers have to operate with a smaller inventory of cars at their stores than American dealers can afford to. While the stock of new cars at the premises of a given dealer is, on average, twenty days in Japan, it reaches fifty-five to sixty days in the United States.[9] Second, in comparison with American dealers, Japanese dealers have, on average, a larger firm size, and, correspondingly, have been assigned by their franchiser a wider area, in most cases one entire prefecture, as the dealer's main area of responsibility.[10] This means that American consumers can more easily than Japanese consumers find within their reach alternative sources of supply that deal with the same brand of vehicles. These two factors, reinforcing each other, make the probability higher that a typical American consumer can find some car that suits his or her taste by shopping around. To the extent that this applies, the need to use the daily change-order system must necessarily be smaller in the United States than in Japan.

Summary of the comparison Since the range of the firms covered in my study is limited, care should obviously be taken in making generalizations from the observed facts reported above. The following picture nevertheless emerges. In achieving flexibility of the production system, one or two of the Japanese car manufacturers in my sample may be constituting the top group in the race, regarding their domestic operations. But their overseas operations are less flexible than not only their domestic operations but also the operations in the overseas markets of the firms that have their base either in the United States or in the United Kingdom, and have been incumbents in these markets longer than the Japanese overseas subsidiaries. In addition, the US-based firm in the sample exerts a reasonable amount of flexibility in its home land, though the degree is somewhat lower, from the viewpoint of production, than that shown by the two Japanese firms in their domestic market.

This picture evokes the following three questions. First, what are the factors that have enabled one or two Japanese automobile manufacturers to show a considerably high degree of flexibility in their domestic operations? Second, what are the factors that would cause difficulty if the US-based car company wished to achieve a higher degree of flexibility than already achieved? Third, what are the factors that have made operations of the Japanese firms in the North American and European markets inflexible to the extent seen above? And what about the future of their operations in these markets? I pursue these questions in the remainder of this chapter. In Sections 4 and 5, to tackle the first two questions, I first analyse how co-ordination is made in the network of firms developed by a representative Japanese car manufacturer, and then compare it with the way in which similar co-ordination is achieved in the network developed by the US-based enterprise I observed. Section 4 deals with the co-ordination between distribution and production of vehicles. Section 5 discusses the co-ordination between vehicle assembly and parts supply. The third of the questions raised above is answered in Section 6. Meanwhile, the question raised on page 130 is answered in Section 4.

4. CO-ORDINATION BETWEEN DISTRIBUTION AND PRODUCTION OF VEHICLES

In the beginning of Section 3, I introduced the concepts of three different methods for making monthly production plan, using Figs. 1 and 2 for explanation. The discussion there started on the assumption that either the full monthly production plan (in the case of method 1) or the plan for the number of the units to be built for each of the car-lines (in the cases of methods 2 and 3) has been determined *by some mechanism* with the lead time L_M, at some point prior to the production month M. For brevity, let us call the plan determined at this time point as '*plan 1*' hereafter.

In this section I examine two mechanisms that I treated as a black box in the last section. One is the mechanism referred to in the last paragraph, through which plan 1 is formed and determined, starting from informational inputs by individual dealers. This mechanism is the subject of the first subsection of this Section. The other is the mechanism through which the planned units of vehicles in plan 1 are allocated to individual dealers. This will be discussed in subsection 3. Subsection 2 gives an intermediate link, discussing the role of dealers expected by the core firm. These three subsections outline the procedure followed by one of the two representative Japanese car manufacturers, which I refer to as J_A hereafter. Then in subsection 4 I compare this procedure with its counterpart developed by the US-based firm, henceforth referred to as A_Y.

The Process through which Plan 1 Is Drawn Up

Plan 1 is a plan for the entire corporation, in which matching is achieved between the monthly demand from all over the world for the vehicles with J_A's brands and the production capacities in Japan and other countries available for producing these kinds of vehicles. The plan is determined as an outcome of a complex process of information-processing and bargaining.

Let us start from the domestic market side. The organizational unit inside J_A responsible for planning and co-ordination of domestic sales and marketing activities is the Domestic Sales Planning Division (DSP, hereafter). Five vehicle distribution divisions, each of which handles one channel, are engaged in distribution and keep direct contact with dealers through their district staff (or field staff).[11] Each of the dealers monthly submits a document called the 'monthly order of vehicles' to J_A, in which the number of units that he wants to lay in to sell during the coming month is listed for all of the car-lines for which he has a franchised dealership. But these numbers are not automatically transmitted to the production side. The DSP and vehicle distribution divisions have the company's own forecast of sales by car-line for the national and regional markets, an assessment of each dealer's attitude and capabilities, and a forecast of the availability of production capacities within the network for the time period concerned. On the basis of these sets of information, and the opinion of the district staff, J_A modifies the numbers ordered by each dealer. In this sense, 'monthly order' may not be a proper word; in reality, it is a request, a necessary informational input to initiate the process, but one that is not expected to be met exactly. On the basis of the modified figures, DSP compiles the list of vehicles to be produced for sale in the domestic market, which this organizational unit tries to secure on behalf of the dealers it represents in the corporation.

The organizational unit inside J_A responsible for the planning and co-ordination of overseas sales and marketing activities is the Overseas Sales Planning Division (OSP, hereafter). In each of the national or regional markets where vehicles with J_A brands are sold, a subsidiary, a branch office, or an agent of J_A, takes on a role analogous to that of DSP in the domestic market. It submits to OSP the list of vehicles ordered compiled in the same way as DSP does in Japan. On the basis of this list, OSP draws up its list of vehicles to be requested from the production side of the corporation for sale in the overseas market.

Plan 1 is determined at a monthly meeting held at the corporate headquarters, the *Vehicle Production Meeting*. One interesting thing to note is that there is no single executive in the corporation who represents total sales and marketing activities of J_A and can co-ordinate DSP and OSP from a higher hierarchical position before the request list for vehicles is presented. DSP and OSP present their respective lists. This means that they are in a position to compete with each other at the corporate level, especially when demand tends to exceed the production capacities, in their endeavour to secure the number of vehicles they want. It is the responsibility of the Corporate Production Control Division (CPC, hereafter) to draft the original plan 1 submitted to the Vehicle Production Meeting. Not only do the demands from DSP and OSP have to be co-ordinated with production capacities, but co-ordination between different car-lines also has to be made, since often the same type of engine is used for different car-lines, which therefore compete for the capacity of the same engine plant. CPC strives, in drafting the plan, to solve these conflicts, playing the role of co-ordinator on the same horizontal level as the divisions and plants to be co-ordinated. Even so, the Vehicle Production Meeting is bound to become a long and heated meeting before an equilibrium solution is reached for the entire corporation. In any event, the corporation has to determine plan 1 by the end of the scheduled target date.

The Role of Dealers Expected by the Core Firm

It should now be clear why the initial informational inputs from dealers cannot be accepted automatically as 'orders'. To reach an equilibrium an adjustment has to be made monthly between the total demand that the distribution side of the network transmits to the planning centre and the total production capacity available. For this purpose, some rationing mechanism has to be used. When demand tends to exceed the production capacity, the orders submitted by dealers have to be curtailed. On the other hand, when the demand becomes less than capacity, organizational units such as DSP and OSP have to strive to encourage their dealers to take more units than they would otherwise have ordered. Since production capacities cannot be very quickly increased or decreased, the distribution side is expected to absorb the burden for this adjustment to a non-negligible degree. This level of generalization applies to all of the core firms I visited, including the American corporation and European subsidiary of the US-based global firm.

The same logic is applicable to the issue of the permissible upper bound of the percentage ratio that the vehicles built on firm orders from consumers can occupy out of the total number of vehicles produced during a given period. The Japanese car manufacturers I visited were not expecting the emergence of a system in which that percentage ratio reached 100. According to them, the current figure of 35 per cent attained by the two core firms seemed a reasonable ceiling; the proper way of selling cars is for dealers to lay in a substantial portion based on their expectation and active plans for sales, not just to play the role of passive electronic terminal for incoming consumers. Underlying this view seems to be a fear that if dealers restrict themselves to playing such a role, the fluctuation of production would become so sharp that the production side could not continue to function.

In sum, core firms commonly insist that their dealers bear some of the burden of smoothing out demand, in order to make the adjustment of the network's production capacities to the demand side easier.

How the Planned Units Are Allocated to Dealers

Nevertheless, the total volume of the vehicles contained in plan 1 has to fluctuate as a reflection of the general condition of the market. How are the planned units in this list broken down to be distributed to various regional markets, and finally allocated to individual dealers who constitute the retail end of the network?[12] The vehicles are allocated to dealers according to the 'weight' given by the core firm to each dealer. The exact method or formula used to calculate this weight can differ between core firms, but the most critical factor is common to all, regardless of the country-origin of the core firm: it is the share of that dealer's sales in the total sales of the core firm. Thus, roughly speaking, if a dealer's share has been 1 per cent over a certain number of consecutive months up to the most recent month, that dealer is allocated 1 per cent of whatever volume the core firm plans to produce in the coming month.[13] The dealer cannot acquire a much larger number by suddenly sending in a larger-than-normal order.[14] In this way, each dealer's continual performance, and the assessment of this performance by the core firm, plays a central role in the manufacturer–dealer relationship; the relationship is something different from the relations that emerge across the spot market.[15]

The Manufacturer–Dealer Interface in the Network Developed by the US Firm

I noted in Section 3 that in the Japanese system dealers seem to be doing somewhat more information-processing within a tighter time schedule, in that they are required to send in orders in a batch every ten days, conforming to the number of units allocated to each dealer at the monthly allocation stage; and that, in contrast, under the Anglo-American order-bank system, dealers are allowed to send in their orders with fewer constraints on timing and quantity-matching.

Examination of the allocation process adopted by A_Y in its domestic market reveals further information in the same direction. This company's allocation is not done at a stroke during the time period assigned for the monthly allocation; while the initial major contact is made during this period, the follow-up effective allocation is done weekly. To the extent that dealers are not required to make their quantitative commitment by each car-line at the time of the monthly allocation, they can enjoy flexibility regarding the number of units per car-line at the expense of reallocation effort exercised by the district offices of the car company.

Further, also at the final specification level, the district offices seem to give a non-negligible level of flexibility to dealers, without disturbing the production side, through their efforts to reshuffle the vehicles scheduled to arrive from the plants to the dealers in their district.

5.   CO-ORDINATION BETWEEN VEHICLE PRODUCTION AND PARTS SUPPLY

In this section, I turn to the upstream side of the network. In subsection 1 I examine how the core firm J_A has its in-house parts manufacturing plants and outside suppliers start manufacturing the necessary parts upon completion of plan 1, and how it secures timely delivery. In subsection 2 I compare this company's practice with the practice taken by A_Y. Then, in subsections 3 and 4, I search for the factors that may explain the difference in the degree of flexibility notable in the production side of the networks developed by the two companies.

How the Core Firm Secures Co-ordinated Supply of Proper Parts

For any automobile manufacturer, it is necessary to send out monthly orders to parts suppliers and in-house parts plants with sufficient lead time to enable them to prepare for production and shipment. But, unless the core firm is operating the production system according to method 1, the specification of each vehicle in plan 1 has yet to be determined, except for the name of the car-line, when plan 1 is finalized. How do the core firms determine the content of their orders to the upstream units?

Both A_Y and J_A base the content of their monthly order on forecasting. On the basis of the trend data available from the sales record of the company, say, over the most recent three months, the probability distribution of different final specifications for each car-line can be estimated. Once the target number of units to be sold during a coming month has been decided for each car-line, the number of vehicles to be produced to each different final specification can be forecasted applying this distribution, and the necessary volume to be procured for each different optional part can be calculated on the basis of this forecast. The monthly order that is issued is based on this calculation. Therefore, there is always a possibility that a discrepancy will arise between the volume of each part requested at this stage and the volume the core firm really finds that it needs as it receives orders with the detailed specifications of vehicles from the downstream side at later stages. A major problem faced by all core firms is how to cope with this discrepancy.

Let us look at the practice taken by J_A in its domestic operation. Upon completion of the forecast that ensues at the finalizing of plan 1, the CPC of the company draws up a schedule of production of vehicles with the projected detailed specifications. On this basis, the company issues the monthly order to each upstream unit in timetable form. At the same time, the CPC sets a guideline for each of the three ten-day production plans to accommodate possible changes of actual demand from the demand forecast. Usually, body types are fixed according to the forecast; for other items in basic specification, such as transmissions and grades of luxury, changes are allowed up to 10 per cent increase or decrease.

Comparing this guideline with the ten-day orders sent from the dealers, DSP makes the request of vehicles for the given ten-day period and sends it to CPC. On the basis of this request, and adding in that portion of vehicles in plan 1 that are going to be built during this ten-day period for the overeas markets, CPC writes up the ten-day production plan and informs each dealer of the date for assembling the individual vehicles concerned via DSP.

For most of the organizational units in the upstream side, the ten-day production plan has no repercussions. They start making the necessary preparations upon receipt of the monthly order, and actual production and delivery is triggered by the receipt of *kanban* or other means of signal transmission, which, in the case of optional parts, is transmitted from the core firm only after the deadline for the daily change-order has passed.

Thus, the *kanban* and other means of signal transmission used in this stage bear the fine-tunings of the monthly order. Not only is the detailed timing of delivery determined by these signals, but changes in the volume of detailed parts may occur at this point. For instance, while 30 pieces of the standard version of a part and 20 pieces of the deluxe version of that part were listed in the monthly order as the requirement for that date, the actual *kanban* may dictate that 28 standard parts and 22 deluxe parts be delivered that day.

Let us compare the practice described above with that taken by A_Y in the United States.

The Manufacturer–Supplier Interface in the Network Developed by the US Firm

Like J_A, A_Y issues the initial list of required parts to suppliers based on the volume calculated from the forecasting of final specifications of vehicles. This list covers five months, to give suppliers the necessary information for preparation. A_Y gives authorization to suppliers to procure raw materials for the parts in the list eight weeks before the actual production week of the vehicles, and to manufacture the parts five weeks before. But, the quantity that A_Y actually asks suppliers later to ship for the vehicle production week may still change from the amount ordered from the suppliers at the time of authorization.

Meanwhile, as dealers send in orders, the forcasted volume in the initial list of required parts is revised weekly, at the same time taking into consideration the inventory of parts at the vehicle assembly plants, and the revised figure is released to suppliers. But there is a limit, as I shall describe below, regarding the point up to which such revision of figures by the car company is allowed. As noted in Section 3, each of the orders for vehicles sent from the sales side of the network has to remain firm for two weeks (or ten working days) in order to maintain stable and undisturbed production. This requirement stems from the fact that, in the United States, car manufacturers are required to make a final commitment to their suppliers regarding the parts they require from them no later than two weeks before the date of assembly.

Thus, the difference in the degree of flexibility between the system operated by A_Y and that operated by J_A boils down to the following point. Whereas in the former system the core firm has to give its final and firm signal to suppliers with at least two weeks' lead time, in the latter system the final and firm signal can be given, for those parts that are finally determined by the daily change-orders, with the lead time equal to or less than three days. To what factors can this difference be ascribed?

Evidently, not all of this difference should be ascribed to a difference in the efficiency of management of the firms in a network. Differences in the geographical distance between the vehicle assembly plant and its suppliers certainly matter. Difference in the means of transportation also matters; for instance, railway transportation in North America often requires five days and sometimes ten. At the same time, we should note that not all of Japanese car manufacturers have achieved the same degree of flexibility as J_A in their domestic operation. This suggests that there must be some factors in the practice developed by J_A, factors that may make a big contribution to the achievement of flexibility by this company. In this regard, I note the company's extraordinary efforts to achieve (1) a levelled production schedule, and (2) a sustainable monthly plan of production. The following two subsections explain these factors.

Levelled Production Schedule

Choices by final consumers are extremely diversified, and orders for vehicles with different specifications are entered at the dealers' terminal in various locations in a way that, if simply arrayed according to the order of receipt, would produce a sequence from which any recurrence of a regular pattern would be extremely difficult to discern. To keep the operation of the production side stable, this original sequence of signals received from dealers has to be transformed into another sequence, featuring some kind of regularity.

A specific way to make such a transformation, which seems to be indispensable to achieve flexible production, is called *levelling production*. This incorporates *levelling in volume* and *levelling in kind*. The former refers to equalization of the volume to be processed per day during a given period. The purpose is to avoid day-to-day fluctuation of the work-load of a worker, a production-line, a shop, and an entire plant. If the company is producing a single standardized good, levelling would end here. But levelling in kind becomes important when there are a number of variations. It is then achieved in the following way. Suppose that a plant is to assemble 10,000 units of a car-line, say, C, during a coming month. Suppose furthur that within this car-line there are three variations, say, C_P, C_Q, and C_R, and the plant is to assemble 5,000 units of C_P, 2,500 units of C_Q, and 2,500 units of C_R. If we assume that there are twenty working days in this month, the philosophy of levelling production dictates that 250 units of C_P, 125 units of C_Q, and 125 units of C_R should be assembled on every working day of the month. Further, it dictates that the sequence of assembly be composed as a recurrence of the following pattern: C_P, C_Q, C_P, C_R. This is the atom, or smallest possible collection which cannot be further divided. By repeating this pattern, the most stable operation under the condition of diversity of products can be secured.

The basic reason is as follows. Suppose that a part or material is necessary only for C_P, while a second part or material is used only for C_Q, and a third only for C_R. Then, if assembly is done in such a way that C_P is assembled continuously in the former half of the month and C_Q (C_R) is assembled continuously in the third (fourth) quarter of the month, the production line for the material for C_P has to have capacities that can meet the demand in the first half of the month; further, it has to be operated at its peak load during the first half of the month, and then, suddenly, it has to be kept idle during the latter half of the month. The same logic applies to the other two production lines for materials. However, if the production at the vehicle assembly plant is levelled in the way described above, production capacities required at each of the three upstream lines can become much smaller, and can be operated much more constantly.[16]

As can be perceived from the description in Section 3, the importance of levelling production is known not only to the management of J_A, but also to that of A_Y. The following two features of the mode of operation of the Corporate Production Control division (CPC) of J_A deserve attention, however. First, the CPC has striven to apply this philosophy not only to the company's vehicle assembly plants, but also to the upstream parts of its manufacturing plants including those of its suppliers. For this purpose, the division has a department whose duty is to provide assistance in prognosis and improvement of the production processes of both in-house and in the suppliers' plants. Second, although several other companies are satisfied with achieving level production of basic specification items such as the body type, the CPC of J_A pursues levelling to the production of detailed specification items, applying a special formula developed in this division. The first feature seems to have contributed to develop the ability of suppliers to manufacture parts with short notice, and the second seems to have served to level the daily requirement of each item from each supplier to an extreme degree, minimizing the repercussion effect of a daily change-order on the production and shipping schedule of parts suppliers. Recall that, as noted in Section 3, acceptance of daily change-orders are made under such a constraint that, for most of optional items, the change of volume caused by daily change-orders must not exceed 10 per cent of the volume initially scheduled for a given period. When levelling of production is pursued as described above, the daily allowance for a change can become clear for each optional item.

Sustainable Monthly Plan of Production

Another aspect of the practice in the network spanned by J_A is that plan 1, the monthly list of the number of planned units by car-line, is regarded by those who are concerned as something to be fulfilled exactly during the month corresponding to the plan, and the figures therein are rarely adjusted after it has been finalized and has triggered various procedures. Since J_A never builds any vehicle without actually receiving an order for that unit, this means two things: (1) that plan 1 is made as a result of very careful assessment of demand and close co-ordination between the sales and the production sides, and (2) that the sales organization of the company has somehow been successful in having its dealers take all of the planned units in plan 1, once the plan has been finalized.

The practice in the network spanned by A_Y is very different in this regard. Similar to the case of J_A, several actions in the network, including the preparation of production at the suppliers, are triggered by plan 1 which is developed each month at the corporate programme meeting. The sales organization of the company pursues an allocation based on this plan. Orders from dealers start to come in based on this allocation. Nevertheless, the following kinds of situation can arise. Each week, the management of each vehicle assembly plant has two figures concerning the number of units to be built during each of the several weeks to come. One is the figure acquired from the weekly breakdown of plan 1; the other is the figure acquired from a weekly summation of the actual orders that the company's sales organization has received from its dealers and transmitted to the plant via processing at the sales planning department. There is no guarantee that these two figures will be in accord. For instance, when actual market demand turns out to be weaker than the assessment made at the time of the corporate programme meeting, the latter figure, which emerges weekly at the desk of the plant scheduling manager, can be smaller than the former for several weeks in a row. Vehicles are built, almost always, based on the actual orders received, similar to the case of J_A. But, since preparation of production has been triggered on the basis of the former figure, an adjustment needs to be made at some point. In the case of the network spanned by A_Y, equilibrium between the preparation of production and the actual demand for vehicles is often regained through a shutdown of a vehicle assembly plant at very short notice; in this company's system, the corporate management can unilaterally decide on plant shutdown without awaiting the corporate programme meeting for the following month.

Thus, in comparison with J_A's system, plan 1 in A_Y's system plays a much weaker role. Although preparation of production starts on the basis of plan 1, this monthly production plan may not be sustained by the sales side. The burden of adjustment is paid by the production side, a method of adjustment that is made possible by the existence of the lay-off system. As to the repercussion of such a method of adjustment on suppliers, they can be paid for the parts that they have been authorized by the car company to manufacture, even if it turns out later that the company does not ask them to ship these parts out according to the plan transmitted earlier, because of the sudden plant shutdown. From the purely financial point of view, therefore, it may not be appropriate to say that the suppliers are being forced to bear much of the burden of adjustment via unilateral cancelling; however, credibility of the time control aspect of the schedule sent from the core firm to suppliers seems to be inevitably weakend by the ever-present possibility of such a sudden downward adjustment. This, in turn, may explain at least in part the practice of North American suppliers requiring at least two weeks' notice before delivery.

Some readers may wonder here if J_A's system applies much more pressure to the company's sales organization and its dealers to take whatever units have been determined in plan 1 to be built in a given month, in comparison with A_Y's system. Such possibility cannot be entirely denied. But it should be noted that, when the market demand is really weaker than the initially estimated value, the sales side cannot sustain for long the plan which is now based on incorrect estimations, whatever pressure or incentives the sales staff may receive. Rather, the following fact may deserve attention.

While plan 1 in A_Y's system is made about two months before the production month, plan 1 in J_A's system is finalized only seventeen working days before the first working days of the production month. This means that the plan is completed only after a long process of information-processing and co-ordination within the organization. Since lay-off is difficult in Japan, plan 1 needs to be drawn up as something sustainable during the month concerned; and, at least in the case of J_A's system, the company seems to have been relatively successful in making its plan 1 have such a feature, to the degree that the plan has worked as a credible signal to suppliers.

Based on the analysis made in the foregoing two subsections, I submit that the following two factors are critically important elements of the organizational skill required on the part of the core firm to achieve a flexible production system: (1) levelling production schedule to the detailed specifications level, and (2) making sustainable monthly production plans.

6. EXPORT AND OFFSHORE PRODUCTION

The basic reason why Japanese automobile manufacturers are using method 1 in their operations in the United States and United Kingdom is that their operations in these countries started from the car-importing business. The vehicles imported into these countries from Japan have to be shipped by sea discontinuously in very large lots, which makes the notion of flexible production largely inapplicable. Although production at the Japanese trans-plants has started recently in these countries, it is still in an early phase. Therefore, marketing activities are handled by the sales subsidiaries set up in these countries by Japanese car manufacturers, the original purpose of which was to deal exclusively with the cars that were made at the manu-facturers' plants in Japan. From the point of view of these sales companies and their dealers, the US and UK plants constitute just one of the sources of their vehicles. In so far as method 1 has worked well in their traditional business, importing and selling made-in-Japan cars, there is no reason for them to rush the transplants to implement methods 2 or 3.

Further, at present, a substantial portion of the parts used in these trans-plants are sent from Japan. To secure a necessary lead time for the manufacture and shipment of these parts, the plants have to receive the monthly order for their vehicles with approximately a two- to three-month lead time before their production. This order is a derivative of plan 1 determined in Japan. Since the lead time from plan 1 to vehicle production in Japan is less than one month, the vehicles to be exported can be built with much less lead time. In other words, if we focus on this lead time, offshore production at present can be regarded as even less flexible than the production of the items to be exported.

However, the emergence of a production system in one geographical area has its own dynamism. Gradually it will come to have a system within it to accommodate the later amendment of orders, receiving signals directly from the sales organization working in the same geographical area. The plants in the United States have already taken some steps in that direction. In this sense, the planning system used there is no longer method 1 in its genuine sense; although the monthly order is received with the detailed specification for each vehicle in the list, part of the specification can be changed at the weekly planning stage.

Theoretically speaking, such accommodation of later changes in orders can be made by two different methods. One is through stockpiling an inventory of parts at the vehicle assembly plant; the other is through gradually increasing the sources of parts in the same geographical area and encouraging those suppliers to develop the skills necessary for close co-ordination. The philosophy formed in Japan over a long time is expected to exert its influence in such a way that the latter method carries more weight with the management of these overseas production subsidiaries, even if it takes a more roundabout and slower course.

7. CONCLUDING REMARKS

In this chapter, limiting the object of analysis to the automobile industry, I analysed the network of firms that a typical core manufacturer in today's economy creates for the production and distribution of its products by developing relations with other firms. I focused on how a fundamental tendency noticeable in contemporary manufacturing affects the inter-firm relations spanned by the core firm. This tendency is a transition from mass production of a single standardized good to flexible production of diversified goods.

An initial statement of the nature of the challenge faced by major car manufacturers in today's economy led us to a natural measure of flexibility which focuses on the method of drawing up the monthly production plan. This measure suggests that one or two Japanese automobile manufacturers have achieved a relatively high degree of flexibility in the operation of their domestic network. Noting this, I proceeded to examine interactions in the network, comparing the domestic network developed by a representative Japanese core firm with that developed by one of the Big Three in their home land.

In the first part of this examination, I investigated how the fundamental plan for production in a month is made using informational inputs from dealers as one of the important factors. This investigation led to a conclusion that the core firm expects its dealers to play a more active role in facilitating an adjustment of the network to the demand for the final product; although achieving progress in flexibility serves to diminish the dealer's risk of

misjudging demand regarding the specification of goods demanded, dealers
are still expected to share some burden of volume adjustment in proportion
to their share of sales.

In the second part of the examination, I turned to the upstream side, to
locate factors that seem especially to have permitted the Japanese core firm
to achieve flexibility in its domestic operation. I spotlighted the following
two factors as critical elements of the organizational skill required on the
part of the core firm to achieve a flexible production system: (1) levelling
the production schedule to the detailed specifications level, and (2) making
sustainable monthly production plans.

Finally, I briefly examined the overseas operations of Japanese manufacturers. Although logistics problems have hindered application of the
same method cultivated in their domestic operations, it can be expected
that production outside Japan will gradually come to have greater flexibility,
as supply bases in the respective areas of production gradually grow.

Two caveats are perhaps in order here. First, the notion of flexibility
contains another aspect, removed from the object of this chapter; that is,
the relatively speedy development of a new model or product. To facilitate
the understanding of interactions between dealers, the core firm, and
suppliers, I limited the analysis in this chapter to ongoing production and
distribution of already developed products. Second, this chapter focused on
practices of some of the large firms that seem most conspicuously to
represent the tendency towards increasing product diversity and the responding challenge to achieve flexibility. It should be noted that core firms
operating on a smaller scale usually offer far fewer variations, and yet some
of them have been able to enjoy strong customer loyalty because of the
high reputation of their cars. Product diversity and speedy responses to
consumers would seem to be just two factors among many that constitute
attractiveness of a firm and its products.

Product diversification and speeding-up of the firms' responses will not
proceed monotonically. Firms face bounds and constraints. Not only social
critiques but also the manufacturers themselves have at times questioned
whether some part of the variations of products or speed of responses might
not be dispensed with. For instance, the company in our sample, J_A, started
in the spring of 1991 to review current variations to curtail any unnecessary
part of them. Similarly, the cycle for development of Japanese cars will
probably be somewhat prolonged in the near future to remove excessive
strain in the organization and to allow more time for fruitful ideas to ripen.
Further, of the two Japanese car manufacturers whose values of L_D in 1989
were compared in Section 3, the latter firm started up a reformed order-
processing system in 1991; it is notable that, although several kinds of
convenience were made available anew for the company's dealers by the
reform, the value of L_D was altered from 4 to 6 taking this opportunity.[17]
This upward adjustment of L_D suggests that the previous practice of setting

its value as low as 4 had been producing excessive strain for the suppliers to this core firm.[18] Yet, with all of these in mind, we can still foresee that the course of future industrial development will not revert to mass production of a single standardized good. As far as flexible production of diversified products is necessitated to some degree, this chapter serves to illuminate some aspects of contemporary business organization that seem to bear importance for economists and policy-makers alike.

As indicated by Aoki (1990; chapter 1 above) and Williamson (1991), a recent and growing concern among economists is to investigate the nature of the complementarities that seems to exist between the mode of (1) the employer–employee relationship, (2) the manufacturer–supplier relationship, and (3) the bank–manufacturer relationship. This chapter urges that a fourth aspect of the corporate network, the manufacturer–dealer relationship, be added to such a research agenda.

NOTES TO CHAPTER 5

1. See e.g. Womack *et al.* (1990). Abegglen and Stalk (1985: chs. 4 and 5) also refer to this point.
2. This information has been taken from the '1991 Car Prices Buyer's Guide' of the *Consumer Review*.
3. This information has been taken from *Jidosha Sangyo no Gaikyo 1990*, April 1990, Public Relations Division, Toyota Motor Company.
4. For instance, the European corporation of a US-based firm that I visited in October 1989 was offering five car-lines as passenger cars, two of which used a common platform. Let us represent these car-lines by code names as A, B/C, D, and E. The number of orderable variations for these car-lines in May 1989 was as follows, excluding variations in colour and trim: A: 1,596; B/C: 11,000; D: 22,000; E: 14,310.
5. Some information on the order-processing method adopted by Toyota is available from Ohno and Monden (1983), Monden (1983, 1991). Monden (1989, 1991) includes information on Nissan's order-processing method. Okamoto (1985*a*) provides information on development of the computerized order-entry system in the Japanese steel and automobile industries. Okamoto (1985*b*) reports the results of his field research on the order-entry system, in which comparisons are made between a number of Japanese car manufacturers. Asanuma (1986) reports the results of his field research on the cause and effects of computerized telecommunication network in the Japanese car industry. All of these reports focus on stage 3 in my terminology; they do not tend to examine the

co-ordination between the core firm and its dealers, which is discussed in Section 4 below.

6. This figure coincides with the number reported by Aoki (1990: 5), based on his research on one of the firms.

7. In October 1990, the average time necessary for Toyota to ship a completed vehicle to the dealer's store which accepted the order from the final purchaser of this car ranged from 2 to 5 days, depending on the geographical location of the store. This means that, from the viewpoint of a purchaser placing the order just at the final deadline for a daily change-order, the average waiting time was about 10 days or less.

8. Abegglen and Stalk (1985: 103–4) noted that freezing the final production schedule for between two weeks and one month has been a usual practice among manufacturers including Japanese firms and cited Yanmar as one of the Japanese firms following this practice.

9. These figures are based on JADA (1990) for Japanese data and on the interview that I conducted at the sales planning department of a US automobile manufacturer named A_y in this chapter in July 1992. See also Womack *et al.* (1990: 184).

10. In 1989, there were 1,740 dealers in Japan which JADA (1990) made the object of its survey on business conditions. On average, each of these dealers sold 3,800 units in 1989 with 187 employees. In the same year, according to NADA (1990), there were 24,575 franchised dealers in the USA, each of which, on average, sold 404 units of new vehicles and 598 used cars with 39 employees.

11. The Japanese term for district or field staff is *chiku tanto-in*. Viewed from the function in the organization of the automobile company J_A, a *chiku tanto-in* is a staff member who has no line authority. But, along the rank hierarchy of the company, it is ranked as equivalent to *kacho* (the department manager). A *chiku tanto-in* normally covers 3–5 dealers. J_A has about 300 dealers and 80 *chiku tanto-in* in the domestic market.

12. Obviously, both adjustment of the initial monthly requests submitted by dealers and later allocation of the planned number of vehicles to be produced cannot be made in a bureaucratic or hierarchical fashion by command. Consent and co-operation from dealers have to be elicited through face-to-face communication. Securing these, as well as developing a longer-term interface, is the responsibility of the field staff, members of whom spend each month about 2 weeks visiting dealers. There seems to be little difference between Japanese-based firms and US-based manufacturers in this respect.

13. More concretely, in the allocation decision, a dealer's sales performance is adjusted, taking into consideration the figures of current inventory and the normal level of inventory at the dealer's store.

14. In greater detail, the practice in J_A's network is as follows. At the start of the cycle of submitting the 'monthly orders of vehicles', each of the dealers is actually asked by the car company to submit the sales plan or monthly requirements of vehicles for the coming three months, M, $M + 1$, and $M + 2$. The figure for month M is for something resembling a firm order; it has the dealer's commitment. If honoured by the car company, the dealer is obliged to lay in that amount. On the other hand, the figures for months $M + 1$ and $M + 2$ are not

firm; they are called 'unofficial notifications'. The dealer can change these figures at the next cycle of 'monthly orders'. In other words, dealers are asked to submit every month a three-month rolling plan. That dealers can change the figures for the months $M + 1$ and $M + 2$ does not mean that dealers can place these orders arbitrarily. For instance, if it turns out that, for month $M + 1$, dealers have to compete with each other to secure allocations owing to a shortage of supply in relation to demand, then the car company will give priority to those dealers who already registered relatively larger figures for $M + 1$ at the cycle of submitting the monthly orders for M. Those dealers who suddenly request a large volume are ranked lower in priority. Thus, dealers that show a steadier performance and greater ability to plan and forecast are valued more highly by J_A than those are more short-sighted and show a volatile performance.

15. Williamson (1981: 1549–50; 1985: 180–2) analysed the conditions under which autonomous contracting gives way to obligational market contracting (e.g. franchising) or forward integration into distribution. The analysis he gave is focused on the safeguards necessitated to protect the system against possible debasement of the quality or reputation of a branded good or service. Further, his argument there boils down to the problem of externality which arises from the difficulty of monitoring the behaviour of each individual distributor. The description I have given here spotlights another aspect of franchising complementary to the one illuminated by Williamson. This description suggests that, to secure the efficiency of the system under a changing environment, dealers are required to develop skills that are specific to the system to some extent, and that the manufacturer can assess such skills only through maintaining a continual relationship; both factors require continuity of the relationship.

16. To understand the basic logic of levelling production, Ohno (1978) is very illuminating. Monden (1983) also provides a useful explanation. Cusumano (1985: ch. 5) gives an informative overview of the historical process through which the philosophy of and methods for production flexibility were developed in the Japanese car industry.

17. Major improvements brought forth for the company's dealers by this reform are as follows. (1) In the previous system dealers were asked to send orders to the car manufacturer in a batch at ten-day intervals. Now they are allowed to send in orders everyday. (2) In the previous system the manufacturer made a production schedule in a batch at ten-day intervals only for the ten-day period under discussion at that planning cycle. Therefore, although dealers could be informed of the planned production and delivery dates for individual vehicles if the corresponding orders were incorporated into the ten-day production plan, they were unable to acquire any prospect for production and delivery for those orders that were not incorporated into the ten-day production plan owing to some production constraint. The manufacturer now accepts orders even if they cannot be accommodated by the nearest ten-day production plan under consideration, and assigns a production date to each order with the planning horizon of 90 days.

18. It is interesting to note that a similar upward revision of the value of L_D has not occurred in the system operated by the other of the two Japanese car manufacturers compared.

REFERENCES

Abegglen, J. C., and Stalk, G., Jr (1985), *Kaisha: The Japanese Corporation*, Basic Books, New York.

Aoki, M (1988), *Information, Incentives, and Bargaining in the Japanese Economy*, Cambridge University Press.

——(1990), 'Toward an Economic Model of the Japanese Firm', *Journal of Economic Literature*, 28: 1–27.

Asanuma, B. (1984*a*), 'Nihon ni okeru Buhin Torihiki no Kozo: Jidosha Sangyo no Jirei', *Keizai Ronso*, 131: 137–58. English translation: 'The Contractual Framework for Parts Supply in the Japanese Automotive Industry', *Japanese Economic Studies*, Summer 1985: 54–78.

——(1984*b*), 'Jidosha Sangyo ni okeru Buhin Torihiki no Kozo: Chosei to Kaku-sinteki Tekio no Mechanism', *Kikan Gendai Keizai*, no. 58: 38–48. English translation: 'The Organization of Parts Purchases in the Japanese Automotive Industry', *Japanese Economic Studies*, Summer 1985: 32–53.

——(1986), 'Joho Network to Kigyokan Kankei' (Information Network and Inter-firm Relationship), *Keizai Ronso* 137: 1–21.

——(1989), 'Manufacturer–Supplier relationships in Japan and the Concept of Relation-Specific Skill', *Journal of the Japanese and International Economies*, 3: 1–30.

——(1992), 'Japanese Manufacturer–Supplier Relationships in International Perspective: The Automobile Case', in P. Sheard, (ed.), *International Adjustment and the Japanese Firm*, Allen & Unwin, Sydney.

——and Kikufani, T. (1992), 'Risk Absorption in Japanese Subcontracting: A Microeconometric Study on the Automobile Industry', *Journal of the Japanese and International Economies*, 6: 1–29.

Chandler, A., Jr (1962), *Strategy and Structure*, MIT Press, Cambridge, Mass.

Clark, K. B., and Fujimoto, T. (1991), *Product Development Performance: Strategy, Organization and Management in the World Auto Industry*, Harvard Business School Press, Boston, Mass.

Cusumano, M. A. (1985), *The Japanese Automobile Industry*, Harvard University Press, Cambridge, Mass.

Fukuoka, Y., and Iwatsuki, N. (1989), 'Toyota no Network System Kochiku ni yoru Kigyo Joho Senryaku no Tenkai' (Development of Corporate Strategy by Toyota through Construction of a Computerized Telecommunication Network System), in *Senryaku Joho System Kochiku no Nerai to Katsuyo* (The Aim and Applications of Strategic Information Systems), Nippon Office Automation Kyokai, Tokyo.

JADA (Japan Automobile Dealers Association: Nippon Jidosha Hanbai Kyokai Rengokai) (1990), *Dai 43 Kai Jidosha Dealer Keiei Jyokyo Chosa Hokokusho* (The Report of the 43rd Annual Survey on Business Conditions of Dealers), Nippon Jidosha Hanbai Kyokai Rengokai, Tokyo.

Jidosha Kogaku Zensho Henshu Iinkai (ed.) (1980), *Jidosha no Hanbai Ryutsu System* (The Sales and Distribution System of Automobiles), Sankaido, Tokyo.

Kawasaki, S., and McMillan, J. (1987), 'The Design of Contracts: Evidence from

Japanese Subcontracting', *Journal of the Japanese and International Economies*, 1: 327–49.

Milgrom, P., and Roberts, J. (1990), 'The Economics of Modern Manufacturing: Technology, Strategy, and Organization', *American Economic Review*, 80: 511–28.

Monden, Y. (1983), *Toyota Production System*, Industrial Engineering and Management Press, Institute of Industrial Engineers, Atlanta, Georgia.

——(1989), *Jitsurei: Jidosha Sangyo no Just-In-Time Seisan Hoshiki* (Cases of the JIT Method in the Automobile Industry), Nippon Noritsu Kyokai, Tokyo.

——(1991), *Shin Toyota System* (New Toyota System), Kodansha, Tokyo.

NADA (National Automobile Dealers Association) (1990), *NADA Data*, NADA Industry Analysis, McLean, Va.

Ohno, T. (1978), *Toyota Seisan Hoshiki: Datsu Kibo no Keiei wo Mezashite* (The Toyota Production Method: How Can We Overcome The Management Philosophy of Scale Economies), Diamond Sha, Tokyo.

——and Monden, Y. (eds.) (1983), *Toyota Seisan Hoshiki no Shin Tenkai* (New Development of the Toyota Production Method), Nippon Noritsu Kyokai, Tokyo.

Okamoto, H. (1985*a*), 'Gendai no Seisan Hanbai Togo System: Tekkogyo to Jidosha Sangyo no Case' (The Contemporary System to Integrate Production and Distribution: Cases of the Steel and Automobile Industries), in K. Sakamoto, (ed.), *Gijutsu Kakushin to Kigyo Kozo* (Innovation and the Structure of the Firm), Minerva Shobo, Kyoto. 114–48.

——(1985*b*), 'Seisan to Hanbai no Interface' (The Production–Distribution Interface: Part I and II), *Doshisha Shogaku* 37: 36–61; 232–51.

Stalk, George, Jr (1988), 'Time: The Next Source of Competitive Advantage', *Harvard Business Review*, July–August: 41–51.

Williamson, O. E. (1979), 'Transaction–Cost Economics: The Governance of Contractual Relations', *Journal of Law and Economics*, 22: 233–61.

——(1981), 'The Modern Corporation: Origins, Evolution, Attributes', *Journal of Economic Literature*, 19: 1537–68.

——(1985), *The Economic Institutions of Capitalism: Firms, Markets, Relational Contracting*, Free Press, New York.

——(1991), 'Strategizing, Economizing, and Economic Organization', *Strategic Management Journal*, 12: 75–94.

Womack, J. P., Jones, D. T., and Roos, D. (1990), *The Machine that Changed the World*, Rawson Associates, New York.

6

The Evolution of Japan's Industrial Research and Development

D. ELEANOR WESTNEY

1. INDUSTRIAL R&D IN JAPAN: THE MACRO-LEVEL PICTURE

Japanese sources regard the late 1970s as a major turning point in the development of industrial R&D in Japan, a transformation that can be traced not only in the pronouncements of industry leaders, but in the national aggregate data on R&D (Aoki 1988; JMA 1987; Takara 1989). In the words of Masahiko Aoki,

The main concern of Japanese firms in the mid-1970s was how to overcome the first negative growth experienced since the end of the war, which was brought on by the first oil shock. One step they took in this direction was to 'slim down' (*genryo keiei*) by reducing the amount of external debt and the number of employees. Although this was a painful experience, it allowed the major Japanese firms to regain their confidence and then, toward the end of the 1970s, to shift all their attention to the critically important research and development (R&D) effort ... Accordingly, there was a quantum leap in the ratio of research expenditure to gross national product from the steady 1.7 percent level in 1975–78 to the 1.80 percent level in 1979. Since then the ratio has continued to increase. (Aoki 1988: 234–5)

Aoki also invokes the rapid increase in patent applications in Japan (and the increase of such applications by Japanese in the United States) to make the case for 'an increasingly active research and development effort by the private corporate sector since the late 1970s' (Aoki 1988: 236). The 1980s witnessed not only an increased commitment of resources to R&D in Japanese industry, but also a growing public commitment to more advanced development and basic research (Aoki 1988: 248; Sentan Gijutsu Riyo Kenkyukai 1989).

Aoki's portrayal of the relative stagnation in R&D investment in the wake of the Oil Shock and the rapid growth after 1979 is borne out by the time-series data of Figs. 1 and 2, which show the changes in industry R&D expenditure from 1965 to 1988 and the number of researchers employed in industry from 1965 to 1989, respectively. The stagnation is most marked in the data on researchers, but the pattern of stagnation or

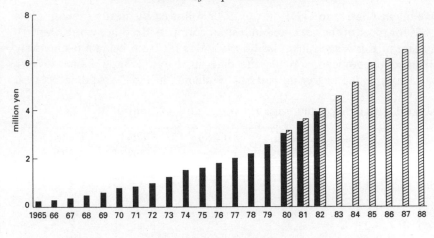

FIG. 1   Industry Expenditure on R&D in Japan, 1965–1988
          Source: Data taken from annual series in *Kagaku Gijutsu Yoran*; the two
          series derive from a change in the mode of calculating the amount beginning
          in 1982, such that the data for 1980–2 differ across the two modes of
          calculation.

slowdown after the Oil Shock until the end of the 1970s, followed by rapid
growth in the 1980s, can be traced in both sets of indicators.

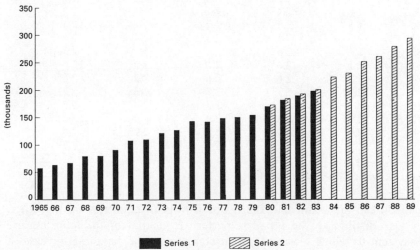

FIG. 2   Industry Researchers in Japan, 1965–1989

That this pattern is not unique to Japan is indicated by the comparative
data in Table 1, which show a similar pattern of stagnation in R&D

investment relative to GNP in the 1970s followed by steady growth in the 1980s for most of the advanced industrial countries. In other words, Japan's increase in R&D investment in the 1980s was far from being a distinctively Japanese phenomenon. While the data in Table 1 show some striking similarities in the aggregate patterns of change in R&D spending between

TABLE 1   R&D Expenditure as a Percentage of GNP, 1961–1989

	France	West Germany	Japan	United Kingdom	United States
1961	1.4	NA	1.4	2.5	2.7
1962	1.5	1.2	1.5	NA	2.7
1963	1.6	1.4	1.5	NA	2.8
1964	1.8	1.6	1.5	2.3	2.9
1965	2.0	1.7	1.6	NA	2.8
1966	2.1	1.8	1.5	2.3	2.8
1967	2.2	2.0	1.6	2.3	2.8
1968	2.1	2.0	1.7	2.2	2.8
1969	2.0	1.8	1.7	2.3	2.7
1970	1.9	2.1	1.9	NA	2.6
1971	1.9	2.2	1.9	NA	2.4
1972	1.9	2.2	1.9	2.1	2.3
1973	1.8	2.1	2.0	NA	2.3
1974	1.8	2.1	2.0	NA	2.2
1975	1.8	2.2	2.0	2.1	2.2
1976	1.8	2.1	2.0	NA	2.2
1977	1.8	2.1	2.0	NA	2.1
1978	1.8	2.2	2.0	2.2	2.1
1979	1.8	2.4	2.1	NA	2.2
1980	1.8	2.4	2.2	NA	2.3
1981	2.0	2.5	2.3	2.4	2.4
1982	2.1	2.6	2.4	NA	2.5
1983	2.1	2.6	2.6	2.2	2.6
1984	2.2	2.6	2.6	2.2	2.6
1985	2.3	2.8	2.8	2.3	2.7
1986	2.3	2.7	2.8	2.4	2.7
1987	2.3	2.8	2.9	2.2	2.6
1988	2.3	2.9	2.8	2.2	2.8
1989	NA	2.9	2.9	NA	2.7

Source: Kagaku Gijitsu Cho (1990).

Japan on the one hand and the major European countries on the other, they also distinguish the Japanese pattern from that of the more mature US system to which it is more often compared. The Japanese increase of the 1980s could be seen as a resumption of an evolutionary earlier trajectory of steady growth, from a system with low levels of R&D spending to one that ranks among the R&D leaders. However, Japan's 'low' levels of R&D spending as a proportion of GNP in the 1960s were low only by comparison with the United States, not with West Germany or France. What is perhaps more striking is that, at a time when Japan's per capita GNP was roughly half that of the European countries, the proportion of its GNP devoted to R&D was very similar.

The aggregate patterns of change in R&D in Japan are most clearly seen in the data on the number of researchers in industry (Fig. 2). Between 1965 and 1975 the number of researchers in industry nearly tripled, from 57,126 to 143,364. However, in the five years following the first Oil Shock, 1975–9, it increased by only 7 per cent. Then, in the following five years (1979–83) the number increased by nearly a quarter, and continued to grow until by 1989 it had reached over half a million.

While the overall pattern of R&D expenditure in the 1970s and 1980s paralleled the experience of the other advanced industrial nations, Table 2 provides evidence of a more distinctively Japanese pattern in the structure

TABLE 2   Structure of R&D Expenditure: Sources and Users
(% of total national R&D expenditure)

	Government		Industry		Universities		Private research institutes	
	Provided	Spent	Provided	Spent	Provided	Spent	Provided	Spent
Japan (1988)	18.4	9.3	76.3	73.9	4.5	12.6	0.7	4.3
USA (1988)	48.0	11.5	47.9	71.8	2.8	13.8	1.4	2.9
W. Germany (1987)	36.6	3.4	62.3*	73.1	—	12.9	—	10.6
France (1983)	53.8	26.4	42.0	56.8	0.2	15.9	0.4	0.9
UK (1987)	38.7	15.1	49.7	67.0	0.6	14.2	1.9	3.7

Source: Kagaku Gijutsu Cho (1990).

of national expenditure on R&D. The comparatively low proportion of total national R&D expenditure provided by the government distinguishes the Japanese technology system from its counterparts in North America and Western Europe. As several observers have noted (e.g. Ergas 1987; Derian 1990), the government has played a far less direct role in R&D expenditure in Japan than in the other advanced industrial nations, with industry shouldering considerably more of the funding burden. The government role in the technology system is important but indirect: it establishes incentives for industrial R&D investments, such as favourable tax provisions for R&D; encourages certain high-profile collaborative R&D projects; and funds and directs the educational system, particularly the universities. As Table 2 indicates, industry spends about the same percentage of national research expenditure in Japan, the United States, and West Germany; however, the direct costs to industry are significantly higher in Japan than in the other two countries.

We would expect that the primary consequence for Japan's science and technology system would be lower industry expenditure on basic research, which tends to rely more heavily on government subsidy, and greater expenditure on the applied research and development that is so much more attractive to industry. In fact, however, the aggregate data collected by the OECD portray Japanese industry as spending a higher proportion of its budget on basic research than in the other advanced industrial nations. Whereas in 1989 the proportion of R&D funding devoted to basic research by US industry was recorded as 3.1 per cent (up from 3.0 per cent in 1987), in Japan the proportion was 6.6 per cent. Given that these figures are subject to great inconsistencies across nations in how basic research is defined and reported, most Western industry analysts express some scepticism about the comparability of these figures. It may even be difficult to interpret within a single country. According to the data published by the Prime Minister's Office, industrial spending on basic research in 1965 amounted to 11.2 per cent of total industry R&D expenditures. But by 1970 this had fallen to 9.3 per cent, and, as Fig. 3 shows, the proportion of industry funding devoted to basic research continued to fall, dropping rather abruptly after the first Oil Shock to 5.2 per cent by 1975 and to a low of 4.6 per cent in both 1978 and 1979.

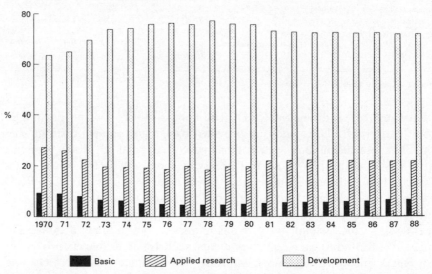

FIG. 3   Industry Expenditure on R&D in Japan: Basic, Applied Research, and Development

Moreover, in spite of the much-touted recognition of the importance of investments in basic research on the part of Japanese industry in the 1980s, even in 1988 the percentage of industry expenditure on basic research had not reached the level reported in the late 1960s and early 1970s. Given the widespread portrayals of the 1960s as a decade in which Japanese firms concentrated on technology imports and the 1980s as a decade in which attention shifted to basic research (Kagaku Gijutsu Cho 1990; JMA 1987), it is difficult to believe that in 1965 firms were allocating nearly twice as much of their R&D budgets to basic research as they were spending in 1988.

However, although these data should be viewed with some suspicion, one inference can safely be made. While the growing allocations of Japanese companies to R&D during these decade has meant that they have been spending increasing absolute amounts on basic research, the aggregate data provide no evidence of a major shift in the pattern of industrial research in Japan. In other words, the increased spending on basic research has not come at the cost of reduced expenditure on downstream development.

Scepticism about Japanese industry's much-vaunted commitment in the 1980s to basic research is also supported by the data on postgraduate education. In the 1950s and 1960s, Japanese industry pushed the government to expand dramatically the size of the faculties and the numbers of students in engineering departments in universities, in order to produce the Bachelors graduates necessary to staff the technology departments in factories. The 1980s saw a steady increase in graduates of Masters programmes, who are trained for product development work in the corporate laboratories of Japan's largest corporations. However, the decade did not witness a comparable expansion of doctoral-level science or engineering programmes; whereas US universities produced 7,651 Ph.D.s in science in 1985, Japanese universities produced less than 10 per cent of that number (see Table 3).

The number of doctorates awarded in Japan includes both those received after following a course of study at a university, and those awarded to researchers employed in a corporation or government laboratory on the basis of research reports submitted to a university (usually the institution from which they received their Bachelors or Masters degree). Recipients of the latter type of degree, who have received their research training on the job, do little or nothing to increase the research capacity of the universities, and it could be argued that they do not bring to the corporate laboratories the specialized research skills and the orientation to fundamental research of a graduate of a university Ph.D. programme. Yet in engineering they have accounted for over 60 per cent of the total number of engineering Ph.D.s awarded (in science their weight has been much lower), and most of the increase in the 1980s in Ph.D.s in engineering. One might expect that an increased industry commitment to basic research would produce the same increase in Ph.D. enrolments as that generated in Bachelors programmes in the 1950s and 1960s and in Masters programmes in the 1970s and 1980s, and yet no such pattern emerges from the aggregate data. Close observation

TABLE 3   Graduates of University Courses and Degree
Recipients, 1975–1988

| | Masters degrees | Doctorates | |
		From university course	Total
Engineering			
1975	5,821		986
1976	6,925		1,079
1977	7,655		1,043
1978	7,609		1,166
1979	7,129		1,195
1980	6,975		1,186
1981	7,368	685	1,236
1982	7,721	621	1,278
1983	8,290	579	1,290
1984	8,609	563	1,291
1985	9,612	552	1,404
1986	10,390	588	1,493
1987	11,093	638	1,547
1988	11,913	721	1,717
Science			
1975	1,482		676
1976	1,663		717
1977	1,630		843
1978	1,676		782
1979	1,667		814
1980	1,710		822
1981	1,896	607	791
1982	1,916	569	764
1983	2,006	582	772
1984	2,082	529	807
1985	2,133	610	860
1986	2,261	564	820
1987	2,508	605	837
1988	2,692	589	881

Source: Kagaku Gijutsu Yoran, annual series.

of any future shifts in these numbers could provide an indicator of whether
the system is actually changing significantly.

Even within Japan, the public commitment of industry to truly fundamental research has been questioned, and the much greater salience of
industry in the funding of Japanese R&D is consequently a matter of some
controversy. One of the major debates in Japanese technology policy since
the mid-1980s is whether or not the public undertaking by government and
industry to generate more fundamental science and technology training, in
order to contribute to the world's stock of knowledge, will require a basic
shift in Japan's science and technology system, involving greater investments

by the government in basic science in government laboratories and in the universities along the lines of the US model (Sakakibara 1988). Some industry leaders have argued that, given the very great conservatism of Japan's leading universities and of the Ministry of Education (which continues to resist funding of research at national universities by other ministries), Japan must find an alternative institutional path to increasing its basic science and technology: a basic research system anchored by corporate basic research laboratories, attached to the large industrial corporations but governed by the norms of open inquiry, individually directed research, and publication that characterize the elite basic research universities of the West. Critics of this approach argue that corporations will have great difficulty in funding the long-term, highly speculative research that contributes to the fund of basic knowledge, and that, even if Japan's corporations were to prove to be outstanding performers in fundamental research, foreigners are unlikely to find them as accessible as universities and therefore are increasingly likely to criticize the Japanese system as relatively inaccessible. On the basis of admittedly unsystematic discussions with Japanese research personnel, I have observed that those in the science-based industries (chemicals, pharmaceuticals, biotechnology) advocate greater government spending and a strengthening of the research base of the universities and public laboratories; whereas those in engineering-based industries (telecommunications, computers, precision manufacturing) are more likely to be sceptical of the capabilities of the universities and to advocate a corporation-centred model for the advancement of basic research.

One other set of aggregate data on Japan's R&D system deserves comment, in part because it has attracted such widespread attention: the rapid growth in patent applications, which Aoki and others have used to demonstrate the growing technological strength of Japanese industry. In 1960, the number of patent applications in Japan was considerably less than that in the United States, and roughly the same (in absolute numbers) as in West Germany and the UK. In 1970, the number of applications reached 100,522 (somewhat greater than in the United States), of which nearly one-quarter (23.2 per cent) were from non-Japanese. The number continued to rise in the 1970s, reaching 144,517 by 1978 (14.8 per cent from foreigners). From 1979 on, however, the number of applications rose dramatically, until by 1988 over 300,000 applications were submitted, over four times the number submitted in the United States, only 9.0 per cent of which were from foreigners (data from Kagaku Gijutsu Cho 1984, 1990).

However, the data on patent applications obscure the fact that in Japan a very high proportion of patent applications have not resulted in patents. Table 4 gives the total number of patent applications in Japan, the United States, West Germany, and the United Kingdom in the five-year period 1983–7. Fewer than 17 out of every 100 applications produces a patent in

TABLE 4   Patent Applications and Approvals, 1983–1987

	Applications	Patents granted	Ratio of applications to approvals
Japan	2,521,965	423,101	0.168
USA	588,233	349,536	0.594
West Germany	378,352	221,529	0.586
UK	164,255	143,189	0.872

Source: based on data in *Kagaku Gijutsu Yoran,* annual series.

Japan, compared to nearly 60 per 100 in the United States and West Germany and over 87 per 100 in the United Kingdom.

Why firms undertake the not inconsiderable expenditure of time and money to submit patent applications with such a low probability of success is an interesting question. One answer lies in the evaluation and reward systems in Japanese industrial laboratories. As Japanese firms expanded their R&D expenditure in the wake of the first oil crisis, many looked to patents as a measure of productivity and performance in their R&D organizations. Today many leading Japanese firms not only provide their technical employees with rewards both for patent applications and for patents received; they also assign patent quotas to each section of their R&D laboratories.[1] Companies, which regularly publish the number of patent applications as a measure of their technological competitiveness, try to make it relatively easy for their employees to apply for patents by providing patent templates and technical support to reduce the amount of time required to write the patent application.

Just as the aggregate data on patents is difficult to interpret without some detailed information about behaviour inside Japan's large industrial corporations, so the data on the changing levels of investments and researchers are difficult to understand without turning to the more micro-level phenomena at the firm level. Research on the organization of Japanese industrial R&D is still somewhat thin, in part because interest in this function is relatively recent on the part of Japanese as well as Western scholars. Some aspects of R&D organization, such as the linkage between R&D and manufacturing within the large Japanese corporation, are increasingly well understood. Others, such as the processes by which an R&D network operates within an industrial group and by which suppliers and customers are drawn into the technology development process, are only beginning to emerge as issues needing investigation. Let us now turn to the firm level, focusing on the large industrial firms that have dominated the development of industrial R&D to date.

2. THE CHANGING STRUCTURE AND ROLE OF INDUSTRIAL R&D

In the United States, the large industrial laboratory within the corporation developed at the turn of the century, pioneered by large firms in electrical equipment (General Electric) and communications (AT&T) (Hughes 1989: 138–9). Between the two world wars, the industrial laboratory was widely adopted and institutionalized in large US corporations. In Japan, while a handful of large corporations had established central research laboratories before the Second World War, it was not until the late 1950s and 1960s that the industrial laboratory became broadly institutionalized.

The data on the establishment of industrial laboratories collected in 1987 by the National Institute for Science and Technology Policy (Fig. 4) show the pattern of establishment of corporate-level research laboratories by

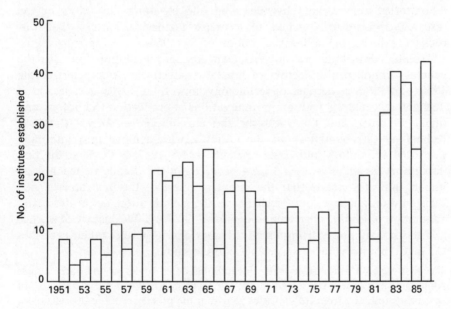

FIG. 4   Changes in the Number of Corporate Research Institutes Established in Japan, 1951–1986
Source: *Historical Review of Japanese Science and Technology Policy.*

Japanese industrial firms. The 1960s witnessed what Japanese called the *kenykujo bu-mu*—the 'research laboratory boom', in which industrial corporations rushed to establish laboratories, usually by elevating the status of their research departments (*kenkyu-bu*) and bringing together technology development groups located in factories. The second wave of laboratory foundings occurred in the 1980s. This pattern of growth followed by consolidation followed by growth had important effects on the organization of R&D within the industrial firm.

In Japan, as in the United States, the pioneers were predominantly firms in electrical equipment (Hitachi established its first *kenkyujo* in 1934) and communications equipment. (The two companies that amalgamated to form Toshiba in 1939 had each previously established a research laboratory, one in 1920 and the other in 1934; three years after the merger of the two companies the two laboratories were amalgamated into one corporate research laboratory; however, in 1944 they were again separated, and a single central laboratory was not re-established until 1961, during the *kenkyujo bu-mu*.) The early adopters had close technical linkages with leading US and European companies, and it is not unreasonable to suppose that the foreign laboratories provided models to some degree. However, the main mandate of the Japanese laboratory was apparently technology transfer and adaptation. In both Hitachi and the Toshiba companies, the first laboratories were created by renaming and elevating the status of the research department attached to a major factory, a pattern that was replicated during the 'laboratory boom' of the 1960s.

Toshiba, describing not only its own company evolution but also the general technological trajectory of Japanese industry, has characterized the 1950s and 1960s as decades of technology import, the 1970s as a decade of 'technology catch-up' with major innovations in production technology and quality control, and the 1980s as the era of *qijutsu-rikkoku* ('making technology the foundation of the nation'), with a move into internally generated technology and basic research (JMA 1987: 201). That the first 'laboratory boom' shown in Fig. 4 occurred in the decade of technology import indicates clearly that the initial mandate of the laboratories, like their prewar Japanese counterparts, was the identification, acquisition, and adaptation of leading-edge technology from the West. The history of science and technology policy from which the data of Fig. 4 were taken describes the first laboratory boom somewhat contemptuously as follows:

The first rush to establish private research institutes began in the early 1960s. Although the rush was supported by the improved international competitiveness of enterprises resulting from technologies gained in the process of trade liberalization, in fact, such establishments were actually real estate investments brought about by high economic growth and the centralization of research and development functions scattered over various business places. (Commission on the History of Science and Technology Policy 1991: 215)

As this description indicates, the first laboratory boom largely involved the consolidation of factory-level research and technology departments into a single site. Both the technology import and transfer mandate and the origins in production-linked groups meant that the new laboratory continued to have strong links to manufacturing and organizational structures that closely paralleled those in production.

However, that the new laboratories tried to deepen their research activities is strongly suggested by the developments of the 1970s, when many companies moved to link their research organizations more tightly with their business divisions. Canon, for example, which set up its central laboratory in 1969, renamed its Central Research Laboratory the Product Technology Laboratory in 1977, with the explicit intention of shifting its activities from the development of 'fundamental technology' to the development of new products in response to the post-Oil Shock environment (JMA 1987: 45). Kubota abolished its Central Research Laboratory (established in 1966) in favour of Technology Research Laboratories in each of its business divisions in 1971-2. The business pressures of the 1970s led most companies to rein in their R&D organizations to some extent and to attempt to tie them more directly to business divisions and to company-wide efforts to improve production efficiency and quality. In the 1970s, for example many companies, followed the early lead of companies such as Matsushita and Hitachi and established Production Engineering Research Laboratories to provide company-wide improvement in production machinery and systems. The growing number of laboratories and technology development groups led many companies to develop Technology Planning Departments to co-ordinate developments, engage in technology planning, and help standardize practices across subunits.

The growing diversification of Japan's large companies at the end of 1970s and into the 1980s led to the next major wave of the establishment of laboratories, as companies set up divisional laboratories attached to production facilities. Again, the establishment of these laboratories was usually based on the technology departments of key factories, with the addition this time of product-related research groups from the central laboratories. These complemented the rejuvenated central research laboratories, which were increasingly given wider-ranging research mandates and longer time horizons. Of the five electronics companies involved in the JMA's thirty-company study of R&D organization in the mid-1980s, for example, Sharp had six laboratories, Mitsubishi Electric had nine, Hitachi and Toshiba both had ten, and Matsushita had fourteen. All five had a corporate laboratory, a corporate-level production technology laboratory, and various divisional laboratories. Many of the latter were established after 1980.

Finally, from the mid-1980s, Japan's largest companies began to establish basic research laboratories (Hitachi was the first, in 1985) and a growing number of research laboratories overseas, some of which were intended to support localization strategies and some of which (such as NEC's Princeton laboratory) themselves had basic research mandates (Herbert 1989; Sakakibara and Westney 1993).

Therefore, in the mid-1980s, when Japanese R&D organization began to attract serious attention from Japanese and Western scholars, the patterns they observed had only just been institutionalized, and in many companies the principal architects of the R&D system were still personally involved in the company. The close links between the central and the divisional laboratories and between the divisional laboratories and the factories described in the studies of the mid-1980s (Westney and Sakakibara 1985; Imai *et al.* 1985; JMA 1987) were reinforced not only by the flows of individuals across subunits that these studies described, but also by their relatively recent evolution, which had involved moving entire groups from one organizational location to another. And the strong structural iso-morphism between R&D and manufacturing, so striking in Japanese com-panies (Westney and Sakakibara 1985; Aoki 1988: 237–42; Westney 1993) is clearly deeply rooted in the close links between the evolution of the R&D function and the factories.

3. THE MANAGEMENT OF R&D WITHIN THE LARGE INDUSTRIAL FIRM

Since the mid-1980s, those scholars who have examined Japanese industrial R&D have focused on understanding what explains the shorter development times of leading Japanese firms (established by Mansfield 1988*b*; 1988*c*), their capacity for effective design for manufacturability (Aoki 1988; Rosen-berg and Steinmueller 1988), and their capabilities in incremental product and process improvement (Dore 1988: 125–144; Rosenberg and Steinmueller 1988; Aoki 1988: 237–47). Among the key factors identified as underlying these capabilities were the strong links between R&D and manufacturing, and the ease with which people were moved across functional boundaries. In the 1980s, often in response to Japanese models, US firms were urged to use cross-functional development teams to speed up product development and make products more responsive to manufacturing and marketing requirements (e.g. Takeuchi and Nonaka 1986; Rosenberg and Steinmuller 1988). And many leading firms—Xerox, DEC, and Hewlett-Packard among them—proceeded to do so, thus apparently reducing the differences between Japanese and US R&D management.

In Japan, however, these cross-functional teams were supported by a human resource management system in R&D which differed substantially from its US counterpart; it included the homogenization of rewards across functions, routinized and permanent personnel transfers from R&D to other functions, and a virtually complete absence of market elements from the so-called 'internal labour market'.

The standardization of reward structures across functions within the large Japanese firm has been a key factor in the organization of R&D. Criteria for base pay, overtime pay, and annual increments for blue-collar workers and the non-supervisory levels of white-collar workers (including all management and technical personnel below the level of section chief) are set in the course of annual negotiations with the company union. As a result, wages, bonuses, and overtime rates are standardized across the functions, and there are strong barriers in the way of using monetary incentives to reward outstanding researchers or to differentiate across functions (Westney and Sakakibara 1985). In interviews in sixteen technology-intensive firms in Japan, Mary Sullivan Taylor found that R&D managers cited resistance from the company union as a major barrier to using salary differentials to distinguish outstanding researchers (Taylor 1989: 139). One explanation of the long hours reported in Japanese R&D organizations therefore, is that overtime pay, to which engineers are as entitled as shop-floor workers, is the only means by which the R&D function can increase the total take-home pay of its employees over those in the production or marketing functions. A 1985 study of computer engineers in Japan and the United States found that, whereas US engineers reported an average work week of 45.3 hours, Japanese engineers in the central R&D laboratories reported 49.38 hours and divisional laboratory engineers, 53.43.

Large US firms, in contrast, often face strong constraints on major differences in salary levels within a given function, but their reward structures are highly differentiated across functions and between blue-collar and managerial employees. The major influence on the salary levels of their R&D employees is not the internal isomorphism across functions that characterizes the Japanese system, but the external technical labour market. In interviews in the 1985 study, several of the US engineers reported that they could most easily increase their pay cheques by generating lucrative offers from other companies. The isomorphism of reward structures across functions in the Japanese firms not only eliminates one potential source of friction in a cross-functional team; it also makes it easier to move employees across functions, either in temporary technology transfer assignments or in the permanent career moves that are a distinctive feature of Japanese R&D organization.

The 'standard' career for R&D employees in most industries, particularly in the electronics and communications industries that have been increasingly regarded as the pace-setters in Japanese R&D, proceeds from the corporate R&D laboratories into divisional laboratories, and then into line management or staff positions in the operating divisions (Westney and Sakakibara 1985; Nihon Noritsu Kyokai 1987; Wakasugi 1989). Relatively few of the recruits to the central R&D laboratories spend their entire lives in R&D, and virtually all of those who do so spend at least part of their careers in assignments to other parts of the R&D organization.

Facilitating these career moves is a highly standardized system of human resource management. In contrast to most US and European firms, recruits to the R&D function go through the same lengthy entry-level training programmes as their counterparts in other functions. Indeed, they do not formally know that they have actually been assigned to any particular part of the R&D organization until they have completed that training. Most large US firms have gone to considerable lengths to create an internal labour market place within their R&D organizations (mimicking external market features by posting training opportunities and position announcements and creating internal job listings, for example), so that employees may be induced to move to areas where they are most needed. Japanese firms, in contrast, rely heavily on hierarchy. In the R&D organization of large Japanese firms, as in other functions, the primary locus of responsibility for planning the employee's career rests with the company, rather than with the individual, as is the case in most US firms. This difference was reflected in many of the indicators in the comparative study of computer engineers cited above (Westney and Sakakibara 1985). In assignment to projects, the most important factor for the US engineers was their own expressed desire to participate; for the Japanese engineers, it was the supervisor of their last project. In training after entry into the company, Japanese engineers were far more likely than their US counterparts to have been assigned to courses by their company, rather than to have undertaken them at their own initiative. Significantly more of the Japanese engineers agreed with the statement that 'The recruitment of engineers is based on long-range personnel planning rather than immediate needs.' And over half the Japanese engineers agreed that their performance was evaluated over a period of five to ten years, compared with just 10 per cent of their US counterparts.

These patterns are similar (or 'isomorphic', to use the language of institutional theory) across firms and, apparently, across industries in Japan, and have been a critically important element in developing the close cross-functional co-ordination that has been so central to their strengths in reducing development times, designing for manufacturability, and incremental product and process innovation, all of which are undergirded by the transfer of engineers across functions and the ability of the firm to assign them to tasks (such as incremental product improvement) that may lack intrinsic interest but have high value to the firm.

Given the fact that isomorphism with company-wide organizational patterns is so strong in Japan, US analysts have tended to assume that the pulls of professionalism and professional identity are extremely weak (see e.g. Saxonhouse 1986: 127–9, and Okimoto and Saxonhouse 1987: 413). The context in which this difference has attracted most attention has been in the area of patterns of technical communication. US researchers, even those in industry, are portrayed as being oriented primarily towards their professional identity, and therefore as willing to publish research results and communicate freely with researchers outside their company. Japanese researchers, on the other hand, are seen as being loyal 'company men', and as therefore being reluctant to share information with 'outsiders'.

However, this perception of the Japanese researcher is based primarily on an economically rational model of professionalization rather than on empirical research: it assumed that researchers communicate within their profession primarily in order to enhance their individual market value (Saxonhouse 1986: 128). In the absence of high levels of cross-company mobility, as in Japan, one would expect incentives for professional communication to be low. There is some empirical evidence that this perception is wrong. In the comparative study of R&D in the computer industry, Japanese company engineers were found to be significantly more likely than their US counterparts to participate in professional societies, to attend professional meetings, and to believe that their company encourages them to publish the results of their work. They are also, surprisingly enough, more likely to value the approval and respect of their professional colleagues outside their own company than are the US engineers (Westney and Sakakibara 1985). The longstanding Western assumption that 'loyalty to the company' and 'professional identity' are at opposite poles of a single continuum needs reassessment: there are two dimensions rather than one, so that researchers can be characterized as strongly loyal to *both* their profession and their company. Companies can create an environment that fosters the 'organizational professional' for whom enhancing a personal reputation in the profession is also a way of enhancing the prestige of the company; and leading Japanese companies have clearly done so.

Although the studies of the late 1980s did much to improve our understanding of the R&D function within the large corporation, the growing interest of US companies in competitive benchmarking in R&D against their Japanese counterparts has begun to raise some issues about the structure of the Japanese firm itself. Moreover, the growing realization by management scholars of the importance of the increasing importance of linkages across subunits in what is becoming an increasingly geographically dispersed function is beginning to direct attention to the linkages between the R&D organization of the large Japanese firm and R&D organizations outside the firm, both within and outside the industrial group. Let us now turn to an examination of the issues involved in these aspects of Japanese R&D organization, although the empirical data base for addressing them is still relatively thin.

4. R&D LINKAGES ACROSS THE BOUNDARIES OF THE FIRM

The greater propensity of Japanese firms to carry out joint research activities has been documented and analysed at some length (e.g. Imai *et al.* 1985; Yamamura 1986; Westney 1988; Wakasugi 1989). In particular, the ability of Japanese firms to work closely with their suppliers has been seen as a critically important element in their short product development times, especially in the car industry. But the issue of R&D networking beyond the boundaries of the firm has a further dimension which has yet to be systematically explored.

As US research managers increasingly try to benchmark their organizations against those of their Japanese counterparts, they are encountering some frustrating problems in drawing the boundaries of the Japanese companies, problems that relate to some fundamental and as yet unresolved issues in our theories of the Japanese firm. To give just one concrete example, at a briefing for US research managers in 1990, the head of the R&D division of a leading Japanese corporation gave three different figures for the number of R&D employees in his firm in the course of a single thirty-five-minute presentation. When questioned by the Americans about this inconsistency, he shrugged and said that the figure depends on how many of his firm's subsidiaries were included in the total. Given the close technical co-operation and the constant flow of researchers across the formal organizational boundaries, including the number of R&D employees in the subsidiaries was probably essential in trying to grasp the scope and scale of his firm's R&D activities.

This problem plagues those researchers who try to draw structural maps of the R&D function in Japanese firms or to develop databases on R&D organization. Most large Japanese companies, particularly in electronics, computers, and telecommunications, which are seen as the leading companies in developing advanced R&D structures, are not single companies but groups of companies under a parent company. Hitachi, for example, has 679 subsidiaries, according to the Toyo Keizai directory of corporate groups; Matsushita has 162, Fujitsu 98. In its report to the Japan Management Association's thirty-company survey of R&D organizations, for example, Matsushita indicated that in 1986 it had 7,160 R&D employees in the parent company, Matsushita Denki Sangyo KK, and 19,400 in its affiliated companies. That these affiliated companies are important in understanding Matsushita's R&D organization is indicated by a grid drawn by Matsushita of its technology development organization in the late 1980s (see Table 5).

The grid takes Matsushita's seven major business fields—audio-visual (AV), information (Info), factory automation (FA), semiconductors (IC), 'living' (primarily white goods and home automation), systems, automobile components (Auto) (primarily electronic), and environmental systems (En) (again, centred on housing); it then identifies which of its six major R&D divisions are involved in which business fields, and which of eight leading subsidiaries are involved in co-operating with those divisions to develop new products and new technologies. How the R&D employees of the group are distributed across the subsidiaries has not yet been systematically investigated. Moreover, in addition to the cross-subsidiary links, Matsushita Denki reported to the JMA that it was regularly involved in joint research

TABLE 5   Matsushita Group Technology Development Organization, Late 1980s

	Major business fields[a]						
	AV	Info	FA	IC	Living	Auto	En
Internal Divisions							
TV Division	X	X			X	X	
Audio-visual (AV) Division	X					X	
Electrical Division					X	X	
Information Equipment Division		X					
Production Technology Division			X				
Semiconductor Research Centre				X			
Affiliated Companies							
Matsushita Telecommunications Management	X	X	X		X	X	
Matsushita Electronics Division		X	X			X	
Matsushita Denshi Kogyo	X			X			
Matsushita Sangyo Kiki		X				X	
Matsushita Refrigeration					X	X	X
Kyushu Matsushita						X	
Matsushita Precision Manufacturing					X		X
Matsushita Housing Construction					X	X	X

[a]AV = audio-visual; Info = information; FA = factory automation; IC = semi-conductors; 'Living' = white goods and home automation; Auto = automobile components; En = environment.

projects with government laboratories and materials and component suppliers and with universities overseas. And Matsushita is by no means atypical.

Those studying R&D in Japanese firms face a set of challenges in coming to grips with the issues of structure and process in Japanese firms. We have long understood that the 'large' Japanese firm is not as large as its Western counterparts, but few writers have come to grips with the implications of this difference in structure; to the extent that they have dealt with the phenomenon at all, they have instead been fascinated by trying to explain *why* the firm is smaller, rather than in trying to understand what difference it makes. But studies of the R&D function in Japanese firms cannot avoid the issue. In 1985, for example, Matsushita Denki, the parent company of the Matsushita group, had 39,403 employees, 7,160 of whom (18 per cent) were defined as being in R&D development. Canon had 15,800 employees, of whom 4,300 (27 per cent) were in R&D. Kao had 5,833, of whom 1,520

(26 per cent) were in R&D (data supplied to the Japan Management Association, published in Nihon Noritsu Kyokai 1987). The structure of the Japanese corporation, where vertical disaggregation is spurred by the very strong pressures to homogenize salaries and rewards within the boundaries of the firm discussed above, means that the 'large' company centres on technology development and final assembly for its core businesses, and also contains the standard corporate staff functions such as planning and finance; it spins off component production, much of sales and distribution, and less strategic businesses into subsidiaries. In consequence, one might argue, the 'large' Japanese firm avoids some of the inertia believed to come from large size (especially constraints on information flows), and by centring the company on technology development and manufacturing it raises the salience of those functions in decision-making and strategy formation.

But in addition, the disaggregation involves the development of an R&D network that extends beyond the forms boundaries of the parent firm, and it is not easy to understand how that network is managed. We now think we understand the typical career path of a researcher in the corporate R&D structures of the parent company—or at least, the typical path in the mid-1980s—but we do not understand the paths of those in the main subsidiaries of the parent company. We do not know the scope of responsibility of the Technology Planning Departments that emerged in the late 1970s and 1980s: do they co-ordinate the activities of only the parent company's technology development units, those of all the subsidiaries, or those of the major subsidiaries? We might assume as a working hypothesis that the isomorphism in structures and the parallel hierarchies observable between R&D and manufacturing in the parent companies also operates across the dispersed R&D units of the affiliated companies. However, the homogenization of rewards assumed to be important in the movement of people and in smooth co-operation within the parent firm clearly does not operate across the group. What implications does this have for co-ordination? At the level of the Japanese technology system as a whole, we do not know whether the R&D capabilities of medium-sized firms within a major group like Matsushita or Hitachi are greater or less than those of their independent counterparts. As interest from Western scholars and businessmen in the medium and small-scale firms in the Japanese technology system grows, these questions will begin to loom larger.

But why should Japanese companies be interested in studying (or in co-operating with the study of) their own extended R&D networks, which apparently operate so well? One possbile answer is that, as they extend their networks across international borders, they find that integrating offshore R&D centres and foreign partners into the networks is more difficult than they anticipated, in part because they do not themselves understand the essential features that make their existing networks function. And, as they move up the value-added chain in research into more advanced development and basic research, they are facing the prospect of changes to their current system, with great uncertainties about how such changes will affect the dispersed R&D network. In the 1990s, therefore, we can expect to see the focus of research on Japanese research shift from the corporate laboratory to the company R&D network.

5. CONCLUSION

The 1980s witnessed major changes in Japan's R&D system. However, as the aggregate comparative data of Table 1 indicated, Japan was not alone in experiencing a decade of change. In response to the recession and increased international competition, US companies engaged in major reorganizations of the R&D function, and in the process turned to their Japanese competitors for ideas for closer integration of R&D, manufacturing, and customers. Some of the longstanding pillars of the US R&D system— AT&T, Eastman Kodak, Dupont—tried to focus their efforts more closely on product development and to link their researchers more tightly to the discipline of the market and the business divisions.

However while many of the studies of Japanese R&D in the 1980s were driven by the desire of management researchers on both sides of the Pacific and of Western managers to understand and learn from the Japanese experience, Japanese research managers were increasingly concerned with the challenges of building more creative research organizations with greater capabilities in basic research and radical product innovations. They looked very deliberately to Western models. A 1986 survey by the Japan Management Association asked Japanese research managers what techniques their companies were using to enhance the creativity of researchers. Five were cited by more than a quarter of the respondents: *bureinsuto-mingu* (a transliteration of 'brainstorming'); *KJ-ho* (KJ method); *PERT-ho* (PERT method); *chekurisuto-ho* ('checklist method'); and *NM-ho* (NM method). The very use of the Western terms indicates how much the companies have turned to Western models; indeed, of the fifteen methods mentioned by the respondents, only four were described by Japanese characters rather than transliterations of Western terms (JMA 1987: 436–8). How widely these methods were actually applied, and the extent to which they changed in adapting to the Japanese environment, is a matter for further research; but the use of the terms alone indicates that Japanese R&D managers in the 1980s were drawing on their Western counterparts for organizational technology, even as they were reducing their propensity to look to them for 'hard' technology.

What we observed—but have not yet systematically analysed—in the 1980s was an unprecedented period of cross-border mutual organizational learning in R&D across the Pacific. Following the changing patterns of R&D organization in Japan over the next decade will require more detailed study of the processes of cross-border learning, as they are enhanced (or perhaps inhibited) by the growing internationalization of the R&D function itself.

NOTE TO CHAPTER 6

1. Based on information from returning MIT–Japan programme interns, several of whom have described the flurry of activity in their research groups when the end of the 'patent year' approaches without the group's having met its quota: researchers 'brainstorm' to develop patent ideas to meet their quota, well aware that many of these proposed patents will never actually be granted or provide much value to the company.

REFERENCES

Abegglen, James (1958), *The Japanese Factory*. Free Press, Glencoe, Ill.

Abegglen, James, and Stalk, George (1985), *Kaisha: The Japanese Corporation*, Basic Books, New York.

Aoki, Masahiko (ed.) 1984, *The Economic Analysis of the Japanese Firm*. New-Holland, Amsterdam.

——(1988), *Information, Incentives, and Bargaining in the Japanese Economy*, Cambridge University Press.

Bartholemew, James (1989), *The Formation of Science in Japan*, Yale University Press, New Haven, Conn.

Brooks, Harvey (1986), 'National Science Policy and Technological Innovation', in R. Landau and N. Rosenberg (eds.), *The Positive Sum Strategy*, National Academy Press, Washington DC, 119–67.

Clark, Rodney (1979), *The Japanese Company*, Yale University Press, New Haven, Conn.

Commission on the History of Science and Technology Policy (1991), *Historical Review of Japanese Science and Technology Policy*, Society of Non-traditional Technology, Tokyo.

Derian, Jean-Claude (1990), *America's Struggle for Leadership in Technology*. MIT Press, Cambridge, Mass.

DiMaggio, Paul J. and Powell, Walter W. (1983), 'The Iron Cage Revisited:

Institutional Isomorphism and Collective Rationality in Organizational Fields', *American Sociological Review*, 35: 147–60.

Dore, Ronald (1988), *Taking Japan Seriously: A Confucian Perspective on Leading Economic Issues*, Athlone Press, London.

Ergas, Henry (1987), 'Does Technology Policy Matter?' in B. R. Guile and H. Brooks (eds.), *Technology and Global Industry: Companies and Nations in the World Economy*, National Academy Press, Washington, DC, 191–245.

Hall, Frank M. and Azumi, Koya (1989), 'Teamwork in Japanese Labs', *Research. Technology Management*, 32 (6): 21–6.

Henderson, Rebecca (1991), 'Successful Japanese Giants: A Major Challenge to Existing Theories of Technological Capability', Working Paper, Massachusetts Institute of Technology.

Herbert, Evan (1989), 'Japanese R&D in the United States', *Research. Technology Management*, 32 (6): 11–20.

—— (1990), 'How Japanese Companies Set R&D Directions', *Research. Technology Management*, 33 (5): 28–37.

Hughes, Thomas P. (1989), *American Genesis: A Century of Invention and Technological Enthusiasm*, Viking Press, New York.

Imai, K., Nonaka, I., and Takeuchi, H. (1985), 'Managing the New Product Development Process: How Japanese Companies Learn and Unlearn', in Kim Clark *et al.* (eds.), *The Uneasy Alliance*, Harvard Business School Press, Boston.

JMA (1987), *see* Nihon Noritsu Kyokai (1987).

Kagaku Gijutsu Cho Gijutsu Seisaku Kyoku (1984), *Kagaku Gijutsu Hakusho: Johoka no Arata na Tenkai ni Mukete* (White Paper on Science and Technology: Facing a New Stage of Information), Okura-sho Insatsu Kyoku, Tokyo.

—— (1986), *Kagaku Gijutsu Hakusho: Kokusai Hikaku to Kongo no Kadai* (Science and Technology White Paper: Topics in International Comparisons Now and in the Future), Okura-sho Insatsu Kyoku, Tokyo.

—— (1987), *Kagaku Gijutsu Yoran (Showa 62 Nenpan)* (Science and Technology Indicators 1987), Okura-sho Insatsu Kyoku, Tokyo.

—— (1990), *Kagaku Gijutsu Yoran (Heisei 2 Nenpan)* (Science and Technology Indicators 1990), Okura-sho Insatsu Kyoku, Tokyo.

Mansfield, Edwin (1988*a*), 'Industrial Innovation in Japan and the United States', *Science*, no. 241: 1769–74.

—— (1988*b*), 'Industrial R&D in Japan and the United States', *American Economic Review*, 78(2): 223–8.

—— (1988*c*), 'The Speed and Cost of Industrial Innovation in Japan and the United States: External vs. Internal Technology', *Management Science*, 34(10): 1157–68.

National Research Council (1989), *Learning the R&D System: University Research in Japan and the United States*, National Academy Press, Washington, DC.

National Science Foundation (1988), *International Science and Technology Update 1988* (NSF 89–307), Washington, DC.

Nihon Noritsu Kyokai (Japan Management Association) (1987), *Senshin Kigyo sanjusha in miru Kenkyujo Un'ei Hasseika Jitsureishu* (Collected Cases of Energising Laboratory Management as seen in Thirty Leading Firms), Nihon Noritsu Kyokai, Tokyo.

Nonaka, Ikujiro (1990), 'Redundant, Overlapping Organization: A Japanese Approach to Innovation', *California Management Review*, 32(3): 27–38.

Okimoto, Daniel, and Saxonhouse, Gary (1987), 'Technology and the Future of the Economy', in K. Yamamura and Y. Yasuba (eds.), *The Political Economy of Japan: The Domestic Transformation*, Stanford University Press, Stanford, Calif., 385–419.

Patrick, Hugh (ed.) (1986), *Japan's High Technology Industries: Lessons and Limitations of Industrial Policy*, University of Washington Press, Seattle.

Reich, Michael R. (1990), 'Why the Japanese Don't Export More Pharmaceuticals: Health Policy as Industrial Policy', *California Management Review*, 32(2): 124–50.

Rosenberg, Nathan, and Steinmueller, W. Edward (1988), 'Why Are Americans Such Poor Imitators?' *American Economic Review*', 78(2): 229–34.

Sakakibara, Kiyonori (1988), 'Increasing Basic Research in Japan: Corporate Activity Alone Is Not Enough', Working Paper no. 8802, Hitotsubashi University.

——and Westney, D. E. (1992), 'Japan's Management of Global Innovation: Technology Management Crossing Borders', in N. Rosenberg, R. Landau, and D. C. Mowery (eds.), *Technology and the Wealth of Nations*, Stanford University Press, Stanford, Calif.

Saxonhouse, Gary (1986), 'Industrial Policy and Factor Markets: Biotechnology in Japan and the United States', in Hugh Patrick (ed.), *Japan's High Technology Industries*, University of Washington Press, Seattle.

Scherer, F. M. (1980), *Industrial Market Structure and Economic Performance*, Rand McNally, Chicago.

Scott, W. Richard (1987), 'The Adolescence of Institutional Theory', *Administrative Science Quarterly*, 32: 493–511.

Slaughter, Sarah, and Utterback, James (1990), 'US Research and Development: An International Comparative Analysis', *Business in the Contemporary World*, 2(1).

Stalk, George Jr, and Hout, Thomas M. (1990), *Competing Against Time: How Time-Based Competition is Reshaping Global Markets*, Free Press, New York.

Sun, Marjorie (1989), 'Japan Faces Big Task in Improving Basic Science', *Science*, no. 243 (10 March): 1205–7.

Takara Soichiro, (1989), *Nichibei Interijensu Senso* (The Japan–US Intelligence War), Bungei Shunju, Tokyo.

Takeuchi, H., and Nonaka, I. (1986), 'The New New Product Development Game', *Harvard Business Review*, Jan.–Feb.

Taylor, Mary Sullivan (1989), 'A Transactions Cost Analysis of Japanese Employment Relationships', Ph.D. dissertation, University of Washington.

Tsusho Sangyo Sho Sangyo Seisaku Kigyo Kodoka (1990), *Sogo Keieiryoku Shihyo: Seizogyo hen* (Indicators of General Management Strength), Okurasho Insatsu Kyoku, Tokyo.

Wakasugi Ryuhei (1989), 'Kenkyu Kaihatsu no soshiki to Kodo' (The Conduct and Organization of R&D), in K. Imai and R. Komiya (eds), *Nihon no Kigyo*, Tokyo Daigaku Shuppankai, Tokyo.

Westney, D. Eleanor (1988), 'Domestic and Foreign Learning Curves in Managing International Cooperative Strategies', in F. Constractor and P. Lorange (eds.), *Cooperative Strategies in International Business*, Lexington Books, Lexington, Mass.

——(1993), 'Country Patterns in R&D Organization: The United States and Japan',

in Bruce Kogut (ed.), *Country Competitiveness and the Organizing of Work*, Oxford University Press.
——and Sakakibara, Kiyonori, (1985), 'The Organization and Careers of Engineers in the Computer Industry in Japan and the United States', Working Paper, Massachusetts Institute of Technology.
Yamamura, Kozo (1986), 'Joint Research and Antitrust: Japanese vs. American Strategies', in Hugh Patrick (ed.), *Japan's High Technology Industries: Lessons and Limitations of Industrial Policy*, University of Washington Press, Seattle, 171–209.

7

R&D Organization in Japanese and American Semiconductor Firms

DANIEL I. OKIMOTO AND YOSHIO NISHI

1. INTRODUCTION

The Semiconductor Industry

Since 1980, more attention in the West has been paid to Japan's performance in the semiconductor industry than to any other industry, with the possible exception of automobiles (Okimoto et al. 1984; Okimoto 1989; Borrus 1988; Finan and Frey 1989; Gilder 1989). How Japan fares in semiconductors, a crucial upstream segment of the epoch-making information industries, is regarded as the most telling test of its ability to make the tough transition from smokestack sectors to high technology.

Japan's successes in heavy manufacturing and assembly have been attributed to the distinctive features of its industrial organization: specifically, its labour and capital markets, employment system, corporate organization, management strategy, subcontracting networks, and close working relationships with business and government. Such features have made it possible for Japan to meet the functional requirements of heavy manufacturing and assembly (e.g. shipbuilding, steel, and automobiles). Japanese industrial organization has been particularly well suited for long production runs, quality control, and the smooth co-ordination of extended supplier and distributor networks.

Are the features that gave Japan a commanding advantage in heavy manufacturing equally well suited to meet the different functional imperatives of high technology? In semiconductors, generating a continuous stream of new technology and bringing one generation after another of new products rapidly to market are essential to compete effectively in global markets. Do such features of Japanese industrial organization as 'no exit' employment lend themselves to the task of adapting to a fast-moving technological and commercial environment? Or do the inherent rigidities built into Japan's system of industrial organization outweigh the advantages (Dore 1987)?

For more than a century, Japan has been stuck with the reputation of being a nation of imitators rather than innovators. At its core, the stereotype of Japan as a nation of copy-cats, incapable of achieving anything more than incremental innovation, is founded on assumptions about the *dysfunctionalism of Japanese organizations*. Such institutions as Japan's educational system, which stresses rote memorization, have been cited as reasons for the puzzling paucity of Japanese contributions to the world's storehouse of seminal discoveries.

Industrial Organization

This paper takes issue with the notion that there is a fundamental incompatibility between Japanese industrial organization and the country's capacity to innovate. The notion is easy enough to dispel. Consider the straightforward empirical facts. Japanese companies control half of the world semiconductor market (Fig. 1). Of the world's ten biggest semiconductor manufacturers, seven are Japanese. As one might expect from such market dominance, Japanese firms have excelled in certain areas of technology such as VLSIs (very large-scale integrated circuits), commodity chips, liquid crystal displays, and semiconductor equipment (e.g. lithography steppers and wire bonders). Thus, causal arguments attributing Japan's

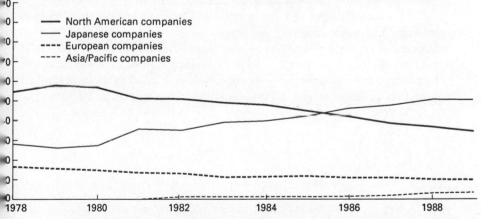

FIG. 1   Regional Shares of the Worldwide Semiconductor Market, 1978–1989
Source: Dataquest Inc., January 1990.

poor R&D performance to distinctive features of Japanese industrial organization are empirically unfounded. Since Japanese firms have proven that they can innovate, the notion that Japanese industrial organization is an insuperable barrier to technological progress can be dismissed.

If Japanese industrial organization is not a stumbling bloc, can we go so far as to say that it actually facilitates innovation? One school of scholars, led by Ken'ichi Imai, argues that old institutions have been adapted to serve positive functions in the processes of innovation, (Imai 1989; Hayashi 1989). This paper can be said to fall into the Imai school in that it calls attention to certain features of Japanese industrial organization—most notably the employment system—that have functioned to advance research and development for certain types of technology. This is seen in the case of floppy disks, discrete devices, and VLSI commodity chips such as DRAMS (dynamic random access memories) and SRAMS (static random access memories).

But this paper diverges from the Imai school in pointing out that some of the same features have also made it difficult to innovate in other areas of technology, such as CPUs (central processing units), MPUs (microprocessing units), and systems and applications software. Hence no simple, clear-cut generalization is possible. What we loosely call 'industrial organization' is so encompassing that it rarely turns out to have only one-dimensional effects. The presumption that the composite elements fit together neatly and function as an integrated system is empirically naive. Organizational features may not only not fit, but may even work at cross-purposes, contrary to structural–functional notions of long-term trends towards evolutionary alignment.

It is possible to argue, of course, that industrial organization in Japan holds together at a higher level of coherence than those of other nations, given the unusual degree of homogeneity and the long period of indigenous gestation; but even Japanese industrial organization contains a mix of positive and negative elements that both impede and facilitate innovation—some of which can be changed, others of which cannot be easily adapted. The positive and negative elements (and their degrees of malleability) affect innovation in different and complicated ways, depending on the nature of the technology in question.

Focus

This paper seeks to identify and assess some of the distinctive features of research and development activities in Japanese semiconductor firms, using comparisons with US firms which have succeeded against tough competition on the basis of continuous R&D breakthroughs. It addresses three broad questions: (1) What are some of the salient differences in R&D approach and organization between Japanese and American semiconductor companies? (2) Why have they developed? and (3) What have been the consequences?

2.   R&D EXPENDITURE

Japanese Corporations: Deep Pockets?

In the United States, where the Japanese have cycled huge capital surpluses, Japanese corporations appear to be cash-rich (Prestowitz 1988). Japanese corporations give the impression of being able to dig deeply into almost bottomless pockets to allocate substantial portions of sales revenue for R&D. Is this image accurate? Do Japanese companies invest a larger share of revenues on R&D than their US counterparts? If so, the higher level of capital expenditure alone might explain Japan's capacity to come from so far behind, so rapidly, to reach the competitive position it now enjoys in the semiconductor industry.

Finding accurate, industry-specific, and company-specific data is difficult; but based on dated figures for the top twenty Japanese and American companies across all sectors for 1983, Abegglen and Stalk found that American firms spend considerably more on R&D in absolute dollar amounts; however, Japanese firms set aside a higher percentage of sales revenue for R&D, which means that, over time, they are raising R&D outlays at a faster rate (Abegglen and Stalk 1985). As time passes, the compound effects of rising R&D expenditure are bound to be felt.

Comparisons of R&D expenditure as a percentage of sales, however, should be broken down into industry- and company-specific categories, since patterns vary by sectors and by company. In some sectors, like chemicals, American and Japanese companies allocate roughly the same percentage of revenue; in others, like aerospace, American manufacturers outspend their Japanese counterparts by a wide margin. Aggregate generalizations thus fail to convey important micro-level information.

What about semiconductors? The semiconductor industry is an interesting but perhaps atypical case. In contrast to chemicals and aerospace, Japanese semiconductor manufacturers have outspent their US competitors by an order of magnitude. Between 1974 and 1984, Japanese firms sustained R&D investment at nearly twice the rate of US companies (based on percentage of sales revenue); moreover, if one includes capital investment in semiconductor plant facilities and equipment, the size of the gap is even greater (Fig. 2). Although the gap has narrowed recently, especially with the economic downturn and the deflation of Japan's speculative bubble in 1992, Japanese companies continue to demonstrate a propensity to invest a larger share of revenues for R&D and new plant facilities.

High and sustained investment rates confirm the image of Japanese corporations as aggressive, free-spending competitors. Japanese semiconductor manufacturers use the vast financial resources at their disposal to pursue long-run goals, even those that may require that they forsake short-term profits. Over the long haul, the pursuit of strategic goals places

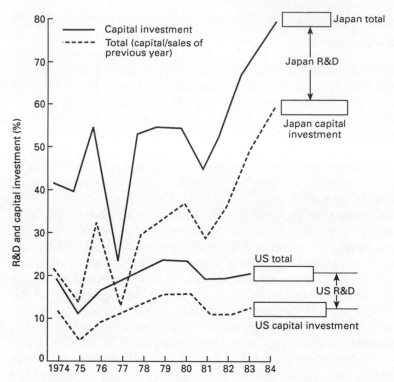

FIG. 2   US–Japanese Semiconductor R&D/Capital Investment, 1974–1984

them in a strong position to expand market share and strengthen their competitive position. What such R&D expenditures also suggest is that large Japanese electronics companies have placed a very high priority on semiconductor research and development. As the most important upstream link to a large and diversified downstream cluster of industries, semi-conductors have been cultivated to serve as the seedbed soil for the growth of consumer electronics, computers, machine tools, telecommunications, and other high-tech sectors.

Stable Patterns

In addition to disparities in R&D spending for the semiconductor industry as a whole, American–Japanese differences at the disaggregated level of individual companies are also striking. R&D expenditure at Japanese companies is measurably more stable over time. The variability in Japanese R&D expenditure is narrower, owing to several underlying factors: (1) company size; (2) high degree of diversification and vertical integration; (3)

cash-rich capital markets; (4) the staying power of intra-industry standards (*yoko narabi*); and (5) long-term employment practices.

The first three factors have been thoroughly analysed already and will not be treated here at any length (see Flaherty and Itami 1984). Suffice it to say that the large, vertically integrated and diversified Japanese corporations—unlike the small- or medium-sized merchant semiconductor houses in the United States—have the capacity not only to raise bigger sums on capital markets (based on the 'main bank' system), but also to siphon off revenues from other product divisions (such as consumer products and home appliances) to underwrite semiconductor research and development. This means that there are big differences not only in the size of the revenue streams, but also in terms of the built-in insulation against cyclical fluctuations in semiconductor demand (since Japanese companies may be able to sell refrigerators when semiconductor sales are down). Thus, the first three factors listed above contribute to the greater stability in Japanese patterns of R&D investments.

To explain why different types of companies tend to cluster together in predictable spending patterns, the psychology of *yoko narabi* (that is, looking at what competitors of comparable size and prestige invest and adjusting one's own R&D levels accordingly) must also be factored into the equation. *Yoko narabi*, together with long-term employment practices (the fifth underlying factor), help to explain why there is so little deviation from the pattern of spending 12–14 per cent of semiconductor revenues for R&D. On a comparative basis, this range is exceedingly high. By contrast, a US company that is renowned for staying ahead of the technological curb, Intel Corporation, reinvests only about 10 per cent of revenues from microprocessor sales for R&D even though Intel's microprocessors have been selling at premium prices.

Remarkably, general R&D expenditure for all products (not just semiconductors) of Japan's electronic giants cluster closely within a narrow band. Traditionally, Hitachi has been the pace-setter in terms of pushing R&D expenditure towards the higher end of the range; but since the mid-1980s Fujitsu and NEC have moved out ahead. Not to be outdone, the other major players—Hitachi and Toshiba—have tried to keep pace, not wanting to fall behind the pack (Fig.3). Thus, the *yoko narabi* nature of budget-making ensures that, at the company level, R&D allocations tend to remain fairly stable.

A factor of even greater weight is the Japanese system of long-term employment. The company's commitment to career-long employment means that the aggregate number of researchers employed by Japanese companies at any point in time remains fairly predictable. Ups and downs in business cycles do not lead to layoffs of full-time employees. *Constancy in the size of a company's research staff*, in turn, means that the level of R&D expenditure will not fluctuate much from year to year. Salary outlays, the

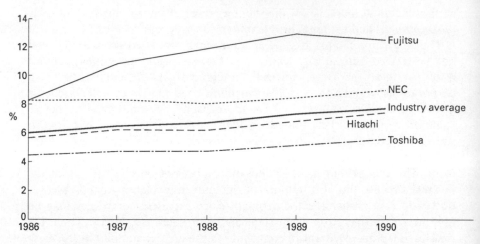

F_IG. 3   R&D as a Percentage of Total Sales: Major Japanese Companies,
1986–1990

biggest portion of R&D costs, stay within a narrow band.

Of course, with retirements and unexpected departures, the size of the
technical work-force can change from year to year; but management seeks
to keep the number in general equilibrium relative to the company's research
needs and goals. Equilibrium is achieved by adjusting the number of college
recruits to offset unexpected departures and the anticipation of expanding
needs. Because the size of the technical work-force represents a *fixed cost*
for Japanese firms, careful planning goes into all decisions affecting the size
and composition of the research staff.

By looking at the 'demographics' of the R&D work-force, we get an
organizational perspective on Japan's high and sustained R&D investments;
the organizational considerations call into question the orthodox explanations based on the presumed far-sightedness and superiority of Japanese
corporate strategy. It may be true that Japanese corporations operate on a
longer time horizon, as many analysts have argued (Abegglen and Stalk
1985; Kotler, *et al.* 1985), but the structural imperative that gives rise to the
longer time horizon is the company's commitment to permanent employment. It is the constant size of its R&D work-force, more than superior
corporate planning and strategy, that explains the continuity of R&D
budgets. Indeed, it is the company's commitment to long-term employment
that forces Japanese management to engage in long-term, strategic planning.

In the United States, by contrast, labour mobility means not only that
continuity in corporate R&D activities is disrupted, but also that the
aggregate number of researchers fluctuates. Such variability is bound to be
reflected in fluctuating R&D budgets. US companies can hire and fire as
business circumstances warrant; and employees can enter and leave freely,

as opportunities arise. To cope with recessions, US semiconductor companies lay R&D personnel off, cancel research projects, and cut back on R&D and capital expenditure.

What Hirschman calls the 'exit option' affects R&D in both positive and negative ways (Hirschman 1970). On the positive side, it gives companies the flexibility to cut fixed and variable costs during recessions, to shift research capabilities quickly, and to bring new technology into the firm by hiring researchers from the outside. On the negative side, it leads to costly disruptions in R&D, erodes company loyalty, plays to short-term incentives, and discourages investment in the development of human capital. On balance, the long-run costs can outweigh the short-term benefits. What is especially damaging is the difficulty of sustaining momentum and continuity in R&D.

Japan's employment system also weighs heavily in all decisions regarding R&D directions, including funding approval for specific R&D projects. In deciding whether or not to invest in certain R&D projects, Japanese managers focus on how best to utilize the company's fixed human resource base in ways that meet the technological requisites of global competitiveness. Making best use of the company's R&D work-force is often the decisive factor in determining whether to go ahead with risky R&D investments, or whether to move into new product markets.

For US firms, by contrast, the overriding concern is to maximize financial returns on investment. To this end, a variety of quantitative methodologies have been adopted to assess risks and returns, especially discounted cash flow (Hodder 1986). Although Japanese companies also subject investments to financial analysis, their analytical tools are not nearly as sophisticated as those taught in American business schools. More reliance is placed on thoroughgoing discussions of the pros and cons of moving in certain technological directions, with careful attention being paid to the hidden and explicit assumptions underlying scenarios of likely outcomes. Instead of letting financial considerations and number-crunching (e.g. net present value or internal rate of return) dictate R&D decisions, Japanese management places greater emphasis on what it will take, technologically, to be a world-class competitor and how to make best use of the research talent to reach the company's goals.

In terms of specific allocations in the R&D budget, anywhere from 18 to 25 per cent (roughly 2.5–3.0 per cent of sales revenues) is earmarked for basic and advanced development research, carried out largely at the company's central research laboratory. The bulk of the R&D budget, anywhere from 75 to 82 per cent (or roughly 10–11 per cent of sales revenues), is spent for applied research and development, most of which is product development and manufacturing technology, done by the various product divisions and at factory sites. The emphasis placed on product development and process technology is perhaps the main reason why Japanese firms can bring new products so quickly to market; and rapid turn-around time is often the key to large sales revenues and future R&D allocations.

Flexibility

In absolute amounts, R&D investment usually increases each year in tandem with the growth of sales revenue. If revenue grows by 10 per cent, R&D investment usually expands by the same amount. While allocations for the central research laboratory as a share of R&D expenditure remain very stable, the amounts allocated to individual divisions can change over time. If certain divisions demonstrate a higher level of productive output, those divisions can obtain merit increases. The same is true of research teams within individual divisions. Working within this merit-based system, semi-conductor divisions with a proven track record can receive stronger support for R&D than other divisions.

Budgets for research groups come from a variety of quarters. Funds for the central research laboratory, where basic and advanced developmental research is conducted, come largely from corporate headquarters. Work at the divisional development laboratories, where product development and process technology take place, is underwritten by each division. Funds for factory engineering laboratories, where manufacturing specifications and processes are ironed out, come out of the budgets for each factory. Having separate funding sources gives the research labs some degree of autonomy, which is necessary in order for each of them to make progress without a lot of centralized micro-management (Aoki 1988). At the same time, budgetary decentralization does not prevent the various laboratories from engaging in close, ongoing interaction, which is also necessary for technology to make its way along the lengthy pipeline from the central research laboratory to the factory floor.

Another feature of R&D budgeting in Japan is the flexibility built into off-budget supplements. Japanese R&D managers have the authority to supplement R&D funds for specific projects in amounts of up to 50 per cent. If, at a critical stage of product development, a research team encounters unforeseen obstacles or cost overruns and needs an immediate infusion of capital to finish its project, the team can go to its R&D manager, who has the authority to approve the funding supplement quickly. Off-budget supplements are much harder to obtain in US companies, where approval is less certain, takes a lot longer, and entails greater bureaucratic red tape. Having supplemental support readily available may be an important and overlooked reason for Japan's capacity to bring products to market so quickly. Japanese firms seem capable of moving faster than American or European firms through the commercialization cycle—from research to development and through to manufacturing and marketing. In an industry like semiconductors, where the technological and commercial environment changes at such high speeds, turn-around time can be of decisive importance (Stalk and Hout 1990).

If R&D expenditures are relatively large and stable, how do Japanese companies make budget reductions when the situation calls for it? Or are they insulated from cyclical perturbations? Looking back at cyclical drops in semiconductor demand, we see that Japanese firms continued to invest more heavily than US firms during the recessions of 1975, 1981, and 1984–5; nevertheless, Fig. 2 shows that Japanese R&D levels fell in the 1975 recession and plummeted in the 1977 recession. This shows that Japanese companies are by no means immune to the impact of business cycles.

If, during severe recessions, R&D budgets have to be trimmed, and if the size of the research staff cannot be pared down, where can cuts be made? Here, as elsewhere, the budget making process is predictable, taking place within the framework of routinized procedures. The easiest target for budget-cutting is the purchase of research equipment and materials. As much as 20 per cent of R&D budgets can be pared through the postponement or cancellation of new equipment purchases. Of course, cutbacks in procurement cannot be continued for more than a year or two without seriously hampering long-term R&D activities; but as a temporary stop-gap measure, such reductions offer a way around having to resort to potentially more damaging cutbacks in research personnel. If the circumstances are severe enough that cutbacks in R&D personnel cannot be avoided, then the usual procedure is to let natural attrition take place through retirements, to offer incentives for early retirement, to send employees out to subsidiaries, and to reduce the number of incoming recruits—all of which lead to a net reduction in the R&D staff without having to resort to layoffs.

Periodic belt-tightening can have beneficial effects. It creates a sense of crisis, which forces R&D teams to become more efficient. Indeed, a sense of crisis can be used as a legitimizing instrument to *improve per capital R&D output*. Using simple accounting procedures, we note that any reduction of R&D expenditure automatically raises the per capita output of research, if the number of researchers is held constant and there is no fall-off in research performance. In US companies, by contrast, the strategy of reducing R&D expenditure by laying off technical manpower does little to improve per capita R&D output. It merely shrinks the manpower pool without improving the efficiency of labour inputs.

Japanese semiconductor companies are not content simply to cut costs. To raise per capita output beyond the limits of simple cost-cutting, they often take steps to enforce more demanding deadlines, to reassess and clarify R&D priorities, to upgrade communications and intra-company co-ordination, and to eliminate extraneous activities. Falling into the last category is 'unofficial' or 'under-the-table' research—that is, work that individual researchers may be allowed to carry on which is not directly tied to a company project. As 'under-the-table' research can consume as much as 10 per cent of a researcher's time, such belt-tightening measures can lead to non-trivial gains in efficiency.

3. ORGANIZATIONAL SETTING FOR R&D

Personnel Recruitment

So much has been written about Japan's employment system that what is by now familiar ground need not be gone over here (see Dore and Sako 1989; Clark 1979; Cole 1979; Chalmers 1989). Instead, this section will focus on lesser known aspects of Japanese corporate organization which affect the course of research and development. Particular attention will be paid to differences in the way Japanese and American companies organize to conduct R&D.

Perhaps the most striking cluster of characteristics in Japan's organizational setting for R&D is what might be labelled the *'C syndrome'*: contact, communication, collective learning capacity, caution, and conservatism. Japanese research teams are organized in ways that bring out these 'C syndrome' characteristics. To a large extent, the origins of the 'C syndrome' can be traced to the structure of long-term employment.

For Japanese semiconductor manufacturers, the employment system brings a preponderant number of technical recruits into the company's work-force. About 90 per cent of the yearly crop of college recruits have earned B.Sc. degrees in engineering or the natural sciences; only 10 per cent of the college recruits have non-technical, BA degrees. Take Toshiba: of the 1,100 recruits from college each year, 1,000 have B.Sc. degrees from Japan's leading universities, a far higher percentage of engineers than among recruits entering Hewlett-Packard or IBM. The 90 per cent figure has been constant over time, even as the absolute number of college recruits has doubled. In 1962 Toshiba hired 540 engineers and scientists out of an intake of 600.

The preponderance of technical employees who spend their entire careers in the same company gives rise to the following consequences: (1) a clear understanding of, and strong orientation towards, technology; (2) extensive in-house training and close, on-going interaction among members of the R&D staff; (3) a large R&D infrastructure that has to be utilized fully; (4) a mix of relative strengths and weaknesses in research capabilities; and (5) a preponderance of managers and executives with scientific and engineering backgrounds.

On the surface, the deeply entrenched features of Japan's employment system—such as the recruitment of engineering graduates from prestige universities—would appear likely to give rise to rigidities. For instance, since the pool of B.Sc. graduates from élite universities is limited, what happens when the growing need for engineers outstrips the supply—which is the case today? Do the blue-chip companies expand their traditional base of recruitment to incorporate non-élite universities, thereby diluting the prestige of their recruits? Does pragmatic need override concern with prestige?

The solution to this manpower dilemma has been quintessentially Japanese. To meet spiralling manpower needs, Japanese corporations have had to broaden their recruiting base to include second- and third-tier universities. However, instead of bringing them straight into corporate headquarters, they have established a maze of small, wholly owned subsidiaries, such as software subsidiaries, where non-élite college recruits are placed. In this way, the prestige of the parent company is protected while its manpower needs are fulfilled. The training that non-élite recruits receive is virtually the same as for the élite group; so, too, is the pay. Once inside the company, there are ample opportunities for lateral mobility into the parent company, not to mention upward mobility into the managerial hierarchy. Interestingly, the experience of the blue-chip electronics corporations indicates that the differences between élite and non-élite recruits are slight in terms of not only overall ability, but also on-the-job performance.

Subsidiaries and Industrial Structure

The creation of small subsidiaries to house non-elite recruits is part of the overall process of 'hiving off' R&D budgets and activities from the centralized core (parent corporation) to small, decentralized clusters on the periphery (subsidiaries). Aoki has called attention to this trend. Such decentralization is sometimes considered Japan's functional equivalent to America's structure of vertical disintegration and its system of venture-capital-driven entrepreneurship. It serves to keep the parent company from ballooning beyond manageable proportions. By 'hiving off' personnel and R&D functions to semi-autonomous subsidiaries, the leanness, core business focus, corporate culture, and organizational integrity of large parent companies can be maintained. Japanese firms do not turn into unwieldy conglomerates.

But the Silicon Valley analogy is somewhat misleading, in that: (1) the semi-autonomous subsidiaries and independent start-ups in America are very different; (2) the impact of subsidiaries on the well-being of large Japanese companies is positive—compared with the disruptive impact of start-ups in the case of established US companies; (3) the US system of venture start-ups has functioned to generate more new products and greater technological innovation than the Japanese system of subsidiaries; (4) the structure of incentives for individuals could hardly be more contrasting; and (5) the role the two systems play in the R&D processes differ markedly.

In the United States, large corporations suffer costly discontinuities when key researchers, engaged in important ongoing projects, leave to form their own companies. Instead of tying up with these entrepreneurial start-ups (though ties are now expanding), large US companies fight to retain control over proprietary technology in order to compete vigorously for shares of burgeoning niche markets. On balance, venture start-ups have functioned to: (1) counteract forces moving the industry towards market concentration; (2) keep barriers to entry low; and (3) serve as a catalyst for innovation and change in the US semiconductor industry. Ironically, Japanese companies have managed to take better advantage of the technology access made possible through the channel of strategic alliances with small US companies than have large US corporations (Okimoto *et al.* 1992). Only recently have large US corporations showed signs of interest in learning how to develop synergies with small, independent companies.

In Japan, the small subsidiaries have been created to serve the interests of parent corporations. Not surprisingly, they have helped perpetuate, rather than shake up, the structure of big-company dominance. So far, at least, they have not played the same catalytic role in new product and software innovation as have the entrepreneurial start-ups in the United States. Small size, flexibility, and informality—organizational assets that new subsidiaries offer—might be the functional requisites that Japan will need to incorporate in order to compete at the cutting edge of technology in the future. For the time being, however, Japanese subsidiaries tend to be engaged in R&D activities in the older, non-mainstream areas of waning commercial value, such as pressure control devices, or in newly emerging, non-traditional areas of still uncertain commercial value, such as applications software for specific hardware devices.

Parent companies seldom rely on their subsidiaries to design and develop pivotal new products or process technologies, such as microprocessing units (MPUs) or state-of-the-art applications-specific integrated circuits (ASICs). Such products parent companies handle in-house, by themselves. Thus, under the present system the subsidiaries tend to be relegated to the peripheral areas of R&D; and, while they may be pulled eventually into the mainstream, their contributions are apt to be of significance only as supplements to the R&D being done within large corporations (except perhaps in the area of applications software).

Corporate Research Laboratories

All the Japanese electronics giants possess the technical manpower and financial resources necessary to support a multi-layered structure of research labs, for which there is no parallel in most US merchant semiconductor houses and electronics firms (see Figure 4). At the core of their research structure are big central research laboratories (CRLs), which have all but disappeared from the corporate scene in the United States except at IBM and AT&T. Japanese executives describe the research done at the CRLs as 'basic', although the term is hard to define, and long-term in nature, with projected time horizons of five to ten years. For financial reasons, the CRLs have been phased out at most US semiconductor firms, and basic

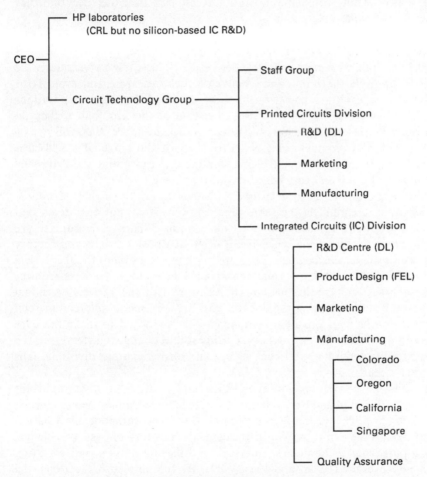

FIG. 4   R&D Organization in Hewlett Packard (HP), USA

research has passed from corporations, like the Bell Lab, into university-based laboratories, like the Center for Integrated Systems at Stanford, and to a lesser extent into industrial research consortia like SRC, the Semiconductor Research Consortium.

In spite of high costs, large uncertainties, and long time intervals before returns on investments come in, Japanese companies have decided not to follow America's lead in phasing out CRLs. They are convinced that they need to maintain an upstream scientific and technological base on which to build downstream products. Being vertically integrated, diversified corporations, with deep pockets and long time horizons, Japanese companies have both the incentives and the resources necessary to maintain the CRLs. The psychology of *yoko narabi*, alluded to earlier, may also be at work; if one or two leading companies operate CRLs, then the others feel that they must do the same.

Japanese universities also do not offer the same research facilities that American universities do. It would be hard, therefore, to shift to the US model of close university–industry ties. Even if Japanese universities were able to upgrade the scope and quality of their research, and even if the leeway for institutional co-operation were stretched, Japanese corporations would still want to keep their CRLs because of the fear that, if they do not preserve the strongest possible research base in-house, they will not be in a position to compete and will drop out of the circle of world-class companies. In contrast to US firms, Japanese corporations are driven by the urge to keep R&D capabilities in-house strong.

Japanese companies expect their CRLs to establish the highest standards of scientific research. At the same time, the CRLs cannot operate as Ivy-towered bastions of detached academic inquiry. These laboratories are supposed to facilitate the work being done at divisional labs and factory engineering research facilities. They are expected to develop the theoretical base for new product designs and new process technology. To do so requires close contact and continuous communication with the various divisional and factory labs, bridging the difficult gap between theory and commercial application. Not all Japanese companies have managed to make the connection. To bridge the gap, Japanese firms rotate young engineers from the CRL to divisional labs and back again, and also encourage divisional labs to fund research projects at the CRL.

Beyond its research mission, the CRLs fulfil a variety of other important functions, as Finan and Frey point out. These include training new engineers, providing overall and long-term research direction, gathering information from around the world, serving as the central repository of basic knowledge, developing core technologies, interfacing with universities, and elevating company prestige (Finan and Frey 1989). By fulfilling such functions, the CRLs have made themselves indispensable to their companies. Not all the R&D projects going on simultaneously in a Japanese company would proceed as smoothly if the CRL were not there, providing conceptual coherence and long-term direction. Compare this situation with that in US companies, where few CRLs even exist today. The comparison reveals a great deal about fundamental differences in the way Japanese and American semiconductor companies approach R&D.

Divisional and Factory Engineering Laboratories

Although the CRLs provide the theoretical underpinnings, the hard work of designing, developing, and manufacturing new products is done at the divisional and factory levels. Divisional laboratories (DLs) in Japan are similar to those in US companies, but what is distinctive about Japanese DLs is the nature of their linkages to other research entities within the firm—sandwiched between CRLs on the one side and factory engineering laboratories (FELs) at production sites on the other. Located at the fulcrum of R&D activities, the DLs can be considered the cornerstones of the corporate R&D structure; they function as the primary mechanism for technology fusion and diffusion within the Japanese firm (Fig. 5).

For DL research projects, the time horizon, from start to finish, is much shorter than for that of the CRLs. The typical time horizon ranges anywhere from one to three years. Within that time frame, DLs are expected to turn out product prototypes which can be produced in small volumes and debugged before being turned over to the factories for mass manufacturing. For commercialization to go forward, the DLs must be able to complete the tasks of designing new products and of ironing out all the problems of process technology within a schedule of very demanding deadlines.

Japanese DLs in the semiconductor industry, especially in commodity markets, such as DRAMs and SRAMs, have performed impressively, judging by the technological and commercial progress made by Japanese semiconductor manufacturers. The secret of the DLs' effectiveness lies in their collective learning capacity. That learning capacity is the by-product of the continuity of the R&D work-force (coming back again to the seminal impact of Japan's employment system). Continuity makes it possible to develop a corps of competent, seasoned research managers. It also facilitates unusually extensive 'body contact' between designers and production engineers at the FELs. The cohesion, continuity, collective learning, contact, and communications that set Japanese R&D apart emerge in large measure out of the practice of long-term employment.

Organizational Innovations

Perhaps the most striking feature of Japanese R&D in the semiconductor industry is the extraordinary degree of communication and 'body contact' that takes place at the various juncture and intersection points in the R&D processes—from basic research to advanced development, from advanced development to new product design, from new product design to new process technology, from new process technology to factory-site manufacturing, from manufacturing to marketing, and from marketing to servicing. Owing to pragmatic organizational innovations, Japanese semiconductor manufacturers have excelled—where many American and

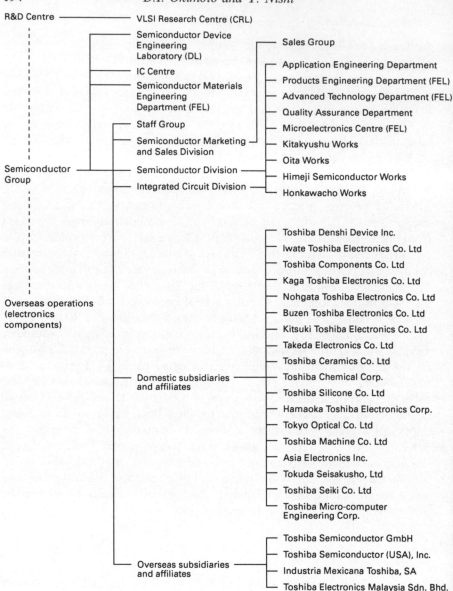

FIG. 5   R&D Organization in a Japanese Company

European manufacturers have faltered—at the seemingly simple but extremely difficult task of making smooth 'hand-offs' at each juncture along the long, interconnected R&D pipeline.

Recognizing the importance of co-ordinating the commercialization cycle,

Japanese companies have come up with some shrewd and innovative methods for facilitating technology transfer between research teams working on different aspects of semiconductor devices. Mention has already been made of the CRLs' functions in the company's R&D system. Equally noteworthy—and of greater commercial relevance—is the extensive interaction and technology transfer that takes place between the DLs and FELs. Not only do engineers from the DLs and FELs work together in joint research teams, but the DLs and FELs continually meet and interact in seeking to iron out problems that inevitably arise in mass-manufacturing new products.

The high priority placed on process technology and low manufacturing costs is reflected in the distribution of engineers within the Japanese company. The largest concentration is usually found at the FELs, located at factory sites where the messy problems of mass production have to be worked out. The majority of Japanese engineers have at least some exposure to manufacturing engineering as part of their job rotation and career training. Not only is there no stigma attached to manufacturing assignments; the ladder of promotion leading up into the higher reaches of executive management—and beyond (including *amakudari*, or post-career executive entry into new companies)—pass through jobs that involve hands-on manufacturing experience. It is almost a requirement for upward career and post-career mobility.

In the United States, by contrast, manufacturing engineers carry the stigma of being second-class citizens. To the manufacturing engineers falls the 'grubby' work of production—for which they receive lower pay and lower prestige compared with the 'glamorous' design jobs. In how many US semiconductor companies can it be said that the majority of engineers are engaged in manufacturing? Few, if any. And, looking at the large number of merchant semiconductor houses in Silicon Valley, we see that only a minority even possess manufacturing facilities, much less factory engineering laboratories.

Owing to the spiralling costs of new wafer fabrication facilities, virtually all of the new start-ups in Silicon Valley since 1986 have been 'fabless'—that is, without fabrication facilities (Okimoto *et al.* 1992). Such 'fabless' start-ups have entered into numerous foundry agreements with Japanese manufacturers, which offer quality, speed, and low-cost production. Few US foundries exist to which these start-ups might turn as alternative manufacturing sources. In helping to keep the system of venture start-ups alive and well, Japanese manufacturers have provided a vital service to Silicon Valley. Scores of US companies like Chips & Technology, Xilinx, Clrrus, and MIPs—story-book Silicon Valley successes—have built major new businesses based on access to the strengths of Japanese manufacturing (Okimoto *et al.* 1992). Of course, Japanese companies have also benefited handsomely from the symbiotic relationship.

In DRAMS, where Japanese companies dominate world production, Toshiba was the first to devise what has turned out to be a highly effective and widely emulated organizational approach to R&D. This organizational innovation, which might be called 'lagged parallel project sequencing', emerged in response to a puzzling phenomenon: why was it that companies that dominated in one DRAM generation (say, 16K) failed to extend their domination into the next DRAM generation (64K)? For many years, dominance in successive DRAM markets fluctuated wildly—in spite of the learning curve benefits of previous success. How could Toshiba position itself to rise to the top and stay there through successive DRAM generations?

Toshiba's semiconductor division devised an organizational response, 'lagged, parallel project sequencing' of consecutive DRAM R&D projects. Toshiba's organizational innovation was designed, first, to combine engineers from development and manufacturing divisions and organize them into small research teams. It also sought to conduct research simultaneously for two consecutive DRAM generations through lagged, parallel sequencing. A team would get started on, say, the 64K DRAM, and two years later another team would launch work on the next generation, 256K DRAM—before the 64K project was completed. Four years later, work would get started on the 1M DRAM at a time when the 64K DRAM was being mass-produced and prototypes for the 256K were being developed. Following completion of the 64K project, the 64K team would switch over to work on the 1M DRAM; then the 256K team would shift to the 4M DRAM project (Fig. 6). Imai and his colleagues have called this lagged, parallel project sequencing the 'sashimi-slice' model of R&D (Imai *et al.* 1985).

From the point of view of achieving rapid turn-around time, the 'sashimi-slice' model offers obvious advantages over the traditional, one-product-generation-at-a-time approach. By bringing together engineers from development labs and manufacturing, the 'sashimi-slice' approach reduces the range of problems that are apt to arise when teams assume the research–development–manufacturing functions separately and in sequence. In the 'sashimi slice' system, manufacturing engineers have a voice in the early design of integrated circuits. Instead of trying to deal with chemical and process bottlenecks *after* the designs are drawn, the Japanese model factors process and production inputs directly into design specifications as they are set. Early interaction enables the research team to the avoid some of the most nettlesome 'hand-off' problems that US companies suffer when design engineers fail to communicate with their manufacturing colleagues, or fail to anticipate the potential bottlenecks that will stall the manufacturing phase. Like Japanese methods of quality control, this approach stresses problem prevention through continuous body contact and thorough-going communications at every stage of the R&D process. It allows research teams to overcome separate, disconnected, and sequential problem-solving, leading to problem detection and subsequent correction.

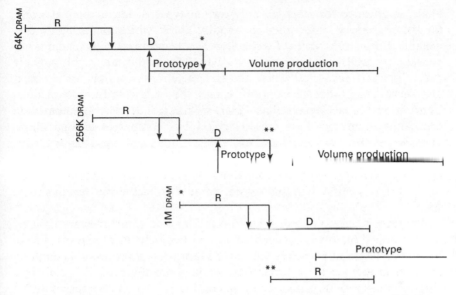

F IG. 6 Typical Research (R), Development (D), and Manufacturing (M) Interactive Diagram in Product-Oriented R&D

The 'sashimi slice' approach also offers the advantage of continuous
collective movement down steep learning curves, as researchers communicate
across project boundaries. Members of the 256K DRAM team can learn
from the experiences of the 64K project as the research moves forward;
they don't have to wait until the 64K project is completed. Collective
learning is also enhanced by the fact that many members of the 64K project
will move on to work on the 1M DRAM project, and the 256K research
team will take on the 4M project. Here again, the value of collective
learning, made possible by the continuity of long-term employment, must
not be underestimated. Thus, the lagged, parallel project approach accel-
erates the speed of commercialization by eliminating 'down time' and
shortening transition times between product generations.

The advantages of the 'sashimi slice' innovation became clear when
Toshiba catapulted to the top of the world's manufacturers of DRAM with
the 256K generation. Once competitors saw what Toshiba had accomplished,
nearly all of Japan's major semiconductor producers revamped their organizational approaches to R&D and followed suit. Like new products and
new process technology, organizational innovations tend to diffuse rapidly
across company boundaries in Japan. Even some of the leading American
companies, such as Texas Instruments, have adopted their own versions of
the 'sashimi slice' model.

It ought to be pointed out, however, that the lagged parallel project model is effective for work on only certain types of technology. It works for DRAMS, SRAM, and other commodity chips, which share highly predictable, linear trajectories of technological advancement. The model is not particularly well suited for products based on nonlinear, highly volatile technological trajectories, where the parameters of research for the next and successive product generations cannot be understood ahead of time. Thus, it is not accidental that Japanese companies have dominated in commodity chips but have lagged behind US companies in logic chips, microprocessors, and software for applications and operating systems. The latter may require a different, perhaps less structured, organizational approach. Whether Japanese companies devise new organizational models to replace, or coexist with, the lagged, parallel project model remains to be seen.

Whatever form new models may take, Japanese companies are unlikely to abandon three organizational characteristics that have helped to make the 'sashimi slice' approach effective: (1) a 'bottom-up' process of submitting research proposals; (2) a broad base of understanding of the company's long-term research directions and goals on the part of all researchers within the firm; and (3) the co-ordinating role played by seasoned R&D managers. These characteristics have existed in Japanese companies throughout the post-war period, and they are likely to be incorporated into whatever new organizational forms take shape.

The 'bottom up' proposal process is widely practised in Japanese companies, particularly in the DLs and FELs. Young researchers are encouraged to submit proposals for research which they consider of high priority. The proposals are handed up to management, which decides on specific projects to fund. Finan and Frey estimate that at least half of all the projects approved for funding make their way up from the lower rungs of the corporate hierarchy (Finan and Frey 1989). This system ensures that research projects will deal with hands-on problem-solving related to process and production technology. It also means that energetic young researchers, who are in the best position to understand technological opportunities, are allowed to help shape the company's research agenda. And because researchers have a strong input in setting the research agenda, a very broad base of understanding develops within the company on long-term research directions and goals. Many occasions arise when this broad base of understanding serves to facilitate the completion of complicated research tasks.

As is well known, the Japanese use a seniority system of pay and promotion based on entry year into the company. Seniority, coupled with long-term employment, give Japan's employment system distinctive qualities. From a Western perspective, the seniority-based long-term employment system ought, logically, to be riddled with all sorts of organizational dysfunctions. Think, for example, about work incentives. How can a will to work be instilled if employees are guaranteed long-term employment?

How can the encouragement of 'free-riders' be avoided? On the surface, Japan's system of seniority-based, long-term employment would seem likely to lead not to the 'C syndrome', discussed earlier, but to the 'I syndrome': inertia, inefficiency, and indifference.

Contrary to Western expectations, however, the system not only works but is the source of order, stability, teamwork, and flexibility, all essential elements of effective R&D. More specifically, the system produces a seasoned and talented cohort of R&D managers. The competence of seasoned Japanese managers at every level may be the most overlooked factor in explaining the effectiveness of R&D in Japanese companies. A comparison of average ages of R&D managers in Japanese and American corporations reveals an older age structure in Japan (see Table 1). Moreover, the comparison shows that, as managers climb up the corporate ladder, the age gap between Japanese and US managers widens. At the level of vice-president for research, the difference can be twelve or more years, reflecting

TABLE 1   Age Composition of Japanese and American Managers

Manager level	Avg. age (Japan)	Avg. age (USA)
1. Project manager	30	25–8
2. Division manager	37	28–31
3. General manager	45	34–7
4. Vice-president	52	40–3

twelve more years of hands-on experience, stronger relationships with the R&D staff, and greater seasoning and maturity. As they move up, Japanese managers learn progressively more about technology and more about the elements of effective management.

In most US semiconductor firms, R&D managers come and go (like fellow employees), causing costly discontinuities that destroy teamwork and morale. If a manager leaves in the middle of a project, the disruption may cause the project to be terminated, or delayed. For small- to medium-sized US semiconductor companies, such disruptions are not uncommon. Even if an acceptable replacement is found and quickly put in place, the damage done can be crippling. Over the years, as companies like Fairchild have found out, the movement of key research managers can take an enormous cumulative toll on the company's core competence and its collective learning capacity.

Japanese companies rely heavily on the intuition and hands-on experience of research managers. As pointed out earlier, they put much less stock than US companies on number-crunching methods of analysis, such as discounted cash flow, in calculating R&D risks and returns. Instead, Japanese companies place their faith in the knowledge of managers, who have gained, over the years, a mature understanding of technology and an experienced perspective on the company's R&D objectives.

Not surprisingly, the differences in Japanese and American styles of management have led to different outcomes. Some analysts even go so far as to cite myopic management for America's economic decline (Hayes and Abernathy 1980). As for the semiconductor industry, a case can be made that the preoccupation of US companies with short-term profits has led to a long-term erosion of their competitive position in world markets *vis-à-vis* Japanese companies. Whether, and to what extent, the argument is valid remains a subject of lively debate, since such intervening variables as capital markets and government policies call simple causality into question.

Technological Choices: Old v. New

In comparing American and Japanese companies, the Japanese appear to be more conservative, less impatient, and more dogged in their approach. When a research project hits an impasse, for example, Japanese managers will urge researchers to stay on course and step up the pace, hoping that, by sheer dint of effort, the bottleneck will be bypassed. By contrast, when an American research team hits an impasse, the manager and his team are more apt to veer off course and try alternative ways of reaching their technological targets. The Japanese manager's instinct is to stick to what is known and bulldoze ahead, while the American manager's impulse is to examine the full range of options and pursue new research roads that circumvent roadblocks. One approach is conservative and patient, the other is experimental and open to new directions.

These differences have come to light at various points in the history of US–Japan semiconductor competition. In circuit designs for memory chips, for example, Japanese companies have shown a clear propensity to stick to conservative, known ways of etching submicron circuits, while US companies, seeing the physical limits of old approaches, have moved boldly to find and develop new technologies. By sticking to the known—to what has worked in the past—Japanese companies have averted some of the pitfalls of high-risk experimentation that have befallen US companies. While the conservative strategy may not have led to bold new breakthroughs, Japanese companies have managed to avoid the dead-end of false starts.

This conservative mindset is evident in the choices made between traditional planar and new trench technologies. Impressed by the future possibilities of new trench technology, several US companies decided to discard the old planar processes in designing the 256K DRAM. American managers believed that the old planar technology was bumping up against hard physical limits, which would be reached with the 1M DRAM. Seeing the handwriting on the wall, they were anxious to get on the new trench track as early as possible so as to be in an advantageous position to dominate the ultra-large-scale integrated circuit (ULSI) markets down the road. If the end is near, why wait?

Japanese semiconductor companies, by contrast, stuck to the more familiar, less risky planar processes and sought to ride this technology to its outer limits—while simultaneously undertaking research on trench technology. As a result, in part, of their commitment to planar technology, Japanese companies were able to dislodge US competitors from their commanding position as the world's largest manufacturers of DRAMS. US companies found, to their dismay, that developing trench technology was more difficult than they anticipated. There was, to be sure, an element of luck; but Japan's success can be attributed to more than pure luck. Shrewd judgement, careful organization, and conservatism had a lot to do with Japan's success.

The planar–trench story seems to be repeating itself in the choices being made today between phased-shift technology and X-ray lithography. Several US companies, foreseeing a dead-end ahead for the current generation of etching technology, have invested heavily in X-ray lithography for submicron circuits in future-generation commodity chips, beginning with the 64M DRAM. Since the early 1980s, IBM has invested more than a billion dollars on research in X-ray lithography, despite the fact that one of its engineers had pioneered the development of phased-shift technology, an alternative method. Enamoured with the prospect of leapfrogging a full generation of technology, IBM and other US companies all but abandoned phased-shift technology, concentrating the bulk of their resources instead on X-ray lithography, a technology that is still far away from commercial application. Meanwhile, all of the major Japanese companies have picked up phased-shift technology—the technology first developed and then abandoned in the United States—and appear ready to utilize it commercially, starting with the 4M DRAM, now in the prototype phase of development. At the same time, as a means of hedging their bets, Japanese firms are also working on X-ray lithography.

Here is another case of Japanese companies choosing the better known, closer-at-hand technologies over bolder, riskier, and more visionary technologies. This should not be taken to imply that Japanese companies lack technological vision; if anything, they tend to be even more visionary than most of their US counterparts. The difference is that the whole organizational setup for R&D in Japanese companies is structured in ways that play to caution, feasibility, incremental advances, and manufacturing considerations. In the cases of the planar *v.* trench processes and the phase-shift *v.* X-ray lithography masks, Japanese companies made clear choices for the known, the feasible, and the more practical. US semiconductor companies, by contrast, gambled on the more advanced, the more challenging and difficult, the more distant, but also potentially the more rewarding technological paths.

In sum, Japanese semiconductor companies perform exceedingly well in R&D tasks where the technological trajectories are predictable, where the theoretical parameters are well defined, and where the transfer of technology from prototype to mass manufacturing requires extensive interaction and communications. A typical technology transfer pattern in Japan would be as follows:

- Define research objectives jointly with development (D) manufacturing (M).
- Transfer 1–2 engineers from D to research (R); work for 1–2 years.
- Return D engineers to D, and transfer 1–2 engineers from R to D.
- Transfer 2–4 engineers from M to D; work for 1–2 years.
- Return M engineers to M, and transfer 2–3 engineers from D to M.

The organizational framework for R&D is well suited to meet the functional needs of research in such areas of semiconductor technology as discrete devices, commodity chips, hardware, and process technology—all of which conform to such characteristics. Japanese corporations have shown a remarkable talent for major organizational innovations that have thrust them to the forefront of industrial leadership, such as the lagged, parallel project approach in semiconductors and the famous just-in-time inventory approach in the case of automobiles. Thus, some of the major features of Japanese industrial organization—especially the long-term and seniority-based employment system—have been adapted and utilized as sources of competitive advantage.

4. STRATEGIC ALLIANCES

Lag Areas

Although Japanese semiconductor companies have moved to the top in memory devices, discrete devices, process technology, and certain types of semiconductor equipment (like lithography steppers), they continue to lag behind US companies in logic chips, microprocessors, operating and applications software, and other types of semiconductor equipment (like ion implanters)—the most advanced areas of semiconductor technology.

Consider microprocessors as an example. Japanese firms have never designed a microprocessor that has become an industry standard like Intel's X86 series, IBM's RS6000 series, or Motorola's 680X0 and 880X0 series. IBM invented the RISC (reduced instruction set computer) microprocessor, which US start-ups like Sun Microsystems and MIPS Computers adapted to gain wide market acceptance. RISC is a major breakthrough in MPU architecture.

Instead of developing its own RISC chip, which would have taken time and substantial money, Fujitsu entered into an alliance with Sun to manufacture its MPU, which is available on an open system basis to any company wishing to adopt Sun's work-station specifications. Other Japanese firms have also concluded alliances with leading US companies to gain access to state-of-the-art microprocessor technology. In microprocessors, America has led and Japan has followed. Why is there this pattern of technological unevenness? Why have Japanese firms had trouble moving up to the higher ends of semiconductor technology?

Part of the problem may be organizational. The organization of Japanese R&D is not designed to encourage bold new conceptualizing, radical departures from the prevailing orthodoxy, and free-wheeling exploration of territories unmapped by known theories. Instead, Japanese organization is geared to operate on the basis of caution, conservatism, and incremental change. It filters out bold new ideas if those ideas cannot be readily proved. It can be accommodating in such areas as hardware, because hardware is predictable and susceptible to design proof; but radical, new concepts seldom pass through the intricate mechanism of consensual deliberation.

Strategic Alliances

How have Japanese firms fared so well if the design of their organizations are inimical to bold new breakthroughs? Historically, the answer resides, to a large extent, in the acquisition and large-scale infusion of knowledge from the outside through the vehicle of strategic alliances. Importing and adapting foreign know how played a crucial role in the speed of Japan's latecomer catch-up (Hayashi 1989; Ozawa 1974; Peck and Tamura 1976). Early on, the vehicle of acquisition took the form of licensing agreements, a rudimentary type of alliance which served to transfer basic, indispensable patents from American to Japanese companies.

From the mid-1980s, the number of American–Japanese alliances has soared. On average, more than a hundred alliances are concluded per year (Fig. 7). The figures understate the actual number, because many alliances are never publicly announced (Okimoto *et al.* 1992). Not only has the number climbed, but the scope of alliances has also expanded. Simple licensing agreements no longer account for the vast majority of strategic alliances; the more popular types include foreign direct investments, joint ventures, and joint development projects, organizationally complex arrangements. Japanese have used investment, joint development, and licensing agreements to gain access to state-of-the-art US technology in MPUs, CPUs, and ASICs, (Fig. 8). Thanks in part to such alliances, Japanese companies have managed to compensate for weaknesses in their organ-

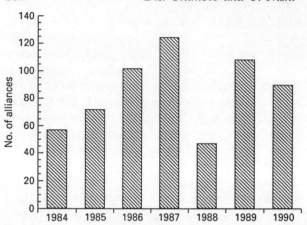

FIG. 7   American–Japanese Semiconductor Alliances, 1984–1990
          Source: Dataquest Inc., 1991.

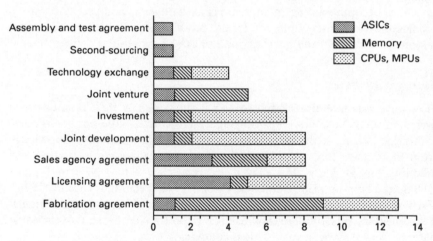

FIG. 8   Agreement Type and Product/Technology, 1990
          Source: Dataquest Inc., 1991.

izational structures. Thus, for Japan's semiconductor industry, strategic
alliances represent probably the most important mechanism for ongoing
access to leading-edge technology.

Whether it be in semiconductors or computers, Japanese companies are
the world's most aggressive participants in global alliances. Take foreign
investments in US high technology. The level of Japanese activity is orders
of magnitude greater than that of European or South-east Asian companies
(Fig. 9). The same holds true for virtually every other alliance type.

Why are Japanese companies so much more active than their American, European, and Asian counterparts?

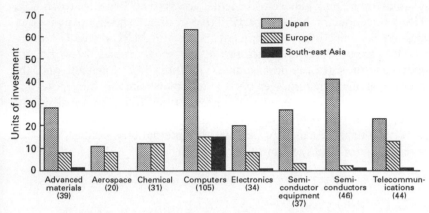

FIG. 9 Foreign Investments in High Technology
Numbers in parentheses refer to industry totals.
Source: Spencer (1991: 10).

The answer may reside again in Japan's industrial organization. The diversified, vertically integrated nature of large Japanese corporations generates an interest in strategic alliances because there are multiplier-effect benefits to be gained with the introduction of new technology. New technologies obtained via strategic alliances can be used to upgrade the quality of both product and process technology for both external and internal captive markets. For diversified, integrated Japanese giants, there may be a kind of 'captive market learning curve' down which these companies can move, as seen in the case of ASICs.

Why so many alliances with American firms? In the semiconductor industry, the most immediate reason is because the US semiconductor industry is still technologically the most advanced in the world. Moreover, the US and Japanese semiconductor markets together account for over 70 per cent of the world market. Sheer size means that, from a probabilistic standpoint, the largest number of bilateral alliances are likely to occur between US and Japanese companies. Beyond the size factor, the large number of US-Japanese strategic alliances reflect the high degree of economic integration and interdependence between the two leading economies of the world. Mention should be made, finally, of the structural complementarity of the two semiconductor industries. Small US venture start-ups need capital, manufacturing facilities, and marketing outlets in Japan's huge market; on the other side of the Pacific, large, vertically integrated, diversified Japanese companies need new product designs and leading-edge technology to cover gaps in their product portfolios and to overcome weaknesses in their R&D infrastructure. The needs and resources of the two sides are symbiotic, leading to a flowering of strategic alliances.

Thanks to the proliferation of alliance linkages, Japanese semiconductor companies are reaping handsome benefits: access to leading-edge technology in US semiconductor houses (particularly in areas where Japanese companies are lagging), joint development projects in MPUs with US firms, the establishment of research facilities in key spots around the world, the employment of software programmers in India and England, and the utilization of manufacturing engineers at factory sites in Singapore and Malaysia. The multiple benefits of globalization will help to offset the handicap of lagging behind in key technologies. As Japanese firms work more with foreign researchers, perhaps the international contact will lead to a reshaping of R&D organization in Japan.

Semiconductors: A Test Case?

If the semiconductor industry is the test case of Japan's ability to make the transition from heavy manufacturing to high technology, the outlook is bright but not entirely free of uncertainties. Corporate organization for R&D in the semiconductor case can be considered a positive factor, on the whole. It has provided a big and rising revenue stream to sustain R&D activities at a vigorous level; it has facilitated the formulation and implementation of R&D priorities and goals; and it has created an organizational setting featuring the 'C syndrome' characteristics: continuity, contact, communications, and collective learning capacity. Enveloped in the 'C syndrome', Japanese R&D teams have made impressive strides in commodity chips, process technology, semiconductor manufacturing equipment, and discrete devices.

The areas of technology where Japan has excelled share several characteristics in common. They are demand-driven, mass manufactured, highly sensitive to cost and quality considerations, process-technology-oriented, and based on incremental innovations. What is crucial to success is the hand-off from prototype development to mass manufacturing. This is precisely where the lagged, parallel project approach contributes to effective co-ordination and fast turn-around time.

On the other hand, two other 'C syndrome' characteristics—caution and conservatism—have impeded progress in the more advanced areas of semiconductor technology: MPUs, CPUs, logic chips, applications, and operating software. The same structure of R&D organization that works so well for commodity chips appears to obstruct progress in the higher end of the value-added chain of technology. Whether Japanese companies will be able to 'tweak' the system in ways that facilitate R&D progress in the higher end of semiconductor technology remains to be seen. If not, Japanese companies may be forced to continue relying heavily on strategy alliances with US partners.

Is Japan's performance in semiconductor technology a reliable indicator of future performance in other areas of high technology? The answer is unclear. In those areas where Japan confronts the same set of functional requisites as the low and mid-range of semiconductor technology, Japanese companies may possess competitive strengths. But in areas where Japanese companies must satisfy a different, more demanding, set of functional requisites, they may face certain disadvantages. Japanese corporations have yet to show themselves capable of achieving high levels of systems into gration, for example, which is essential for R&D success in such sectors as the aerospace industry. And what about technologies that have still different characteristics, such as pharmaceuticals and chemicals? Clearly, making bold predictions on the basis of Japan's experience in the semiconductor industry is premature, given the fact that the semiconductor competition is still unfolding and the record of performance to date, although largely positive, is somewhat mixed.

REFERENCES

Abegglen, James C., and Stalk, George, Jr (1985), *Kaishia: The Japanese Corporation*, Basic Books, New York.

Aoki, Masahiko (1988), *Information, Incentives, and Bargaining in the Japanese Economy*, Cambridge University Press.

Borrus, Michael G. (1988), *Competing for Control: America's Stake in Microelectronics*, Ballinger, Cambridge, Mass.

Chalmers, Norma J. (1989), *Industrial Relations in Japan: The Peripheral Workforce*, Routledge, London.

Clark, Rodney (1979), *The Japanese Company*, Yale University Press, New Haven, Conn.

Cole, Robert E. (1979), *Work, Mobility, and Participation: A Comparative Study of American and Japanese Industry*, University of California Press, Berkeley, Calif.

Dore, Ronald P. (1987), *Taking Japan Seriously*, Stanford University Press, Stanford, Calif.

—— and Sako, Mari (1989), *How the Japanese Learn to Work*, Routledge, London.

Finan, William F., and Frey Jeffrey (1989), *The Effectiveness of the Japanese Research–Development Commercialization Cycle: Engineering and Technology Transfer in Japan's Semiconductor Industry*, Semiconductor Research Corporation, Research Triangle Park, North Carolina.

Flaherty, M., Itami, Therese, and Itami, Hiroyuki (1984), 'Finance', in *Competitive Edge*, 134–76.

Gilder, George (1989), *Microcosm*, Simon & Shuster, New York.

Hayashi, Takeshi (1990), *The Japanese Experience in Technology: From Transfer to Self-Reliance*, United Nations University Press, Tokyo.

Hayashi, Yuichiro (1989), *Nettowaakingu no Keizaigaku*, NTT Shuppan, Tokyo.

Hayes, Robert, and Abernathy, William (1980), 'Managing Our Way to Economic Decline', *Harvard Business Review*, 58(4): 67–77.

Hirschman, Albert O. (1970), *Exit, Voice, and Loyalty: Responses to Decline in Firms, Organizations, and States*, Harvard University Press, Cambridge, Mass.

Hodder, James E. (1986), 'Evaluation of Manufacturing Investments: A Comparison of US and Japanese Practices', *Financial Management*, Spring: 17–24.

Imai, Ken'ichi (1989), 'Kigyo Guruppu' (Manufacturing *Keiretsu* Groups), in Ken'ichi Imai and Ryutaro Komiya (eds.), *Nihon no Kigyo*, Tokyo Daigaku Shuppankai, Tokyo. 136–42.

——Nonaka, Ikujiro, and Takeuchi, Hiortaka (1985), 'Managing the New Product Development Process: How Japanese Companies Learn and Unlearn', in Kim B. Clark *et al.* (eds.), *The Uneasy Alliance: Managing the Productivity–Technology Dilemma*, Harvard Business School Press, Boston.

Kotler, Phillip, Fahey, Liam, and Jatusripitak, S. (1985), *The New Competition*, Prentice-Hall, Englewood Cliffs, NJ.

Okimoto, Daniel I. (1989), *Between MITI and the Market; Japanese Industrial Policy for High Technology*, Stanford University Press, Stanford, Calif.

——Sugano, Takuo, and Weinstein, Franklin (eds.) (1984), *Competitive Edge: The Semiconductor Industries in the US and Japan*, Stanford University Press, Stanford, Calif.

——Tatsuno, Sheridan, Kvamme, Floyd, Nishi, Yoshio, and Dewath, Edward (1992), *US–Japan Strategic Alliances in the Semiconductor Industry*, Asia/Pacific Research Center, Stanford, Calif.

Ozawa, Terutomo (1974), *Japan's Technological Challenge to the West, 1950–1974: Motivation and Accomplishment*, MIT Press, Cambridge, Mass.

Peck, Merton, and Tamura, Shuji (1976), 'Technology', in Hugh Patrick and Henry Rosovsky (eds.), *Asia's New Giant*, Brookings Institution, Washington, DC, 535–58.

Prestowitz, Clyde V. Jr (1988), *Trading Places*, Basic Books, New York.

Spencer, Linda (1991), *Foreign Investments in the United States: Unencumbered Access*, Economic Strategy Institute, Washington, DC.

Stalk, George, Jr, and Hout, Thomas M. (1990), *Competing Against Time*, (Free Press, New York. 1990).

8

SMEs, Entry Barriers, and 'Strategic Alliances'

D. HUGH WHITTAKER

1. INTRODUCTION

The structure of Japan's industry has come under increasing scrutiny in recent years, not least by US trade negotiators in the Structural Impediments Initiative talks. Besides speaking for foreign companies trying to enter Japanese markets, and Japanese consumers, the US team for the Structural Impediments Initiative might have wished to add small Japanese companies, since these have long been held to suffer from the dominance of large firms in the industrial structure and to be exploited in *keiretsu* relationships. The authors of Japan's 1990 Economic White Paper (Keizai Kikakucho 1990), however, argued that, while there might be some obstacles to open trading, and an opaqueness in the rules of business interaction that should be removed, Japan's industrial structure *is* in fact open to new entry and to the forming of new trading links. Their stout defence of the economic rationality of Japan's industrial structure was a far cry from the famous dual-structure exposition of the 1957 Economic White Paper. Moreover, business journals in 1990 were carrying articles on the vast 'reserve army' of candidates for listing on the over-the-counter and 'second section' of the stock exchanges (e.g. *Shukan Toyo Keizai*, 25 August, 1990: 'Here are the Companies Expected to Make Public Offerings ... Where is the Next Nintendo?'), which would further serve to indicate the rapid growth and confidence of many smaller firms.

Can new players enter the corporate major league in Japan? In short, yes. A list of those in the process of doing so may be gleaned from Nakamura's new *Chuken kigyo ron* (Nakamura 1990). Also, despite higher start-up costs in many industries, it is thought that environmental changes portend a substantial increase in the coming years, as the size and versatility of smaller firms offer them increasingly the competitive advantages. The picture is by no means unambiguously rosy, however, and this paper is reserved in its assessment. Obstacles in setting up venture businesses (in the US conception of the term) are well known; but even established smaller

I would like to thank Abe Hiromi and the Nikko Research Centre for providing information for Section 3 of this paper.

firms, which provide a platform for entry into new markets, face a number of challenges in their expansion and diversification strategies. Large firms continue to shape the patterns of entry in a variety of ways. Such a view need not be based on a dual-structure or neo-dual-structure view of the Japanese economy.

The following section of this paper reviews accounts of the changing position of small- and medium-sized enterprises (SMEs) in the Japanese economy. SMEs in manufacturing, defined as those having less than 300 employees and capitalized at less than ¥100 million, consituted 99.5 per cent of establishments in 1986, unchanged from 1975; the proportion of employees was 74.4 per cent, up from 70.5 per cent; shipments and value added were little changed at around 52 and 56 per cent respectively (Chusho kigyo cho 1990a: apps. 2–9). Rather than a (quantitative) resurgence in small firms noted in many countries, then, the accounts concern qualitative changes in their position.

Section 3 puts these into perspective by looking at leadership in various markets, from the large and mature to the lower-volume, new, and '2.5' firms. This is followed in Section 4 by a discussion of problems commonly encountered by SMEs, ranging from factor markets, particularly people, to management, marketing, succession, and, finally, problems in starting new companies.

Government policies aimed at alleviating these problems are briefly examined in Section 5, where the prospects of 'inter-industry' and 'fusion' networks opening up new growth opportunities are considered. Network-relations-building economies of scope, as opposed to scale-oriented pyramid-type relations, are considered by some to be an important weapon of newly emerging firms and groups, prototypes of a new industrial organization. Such networks generate difficulties of their own, however, and constitute no panacea to SME problems. In Section 6 a brief look at changes in the industrial structure of Ota Ward, Tokyo, will attempt to put the overall discussion into perspective.

The arguments are based on existing literature as well as extensive interviews in small firms in the Ota/Jonan area between 1986 and 1990. The focus is on manufacturing.

2. THE CHANGING POSITION OF SMES

In the *chusho kigyoron* (SME theory/debate) literature, one finds progressively fewer references to domination by monopoly capital, exploitation, and dual structure, although there is now a 'new dual structure' literature. One strand of the more recent writings stresses the economic rationality of inter-firm relations especially between large firms and SMEs, so much so that these are held to be a key element in the growth to world dominance of the automobile and appliance industries. The word *shitauke (kigyo)*, generally translated as 'subcontractor' but implying a hierarchical arrangement, is abandoned in favour of 'supplier', and *oya*, or 'parent', for 'manufacturer'. Manufacturers have come to depend on suppliers as much as the obverse; the long-term relationships are mutually beneficial. This evaluation now provides a model for worldwide emulation (e.g. Womack *et al.* 1990).

Another strand, which is closer to the subject of this paper, draws attention to the SMEs that are not subcontractors, and to those that have escaped from *shitauke* reliance. The two strands overlap, in that subcontractors, which responded positively to constant pressure from 'parents' to reduce costs, raise their technical level, rationalize production, and finally participate in design and development, then found they had a springboard from which to sell their components or know-how more widely, and ultimately to launch their own products.

In 1987, 55.9 per cent of SMEs did some form of subcontracting, down from 65.5 per cent in 1981 and just lower than the 58.7 per cent in 1971. It is difficult to make a definitive statement from these figures alone, but the authors of the 1990 SME White Paper make the following interpretation:

Along with this growing gap in management ability, a structural change is underway among subcontractors in which those not able to meet the demands of 'parent' companies are getting fewer orders and are being forced to change or close their businesses, while others have strengthened their managements and reduced their dependence on their 'parents' and have even become independent companies. This structural change is thought to have contributed to the recent decline in the number and proportion of subcontractors. (Chusho kigyo cho 1990*a*: 157–8)

Even among subcontractors in manufacturing, 24.1 per cent are said to have an own product (*jisha seihin*), and 57.8 per cent of these intend to increase the importance of such products for their business, while 40 per cent of those without their own product would like to develop one (Chusho kigyo cho 1990*a*: 160).

The changing position of SMEs is said to be facilitated by owners/managers responding positively not only to 'parent' or customer pressures, but also to changes in the environment. For example, changes in markets, such as segmentation in mass markets, with heightened and diversified consumer preferences, have reduced product cycle times and forced large manufacturers to rely on their suppliers, not only in terms of cost, delivery and quality, but increasingly for sub-assembly work and even for the design and development phases of the product cycle. Suppliers that have been able to strengthen these functions have gained a base for greater equality and independence; 37.6 per cent of manufacturing subcontractors were said to have their own design sections, and 26.4 per cent an R&D

section in 1989 (Chusho kigyo cho 1990*a*: 160), although just what constitutes an R&D or design 'section' no doubt varies widely.

Second, structural changes such as the 'servicization' (growth of services) and '2.5-ization' (the fusion of manufacturing and services) of the economy, the trend towards 'knowledge intensity', and the shift to domestic-demand-led growth have also opened up small new and niche markets which may not be attractive for large firms to enter, or in which small firms may actually have an advantage. These provide a toehold and springboard for later expansion.

Third, other developments, such as the 1985 yen shock, increased the incentives for subcontractors to reduce their dependence on 'parents' because of the tremendous pressure to cut costs and the heightened uncertainty as 'parents' rushed to set up operations overseas. At the same time, sky-rocketing land prices helped those with land because it increased collateral for borrowing funds for new equipment and projects.

Finally, although new technology is a double-edged sword, in the context of the above changes it has provided new opportunities for SMEs. Micro-electronics-based technology in manufacturing, for instance, has increased flexibility and helped small firms overcome some of their space and skills problems, while affordable CAD systems have increased possibilities in design. On-line systems provide information and facilitate new 'networking' arrangements which may help overcome traditional marketing problems. Sato argues:

In these advanced technological developments, SMEs are becoming leading figures. Venture companies are without a doubt playing a part in technological development. Independents, subsidiaries, large, medium, small—there are many kinds of new ventures. Using advanced technology, developing it, manufacturing it—SMEs are significant in many aspects. (Sato 1990: 15)

Some of the changes are encapsulated in the story of MZ Manufacturing Company, variations of which are widespread and widely reported. This particular case comes from Seki and Kato (1990: 59–60; see also Section 6).

MZ was founded in the post-war period by an engineer who left an instruments maker to start out on his own. He did repairs and machining for his old company at first, but with his son decided in the 1960s to develop his own product, using subcontracting work as the financial and technical base to do so. After some consideration they decided to develop a durometer. Their plans coincided with the beginnings of instrument digitization, and they became the first to produce a digitized durometer in Japan in 1968. They became specialists, and quickly applied microelectronics technology to their instruments in the 1970s while established instrument-makers were still changing over. As a rcsult, they gained 60 per cent of the domestic share in digitized durometers, and now export 60 per cent of their production to twenty-two countries. From the durometer base they have branched out into systems developments, and employ fifty people in their Ota factory in Tokyo (with six in design and development) and a further ten in a software spin-off in Akihabara.

Note the small size of the company. Smallness may now be seen as an advantage rather than a handicap, since small firms can respond quickly to changes in environmental conditions. In particular, firms that forge flexible links with other compact, purposeful firms in networks are well adapted to the new environment. Kiyonari conceptualizes the changes in Fig. 1. And

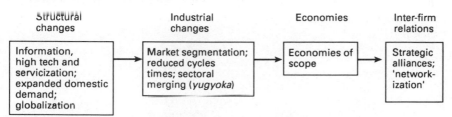

| Structural changes | Industrial changes | Economies | Inter-firm relations |

| Information, high tech and servicization; expanded domestic demand; globalization | → | Market segmentation; reduced cycles times; sectoral merging (*yugyoka*) | → | Economies of scope | → | Strategic alliances; 'network-ization' |

FIG. 1   Changes in Industrial Structure and their Impact
   Source: Kiyonari (1990:228)

Nakamura argues:

In other words, in the changing industrial structure and corporate restructuring responses to it, the breakdown of industrial divisions (*yugyoka*) makes diversified patterns of economic behaviour by individual actors indispensable. This will be achieved by independent, positive companies loosely coupled with others to reinforce each other and positively use external resources to bring about economic efficiency. We can see the beginning of the transformation of Japan's industrial organization towards network organization, which is quite different from the pyramid type symobolized by large peak firms and their *keiretsu* subcontractor systems. (Nakamura 1990: 57)

Ultimately, according to Hashimoto,

In these developments, what kind of enterprises will take the lead will be an important factor in influencing the tempo of change and future economic and industrial structure. If we posit that demand will be towards the small-scale, segmented, diverse and domestic, it will be difficult for economies of scale to operate, and it is possible that SMEs will become the 'captains of industry'. (Hashimoto 1989: 22)

There are grounds for accepting that the literature reflects objective changes in SMEs and inter-firm relations. The post-war dependence relationships fostered by large-firm domination of technology, capital, and marketing, strengthened during the *keiretsu* formation of the early high-growth period, with qualitative upgrading during the later high-growth period, were modified during the low-growth period, especially with product diversification strategies. Others would argue that there has been a lag as dualist approaches remained orthodox long after changing conditions superceded their relevance. The battle for recognition of Nakamura's third type of company—the *chuken kigyo* (core firm)—is illustrative of this. Some have even questioned whether the monopoly capital/dualism/*keiretsu*/dominance literature was ever relevant at all (e.g. Miwa 1990).

Accompanying the process of re-evaluation and reinterpretation, on the other hand, lies the fear that the pendulum might now be swinging too far in the opposite direction; that the emerging orthdoxies may be almost as partial as the old ones (e.g. Kameyama 1989). And there are grounds for such fears.[1]

3. THE END OF GIANT FIRMS?

Are Japan's giant firms to be the dinosaurs of a new age, then? A certain scepticism is in order regarding blithe claims that economies of scale are giving way to those of scope, and that this automatically works to the disadvantage of large firms. Why should large firms not use their key technologies and extensive 'networks' to make use of economies of scope as well? And are economies of scale really breaking down? This was the key question asked by Pratten in his recent study of the growth of small, high-tech firms in Cambridge and East Anglia in the UK. His conclusion was that the case for extensive dimunition of economies of scale is weak; rather, few of the small firms were operating in direct competition with large firms:

In brief, the explanation for the existence of many of the small firms is that they operate in market niches ... the question left unanswered was why big firms did not fill the niches in which these small firms operate. (Pratten 1991: 50).

In Japan, there are periodic outcries that large firms *do* invade small firms' niches, supporting the view of differentiated spheres of operation, while illustrating the relative nature of markets, niche and otherwise. Rather than engage in an abstract discussion of economies and markets, competition and competition avoidance, a brief look at actual market leadership may shed light on the situation.

In established industries with high sales volumes, large firms clearly remain dominant. The top ten electrical machine makers in 1990 were all very large firms, and were exactly the same as the top ten in 1970, although some of the rankings have changed (Table 1). The same applies to, e.g., the top trading companies, except that no. 10, Ataka, has been absorbed by C. Itoh.

TABLE 1   Top Ten Electric Machine Makers, f1970 and 1990[a]

1970	Sales (¥bn)	1990	Sales (¥bn)
1. Hitachi	675.0	Hitachi	3,788.8
2. Toshiba	550.2	Toshiba	3,227.7
3. Mitsubishi Electric	376.1	NEC	2,961.1
4. NEC	195.7	Mitsubishi Electric	2,300.8
5. Matsushita Electric	119.9	Fujitsu	2,337.8
6. Fujitsu	119.4	Nippon Denso	1,379.3
7. Fuji Electric	103.3	Matsushita Electric	971.5
8. Nippon Denso	85.3	Fuji Electric	591.9
9. Oki EI	57.5	Oki EI	582.1
10. Matsushita CI	43.7	Matsushita CI	441.7

[a]Excluding appliances.
Source: Nikko Research Centre (NRC) mimeo.

The pump industry is less dominated by giant firms, although some have a major presence. There are a number of *chuken* manufacturers—medium- to large-sized firms operating mainly within that industry in the top ten (Table 2). None of these was established after 1955, however, and no new entrants are envisaged. It is a mature industry, characterized by evolutionary rather than revolutionary innovation. Reputation is important, and start-up costs are considerable.

TABLE 2   Top Ten Pump Makers, f1990

	Total sales (¥bn)	Pump sales (¥bn)
1. Ebara Corp.	245.0	140.0
2. Hitachi	3,788.8	(40.0 est.)
3. Kubota	708.9	30.0
4. Tsurumi Mfg. Co.	24.8	24.8
5. Torishima Pump Mfg.	22.3	21.0
6. Mitsubishi Heavy Industries	2,327.1	20.0
7. Dengyosha MW	17.7	13.0
8. Nikkiso	35.8	10.0
9. Shinmeiwa	122.8	8.3
10. Awamura Mfg. Co.	6.6	5.5

Source: NRC mimeo.

The machine tool industry has even fewer very large participants, and is dominated by *chuken* firms (Table 3). The small average size of the firms may be attributed to the overall size of the market, small volume and large variety, and vulnerability to economic cycles (cf. Nihon kogyo shinbunsha

TABLE 3   Top Ten Tool Makers, f1990

	Total sales (¥bn)	Machine tool sales (¥bn)
1. Yamazaki Mazak	130.0	130.0
2. Okuma Machinery Works	118.1	111.0
3. Mori Seiki	100.3	98.3
4. Toyoda Machine Works	179.0	62.7
5. Hitachi Seiki	60.5	54.5
6. Makino Milling Machine	62.2	52.2
7. Toshiba Machine	132.1	48.9
8. Osaka Kiko	42.3	36.4
9. Nippei Toyama	38.7	34.4
10. Okuma & Howa Machinery	31.6	31.6

Source: NRC mimeo.

1988: 306). Again, none of the top ten was established after 1955. The advent of NC/CNC (numerically controlled/computer numerically controlled) machine tools did provide new opportunities, however. Fanuc, which was a spin-off from Fujitsu in 1972 and soon became the world's largest maker of CNC controllers, is the most striking example, but the number 11 machine tool maker (in terms of sales, 1990), Sodick, is also notable. Founded as recently as 1976, this firm received investment from the venture capital firm JAFCO and now has over 800 employees, although its growth has been punctuated by disputes over patent infringements in its market base, electric discharge machines. While established in 1919, Yamazaki's rise has also been meteoric, propelled by a new international orientation and mastery of CNC technology.

What about newer industries? In the strategic semiconductor industry, where there are clear economies of scale and where resources for very rapid expansion are critical, not surprisingly, large established firms dominate (Table 4). A more pertinent area to look at is semiconductor equipment, where the market is much smaller and there is considerable customization. A cursory look at the companies listed in Table 5 would show that, apart from Nikon and Canon, the other top makers indeed have fewer than 2,000 employees, and some fewer than 1,000. (The top ten for 1990 was almost the same as in 1985, although Kokusai Electric may have moved up a notch.)

There are difficulties in defining the market, however, and in-house production by major semiconductor makers like Hitachi would make them major equipment producers (in the middle of the top ten) in their own

TABLE 4   Top Semiconductor Makers, f1980, f1990

1980	Sales (¥bn)	1990	Sales (¥bn)
1. NEC	166.0	NEC	725.0
2. Hitachi	130.0	Toshiba	700.0
3. Toshiba	110.0	Hitachi	580.0
4. Sharp	57.0	Fujitsu	415.0
5. Fujitsu	56.9	Mitsubishi Electric	375.0
6. Matsushita EI	50.0	Matsushita EI	280.0
7. Mitsubishi Electric	44.0	Sanyo Electric	195.0
8. Tokyo Sanyo	31.0	Sharp	190.0
9. Oki EI	19.2	Oki EI	160.0
		Soni	160.0

Source: NRC mimeo.

right. The major semiconductor makers are also shareholders in some of the equipment companies: NEC of Ando Electric, Hitachi of Kokusai Electric, and Fujitsu of Advantest. And even where they are not major shareholders, there are close links for joint product development. Tokyo Electron thus has strong links with the major makers Toshiba and NEC.

Only two of the top ten—Tokyo Electron and Shinkawa—were founded after 1955. Tokyo Electron started out in 1963 as a high-tech trading company, importing equipment from the United States and gaining production experience in modifying the equipment for Japanese customers. Shinkawa started in 1959, soon becoming a major wire bonder maker. Its

TABLE 5   Top Ten Semiconductor Equipment Makers, f1985

	Sales (¥bn)
1. Tokyo Electron	99.0
2. Nikon	44.2
3. Nihon Shinku	41.5
4. Advantest	39.9
5. Canon	33.0
6. Ando Electric	23.4
7. Shinkawa	21.1
8. Disko	17.5
9. Kokusai Electric	16.8
10. Tokyo Seimitsu	14.0

Source: NRC mimeo.

largest shareholder in 1990 was the semi-public venture capital Tokyo Small Business Investment Company. Many of the others were already *chuken* makers in their respective (niche) fields, for which growth prospects were limited. They successfully diversified into semiconductor equipment. This is not a picture of independent start-ups muscling in on new markets, but that is not surprising, given the limited number of user companies.

How about a new industry where the customers are much more diverse, like computer-aided design (CAD)? It is difficult to list the top makers by sales for CAD because (1) several US companies figure prominently; (2) large companies like Fujitsu and NEC produce many of their own systems and also sell them, but they register as computer systems; (3) the elements of CAD defy easy definition to compile figures under. The sales of well-known specialists such as Mutoh, Graphtec, and Max constitute a relatively small portion of the overall market. (These three companies, incidentally, were founded between 1942 and 1952, and have diversified into CAD; they are not newly-founded CAD companies.[2])

That does not mean, of course, that there are not any successful new small firms within these industries, or that some of them are not major players in sectors of these markets. But very often extant firms, especially in manufacturing, provide the springboard for diversification. These have been founded in the post-war period, have established a competent technological base with a stable market and core of employees, and quite often the second-generation president has led the successful diversification, as we saw with the company MZ. An existing firm provides manufacturing capabilities, an income base to support new development, the network of contacts, and a track record that can engender trust (with customers as well as finance sources), as well as the all-important human resources.

Another factor here is the conservative nature of venture capital funding, described by Clark (1987). It is difficult for a researcher to leave a company and independently attract venture capital (or researchers) for a new technological development on a high-risk–high-return basis. Established companies are more likely to get 'venture' funding prior to going public, unless they have large-firm backing. In the fine ceramics industry, market leader Kyocera, founded in 1959 and now with 13,000 employees and sales of over ¥350 billion, is a widely cited success story (cf. Nakamura 1990: 135–44), but the other two market leaders were pre-war Morimura *zaibatsu* companies. In fact, eight of the top ten derive from pre-war materials makers (the other exception being Asahi Sashi, founded in 1950). The same applies in biotechnology, in contrast to the 1980s situation in the United States:

Although the Japanese government has made biotechnology a national priority, and even though business surveys rank biotechnology as the industry with the most potential for the future, the industry comprises only firms that have entered from established positions in related fields. By contrast, 111 new US firms were formed between 1977 and 1983 with the explicit intention of exploiting the technological and commercial potential of biotechnology. Venture capitalists in the United States have invested $2.0 billion into these biotechnology ventures, not to mention other sources of financing. This is about 13–14 times the entire amount of venture capital available in Japan for all industries. (Okimoto and Saxonhouse 1987: 401)[3]

Information-processing and services is a new, rapidly growing (annual growth rate of almost 25 per cent between 1985 and 1990), '2.5' industry. The interest of large firms in this strategic area is thus hardly surprising. As Table 6 shows, eight of the top ten firms have been established by large makers or users. The two independents, however, were established in the 1960s and listed in 1982, with CSK growing particularly rapidly from its dispatching base into a major and diversifying firm, with its own group and franchisees, and INTEC expanding from its mainframe service base in Toyama.

TABLE 6   Top Ten Information Service Companies, f1989[a]

Company	Group
1. NTT Data Telecommunications	NTT
2. Nomura Research Institution	Nomura Securities (user)
3. Hitachi Information Systems	Hitachi (maker)
4. CSK	(independent)
5. Japan Research Institute	Sumitomo Bank (user)
6. Hitachi Software Engineering	Hitachi (maker)
7. QUICK	Nihon Keizai Shinbun (user)
8. Toyo Information Systems	Sanwa Bank (user)
9. INTEC	(independent)
10. Nippon Steel Information Telecommunication Systems	Nippon Steel (maker)

[a]Excluding information network companies.
Source: Nikko Research Centre (1991: 320–1).

This very brief tour of markets has suggested that large firms remain dominant in their respective markets (despite 'segmentation') and have diversified into others, either directly or by creating new companies. They are major influences in yet other markets in their roles as customers and co-developers. Established *chuken* and smaller firms remain major players in their own respective markets, and have also diversified into new areas (not always strictly 'niche' and with growth potential, as Nakamura argues, but still usually relatively protected from large firm entry), with the addition of a small number of successful new independent businesses, some of which start with a base of foreign technology. A closer look may reveal that new 'networks' have aided penetration into new markets. Such observations are rather mundane, but are worth making since aggregate discussions of large and small firms can obsure the distinctions, and studies of small successful firms sometimes lack a wider perspective. The distinction between established *chuken* and SME diversification on the one hand, and independent start ups on the other, is especially worth making, given the implications for entry and growth problems discussed below.

The picture is not one of outright dominance by large firms, or even of reproduction of the status quo in new fields; but neither is it one of industrial *gekokujo*, with small firms turning the tables on large firms. There are, of course, variations from industry to industry. Market-leader discussions are open to the criticisms that they bias the picture against small firms, and that they fail to capture the dynamic character of industrial restructuring and new cross-market growth. Regarding the former, however, in a country where rankings are extremely important, small firms often rank in the top five or ten of small markets, again as suggested by the MZ example. Focusing further down the market size scale would produce a reasonably similar picture.[4] The second criticism should not be construed as an open invitation to speculation, especially in view of the problems faced by SMEs, which we shall now consider.

4. PROBLEMS FACING SMES

Despite favourable environmental changes, SMEs face a number of problems stemming largely from their size. Most are not unique to Japan, although their particular manifestation and intensity may be distinctive. They will be discussed initially in terms of inputs from factor markets (money, materials, and people), management problems in integrating these, and problems in marketing outputs. As we have seen, many of the successful SME new market entrants are well-established firms. I shall touch briefly on the important issue of successors, as well as new start-ups.

Financing

Difficulties in raising funds and high interest rates are not problems restricted to Japanese SMEs. As controversy in 1991 suggests, many small British firms would identify with the saying 'Banks want to push umbrellas on to you when the weather is fine and take them away when it starts to rain.' Capital shortages and high demand from large companies in the past meant that the large city banks were seldom considered even fair-weather friends, and in downturns SMEs were doubly squeezed by large firms delaying payment for goods or services delivered. Again, this phenomenon is not unique to Japan, but was intense there.

Government and SME financing institutions helped ease the situation, especially in downturns; and from the late 1970s, as large firms increased their retained earnings and embarked upon 'securitization', city banks became more eager to court SMEs. The position of SME owners with land was also strengthened by the collateral that rocketing land prices conferred. Roughly 23 per cent of SME loans came from city banks in 1980, but 32 per cent in 1988. (Over the same time, the proportion supplied by the three government insititutions decreased from 13 to 8 per cent: Chusho kigyo cho 1986, 1990*a*: app. 30).

Large manufacturing firms have thus loosened their ties with banks (*ginko banare*), while SMEs have increased their reliance on bank loans. Although 'securitization' has not penetrated the SME world deeply, a small but visible number of SMEs are being listed, with numbers on the OTC (over the-counter) market expected to rise from around 500 in 1990 to at least 1,000 by the end of the century. Recent new listings are concentrated especially in high-technology manufacturing and new businesses and services (Hamada *et al.* 1990).

Overall, financing nowadays is not the most serious problem for existing SMEs, particularly those with land. As Kiyonari says, instead of management problems stemming from difficulties in obtaining finance, present difficulties in obtaining finance are more likely to stem from management problems (Kiyonari 1990; 203). This may change somewhat in the post-bubble economy.

Materials

Small firms that have to buy materials from certain large firms, whether for oligopolistic or trading reasons, may be confronted with high prices. And when they have to sell their products to large firms, as many do, they may be confronted by low prices—again, a double squeeze. If the price of raw materials rises—fuelled, for example, by an increase in oil prices—they are not permitted to pass on the increase. Indeed, they are forced to reduce costs as large firms implement new cost-cutting programmes. Many small firm owners who experienced price cuts yet again following the yen rise claim that they have finally reached their limit. As they gain greater independence and diversify their materials suppliers and customers, they are becoming less vulnerable in this respect.

People

Probably the greatest problem facing small firms in Japan today derives from the labour markets. Traditionally there has been a strong correlation between academic achievement and the size of firm that school- or college-leavers have sought to enter; the larger the firm, the higher the wages and the greater the job security, career prospects, and prestige, so the higher the academic quality of applicants the firm has been able to recruit. It would be safe to say that this correlation has been stronger in Japan than in other countries, and it has been strengthened by the practice of 'lifetime' employment in the larger firms.

This does not mean that small firms could not find skilled workers, or that they lack entrepreneurial talent, which not infrequently resides in founding owners or their successors. Incentives for starting up or taking over parents' firms have been sufficient to ensure that. The situation has become increasingly difficult for SMEs, however. Despite the changing image of SMEs, many school-leavers are reluctant to be employed by one, particularly if it is family-run. And those that are may not be prepared to work as hard to learn a trade as in former times. In the words of one small engineering firm owner,

'Parents used to come around and bow down and ask us to teach their boys skills, and to belt them if they didn't learn. You can't do that now—they'd quit. They quit to drive rubbish trucks where they can get as much without worrying about 1/5,000 or 1/10,000 tolerances. They don't think long-term any more.'

This is related not just to a youthful aversion to the 3 Ks (*Kiken*—dangerous; *kitanai*—dirty; *kitsui*—demanding), but to a general preference among youth for office jobs, to growing affluence, and to fewer situations arising in which talented or hardworking youths are forced to leave school early through family circumstances, thus missing out on the chance to work in a large firm.

Intensifying this has been the very tight labour market situation in most parts of Japan. According to a survey carried out in Tokyo and surrounding prefectures in March 1991, 62 per cent of SMEs which wanted to recruit new graduates were unable to recruit *any* (*Asahi shinbun*, 26 April 1991). The figure was highest for construction companies (69 per cent), followed by manufacturing (68 per cent) and transportation (64 per cent), with retail and services below 50 per cent. Mid-career workers and even part-timers are hard to recruit, and by occupation the shortage is not just of engineers, but also of general shop-floor workers. Reports tell of closures caused by worker shortages, and wages and conditions have had to be improved. Newspapers carry frequent reports of the desperate and novel means managers are using to try to attract workers; and of course, illegally employed foreign workers are working mostly in SMEs.

Management

SMEs also face numerous management challenges in effectively integrating production factors, strategy development and co-ordination, and growth-related problems, and in adapting to environmental changes. Founders may bring engineering skills with them, but they lack experience in financial management, human resource management, and marketing. They may be forced to spend all their time on day-to-day production matters with no time to develop longer-term objectives. Their skills might be enough to manage forty employees, but be stretched at a hundred. Partners in a business venture might bring vital knowledge and contacts with them, and recruit some other mid-career workers, but be unable to integrate their vision sufficiently to persuade a university professor to recommend good graduating students, an important step in the creation of a corporate identity and take-off as a growing concern. Again, this relates not just to labour shortages, but also to labour market characteristics, which is part of the reason why corporate growth is slower in many independent start-ups in Japan than, for example, in the United States or even the United Kingdom, and why so many of the top firms in new industries are long-established.

Marketing

Large firms naturally have greater ability to advertise, greater marketing resources, name recognition advantages, and deeper pockets to finance head-on competition. Also, small firms may come up against the distribution impediments and bureaucratic obstacles that many foreign firms complain of. As was argued, however, many of these smaller firms operate in intermediate and niche markets, where the number of customers is smaller and more readily identifiable. Still, they may have trouble establishing themselves, only gradually gaining sizeable orders from new customers, and may be forced to accept disadvantageous trading conditions for some time. These marketing resource and name recognition handicaps apply also to the new business and service areas, but are alleviated somewhat by a business media hungry for stories on promising new trends market sectors, and firms. Furthermore, lack of marketing and sales specialists may be compensated for by building up close relations with customers, and developing a responsiveness to their needs.

Successors

An important concern of many SME owners is that of succession. Where the owner has a recognized successor, there is an incentive to pass on a going concern. Often the introduction of mechatronic equipment in engineering firms has been carried out by the owner's son (who may well have been to university and studied engineering or economics, and may have worked in a larger firm for a spell), not to mention the implementation of own-product strategies. Roughly 40 per cent of SME founders are now over 60 years old, and it has been estimated that 84 per cent of closures in 1988 took place in SMEs where there was no successor (Chusho Kigyo cho 1990*b*: 49). Changing generational preferences also make this an important issue for owners, as is suggested by the quote at the end of this section.

Start-ups

Start-up problems are not restricted to venture firms. Whereas once it was relatively easy to set up a new manufacturing business, subcontracting at first for one's former employer before branching out, the obstacles to this course of action have grown. It is very difficult now to start out with one second-hand lathe in a tiny back-street workshop. Technological requirements have become very stringent, and manufacturers have become increasingly selective about who they give orders to. A CNC lathe or machining centre may now be required to secure orders. And there is the critical problem of finding workers. As a result, small firm owners say that fewer of their workers are likely to become independent:

'In the past about fifteen of our workers have become independent. We shared some of our business with them. Nowadays you need about ¥100 million to set yourself up, the machines are complicated, and the processes more difficult. None of the workers here now will become independent.'

New establishment rates in manufacturing have declined steadily since the late 1960s, where they averaged 6.0 per cent per year versus a closure rate of 2.5 per cent, to 3.1 and 3.0 per cent in the 1981–6 period. In all industries, the start-up—closure gap closed from 3.3 to 0.7 per cent over the same period (Somucho, various years; see also Chusho kigyo cho 1990*b*: 73). This is especially evident in the major cities; in Tokyo the number of factories fell by 9 per cent between 1985 and 1988. The number in Ota Ward fell by the same proportion, with a drop in employment of 16 per cent (Ota Ku 1990: 17). Moreover, many of the start-ups in Ota were actually by established SME owners.

In sum, while in theory existing SMEs are in a better position than in the past, they face numerous challenges. Those that have been able to respond positively through good management or good fortune have survived and indeed prospered, while others have not fared so well; hence the widely remarked 'polarization' of SMEs, between those growing and gaining greater independence and those slowly 'sinking'. As well, the successor problem, generational attitude changes, and difficulties in setting up new firms have raised the spectre of 'hollowing out from below'.

The key issue for many SMEs is people. Securing the right staff influences an increasing range of management decisions, as is indicated by the following comments by small factory owners in Ota Ward:

'I try to hire young females for the office. They make the workplace brighter, and where there are young women, you can get young men.'

'Look at Company X over there. They've designed their building in an outrageous way, but it's worked. They're getting young people.'

'One of the main reasons we're setting up a branch factory in Yamagata is because you can still get people there.'

'A survey in Nikkei the other day said 36 per cent of shop-floor workers at Toyota wouldn't want their children to do the same job. What would it be for *machi koba* ('street-corner' factories)? More like 100 per cent. There are three ways to go—same as now, and slowly sink; new product; or specialist technique (*gijutsu*). With technological development, you can make use of your own experience in production and do it with your own know-how. But it's only worth it if you've got someone to take over. That's what drives me on. Unless I can make it interesting for my children, they won't stay.'

Parents ('parent' companies) have often provided an impetus for change in such factories. Now, it would seem, children do. Shortages of workers have spurred new investment, changes in working conditions, even the quest for new lines of business and products/processes. They are also an important consideration in the inter-firm link-ups or 'networking'. For many small firms, this is the only realistic means of expansion, even survival. The last factory owner quoted, besides his main machining business, has formed a small development company and is seeking patents for four 'environmental' machines developed jointly with other factory-owner friends: 'I'm lucky, because I know a lot of people; I hear a lot of problems, and can get a lot of people together. That's the road to survival.'

5. GOVERNMENT SME POLICIES AND NETWORKS

SME problems are old and new. There was a spate of 'labour shortage closures' in the late 1960s, for instance, when the 'growing gap' between successful innovators and 'the rest' was also widely commented on, and not for the first time. Policies that address the problems are similar; they embody a range of old and new and sometimes contradictory perceptions about SMEs.[5] At the risk of oversimplification, the predominant policy line by the late 1950s largely reflected the dual-structure views expressed in the 1957 Economic White Paper, with protection policies added for political reasons. Small, backward SMEs had to be encouraged to 'modernize', that is to increase their size and capital intensity, or convert if they couldn't. 'Modernization bankruptcies' brought some recognition of the limitations of encouraging small firms across the board to behave like large ones, but real changes did not come about until after the 1972 SME Policy Deliberation Council's report, which stressed the shift to a 'soft', knowledge-intensive economy from 'hard', volume, scale-merit orientation, as well as the need to respect SME diversity.

By 1980 (cf. the 1980s 'Vision'), a combination of strong small-firm performance during the economic turbulence of the 1970s and changes in the economy led to the recognition that, not only was there a variety of small firms, but that a good many were active and 'vital', very well suited, in fact, to the new age (Arita 1990: 111, 126). It was no coincidence that this re-evaluation was concurrent with those taking place in other countries. A number of measures based on this thinking were introduced or strengthened in the 1980s. Of particular concern here are those measures encouraging 'networking', such as 'inter-industry exchange' and 'fusion' (*yugoka*).

Rather than nudging small firms in the same industry together to achieve economies of scale, a range of new programmes was launched by central, regional, and local authorities to encourage SME collaboration across industries. The rationale, supplied in part by academics, was (1) the familiar notion that SMEs are limited in terms of management resources, technology development capabilities, human resources, marketing know-how, and information. Encouraging SMEs to co-operate with each other could make up for these shortcomings; but (2) rather than pursue ever greater efficiency within their established areas, or combining resources in these areas to achieve greater economies of scale, key management issues for SMEs now include how to cope with the changing nature of markets, given the breakdown of traditional boundaries, changing customer preferences, and structural changes such as 'servicization'. Through *inter*-industry exchange and co-operation these issues can be grasped and tackled more effectively. 'Loosely coupled networks' may in fact be capable of greater creative response to the challenges than traditional 'hierarchical' organizations (Ogawa 1990: 46–7).

In other words, the programmes address problems that SMEs face in their responses to environmental change; their efforts to develop their own products and gain greater independence; risk-sharing and finance; lack of human resources and marketing weaknesses; etc.; and they come complete with theoretical backing. As befits the 'information age', SME information centres with on-line data facilities have also been established, and encouragement is now given to small firms to introduce networking information technology.

The first programme was the 'technology exchange plaza', launched in 1981 by the Japan Small Business Corporation as an extension of its technology transfer promotion activities. It was funded half by the national and half by the prefectural governments, and backed by JSBC information facilities and consultants (Kokudo cho 1990: 25). The number of small-firm groups engaged in 'plaza', and subsequently 'inter-industry exchange' and cross-industry 'fusion' (*yugoka*), activities has increased rapidly, from around 700 reported in 1987 to 1,527 in 1988 and 1,927 in 1989, involving over 65,000 firms.

There are various types of groups, some organized by private initiative, others at the initiative of various public bodies or chambers/associations of commerce and industry; some under plaza sponsorship, some open to new entry, others closed, etc. As for objectives, according to one survey, 61 per cent seek primarily information exchange and 15 per cent technology exchange; 9 per cent view them primarily as a means of training successors, 6 per cent as a study group on a particular issue, 6 per cent to receive joint orders, and 3 per cent for joint technology development. The Yokohama Technology Communication Plaza, consisting of thirty-eight companies and organized under the auspices of the Yokohama SME Guidance Centre, seeks primarily to exchange technology information and jointly to solve technology-related problems. The Yokohama YK Project organized under the sponsorship of the Yokohama Industry Hall (*kogyokan*), on the other hand, involves some 200 firms and saw the development and commercialization of some twenty new products between 1982 and 1987 (Kokudo cho 1990: 29).[6]

To the cynic, the programmes and the publicity efforts surrounding them smack of government agencies perpetuating their reason for existence, and dressing up their schemes in roughly tailored academic garb. In their defence, they help to generate interest in important trends and issues, discussion, and, where necessary, support. In this way, they may really be 'catalysers' (as the government consultants for *yugoka* are called) for private initiative. As far as the small-firm participant is concerned, what matters is not the theoretical rationale but the possibility of gaining new contacts, useful information, and perhaps a new application for a technology or a partner for product development. As such, the programmes may provide a useful supplement to their own efforts, but are by no means a panacea to their problems.

In fact, they generate problems of their own. Commonly cited are the failure of those involved to 'fuse' or even offer know-how. Sometimes there is too much emphasis on product development; there are difficulties in operationalizing projects, marketing failures of products developed, and organizational problems (Tokyo shoko shidojo 1990: 28–32). 'Loosely coupled networks' may be appropriate for stimulating creative projects, but not necessarily for managing the results (day-to-day production of the products, marketing, etc.: Tokyo shoko shidojo 1989: 53–4).

Looking at the programmes in context, over the past five or six years a considerable literature on networks has appeared in Japan. Some of it incorporates *keiretsu* relationships and argues for the economic rationality of these. Other accounts see networks as a new form of organization, looser and more flexible than those typically found in *keiretsu*, and better suited to take advantage of environmental change. Within this current, some see small-firm networks (government-initiated or otherwise) as a means for small firms to develop greater independence from large firms and for solving handicaps associated with size. A sober assessment must conclude that, while they may provide firms with new opportunities for growth, small-firm networks are not yet harbingers of a new industrial structure in which large firms are relegated to history.

6. SMALL FACTORIES IN OTA WARD

It is fitting to conclude with some comments on changes in the industrial structure of Ota Ward, Tokyo, which is in an area in a number of ways at the forefront of industrial restructuring, and has the greatest concentration of factories at the city level in Japan. Roughly 90 per cent of Ota's 8,000 factories have twenty or fewer employees, and 80 per cent are in the general, precision, electrical, transport machine, and metal product industries. Ota is part of the Keihin industrial belt, home to many of Japan's large engineering firms.

In the 1960s, many of the large firms relocated their mass production facilities away from Tokyo because of high costs and restrictive factory laws. In the aftermath, some of the suppliers that stayed behind successfully developed their own products. Where once they machined high-volume parts for automobile and appliance makers, for instance, they now made low-volume automation machines for the same manufacturers based on their own production experience. These companies, often with 100 or fewer employees, became 'new core' producers, securing orders nationwide, and now worldwide, and subcontracting out work locally. Other subcontractors cut their ties with appliance makers after one too many 'cost-down' beatings, and instead began to work for the new core firms or other *chuken* makers (which did not apply the same pressure, and often paid in cash; also, their work often had a higher value-added component) or else developed products themselves. Others did prototype work for the R&D factories the large firms left behind. High land and wage prices and worker shortages have exerted constant pressure towards higher value-added work.

Seki and Kato (1990) divide the metal/machining factories into four types, and describe the close links between them (p. 115). The product makers (the 'new core' firms) comprise 10.6 per cent of the factories and 40.3 per cent of employees, processing/machining factories 44.5 and 23.0 per cent of employment, heavy processes (forging, welding, press work, etc.) 28.8 and 21.2 per cent, and related functions (materials, plastic moulds, assemblers, etc.) 16.2 and 15.4 per cent. The historical and geographical position, recent evolution, and the balance between these types, they argue, lend Ota its position as a 'national technopolis'. But it is a fine balance, and there are fears that it will be upset by 'hollowing-out' from below (or from the sides, if one is to avoid hierarchical terms).

Two examples of the 'new core' firms are FK, with 75 employees, and SS, with 100.[7] The father of the present president of FK started out by machining metal car parts for Mitsubishi and Isuzu at the end of the war, but in the mid-1950s decided to make his own product—custom machines for making those same parts. The change over took ten years but was ultimately successful, and now FK sells the machines to major car makers not only in Japan but in Korea as well. It farms work out to 100 subcontractors and has purchasing relations with a further 200. SS, in the neighbouring Shingawa Ward, started out as a tool trading company in the pre-war period, and after the war took on some machining work for its biggest client. At the client's request, it also attempted a machine for an automated assembly line. It has since grown into one of the top three firms in the automated assembly line equipment market, with many orders recently for large firms' overseas transplants. The structure of SS's subcontracting has changed over the past twenty years, from a single tier of firms each with around ten employees, to a multi-tier structure with the top firms having between thirty and fifty employees. SS has established factories in Kanagawa Prefecture, and has recently teamed up with two other firms to move into automated warehousing hardware.

Various types of small-firm networks can be found in and around Ota Ward, from the manufacturing and development networks just described to information exchange clubs and organizations and even an on-line network. Small size, agility, and networking have indeed helped establish the new core firms. But while Ota's firms have gained greater direct independence from the giant firms, ultimately they also rely on these firms to buy their products and processes. Because so many of their goods are intermediate, they are more reliant than those SMEs, for example, in the eastern (Joto) part of Tokyo, which are not so high-tech or specialized and produce more final-demand products.

Small firms in Japan can and do become independent product makers, even major ones in their particular markets and market sectors. On occasion, too, these bases provide a springboard to growth and diversification, through *chuken* to major league status. As we have seen, such firms are often established SMEs, which gain the vital entrepreneurial input and enter the right market at the right time. Industrial growth and change have generated numerous opportunities for such SMEs, while competitive pressures punish those who lag.

But giant and large firms still exert strong influences, through the product markets they dominate, the new ones they enter (directly, or through spin-offs, start-ups or joint ventures), through co-development projects, the products and services of smaller firms that they purchase, and through their influence on labour markets, policy-makers, and so on. Small firms are not confined to the back seat of Japanese industry; but neither have they, individually or in networks, seized the driving wheel.

NOTES TO CHAPTER 8

1. With regard to the economic rationality of Japan's industrial structure, even if it is based on economically rational principles, it is a very limited concept of rationality, which only superficially considers the apportionment of benefits and burdens (e.g. Okumura 1990).
2. Observations on the semiconductor equipment and CAD industries were provided by NRC analyst K. Tatsuzawa.
3. Okimoto and Saxonhouse (1987) found that R&D expenditure by smaller firms (less than 1,000 employees) in Japan constituted a greater proportion of total R&D expenditure than in the USA, but this was due to their numerical strength; the research *intensity* (% of sales) was overall lower, and a smaller proportion of so-called major innovations came from smaller firms.
4. Thus, the term 'spectrum economy' used by Dore and others is appropriate, one with rather fine gradations. In line with this thinking, I have avoided arguments based on aggregate dualist SME *v.* large-firm figures. SMEs might be more profitable than large firms (a fact that was pointed out by Komiya 30 years ago). On the other hand, the value-added productivity (value added per employee) differential between large and small firms has *increased* in the post-Oil Shock period, as capital productivity has failed to keep up with capital investment increases in SMEs. Such aggregate observations might be suggestive, but can be misleading if used carelessly. Further size breakdowns are necessary, and controls must be added, e.g. for industry and capital intensity.
5. The notions of 'too small, too many' and 'excessive competition' which underpinned many SME policies, for instance, were mixed with the (Occupation Authority GHQ-derived) view that SMEs should be encouraged to promote healthy competition and prevent unhealthy concentration (Arita 1990).
6. One *yugoka* group reported in the 1988 SME White Paper consisted of 5 manufacturing SMEs—in medical instruments, wireless communications, switching devices, inspection equipment, and machine design—which developed an intelligent underwater robot. Partly because of the grant conditions, in 1989 only 94 groups were official programme participants of *yugoka*. At the end of 1988, 57% were reported to be in the initial 'exchange' 'operationalization' or business phase (Chusho kigyo cho 1989: 83–5; 1990).
7. The following is based on my own interviews with managers of Ota Ward enterprises in 1989–90.

REFERENCES

Arita, T. (1990), *Sengo nihon no chusho kigyo seisaku* (Japanese Postwar SME Policies), Nihon hyoronsha, Tokyo.

Asanuma, B. (1990), 'Nihon ni okeru meka to sapuraiya to no kankei' (Maker–Supplier Relations in Japan), in M. Tsuchiya and Y. Miwa (eds.), *Nihon no chusho kigyo* (Japanese SMEs), Tokyo daigaku shuppankai, Tokyo.

Chusho kigyo cho (ed.) (1989), *Chusho kigyo hakusho* (SME White Paper), Okurasho insatsu kyoku, Tokyo.

——(ed.) (1990*a*), *Chusho kigyo hakusho* (SME White Paper), Okurasho insatsu kyoku, Tokyo. See also various other years.

——(1990*b*), *90 nendai no chusho kigyo bijion* (1990s SME Vision), Tsusho sangyo chosakai, Tokyo.

——(1990*c*), *Dainanakai kogyo jittai kihon chosa hokokusho* (Seventh Industrial Situation Basic Survey Report), Tsusan tokei kyokai, Tokyo.

Clark, R. (1987), *Venture Capital in Britain, America and Japan*, Croom-Helm, London.

Hamada, Y., Kumagai, K., and Nishizawa, A. (1990), *Kabushiki tento shijo* (The OTC Market), Toyo keizai shinposha, Tokyo.

Hashimoto, T. (1989), 'Keizai, sangyo kozo no tenkan' (Changes in the Economy and Industrial Structure), in Kokumin kin'yu koko (ed.), *Gendai shitauke kigyoron* (Perspectives on Modern Subcontracting Firms), Chusho kigyo risarchi senta, Tokyo.

Imai, K. (1986), 'Netowaku soshiki: tenbo' (Network Organization: Prospects), in *Soshiki kagaku* (Organization Science), *20*(3): 2–12.

Johanson, J., and Matsson, L.-G. (1987), 'Interoganizational Relations in Industrial Systems: A Network Approach Compared with a Transaction Cost Approach', *International Studies in Management and Organization*, 17(1): 34–48.

Kameyama, N. (1989), 'Komento' (Comments), in M. Tsuchiya and Y. Miwa (eds.), *Nihon no chusho kigyo* (Japanese SMEs), Tokyo daigaku shuppankai, Tokyo.

Keizai kikakucho (EPA) (ed.) (1990), *Keizai hakusho* (White Paper on the Economy), Okurasho insatsu kyoku, Tokyo.

Kiyonari, T. (1990), *Chusho kigyo tokuhon* (SME Reader), 2nd edn., Toyo keizai shinposha, Tokyo.

Kokudo cho (ed.) (1990), *Chiiki sangyo kodoka to igyoshu koryu* (Regional Industrial Upgrading and Exchange across Industries), Okurasho insatsu kyoku, Tokyo.

Miwa, Y. (1990), *Nihon no kigyo to sangyo soshiki* (Japan's Enterprises and Industrial Organization), Tokyo daigaku shuppankai, Tokyo.

Nakamura, H. (1990), *Shin chuken kigyo ron* (New Core Firm Theory), Toyo keizai shinposha, Tokyo.

Nihon kogyo shinbusha (1988), *Nihon kogyo nenkan* (Japan Industrial Yearbook), Tokyo.

Nikko Research Centre (1991), *Analysis of Japanese Industries for Investors 1991*, Nikko Research Centre, Tokyo.

Ogawa, M. (1990), 'Chusho kigyo no netowaku katsudo ni miru kigyo no joho kodo' (Corporate Information Behaviour Seen in SME Network Activities), in

Tokyo shoko shidojo (ed.), *Shoko shido* (Industry and Commerce Guidance), no. 441, 45–62.

Okimoto, D., and Saxonhouse, G. (1987), 'Technology and the Future of the Economy', in K. Yamamura and Y. Yasuba (eds.), *The Political Economy of Japan*, i, *The Domestic Transformation*, Stanford University Press, Stanford, Calif.

Okumura, H. (1990), 'Seitoka dekinai *keiretsu* no gorisei' (Keiretsu Rationality Can't be Justified), *Ekonomisto*, 10 July: 78–89.

Ota Ku (ed.) (1990), *Ota ku no kogyo* (Industry in Ota Ward), Tokyo.

Pratten, C. (1991), *The Competitiveness of Small Firms*, Cambridge University Press.

Sato, Y. (1990), 'Rekishi no naka de henyo suru chusho kigyo' (SMEs Changing within History), in M. Tsuchiya and Y. Miwa (eds.), *Nihon no chusho kigyo* (Japanese SMEs), Tokyo daigaku shuppankai, Tokyo.

Seki, M., and Kato, H. (1990), *Gendai nihon no chusho kikai kogyo* (Modern Japanese SME Machinery Industry), Shinhyoron, Tokyo.

Somucho (ed.) (various years), *Jigyosho tokei chosa hokoku* (Establishment Statistical Survey Report), Nihon tokei kyokai, Tokyo.

Tokyo Shoko Shidojo (1989), *Chosa kenkyu: Chusho kigyo no yugoka katsudo to un'ei* (Survey Research: SME 'Fusion' Activities and Administration), Tokyo.

——(1990), *Chosa kenkyu: Tokyo no chusho kigyo to yugoka* (Survey Research: Tokyo SMEs and 'Fusion'), Tokyo.

Tsuchiya, M., and Miwa, Y. (eds.) (1990), *Nihon no chusho kigyo* (Japanese SMEs), Tokyo daigaku shuppankai, Tokyo.

Womack, J., Jones, D., and Roos, D. (1990), *The Machine that Changed the World*, Rawson Associates, New York.

9

Japanese Human Resource Management from the Viewpoint of Incentive Theory

HIDESHI ITOH

1. INTRODUCTION

This paper concerns the management of human resources in the stylized large Japanese firm. The emphasis is on issues of internal incentives, on how the Japanese firm provides its employees with incentives to behave in harmony with goals of the firm. The paper takes an economic approach; by drawing freely on the insights from the growing literature on the economics of organizations (incentive theory), I attempt to explain the economic rationale of some of the distinct features of Japanese human resource management (HRM) practices, particularly on pay and promotion systems, as well as to discuss possible reasons why they are different from Western management practices. Of course, this does not imply that I intend to refute other paradigms, such as those by sociologists, anthropologists, or historians: the economic approach is but one of many alternative ways of looking at Japanese management practices.

It is not my intention to present an exhaustive survey of the economic literature on Japanese firms. There are large bodies of comparative empirical studies that attempt to 'demystify' Japanese management, identifying what distinguishes the Japanese firm from its Western counterpart. Today's informed readers probably know that what is unique in Japan is a much more subtle matter than popular writings have suggested. In Section 2, I briefly review some stylized facts about the Japanese human resource management by referring to the recent empirical research. However, my aim throughout the paper is not to contribute to our further understanding of what is and is not unique in Japanese firms; basically, I take the characteristics summarized there for granted, and focus here on their causes and economic rationality.

The author would like to thank Masahiko Aoki, Banri Asanuma, Osamu Hayashida, Hiroyuki Itami, John McMillan, Tsuyoshi Namikawa, Masuyuki Nishijima, Isao Ohashi, Toshiaki Tachibanaki, and Yuji Yumoto for helpful comments and discussions, and Akiko Yamazaki for editorial assistance. Financial support from the Japan Economic Research Foundation is gratefully acknowledged.

In Section 3, I consider some of the implications arising from the distinct characteristics of Japanese work organization structures for incentive issues. One of the main messages of the paper is that the reward structure of the Japanese firm is designed so as to alleviate various incentive problems associated with the structure of its work organization. Differences in pay, promotions, and employment relations from the Western firm can also be attributed to differences in work organization. I consider some possible reasons why work organization structures are different between Japan and the West, but the discussion is highly incomplete because of the very preliminary stage of the economic study of organization structures.

The premise of the paper is as following. It is the substantial lifetime pay differences stemming from different rates of promotion that motivate employees in the Japanese firm. Unfortunately, the empirical research testing this hypothesis is scarce. In Sections 4–6, therefore, I focus on its theoretical justification and implications. Section 4 concerns the lack of pay-for-performance. The hypothesis implies that Japanese employees are not rewarded immediately and transiently after some (objective or subjective) measures of individual performance become available. Again, no empirical research is available, yet the recent development in the principal–agent paradigm provides some illuminating logic leading to such a feature, particularly in the Japanese firm, given its organization structures.

If pay-for-performance is absent in the short run, incentives must be provided for employees over their career, and to do so long-term attachment between employers and employees is necessary. In Section 5 I discuss the nature of long-term relationships in Japan. My standpoint there is that it is structures and practices adopted by the Japanese firm that are responsible for the strong degree of employer–employee attachment over long periods.

Section 6 then concerns promotion schemes—reward attached to discrete 'hierarchical ranks'. I consider several economic theories that explain why pay is attached to discrete ranks rather than individuals, and the implications of this for the promotion patterns characterizing the Japanese management practices, i.e. 'wide' career (experience in a broad range of tasks), and slow promotion. Section 7 contains concluding remarks.

2. STYLIZED FACTS

The purpose of this section is to summarize some of the representative features of the HRM practices of the stylized Japanese firm, compared with the Western firm. The summary here is brief and is not intended to be complete; in particular, few supporting data will be shown. Aoki (1988), Hashimoto (1990), Koike (1988), and Lincoln and McBride (1987) offer more extensive surveys of the empirical studies, and detailed description and supporting data for the characteristics presented below.[1]

I have chosen to review the following topics: long-term employment relationships; compensation policies; promotion schemes; and work organization. Note that not all Japanese firms or their employees share the features summarized below. My major focus is on regular male (both blue-collar and white-collar) workers of large private companies in Japan.[2]

Fact 1 Long-term employment relationships are more prevalent in Japan.

Long-term employment relationships are common not only in Japan but also in many Western countries. However, careful empirical studies seem to show that this feature is more prevalent in Japan. For example, an average worker in Japan stays longer with the same employer than an average worker in the United States does, and does not change jobs as often as the latter (Hashimoto and Raisian 1985). Whittaker's (1990) comparison between Japan and Britain shows that a greater proportion of Japanese workers have 'long tenure' than British workers. Koike (1988) and the *OECD Employment Outlook* (OECD 1984) contain similar results, and comparisons with other European workers as well.

The durable attachment of a worker to an employer occurs when the employer does not dismiss the worker and when the worker does not leave the firm. The first of these two conditions is known as 'lifetime' employment; except for extreme situations, the firm does not dismiss its workers (until mandatory retirement, of course).[3] The lifetime employment thus only binds the employer. Note, however, that this is not a contractual state: no explicit clause regarding this policy is found in the employment contract. In fact, Japanese labour law prohibits contracts from covering more than one year, and the usual practice is not to specify the employment period. Thus, the enforcement of the no-dismissals policy in Japan must somehow rely on non-contractual implicit mechanisms such as reputation, which make the policy self-enforcing.[4]

The second condition for long-term employment relations, i.e. that Japanese workers do not separate from their employers in mid-career as often as workers in Western countries do, depends on the competitiveness of the external labour market. This is determined partly by exogenous factors and partly by endogenous factors such as the structures and practices of firms. The discussion in Section 5 emphasizes the latter factors.

Fact 2 (*a*) Not only white-collar but also blue-collar workers are paid monthly salary and biannual bonuses. (*b*) Salary rises at regular intervals (usually every one to two years), and also at the time of promotion to higher hierarchical 'ranks', on the basis of age and tenure (and merit assessments, particularly for the latter). (*c*) Wages are *not* attached to particular jobs; i.e., ranks are only loosely associated with specific job classifications.

Word 'rank' in Fact 2 is worth clarifying. There are two kinds of discrete hierarchical ranks, which I call *vertical ranks* and *horizontal ranks*.[5] The former are associated with hierarchical titles (*yakushoku*) such as section chief, department head, and so on; hence promotion to a higher vertical rank (*shōshin*) implies changes in authority and/or responsibility. The horizontal ranks, on the other hand, are artificially created grades (*kyū* or *shikaku*) which are use for differential treatment of individuals in terms of status and/or pay only. Promotion to a higher rank in this sense (*shōkyu* or *shōkaku*) implies no essential change in authority, responsibility, or jobs performed. These two sort of ranks are interrelated to some degree, since a hierarchical job title often has a specific grade as a prerequisite; i.e., promotion to a higher vertical rank may not be possible before a particular horizontal rank is reached.

Figure 1 illustrates the stylized pay scheme in Japan. A new employee is first assigned to the lowest rank (rank 1 in the figure), and is paid the salary that is attached to that rank. His salary increases regularly with tenure or age, along the curve. The pay rise also depends on merit assessment, which is why each curve in the figure has some breadth: workers with the same tenure and age possibly receive different wages according to their merit ratings. The slope of each curve becomes less flat as the worker's age and tenure increase. At some point in his career, the worker is promoted to a higher rank (rank 2), with a steeper wage–seniority curve, based on seniority and merit assessment. After he stays with that rank and receives regular pay rises according to the curve, he may be promoted to the next level (rank 3); and this career development continues. Fact 2 mainly concerns each wage–seniority curve. Promotion is the subject of Fact 3 below.

Koike (1988) claims that many of the features in Fact 2 are common among white-collar workers in a number of Western countries, while only in Japan do these features extend to production workers: the uniqueness of the Japanese firm is in its 'white-collarization' of blue-collar workers. Ishida (1990) argues, mainly on the basis of a comparison with British workers, that wages contingent on merit ratings are the most distinct characteristics of the pay system for Japanese production workers, in contrast with wages attached to jobs for production workers in the West. Several systematic empirical studies show that many of these characteristics are more prevalent in Japan. Hashimoto and Raisian (1985) find that: (1) wages typically rise more rapidly with tenure for Japanese workers than for American workers; and (2) firm-specific experience (tenure) has a greater effect than general experience (total years of work experience) in Japan, while the reverse is true in the United States. Kalleberg and Lincoln (1988) find that personal characteristics such as age, tenure, and marital status are important determinants of earnings for Japanese production workers, while job characteristics play a greater role for American workers. In accordance with this last evidence, Ono (1989) argues that much of the positive slope of wage–

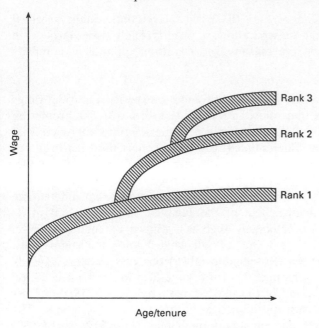

FIG. 1   The Stylized Pay Scheme in Japan

seniority curves reflects the firm's intention to guarantee the living expenses of workers.

There is no systematic research that attempts to measure the effects of merit assessments on salary increases in Japan. However, casual observation seems to indicate that the salary increase upon promotion is much more important than the regular annual pay raise. Although his data are old (1966), Fujimura (1989) reports that for most employees (about 80 per cent for firms with more than 5,000 employees, 65 per cent for firms with 1,000–4,999 employees) the difference between the highest and the lowest regular salary increases is within 5 per cent range. Tachibanaki (1987, 1988), using the 1975 survey data on Social Stratification and Mobility in Japan, find that the hierarchical (vertical) ranks have the most important influence on earnings differentials.

Other distinct features of compensation practices in the Japanese firm are biannual bonuses and lump-sum payments at the time of separation. The role the bonus system plays in Japan is an issue that has frequently been discussed and examined by economists. The bonus may be a worker's share of returns to firm-specific human capital (Hashimoto 1979), a sort of profit-sharing mechanism stabilizing employment (Freeman and Weitzman 1987), or an effort incentive for the worker (Ohashi 1989; Okuno 1984). Aoki (1988) alerts us by noting that much of the bonus payment depends on merit assessments, more than the basic salary contractually specified does. He also notes that the separation payment typically rises sharply with tenure and depends on the reasons for separation (private or company reasons).

Fact 3 (*a*) Workers in the Japanese firm tend to experience a wider range of closely related jobs than those in the Western firm. (*b*) The promotion pattern of white-collar workers in Japan is a late selection approach; that is, the majority are not differentiated from their cohort until ten to fifteen years of tenure, and then only a minority are selected to go on to upper management positions.

Koike (1988) argues that these are two of the features that differentiate the human resource management of the Japanese firm from that of its Western counterpart. Unfortunately, there is not much systematic evidence. Koike (1988) offers some evidence of (*a*), while I know no comparative study of promotion speed. Rosenbaum (1979) observes patterns of early selections of 'stars' in personnel data of a large firm in the United States; according to his data, 2 out of 671 newly hired employees in 1962 (0.3 per cent) attained the highest position after thirteen years of tenure. The personnel data of a large oil company in the United States in Forbes (1987) show that the ration is 2 per cent (4 of 180 reached the highest position after eleven years of tenure). On the other hand, Hanada (1989) offers career trees of five Japanese firms; the ratio of the employees in the same cohort who reached the highest rank after fifteen years of tenure are 3, 65, 74, 81, and 100 per cent: except for one firm, then, property (*b*) is evident.[6] For other evidence on (*b*), see Pucik (1985) and papers in Koike (1991).[7]

Although seniority is still an important determinant of promotion decisions, merit ratings appear no less important.[8] In the long run, substantial pay differences among workers with the same experience and education seem to emerge, differences that originate mainly from different promotion rates. Weiss (1984, 1988) find such a pattern in large Japanese manufacturers and argue that its motivational effect is a 'reality' of Japanese productivity. One comparative study of large earnings data in Japan and the United States, Kalleberg and Lincoln (1988), finds that promotion expectations of workers are positively and strongly related to their earnings in Japan, though no such relation is found in American data.

Fact 4 (*a*) Job demarcation in work organization of the Japanese firm is more ambiguous and fluid. (*b*) More *de facto* responsibility is delegated to the lower tiers of hierarchy in Japan.

The first feature can be summarized as follows. The Japanese firm tends not to use detailed job classifications or to offer a clear job description to each individual worker. Jobs are assigned to groups of workers who closely collaborate to perform them, via mutual help and information-sharing. A group leader often has some degree of discretion over job assignments within the group. Workers perform multiple tasks via intra-group job rotation. Concerning the second feature, what is delegated may be a task to cope with an unforeseen and urgent problem (Koike 1988), co-ordination among workshops (Aoki 1988), or production decisions such as scheduling and quality control (Cole 1989; Monden 1983).

There is ample anecdotal case-study evidence on these features; even quantitative evidence based on systematic data exists, which for the most part accords with the description given above (Lincoln *et al.* 1986; for other quantitative studies, see the survey by Lincoln and McBride 1987).

3. WORK ORGANIZATION STRUCTURES

Because the focus of the paper is on internal incentives, for the most part I take the characteristics of organization structures as given in my argument. Theoretical comparative analyses of different organization and information structures, with reference to Japanese work organization, are found in Aoki (1986, 1988, 1990) and Itoh (1987, 1988). These papers take the team-theoretic approach, assuming away incentive problems, and identify several environmental factors that affect the choice of organization structures. The Japanese-type work organization with the properties mentioned in Fact 4 is more effective if scale economies are less important, environmental changes are continual but not too drastic, or workers have sufficiently high learning capabilities. The results suggest possible explanations of the differences in work organization between Japan and the West. For example, there may be reasons in Japan that discount the importance of scale economies, such as the smaller domestic markets than those in the West and the high land prices and the scarcity of land supply, which raise inventory costs more in Japan and hence discourage high buffer inventories.

There is some preliminary theoretical research on organization structures from the viewpoint of incentives, as well. Prendergast (1991) studies the delegation of responsibilities. He shows that managers may have an incentive to exert too much authority over their subordinates in order to improve their own career prospects; he then shows that the problem is mitigated when the labour market is non-competitive, e.g. because firms collude in hiring. Itoh (1991, 1992) shows that work organization with ambiguous job demarcation may be preferred by the employer from a purely incentive reason: having workers engage in several activities keeps worker motivation high even though each task is so monotonous and boring that they might be tempted to free-ride on others' help.[9] This result depends on costs of workers doing multiple tasks. Sometimes it is too costly to force workers to exert effort on an additional task quite different from their other, usual tasks. In fact, Holmström and Milgrom (1991) present the opposite case, maintaining that it is always optimal for the firm to make a worker specialize in a set of similar activities in terms of the measurability of performance, because such a job design reduces the distortion in how the worker allocates his attention among these activities. Tirole (1986) argues that job rotation across work-groups can discourage coalitional behaviour detrimental to the organization, such as the manipulation of information by supervisors, while Itoh (1992, 1993) argue that job rotation *within* work-teams facilitates mutual monitoring and sanctioning among members, and that the resulting co-operation among workers benefits the employer by reducing incentive costs.

Although these studies suggest that the optimal organization structure be determined partly by incentive considerations, they are still preliminary, and hence in this paper I mainly consider just one direction: from structures to incentives.

The differences in work organization structure provide the following implications on incentive issues:

1. The Japanese firm suffers from the lack of objective individual performance measures of production workers, and thus relies on subjective performance measures more than the Western firm.
2. Co-operation among workers in performing tasks is more important in the Japanese firm because its structure is highly dependent on their lateral interactions.
3. The Japanese firm counts more on effort and capability at lower levels in the hierarchy (via more extensive delegation) than the Western firm.

These claims being given, I analyse the reward system (compensation and promotion) in the Japanese firm in the subsequent sections.

4. WEAK LINK BETWEEN PAY AND PERFORMANCE IN THE SHORT RUN

The summary in Section 2 indicates that compensation for an employee in the Japanese firm is not, *in the short run*, sensitive to any of his performance measures that may be available. By the 'short run', I mean such a short period that no selection decision for promotion is made. Then each employee is paid a fixed basic salary associated with his pay rank, with biannual bonuses and various allowances. In general, the basic pay increases regularly every year while the major determinants of the amount of the pay rise seem to be personal characteristics such as age, tenure, marital status, and so on (for quantitative evidence, see Kalleberg and Lincoln 1988). Although the bonuses depend on corporate performance, in large firms the perceived connection between bonuses and individual performance will be weak since the corporate performance measures such as profits are much too aggregated to reflect individual effort. Merit assessment is said to be an important determinant of an employee's earnings, and even more important in promotion decisions, whereas the incentive effect of the merit rating on bonuses and regular increases in basic wages appears to be limited.

The purpose of this section is to offer theoretical justification for this seemingly weak tie between pay and performance in the short run. Note that this observation may be valid in Western firms as well. Baker *et al.* (1988) point out this anomaly by referring to empirical evidence from American data. Because I am not aware of any comparative empirical research on the extent of this feature in various countries, no attempt to explain international differences is made here; I merely make some predictions.

I assume that some sources of information about individual performance, either objective or subjective measures, are available: if neither objective measure nor subjective assessment is available, the lack of pecuniary reward for individual performance is obvious.[10] However, I must remind readers that, as argued in the preceding section, objective measures even for production workers are hard to obtain under the Japanese work organization. The main point argued here is that, given the work organization practices of the Japanese firm, it is often in the interest of the firm not to reward workers immediately and transiently after their performance measures become available.

4.1 The Trade-off between Incentives and Risk-Sharing

The principal–agent paradigm has provided a theoretical basis for rewarding individual contributions. The standard moral hazard model illuminates a trade-off between incentives and risk-sharing (or fairness, in the sense that one would not like one's rewards to be affected by uncontrollable factors).[11] Suppose that an employee is offered a fixed (time-based) salary, the level of which is competitive and high enough for him to accept it. Such a pay scheme has an advantage that the income of the employee is not subject to exogenous risk, given that he is risk-averse (or has limited wealth). However, he is going to work in the way he likes best, as long as he is not caught by the firm for not behaving appropriately. Implicit here is the assumption that there is a conflict in interests between the firm and the employee, stemming from costs or unwillingness to exert effort, incongruity in risk preferences, differing information concerning tasks, and so on. To induce desirable behaviour, the firm must design compensation sensitive to the employee's actions via the use of objective performance measures, such as the number of units produced, sales, divisional profits, and so on, and subjective measures, such as merit ratings by supervisors. These are however quite noisy measures of the employee's effort and hence make his income less predictable, subject to the factors that he cannot control. The result is higher average pay, because the firm must compensate for the risk premium so as to keep him working for the firm.

This argument offers one explanation of the lack of performance-based pay: it is sometimes too costly in terms of risk-sharing to provide incentives through immediate pay-for-performance. Suppose that the firm can force an employee to select at least some minimum level of effort. Inducing him to work a little bit harder than that level is not costly if the minimum level is modest (e.g. being present in his private office). However, if the minimum level is so high (e.g. because he works with others, including his boss, in a large room) that a small increase of effort from the lowest possible level is painful (i.e. his marginal disutility is large), there is a fixed cost of providing incentives to work harder arising from the risk-bearing. Thus, if the minimum enforceable effort level is already high, the firm may not provide incentives via pay-for-performance, unless a substantially higher level of effort is required. The argument depends on the costs of monitoring inputs (effort) and outputs (performance). Since the latter costs are higher under the Japanese work practices such as ambiguous job content and regular job rotation within groups, it is expected that the practice of paying production workers according to objective measures will be less widespread in Japan.

4.2 Missing Incentives for Multi-Task Workers

When a worker is assigned to several different tasks, or if his single task has several aspects that cannot be characterized by a single activity, the incentive problem has a new dimension: allocation of effort to various tasks/activities. A production worker may have to care about his production rate, quality, machine condition, conditions of other workers, and so on. A salesman may need to attend to his sales volume as well as his reputation among consumers in his territory. A division manager will have to attend to not only short-run earnings but also the long-term growth of the division. Various members of organizations are also expected to perform some routine work and at once to respond flexibly to unanticipated contingencies as they arise.

Some tasks or dimensions are easier to measure than others. If a worker's compensation is contingent on the performance measures of such activities, his allocation of effort may be biased towards those activities at the cost of others that are not easily measured. The point is not that pay-for-performance does not motivate workers, but that it sometimes motivates them too much towards some specific direction. Thus, if crucial activities are not measurable, it may be in the employer's interest to offer a fixed salary, or at best to tie individual pay with a broader performance measure such as profits, even if good personalized measures for specific, but less important, actions are available. This result has been formally obtained by Holmström and Milgrom (1991).

This theory suggests at least two possible reasons why pay-for-performance, particularly for blue-collar workers, is not common in Japan (relative to other industrialized nations, although I am not aware of empirical evidence). First, Japan's status as a 'late developer' forced Japanese firms to adapt to rapidly changing environments. As a result, workers' timely and flexible responses to unforeseen contingencies were likely to be more valuable to the firms than their routine, deterministic behaviour towards specific objectives.[12] Second, as mentioned in the previous subsection, job demarcation in the Japanese firm is ambiguous, and each of its production workers performs a wider range of jobs than more specialist-oriented workers in the Western firm. Therefore, we expect that compensation strongly tied with specific measures, even if they are available, may be discouraged in Japan.

4.3 Subjective Merit Assessment and Side Trades

The remaining explanation of the lack of pay-for-performance is associated with subjective measures. Performance in many jobs, particularly for white-collar workers, cannot be measured objectively. Subjective measures are then introduced. Aoki in fact claims that the 'importance of merit assessment ... is one of the distinctive characteristics of the Japanese payment scheme and contrasts with that in the unionized [American] firm, where managers have much less discretionary power over an individual's earnings, which instead depend on the job evaluation system (one single wage rate for one job) and the seniority rule' (Aoki 1988: 56). However, he also states: 'The relative weight placed on the assessment of individual assessment in pay determination within the same grade differs from one firm to another. The union usually demands egalitarian treatment, and some firms have only a single basic pay rate for each grade ... The merit assessment has more weight in the promotion decision.' (p. 55). Although no study of actual data concerning the effects of merit ratings on regular increases in basic pay (as well as on bonuses) exists,[13] its incentive effect seems to be not so large in the short run as theory suggests.

In the rest of this section, I discuss some possible problems arising from a strong link between pay and merit ratings in the short run. The point is that supervisors/performance-raters are also self-interested agents, and hence their incentives matter in the design of pay structures.[14]

The first problem is that pay-for-performance makes it possible for supervisors to abuse their positions so as to benefit themselves at the expense of their employer. To illustrate the problem, consider the following simple three-tier hierarchy of an employer, a supervisor, and two workers, drawn from Laffont (1990). Each risk-averse worker i ($i = 1,2$) exerts effort. His individual production level x_i is a random variable whose value is either H (high) or L (low) with $H > L$. The probability of $x_i = H$ is increasing in worker i's effort level. However, x_i is not observable to the employer: the only objective measure verifiable to him is a broad measure of total profits, $x = x_1 + x_2$. The employer can hire a supervisor who can observe and report on individual production levels, which can be interpreted as merit ratings. Suppose that compensation is fixed at the beginning of each year. Thus, the first-year compensation is constant, while the second-year compensation can be contingent on the first-year performance.

This is a variant of the moral hazard model of the two-tier hierarchy where the trade-off between incentives and risk-sharing is the point. If the supervisor is honest, the firm will offer each worker pay-for-performance in which his next-year's pay is higher when his individual production level is high than when it is low. However, such a pay structure creates opportunities for covert side-trades between the supervisor and the workers: the supervisor can form a coalition with one of the workers at the expense of the other, or he can extract private benefits from each worker by threatening to favour the other.[15]

Note that this sort of manipulation by the supervisor becomes possible only when each worker's compensation is tied to his *individual* rating. Laffont (1990) shows that it is sometimes optimal not to use the personalized pay scheme dependent on the supervisor's report but instead a pay scheme contingent only on broader, more general, objective measures. The latter non-personalized pay structure has the shortcoming that the employer is not availing himself of valuable information possessed by the supervisor to provide incentives for workers. The cost of ignoring such information will be higher if individual ratings contain additional information, e.g. about workers' unknown abilities. It is therefore in the firm's interest not to discard the supervisor's information completely, but rather to use it after some interval, e.g. when making promotion decisions. The delayed use of such subjective information may recreate an opportunity for detrimental deals on the side-trades as described above. However, the chance of a successful trade seems to be smaller because such deals are now more difficult to enforce. When the supervisor and a worker form a coalition, the former will demand some favour in exchange for a counter-favour (good rating). The strong link between pay and ratings makes it easy for the worker to know whether the promise is kept. However, when the rating is used only much later in his career, the feasibility of side-trading will be limited.[16]

According to Edwards (1979), who analysed the historical evolution of the organization control systems in the United States, the arbitrary power of foremen/supervisors and the resulting problems of favouritism, idio-syncrasies, prejudice, and so on were in fact observed in the early decades of the twentieth century. And the system was abandoned, along with other systems, in favour of 'bureaucratic control' systems that combine formal bureaucracy and organizational commitment as rewards.[17] On the other hand, close personal relations with bosses are still common in the Japanese firm. Yoshino (1968) emphasizes the prevalence of informal groups in Japanese corporate organizations, and discusses adverse effects of the informal cliques that arise from common cohort, birthplace, or school ties on formal organization structures, employee morale, and decision-making. Lincoln and Kalleberg (1990) offer quantitative evidence based on their systematic data that strong vertical ties (between workers and supervisors) are far more prevalent in factories in Japan than in those in the United States. It should be pointed out that these observations do not necessarily imply that collusive behaviour detrimental to the organization actually prevails. Tirole (1986) argues that observed collusive behaviour is only the tip of the iceberg, because organizations can anticipate and react to the possibility of coalitions to restrict their formation. Aoki (1988) observes in the Japanese firms several devices that are intended to mitigate the danger of unfair treatment by supervisors: formalization and standardization of assessment procedures by the personnel department; job rotations, both at the supervisory and the subordinate level; monitoring by the personnel department via grievances; and the importance of maintaining the reputation of supervisors among subordinates for the former's career.[18]

4.4 Team Production and Supervisors' Career Concerns

The other problem associated with subjective performance appraisals and pay-for-performance concerns the assessment of supervisors. Supervisors in general perform not only supervisory tasks but also productive tasks such as co-ordination, training, and so forth. Then they are judged, in part, by their subordinates' performances, because these contain valuable information about the supervisors' effort or ability. Thus, when a supervisor's compensation depends on his report concerning his subordinates' performance, his incentives in making the report may be perversely affected.

For example, the supervisor may tend to overstate team performance when the performance measure is not verifiable; he may incline to overgenerosity in reporting the quality of subordinates when he is responsible for education and training; he may work too much to cover up any problems in his workplace; he may possibly pass responsibility for poor team performance, once detected by the employer, on to subordinates; he may tend to give subordinates undifferentiated ratings, in particular when grievance systems activate. I know of no formal model deriving these effects, nor any empirical evidence from Japanese data. However, the implication is that it is sometimes in the interest of the employer not to reward supervisors contingent on their reports in the short run.

Because of these problems in transient pay-for-performance in the short run, the firm may be motivated to engage in long-term relationships with employees and to use promotions as an incentive device. The subsequent sections consider this possibility. An alternative solution is to use dismissal as a discipline device. For example, the presence of involuntary unemployment makes mid-career separation costly for workers, and hence they can be motivated to work without pay-for-performance by termination-type contracts in which each worker is dismissed when found shirking, and otherwise is paid a fixed wage.[19] This approach seems difficult to pursue in Japan because dismissals are costly, as was discussed in Section 2. The implication is that Japan and the West may be located in quite different equilibria in labour markets, one with long-term relationships and the other with short-term termination contracts.[20] Both equilibria may be characterized as the lack of immediate pay-for-performance, but the solution to this problem can be quite different from one to the other.

Before moving on, I would like to comment on my argument in this section. Here I have not considered the incentive effects that promotions may have on workers; promotions as an incentive scheme are supposed to result from the lack of pay-for-performance. Note, however, that the reverse may be true: incentive effects arising from promotions may be a cause of the absence of pay-for-performance. Suppose that workers (as well as the internal or external labour market) do not know their ability. Then the market (in the case of internal labour market, the current employer) uses their current performance to update its beliefs about their ability, and to determine their future compensation and promotions based on these updated beliefs. The workers are then concerned about the effects of their current performance on their future careers. This implicit incentive effect, called 'career concerns', can complement the explicit incentives through pay-for-performance. Gibbons and Murphy (1992) show that pay schemes optimize total incentives, i.e. the mixture of the incentives from career concerns and those from pay-for-performance. Career concerns are strong when workers are young and have many potential promotion opportunities; for these workers, the link between pay and performance is weak. On the other hand, pay-for-performance is important for those whose career concerns are weak, e.g. because they are close to retirement. It is desirable to test this prediction using Japanese data.[21]

5. EXPLAINING LONG-TERM EMPLOYER–EMPLOYEE ATTACHMENT

The previous section offered several possible reasons why the Japanese firm does not adjust pay immediately and transiently after some objective or subjective performance measures of workers are obtained. If the transient pay-for-performance does not provide incentives, then what does? The answer seems to be: promotions and the resulting substantial differences in lifetime earnings among workers in the Japanese firm, observed and emphasized by Tachibanaki (1987, 1988) and Weiss (1984, 1988). Obviously, these incentives are effective only under strong long-term attachment between employers and employees. In this section we consider how long-term employment relationships are sustained in Japan.

The long-term employment relationships in Japan have often been explained by reference to some exogenous factors such as traditional Japanese values stressing groupism and loyalty, or the lack of the competitive labour markets for those who leave firms in mid-career in Japan. There is in fact some evidence, consistent with the latter, that Japanese management practices prevail more in low-growth areas (with fewer outside opportunities) than in high-growth areas (with active labour markets) in a given country. (See e.g. Trevor 1983 for evidence in Britain.) However, in this paper I take the proposition that it is the structures and practices adopted by the Japanese firm that are responsible for the strong degree of employer–employee attachment over long periods.[22] From this view, the lack of an active labour market for mid-career job-changers in Japan can be characterized as an equilibrium outcome different from the equilibrium outcome in the West.

The robust long-term attachment occurs either because it is in the employee's interest not to leave the current firm for a new employer in mid-career, or because it is in the employer's interest not to hire former employees of other firms. The following subsections deal with these two possibilities.

5.1 A Barrier to Exit by Wages Increasing with Seniority

An employee does not leave the current firm, even if he can find a new employer who is ready to offer better terms, because it is costly for him to do so. The best-known cost is the loss of firm-specific human capital in which the worker has invested. Several empirical studies show that tenure has a stronger effect on the slope of wage profiles in Japan than in the United States, and the resulting steeper wage profiles reduce labour turnover (Hashimoto and Raisian 1985, 1989; Mincer and Higuchi 1988). However, this result is also consistent with the agency-theoretic explanation of upward-sloping wage–tenure profiles initially presented by Lazear (1979, 1981): to discourage mid-career separation (as well as to provide effort incentives), firms pay workers compensation less than the value of their marginal product when they are young, and greater than their marginal product when they are old (see also Murphy 1986).

I know of no empirical study testing these two competing hypotheses by using Japanese data.[23] There are, however, some empirical observations in Japan that are mystifying from the perspective of specific human capital theory. First, there is a compensation paid at the time of separation, the amount of which increases sharply with tenure, and is higher when the separation is for company reasons rather than for private reasons. This practice significantly increases mobility costs. However, this amount cannot be explained by a sudden increase in specific skills.

More importantly, many personnel practices of the Japanese firm are easily explained if we assume that old workers receive compensation more than the value of their marginal product. First, there is mandatory retirement. Although now rare in the United States, this is still common among large firms in Japan (as well as in Canada, Britain, etc.). The well-known explanation of mandatory retirement by Lazear (1979) relies on the feature of his model that old workers are paid more than their value, and hence that a date at which the contract is terminated must be fixed in advance. Second, with upward-sloping wage profiles bearing the above feature, the firm has an incentive to dismiss old workers. In order to maintain the wage profiles (to discourage mid-career separation), the firm therefore has to invest in its reputation. The lifetime employment policy can be interpreted as such an example. Third, this feature is also compatible with the practice of the Japanese firm that when layoffs are inevitable senior workers are laid off first. The Japanese firm attempts to avoid layoffs in order to maintain its reputation-sustaining upward-sloping wage profiles. However, when cutting labour costs becomes unavoidable, it is in the firm's interest to lay off those who are overpaid relative to their productivity.

Under the theory of specific human capital, senior workers are compensated less than or equal to the value of their marginal product (Becker 1975; Hashimoto 1981). The reasoning is that, because specific training is productive only in the current firm, the firm bears part of the cost and collects part of the return on specific training. The agency perspective can complement the specific human capital story in order to explain these features of the Japanese firm. Many empirical studies of the Japanese labour market simply assume away the agency hypothesis in favour of the theory of specific human capital[24] to explain the finding that earnings increase with tenure. More rigorous tests of alternative hypotheses are required.[25]

5.2 Perverse Effects of Mid-Career Recruiting

Although no empirical test is available,[26] there are several possible reasons why firms may be reluctant to hire those who have left other firms (except at the bottom of the rank). First, outsiders may not be as productive as insiders because of the latter's accumulation of firm-specific human capital. An employer hiring a new employee must start investing in specific training, which is costly relative to those who have already acquired the specific skills, because these training costs must be recovered. If it is true that Japanese firms invest more in specific training than do Western firms, then this reason explains the lower labour turnover in Japan. The problem is that it is not clear whether there in fact exist substantial differences in the necessary skills among, for example, large firms in the same industry segment.

Second, there may be collusion among firms. Aoki asserts that 'Japanese firms, particularly large and established ones, have bound themselves to an implicit code of not hiring former employees of other firms, particularly skilled ones ...' (Aoki 1988: 83). They could punish those who deviate from that code, and are detected, by reverting to fierce competition for hiring workers. The question is, what enables large Japanese firms to sustain collusion more easily than Western firms?

The third possible reason is that hiring a new employee at a high hierarchical rank may have negative effects on existing employees' motivation: the number of promotions available for the junior workers may be reduced, or obtaining a skilled worker from outside may send some negative signal to insiders concerning their capabilities. This possibility is pursued more in the next section in association with slow promotional patterns in Japan.

Fourth, firms may infer that a job-changer is of low ability or a 'bad' type. Gibbons and Katz (1991) present a model in which the current employer has better information about worker ability and the market infers that job-changers are of low ability. In MacLeod and Malcomson's (1988) model of promotion, which is discussed in the next section, it is assumed that the market cannot tell whether a worker who has left a firm was dismissed or left voluntarily. The authors can however show that there exists a sequential equilibrium in which the market believes that the final rank of the worker at the previous firm was too high in terms of his ability. A job-changer may have difficulty in finding a job, even if the market knows that he has separated voluntarily, because he is viewed as a 'bad' worker, i.e. one who tends to move on.

6. PROMOTIONS AND PAY ATTACHED TO RANKS

Promotions in this paper are defined as pay increases that result from moving up to a higher vertical or horizontal rank as defined in Section 2. In other words, pay is attached primarily to a finite number of grades or hierarchical job titles, not to individuals. This implies that a substantial part of information concerning individuals is not used immediately for rewarding them: two workers with moderately different performance histories receive approximately equal salaries (via assignment to the same rank). The discussion in Section 4 is relevant; there I described several perverse incentive effects of using detailed individual performance information for rewarding workers without delay. Some of the arguments are extended to explain the speed of promotions in this section.

Note that promotions to the upper hierarchical ranks serve a purpose other than providing incentives: i.e. a better matching of individuals to tasks (here including hierarchical titles) upon having learned more about their ability. More information is accumulated over time about workers' potential abilities and characteristics, and their productivity increases via improvement in job-matching. Pay that is not attached to individuals is again a puzzle from the viewpoint of this second purpose, because it does not fully use workers' productive skills or information concerning their abilities.[27]

In the rest of this section, I present theories of promotion and their implications concerning the distinct characteristics in the Japanese firm, i.e. 'wide' career and slow promotion. First, I focus on the learning aspect of promotions and argue that pure learning models cannot explain the slow promotion rate in the Japanese firm. I then consider the theory of rank-order tournaments, which focuses on promotion as a pure incentive device. Finally, I consider interactions between these two theories.

6.1 Promotion as a Learning Device

In this section, I abstract away incentive problems to focus on the learning aspect. I assume that each worker's ability is initially unknown to the firm as well as to himself. The current employer, by observing some performance measures such as merit ratings, accumulates information concerning the worker's true ability. The average productivity of the worker then increases as more information is accumulated, via reassignment to various jobs including hierarchical titles. (The discussion in this section thus concerns vertical ranks.) For the time being, suppose that potential employers in the outside labour market can observe the same performance measures as the current employer does. Then in each period, the worker is assigned to the position best suited to him based on the market belief in his ability in that period, and is paid the expected value of his marginal product at that position. Because the risk-averse worker dislikes any fluctuation of his earnings, the firm may instead offer a long-term contract in order to insure him against uncontrollable risk: then no demotion or pay cut occurs, while the worker's wage increases, often with promotion to higher ranks, only when his previous performance was so good that the updated belief about his ability increases his expected productivity sufficiently and consequently potential employers are willing to offer him higher wages to tempt him away (see Harris and Holmström 1982).

Note that, in the case of symmetric information discussed above, pay is attached to individuals: workers who are assigned to the same rank, but have different performance histories are paid different wages at the same position. This conclusion, however, is sensitive to the assumption that the performance measures of the workers are observable to potential employers as well as to the current firm. It is often the case that the current employer has better information about its employees than the others, e.g. because the latter cannot observe the results of merit ratings. On the other hand, it is likely that the outside firms can observe employees' hierarchical ranks and compensation offered by the current employer (e.g., an employee can communicate his title and pay in a verifiable way, while it is difficult for him to convince them of his performance in the current firm), and can use these as an imperfect signal about ability. Waldman (1984) analyses such a case and shows that pay attached to ranks arises as an optimal structure.

To see this, suppose for simplicity that there are two periods and two ranks, rank 1 and rank 2. Rank 1 is the 'port of entry' to which all the new employees are assigned at the beginning of period 1. At the end of period 1, some performance measure of the employee becomes available, and (for simplicity) it reveals his true ability perfectly. If his ability is sufficiently high, he is more productive at rank 2 than at rank 1. However, the current firm must consider the fact that the market can, by observing the promotion, infer that he is sufficiently able. Firms in the market may then attempt to bid him away from the current employer, and so his present firm, in order to retain him, is required to pay compensation compatible with the offers by the outside firms. Because the outside offers are contingent only on job assignment (rank 1 or 2), there is no reason for the current employer to use superior information about ability for compensation schemes.

Two important results arise from his model. First, there are fewer promotions than would be optimal if ability information were known to the market as well; the intuition is that, because of the discontinuous jump in pay upon promotion, it is too costly to promote those who are only a little more productive at rank 2 than at rank 1. Second, as the level of firm-specific human capital increases, this inefficient assignment diminishes, because the efficient assignment becomes more valuable to the current firm.

These results also have important implications on the speed of promotions when the model is extended to the case of more than two periods. Bernhardt (1989) and Waldman (1990) show that promotions are delayed relative to the efficient assignment under symmetric information, and that this delay is negatively related to the proportion of skills that are firm-specific. This result, however, is not consistent with empirical evidence. Specific training is more important in the Japanese firm and general training is more important in the American firm (Hashimoto and Raisian 1985, 1989; Mincer and Higuchi, 1988), while promotions are more delayed in the Japanese firm. The problem of the model, when it is applied to the Japanese management practices, appears to be the assumption of a competitive labour market. If the market is non-competitive, then the current employer has no incentive to conceal information concerning worker ability, and hence assigns workers efficiently, resulting in no delay in promotion. Competition among divisions within a firm could mimic the competition in the external labour market, but casual observation does not reveal such competition as a typical practice in the Japanese firm.

6.2 Promotion Lottery as an Incentive Device

I next focus on promotions as an incentive scheme. Lazear and Rosen (1981) view salaries as prizes of promotion lotteries and grades as names for prizes. Consider the standard principal–agent model, in which several risk-averse workers exert unobservable effort which, along with uncontrollable factors, determines individual performance. The workers with best performance among them, whose proportion is specified by the contract, are promoted to a higher rank with a higher pay (winning prize) *fixed in advance*.[28] This contest works as a strong motivator. Note that the workers' abilities are assumed to be common knowledge, and hence we assume away the learning aspect of promotions.

There are three often argued reasons why this rank-order tournament scheme may be preferred by the firm. First, it requires much coarser information of ordinal ranking among workers' performance than cardinal performance measures, and hence its monitoring costs will be smaller. Second, workers' earnings are less affected by uncontrollable 'noise' because their performance ranking is insensitive to common random factors. For example, if the performance of each worker depends on his effort, his machine condition, and the production system of the factory, the last of which is uncontrollable *and* common to all the workers, the last two factors are simply a noise to him, and his pay fluctuations should not be contingent on them. While the last common noise factor affects his *absolute* performance, it does not affect his *relative* performance. And his ranking among the workers is one example of his relative performance, which filters out the common uncontrollable factor. Note however that this is not a strong reason to choose pay attached to grades rather than individuals, because the employer could use more elaborated relative performance measures, such as bonuses contingent on the performance of a worker relative to the mean performance among the workers (Holmström 1982).

Third, the effectiveness of the rank-order tournament scheme is not affected by the subtle condition of whether or not individual performance measures are verifiable (Carmichael 1983; Malcomson 1984). If they are not verifiable, and hence if labour contracts contingent on those measures are not enforceable explicitly, the firm has incentives to renege on what is specified in the contracts. For example, the firm may decide not to raise wages upon observation of good performance, as is specified by the contract, by reporting that performance was not good *enough*. However, under tournament schemes, the firm has nothing to gain by being dishonest: misreporting a worker's performance as bad when it is actually good simply increases the probability that other workers will win the competition. For this argument to work, the prize must be attached to a hierarchical title which *must be filled*; or, when it is attached to a pay grade, the proportion of workers to be promoted there must be verifiable. These conditions seem easier to satisfy than verifiability of performance measures.

Of course, repeated interaction and reputation can make contracts contingent on unverifiable measures self-enforcing. Such implicit contracts are costly, however, because the firm must earn a surplus by abiding by implicit agreement with workers (MacLeod and Malcomson 1989). Since the rank-order tournament schemes do not require such a surplus, they have the advantage over pay attached to individuals in the long run.

Problems of the rank-order tournaments Because the rank-order tournament scheme is but one special form of pay-for-performance, it is subject to the same problems as discussed in Section 4: fixed costs of risk-sharing, danger of tying pay with specific objective measures (including influence costs), and, in particular, perverse effects of merit ratings. Several practices observed in the Japanese firm can be interpreted as ways to mitigate the problems associated with subjective merit ratings. Aoki (1988) observes rotation of both supervisors and subordinates in the Japanese firm. Yoshino (1968) finds that in the Japanese firm 'one is rewarded for his competence only after he proves his ability to the satisfaction of *everyone concerned*' (p. 237; emphasis added). These organizational responses to the vertical collusion problem naturally lead to the distinct management characteristics in Japan, i.e 'wide' career (broad range of tasks) and slow promotion. Another way to alleviate the problem is to introduce some exogenous criteria such as seniority in promotion decisions, which again is compatible with Japanese management practice.

There are some extra costs of tournaments themselves. First, workers who compete for higher positions have no incentive to co-operate. Under tournaments, each worker can increase his winning probability by engaging in 'sabotage', reducing the performance of his competitors (Lazear 1989; Itoh 1992). Thus, if co-operation among workers is critical, as in the work organization of the Japanese firm, those who compete for promotions should be separated. Second, contestants have incentives to collude to choose lower effort levels. Thus, they should again be separated, or their tasks should be designed so as to prevent them from mutually monitoring their effort, if the firm would like to encourage workers to co-operate as a work-group where mutual monitoring and sanctioning enforce their co-ordinated effort.[29] In the Japanese firm, employees in the same category in terms of year of graduation from college are subject to the same promotion process. Although I have no data, extensive rotations enable them to work in various departments, regional offices, or factories, and as a result there is little chance that they will work together in the same place, particularly in large firms. Such a practice makes it possible for the Japanese firm to attain effective co-operation and competition simultaneously.

Third, incentives for those who have lost contests are absent under tournament schemes. Consider a sequence of elimination tournaments in which winners of a tournament proceed to the next tournament, in order to attain higher positions, while losers are completely eliminated from competition. Competition for higher ranks in hierarchical organizations appears to be well represented by such a sequence of elimination tournaments (Hanada 1989; Rosenbaum 1979).[30] If the firm wants the losers to continue to exert high effort for the duration of their careers, then it may be in the interest of the firm to reduce the speed of promotion, in order to keep effort incentives of all the members high, by increasing the proportion of workers to be promoted early in their careers.

Note that the slow promotion of this sort has costs as well. First, delay in promotion will increase costs of misassignment of able employees to lower-level jobs. Second, talented employees may leave to receive higher compensation elsewhere. Third, if workers have control over riskiness of their decision-making (e.g. if they choose risky projects), their choice may be biased, from the firm's viewpoint, against risky actions under elimination tournaments with many winners in early rounds. It may therefore be in the interest of the firm not to slow promotions, but to change the structure of elimination tournaments so that early losers can be given second chances to catch up with early winners later in their careers. This argument is also found in Hanada (1989).

The optimal speed of promotion will be determined by the trade-off between the benefits and costs mentioned above. The argument here predicts slower promotion in the Japanese firm because mid-career separation of able workers seems more costly in Japan, and because the incentives of the losers seem particularly important for Japanese-type work organization, in which much responsibility is delegated to lower levels of hierarchy.

6.3 Interaction of Learning and Incentives

If the incentive effects of promotion are important in the Japanese firm, the results to be drawn from the pure learning model of promotion in Section 6.1, which are not consistent with the observation of the Japanese practices, may be due to this lack of incentive problems there. I here present several recent studies of promotion that incorporate both learning and incentive facets into rigorous models.

Prendergast (1992) introduces into a learning model workers' incentives to acquire costly firm-specific skills. Only the current employer (not the workers) can learn about their abilities, and the issue is whether or not the firm reveals information concerning ability to workers before training. An employer can do so credibly by promoting and giving pay rises only to workers with sufficiently high ability. However, some of the other workers will then be discouraged from acquiring skills. This case is interpreted as the American mode of career development. Alternatively, the employer can conceal information about ability from workers by offering the same terms to all of them. All workers are then motivated to acquire skills. This case is embodied in the Japanese method of slow promotion.

Prendergast shows that, without competitive external labour markets, the Japanese mode is preferred to the American if the returns to specific training are sufficiently high, because the former alleviates the firm's incentive to ᵉⁿᵃᶜᶜᵉⁱᵃᵗᵉ workers' labour in order to induce them to acquire skills. This result seems compatible with the observation that specific skills are more important in Japanese work organization. He also shows that, if the external labour market is competitive, the advantage of the Japanese system under no labour market disappears because bids from the market reveal ability information to workers.[31]

Prendergast (1992), in a different model, considers career concerns, which arise in the learning model when the moral hazard problem is present; i.e., workers can exert unobservable effort to influence the beliefs about their ability held by the internal or external labour market. Two workers with symmetric uncertainty about each worker's ability join a firm. The employer observes some signals about each worker's ability, which fact determines the 'leader' and the 'follower'. The firm then trains the two workers through on-the-job training, and while the workers exert effort additional signals on ability become available. On the basis of the updated beliefs about ability and the returns on training, one of the two is promoted to a higher rank with higher pay.

Prendergast shows that, when no competitive labour market exists, the firm designs on-the-job training such that the leader is handicapped; the follower is given more training so that their race is 'tight'. This case seems closer to the Japanese practice that everyone is given a chance to receive training and to demonstrate his potential capability. On the other hand, when the labour market is competitive, the leader is given more training, which result Prendergast interprets as the 'star treatment' typical in the American firm.

Note that in both models Prendergast takes the competitiveness of the external labour market as an exogenous factor. However, the lack of the competitive labour market may arise endogenously from his models. (See Section 5.2 for relevant discussion.) Suppose that in the first model the Japanese mode of slow promotion is optimal with no labour market, and that offers by a firm to outsiders are observable to *its own* employees. Then such offers before training reveal ability information to its own employees, which discourages them from acquiring skills. It may therefore be in the interest of firms not to offer outsiders high job ranks when the Japanese-type pooling scheme is optimal in the absence of a competitive labour market. Similarly, in the second model if the firm attempts to hire a leader away from other firms, then, anticipating such a possibility, the employees will reduce their effort because the marginal return to effort decreases as the probability of winning a high rank is reduced.

The implication from this argument is the same as that given at the beginning of Section 5: Western management and Japanese management may represent two different equilibria, one of which has a competitive labour market and the other a non-competitive one.

Another model worth mentioning is the self-selection model by MacLeod and Malcomson (1988), which Aoki (1988) uses to explain the economic rationale of wages attached to pay grades in the Japanese firm. They consider the adverse-selection case, where the ability of each worker is his private information. Because performance measures are not verifiable, self-enforcing contracts are of termination type: if the performance of a worker is unsatisfactory, he is dismissed, while if his performance is satisfactory, his pay is independent of his current performance level. MacLeod and Malcomson show that the equilibrium rank hierarchy has a finite number of pay grades, despite a continuum of possible ability levels. The intuition is that, in the equilibrium they consider, when a worker separates from the employer, the market infers that he was assigned a pay grade too high in terms of his true ability. Thus, in the new firm he is assigned a grade just below his previous one. The number of grades must therefore be finite, and the utility difference between grades must be discrete, in order to make shirking and the resulting separation costly. In equilibrium, each worker self-selects the grade appropriate to his ability, and hence no separation occurs. From the firm's point of view, self-selection is optimally attained by first assigning all workers to the lowest grade, and then promoting them one grade each period if their performance satisfies the promotion criteria, until each of them reaches his optimal grade. The firm makes positive profits from each worker before he reaches this grade.

This model explains the optimality of promotion schemes, but does not provide clear insights on the speed of promotions.[32] More seriously, the use of termination-type contracts in Japan appears to be limited, because it is costly for the firm to dismiss workers: as mentioned in Section 2, the 'lifetime' employment policy binds employers both implicitly and explicitly. MacLeod and Malcomson consider contacts of the termination type because they are only self-enforcing contracts given that performance measures are not verifiable. Although this theory may characterize the equilibrium in labour markets in the West, I conjecture that the Japanese firm, because of additional constraints, takes another route, using unverifiable performance measures (in particular, subjective merit assessments) by mitigating the verifiability problems by some means.

6.4 Notes on Seniority as a Promotion Criterion

Before ending this section, I want to comment on the question, why is seniority an important determinant of promotions in the Japanese firm? Seniority seems to provide some upper bound on the speed of promotion. However capable a worker is known to be, he has to wait for promotion to high hierarchical ranks until he becomes sufficiently 'senior' (as measured by tenure or age). One obvious reason for this is specific human capital; even if a worker's potential ability is high, he needs ot accumulate specific skills before being promoted. A related reason is that the seniority rule enables senior employees smoothly to transfer their skills and information to young employees, as well as to evaluate the latter honestly. Without this rule, the senior workers would have incentives for reducing the promotion prospects of the young. This argument is more relevant in the Japanese firm because of the importance of on-the-job training and merit assessments in its work organization. The similar argument holds for hiring decisions. To provide senior employees with incentives to hire able individuals, the firm must give the senior workers some guarantee that those capable young employees will not jeopardize their positions. Given the high costs of mid-career separation, such a consideration is likely to be more serious in Japan.

7. CONCLUDING REMARKS

The existing literature on Japanese firms focuses mainly on 'what' questions: what is different, and what is similar in the Japanese management practices? This paper instead focuses on 'why' questions concerning internal incentives in the Japanese firm from economic perspectives.

Three main conclusions can be drawn from this paper. First, if we take work organization structures of the Japanese firm as given, then the reward structures and employment relationships are quite consistent with the insights from the recent literature on economic theories of organizations. More rigorous studies of pay and promotion schemes are required, but the lack of theoretical studies of organization structures appears to be a more serious problem from the theoretical point of view. Successful models could explain simultaneously the distinct features of work organization and employment structures in the Japanese firm, along with market conditions. They would also offer a more consistent explanation of the differences between the Japanese firm and the Western firm; for example, they might characterize the contrast as two different equilibria in the models.

Second, although much comparative empirical evidence on the Japanese management practices is now available, rigorous tests of alternative theories are still sparse. It seems to me that most of those who study Japanese human resource management have focused exclusively on the theory of firm-specific human capital, regarding incentive issues as irrelevant in the Japanese firm, for some exogenous reasons. I think that specific skills are important determinants of the Japanese practices, but, as I have argued above, they are not likely to be the whole story: some empirical observations can be explained in a more consistent way by incentive theory. Our increased understanding of Japanese HRM practices will improve substantially when we can obtain micro personnel data from Japanese firms and test several theories.

Third, many distinct features of the Japanese human resource management, along with other features of organization and market structures, are likely to constitute a 'system': they are closely interrelated, and one aspect of the Japanese system could not exist without all the others.

NOTES TO CHAPTER 9

1. I have attempted to choose English references whenever available. However, I apologize to those readers who do not have Japanese language proficiency for sometimes (inevitably) referring to the literature written in Japanese.
2. Of course, this does not imply that medium–small firms or temporary/female workers are unimportant in the Japanese economy.
3. The Japanese firm usually resorts to shorter work hours, work-sharing, and transfers prior to dismissals.
4. Despite this contractual incompleteness, however, judicial mechanisms sometimes enforce the lifetime employment policy in Japan. The Supreme Court has often ruled against dismissal decisions by firms unless they are sufficiently reasonable (Tsuchida 1989).
5. These roughly correspond to 'vertical hierarchies' and 'horizontal hierarchies' in Stiglitz (1975), respectively. Aoki's (1988) 'ranking hierarchy' is more associated with the latter, horizontal, one.
6. However, his data also show that, even though many individuals reach the highest position among them after 15 years, there is non-negligible diversity (a few years) in their speed. In addition, both Rosenbaum and Hanada find that employees promoted in the earliest period have a much better chance of being further promoted than those not promoted then.
7. Note that, because of the nature of personnel data, most of the empirical literature mentioned here looks at career development during the high growth period in Japan, the 1960s–1970s. It is often said that Japanese labour practices are now changing, towards faster promotion, less dependence on seniority, and so on. I do not consider this issue here because of the lack of enough systematic, quantitative evidence at this time.

8. For example, the empirical study by Tachibanaki (1988) finds that seniority is an important, but not a necessary, condition for promotion.

9. Monden (1983) regards this effect as one of the advantages of regular job rotation in the Toyota production system.

10. In addition, I implicitly assume that these measures are verifiable in courts, and hence that employment contracts can be written such that pay is contingent on them. Otherwise, pay cannot be contingent on current performance because there is a hazard of employers' reneging the contracts that contain such pay-for-performance clauses. Note that in such a case pay can still be contingent on past performance because it can be self-enforceable via reputation (see MacLeod and Malcomson 1989 for a formal model), and hence the problems discussed here are still valid.

11. See Hart and Holmström (1987) for a survey.

12. There is empirical evidence that, even today, managers of large Japanese firms perceive their environments to be more volatile than those of large American firms do (Kagono *et al.* 1985).

13. Fujimura (1989) is one exception.

14. The extensive use of subjective measures also affects workers' incentives; they may allocate too much energy in an effort to influence their supervisor's ratings, at the cost of other productive activities (Milgrom 1988; Milgrom and Roberts 1988). This is a variant of the problem of allocational inefficiency discussed above, and hence is not pursued further in this section.

15. A related problem also arises in a simpler case where there is only one worker. Tirole (1986) analyses such a model to show that, when the employer uses the supervisor's information to reward the worker, the supervisor acts as an advocate and conceals evidence that is unfavourable to the worker.

16. As Tirole (1986) notes, job rotation across divisions, factories, or offices that breaks the long-term attachment of a worker to a particular supervisor further restricts side-transfers.

17. Ishida (1990) observes the similar problems in British firms, including Japanese factories in Britain.

18. On the other hand, some organizational practices of the Japanese firm seem to encourage on-/off-the-job interaction with supervisors as well as with co-workers. For example, job rotation *within work-groups* facilitates mutual monitoring and interdependence, and hence creates opportunities for worker co-operation via side-trades, which can be beneficial to the organization; see Itoh (1992, 1993).

19. See MacLeod and Malcomson (1989) and Shapiro and Stiglitz (1984) for formal models.

20. See Okuno-Fujiwara (1987) for a formal model along this line.

21. Casual observation seems to accord with the prediction: as a worker moves up in the ranks, his pay depends more on his performance measures.

22. For a systematic empirical study of work organization and attitudes in the USA and Japan from this perspective, see Lincoln and Kalleberg (1990).

23. See Hutchens (1987), Krueger (1991), and Lazear and Moore (1984) for tests using the US data.

24. Or the 'living-expenses guaranteed hypothesis' by Ono (1989), mentioned in Sect. 2.

25. For example, Mincer and Higuchi (1988) do not pursue the agency hypothesis by attributing to 'the traditional reputation of Japanese workers for discipline and loyalty to the firm'. They also assert that, because assessment by supervisors plays a larger role in the careers of Japanese workers, upward-sloping wage profiles are unnecessary in order to deter shirking. However, my focus here is on the wage profiles as a barrier to exit.

26. Tachibanaki and Taki (1990) find in Japanese data that those who have moved to bigger firms receive higher wages while those who have moved to smaller firms have decreased their earnings. However, it is not clear which of the four stories below these findings favour.

27. The theory of human capital also suggests pay attached to individuals. Williamson *et al.* (1975) offer one explanation of pay attached to particular jobs (not ranks) within the framework of human capital theory. Their argument hinges on the assumption that a worker accumulates specialized skills and information about his job, and can acquire monopoly power against the employer. This explanation appears persuasive when applied to production workers in the unionized Western firm where a strict one-wage-rate per job is the rule. However, it has problems as an explanation of the Japanese practice. First, Japanese workers are less likely to obtain monopoly positions with respect to their jobs, because of their wide careers: it is much less costly to replace a worker by somebody else in the same firm in Japan than in the West, given the differences in organization structures. Second, the use of subjective merit assessment for production workers in Japan is hard to explain under this theory.

28. If one assumes that there are 'many' employees (a continuum of them), then specifying the proportion to be promoted is equivalent to specifying a threshold level of absolute performance.

29. The conditions for the firm to prefer doing so are obtained in Holmström and Milgrom (1990), Itoh (1993), and Ramakrishnan and Thakor (1991).

30. See Rosen (1986) for a model of elimination tournaments.

31. The current firm's incentive to conceal information from the market will not completely preclude information leakage. On the other hand, if the American system is optimal with no labour market (e.g. because specific training is too costly), the bids from the labour market do not have detrimental effects, while the incentive to conceal appears. The net result may be slower promotions with the competitive labour market than without, for the reason discussed in Section 6.1.

32. One possible explanation comes from the feature of their promotion process that the firm can increase its profits by shirking and delaying promotion. In the equilibrium MacLeod and Malcomson consider, the market beliefs are optimistic enough to enable employees to deter such shirking by the employer costlessly by quitting the firm. However, if a worker's cost of mid-career separation is high (e.g. because the market beliefs about the ability of job-changers are quite pessimistic), he will prefer staying and accpeting delay to separating from the firm, and hence promotion delay may prevail. Alternatively, slow promotion and 'wide' career could arise from their model because the performance measures are often subjective and hence the problems associated with merit ratings are inevitable as well.

REFERENCES

Aoki, M. (1986), 'Horizontal vs. Vertical Information Structure of the Firm', *American Economic Review*, 76: 971–83.

—— (1988), *Information, Incentives, and Bargaining in the Japanese Economy*, Cambridge University Press.

—— (1990), 'The Participatory Generation of Information Rents and the Theory of the Firm', in M. Aoki, B. Gustafsson, and O. E. Willamson (eds.), *The Firm as a Nexus of Treaties*, Sage, London.

Baker, G. P., Jensen, M. C., and Murphy, K. J. (1988), 'Compensation and Incentives: Practice vs. Theory', *Journal of Finance*, 43: 593–616.

Becker, G. S. (1975), *Human Capital: A Theoretical and Empirical Analysis, with Special Reference to Education*, 2nd edn., University of Chicago Press.

Bernhardt, D. (1989), 'Skill Profiles, Observability and Firm Hierarchies: A Theory of Promotion and Compensation', Discussion Paper no. 764, Department of Economics, Queen's University.

Carmichael, L. (1983), 'Firm-Specific Human Capital and Promotion Ladders', *Bell Journal of Economics*, 14: 251–8.

Cole, R. E. (1989), *Strategies for Learning: Small-Group Activities in American, Japanese, and Swedish Industry*, University of California Press, Berkeley, Calif.

Edwards, R. (1979), *Contested Terrain: The Transformation of the Workplace in the Twentieth Century*, Basic Books, New York.

Forbes, J. B. (1987), 'Early Intraorganizational Mobility: Patterns and Influences', *Academy of Management Journal*, 30: 110–25.

Freeman, R. B. and Weitzman, M. L. (1987), 'Bonuses and Employment in Japan', *Journal of the Japanese and International Economies*, 1: 168–94.

Fujimura, H. (1989), 'Seiseki Satei no Kokusai Hikaku' (International Comparison of Merit Ratings), *Nihon Rōdō Kyōkai Zasshi*, no. 362: 26–37.

Gibbons, R. S., and Katz, L. F. (1991), 'Layoffs and Lemons', *Journal of Labor Economics*, 9: 351–80.

—— and Murphy, K. J. (1992), 'Optimal Incentive Contracts in the Presence of Career Concerns: Theory and Evidence', *Journal of Political Economy*, 100: 468–505.

Hanada, M. (1989), 'The Principle of Competition in Japan's Personnel System', *Japanese Economic Studies*, 17: 3–22.

Harris, M., and Holmström, B. (1982), 'A Theory of Wage Dynamics', *Review of Economic Studies*, 49: 315–33.

Hart, O., and Holmström, B. (1987), 'The Theory of Contracts', in T. F. Bewley (ed.), *Advances in Economic Theory, Fifth World Congress*, Cambridge University Press, 71–155.

Hashimoto, M. (1979), 'Bonus Payments, On-The-Job Training, and Lifetime Employment in Japan', *Journal of Political Economy*, 87: 1086–1104.

—— (1981), 'Firm-Specific Human Capital as a Shared Investment', *American Economic Review*, 71: 475–82.

—— (1990), 'Employment and Wage Systems in Japan and their Implications for

Productivity', in A. S. Blinder (ed.), *Paying for Productivity: A Look at the Evidence*, Brookings Institution, Washington, DC.

—— and Raisian, J. (1985), 'Employment Tenure and Earnings Profiles in Japan and the United States', *American Economic Review*, 75: 721–35.

—— —— (1989), 'Investments in Employer–Employee Attachments by Japanese and US Workers in Firms of Varying Size', *Journal of the Japanese and International Economies*, 3: 31–48.

Holmström, B. (1982), 'Moral Hazard in Teams', *Bell Journal of Economics*, 13: 324–40.

—— and Milgrom, P. (1990), 'Regulating Trade among Agents', *Journal of Institutional and Theoretical Economics*, 146: 85–105.

—— —— (1991), 'Multi-Task Principal–Agent Analyses: Incentive Contracts, Asset Ownership and Job Design', *Journal of Law, Economics, and Organization*, 7 (Special Issue): 24–52.

Hutchens, R. M. (1987), 'A Test of Lazear's Theory of Delayed Payment Contracts', *Journal of Labor Economics*, 5: S153–70.

Ishida, M. (1990), *Chingin no Shakai Kagaku: Nippon to Igirisu* (Social Science of Wages: Japan and Britain), Chūō Keizaisha, Tokyo.

Itoh, H. (1987), 'Information Processing Capacities of the Firm', *Journal of the Japanese and International Economies*, 1: 299–326.

—— (1988), 'Information Structures, Task Structures, and Coordination Systems', Working Paper no.4, Faculty of Economics, Kyoto University.

—— (1991), 'Incentives to Help in Multi-Agent Situations', *Econometrica*, 59: 611–36.

—— (1992), 'Cooperation in Hierarchical Organizations: An Incentive Perspective', *Journal of Law, Economics, and Organization*, 8: 321–45

—— (1993), 'Coalitions, Incentives, and Risk Sharing', *Journal of Economic Theory*, 60: 410–27.

Kagono, T., Nonaka, I., Sakakibara, K., and Okumura, A. (1985), *Strategic vs. Evolutionary Management: A US–Japan Comparison of Strategy and Organization*, North-Holland, Amsterdam.

Kalleberg, A. L., and Lincoln, J. R. (1988), 'The Structure of Earnings Inequality in the United States and Japan', *American Journal of Sociology*, suppl. to 94: S121–53.

Koike, K. (1988), *Understanding Industrial Relations in Modern Japan*, Macmillan, London.

—— (1991), *Daisotsu Howaito Karā no Jinzai Kaihatsu* (Human Resource Development of College-Graduate White-Collar Workers), Tōyō Keizai Shinpō Sha, Tokyo.

Krueger, A. B. (1991), 'Ownership, Agency, and Wages: An Examination of Franchising in the Fast Food Industry', *Quarterly Journal of Economics*, 106: 75–101.

Laffont, J.-J. (1990), 'Analysis of Hidden Gaming in a Three-Level Hierarchy', *Journal of Law, Economics, and Organization*, 6: 301–24.

Lazear, E. P. (1979), 'Why Is There Mandatory Retirement?' *Journal of Political Economy*, 87: 1261–84.

—— (1981), 'Agency, Earnings Profiles, Productivity, and Hours Restrictions', *American Economic Review*, 71: 606–20.

—— (1989), 'Pay Equality and Industrial Politics', *Journal of Political Economy*, 97: 561–80.

—— and Moore, R. L. (1984), 'Incentives, Productivity, and Labor Contracts', *Quarterly Journal of Economics*, 99: 275–95.

—— and Rosen, S. (1981), 'Rank-Order Tournaments as Optimal Labor Contracts', *Journal of Political Economy*, 89: 841–64.

Lincoln, J. R., and Kalleberg, A. L. (1990), *Culture, Control, and Commitment: A Study of Work Organization and Work Attitudes in the United States and Japan*, Cambridge University Press.

—— and McBride, K. (1987), 'Japanese Industrial Organization in Comparative Perspective', *Annual Review of Sociology*, 13: 289–312.

—— Hanada, M., and McBride, K. (1986), 'Organizational Structures in Japanese and US Manufacturing', *Administrative Science Quarterly*, 31: 338–64.

MacLeod, W. B., and Malcomson, J. M. (1988), 'Reputation and Hierarchy in Dynamic Models of Employment', *Journal of Political Economy*, 96: 832–54.

—— —— (1989), 'Implicit Contracts, Incentive Compatibility, and Involuntary Unemployment', *Econometrica*, 57: 447–80.

Malcomson, J. M. (1984), 'Work Incentives, Hierarchy, and Internal Labor Markets', *Journal of Political Economy*, 92: 486–507.

Milgrom, P. R. (1988), 'Employment Contracts, Influence Activities and Efficient Organization Design', *Journal of Political Economy*, 96: 42–60.

—— and Roberts, J. (1988), 'An Economic Approach to Influence Activities in Organizations', *American Journal of Sociology*, suppl. to 94: S154–79.

Mincer, J., and Higuchi, Y. (1988), 'Wage Structures and Labor Turnover in the United States and Japan', *Journal of the Japanese and International Economies*, 2: 97–133.

Monden, Y. (1983), *Toyota Production System: Practical Approach to Production Management*, Industrial Engineering and Management Press, Norcross, Ga.

Murphy, K. J. (1986), 'Incentives, Learning, and Compensation: A Theoretical and Empirical Investigation of Managerial Labor Contracts', *Rand Journal of Economics*, 17: 59–76.

OECD (1984), *OECD Employment Outlook*, Paris.

Ohashi, I. (1989), 'On the Determinants of Bonuses and Basic Wages in Large Japanese Firms', *Journal of the Japanese and International Economies*, 3: 451–79.

Okuno, M. (1984), 'Corporate Loyalty and Bonus Payments: An Analysis of Work Incentives in Japan', in M. Aoki (ed.), *The Economic Analysis of the Japanese Firm*, North-Holland, Amsterdam.

Okuno-Fujiwara, M. (1987), 'Monitoring Cost, Agency Relationship, and Equilibrium Modes of Labor Contract', *Journal of the Japanese and International Economies*, 1: 147–67.

Ono, A. (1989), *Nihonteki Koyō Kankō to Rōdō Shijō* (Japanese Employment Practices and Labor Markets), Tōyō Keizai Shinpō Sha, Tokyo.

Prendergast, C. (1991), 'A Theory of Worker Responsibility', mimeo, Graduate School of Business, University of Chicago.

—— (1992), 'Career Development and Specific Human Capital Collection', *Journal of the Japanese and International Economies*, 6: 207–27.

Pucik, V. (1985), 'Promotion Patterns in a Japanese Trading Company', *Columbia Journal of World Business*, 20: 73–79.

Ramakrishnan, R. T. S. and Thakor, A. V. (1991), 'Cooperation versus Competition in Agency', *Journal of Law, Economics, and Organization*, 7: 248–83.

Rosen, S. (1986), 'Prizes and Incentives in Elimination Tournaments', *American Economic Review*, 76: 701–15.

Rosenbaum, J. E. (1979), 'Tournament Mobility: Career Patterns in a Corporation', *Administrative Science Quarterly*, 24: 220–41.

Shapiro, C., and Stiglitz, J. E. (1984), 'Equilibrium Unemployment as a Worker Discipline Device', *American Economic Review*, 74: 433–44.

Stiglitz, J. E. (1975), 'Incentives, Risk, and Information: Notes towards a Theory of Hierarchy', *Bell Journal of Economics*, 6: 552–79.

Tachibanaki, T. (1987), 'The Determination of the Promotion Process in Organizations and of Earnings Differentials', *Journal of Economic Behavior and Organization*, 8: 603–16.

——(1988), 'Education, Occupation, Hierarchy and Earnings', *Economics of Education Review*, 7: 221–9.

——and Taki, A. (1990), 'Wage Determination in Japan: A Theoretical and Empirical Investigation', in H. Konig, (ed.), *Economics of Wage Determination*, Springer-Verlag, Berlin.

Tirole, J. (1986), 'Hierarchies and Bureaucracies: On the Role of Collusion in Organizations', *Journal of Law, Economics, and Organization*, 2: 181–244.

Trevor, M. (1983), *Japan's Reluctant Multinationals: Japanese Management at Home and Abroad*, Frances Pinter, London.

Tsuchida, M. (1989), 'Nihonteki Koyō Kankō to Rōdō Keiyaku' (Japanese Employment Practices and Labor Contracts), *Nihon Rōdōhō Gakkaishi*, 73: 31–70.

Waldman, M. (1984), 'Job Assignments, Signalling, and Efficiency', *Rand Journal of Economics*, 15: 255–67.

——(1990), 'A Signalling Explanation for Seniority Based Promotions and Other Labor Market Puzzles', mimeo, University of California at Los Angeles.

Weiss, A. (1984), 'Simple Truths of Japanese Manufacturing', *Harvard Business Review*, 62: 119–25.

——(1988), 'Incentives and Worker Behavior: Some Evidence', in H. R. Nalbantian (ed.), *Incentives, Cooperation, and Risk Sharing*, Rowman and Littlefield, Totowa, NJ.

Whittaker, D. H. (1990), *Managing Innovation: A Study of British and Japanese Factories*, Cambridge University Press.

Williamson, O. E., Wachter, M. L., and Harris, J. E. (1975), 'Understanding the Employment Relation: The Analysis of Idiosyncratic Exchange', *Bell Journal of Economics*, 6: 250–80.

Yoshino, M. Y. (1968), *Japan's Managerial System: Tradition and Innovation*, MIT Press, Cambridge, Mass.

10

Co-ordination, Specialization, and Incentives in Product Development Organization

HIDESHI ITOH

1. INTRODUCTION

What does an effective form of organization for developing complicated new products look like? Recent empirical research in the auto industry worldwide provides an interesting answer: project organizations with broad task assignments among engineers and powerful product managers (called 'heavyweight' product managers) achieve better performances in product development (Clark *et al.* 1987; Clark and Fujimoto 1991; Womack *et al.* 1990). The purpose of this paper is to seek to understand this seemingly paradoxical observation.

In order to design a new car, numerous decisions on the target market of consumers, specifications, appearance, performance, and so on must be made. Furthermore, various dimensions of the car must fit well together: decisions must be co-ordinated. Failure to attain the proper co-ordination of various attributes of the car will be very costly. One key role of a product manager is certainly to ensure co-ordination. The heavyweight product manager system, in which a product manager is responsible for all aspects of the project and has strong influence over participating engineers, will probably achieve a more effective centralized co-ordination among engineers. Why, then, are engineers under the heavyweight product manager system less specialized? Similarly, if engineers perform multiple tasks together so that they can share knowledge easily and co-ordinate their activities autonomously, the need for centralized co-ordination by the product manager should be reduced.

Given the empirical results, I will discuss two basic reasons why this combination of a small degree of specialization and strong product managers is optimal. The first scenario views the product manager's role as that of a strategic business decision-maker. As Clark and Fujimoto (1991) argue, one of the most important roles of the heavyweight product manager is to create and communicate a core concept of the new product that matches consumer expectations. He will need to allocate his limited attention to information-gathering about consumer needs and to communicating the concept to engineers, in addition to the already complex tasks of co-ordination across detailed functional activities and components.

It is usually the case that engineers are expected to have a priori information about how the details must be co-ordinated and implemented. Broad task assignments and job duplication further encourage interaction and communication among engineers, and enable them to attain an internally consistent combination of activities without relying too much on the product manager. However, there are in general many combinations that are internally coherent, and not all of them are globally optimal. For example, technological progress or changing customer expectations can alter the most effective combination discontinuously. Creating an explicit concept and communicating it to engineers ensures that the combination chosen by the engineers is globally optimal. Today the integrity of the car and its ability to meet ambiguous and changing customer expectations appear to be more important than individual functional performances. The possibility that lateral co-ordination may achieve a combination that is internally consistent but not optimal is more serious. In that case, the product manager should attend more to concept creation and infusion, and less to detailed engineering co-ordination *per se*. The result is that less specialized (for the purpose of lateral co-ordination among engineers) but more centralized (in terms of business decision-making, i.e. concept creation) product development organizations perform better.

The second scenario focuses on the incentive dimension of product development. Another important role of the heavyweight product manager that is absent in other types of organization is to provide project members with strong incentives to co-operate for the success of the project. Although I do not offer any answer to the question of how the product manager, without formal authority, can so influence engineers, I will argue that, provided that strong incentives can be provided, the heavyweight product manager will (rationally) induce participating engineers to perform a wide range of tasks with some job duplication. The key factors are team production and complementarities. Complementarities across tasks and engineers are inherent in complex product development such as designing a new car: as an engineer performs more of an activity, his marginal returns to doing more of any other activity, as well as the other engineers' marginal returns to the first activity, increase. This feature not only creates the possibility of co-ordination failure discussed above, but also makes the performance measurement of each task difficult. Then the organization can reduce the cost of inducing engineers to work hard for the success of the project, by increasing the number of tasks performed by each individual engineer and creating joint responsibility, so that some tasks are performed jointly by several engineers. Without the heavyweight product manager, such broadening of task assignments would increase the incentive costs.

These two points are also important in understanding the internal organization of Japanese firms in general. It is often said that in the stylized Japanese firm more responsibilities are delegated to workers than in the Western counterpart, e.g. co-ordination tasks, responses to emergent events, and so on; and there is some systematic empirical evidence for this. (See Aoki (1988) and Lincoln and McBride (1987) for a survey.) However, one should also note that such decentralization works well only within some acceptable conditions that are set by a central unit. For example, it is the careful prior production scheduling by the central planning office and the factory engineering office that enables the horizontal co-ordination through *kanban* to perform the fine-tuning of production across horizontal shops effectively and flexibly (see Monden 1983).

On the incentive side, Aoki (1988) summarizes my point in his 'First Duality Principle'. In order for firms to be internally integrative and organizationally effective, either their co-ordination or their incentive mode needs to be hierarchical—but not both. Japanese firms tend to be less hierarchical in the co-ordination of operation decisions while they rely on centralized incentive systems. The product development organization adopted mainly by the Japanese makers is consistent with this pattern: engineering co-ordination is decentralized to less specialized functional structures with intensive lateral information flow, while incentives are centralized through the heavyweight product manager. A problem of many projects in the West may be that they are decentralized in both co-ordination and incentives.

The rest of the paper is organized as follows. Section 2 summarizes the empirical evidence on product development in the world auto industry. Section 3 is devoted to the informal study of specialization in organizations. Then, on the basis of the discussion in Section 3, Sections 4 and 5 develop in detail two theories of the optimal organization structure mentioned above. Section 6 contains a summary and concluding remarks, with some thoughts on international differences.

2. EMPIRICAL FINDINGS

Two large-scale research projects have recently reported interesting findings on product development organization. The work by Clark and Fujimoto (Clark *et al.* 1987; Clark and Fujimoto 1991) surveyed almost all the US, Japanese, and European auto makers, and collected data on a number of product development projects, each engaged in the development of either an entirely new model or a major model change in which over half the parts were newly designed. The regional data collected by Clark and Fujimoto revealed that, even after adjusting for differences in size and scope of projects, the average Japanese project attained better performance (significantly shorter lead time), using fewer engineering hours, than the average US and European counterparts. They then conducted further analysis to find factors explaining this difference.

The larger-scale research project by IMVP (International Motor Vehicle Project) at MIT was pursued to understand a new production system called the 'lean system', adopted mainly by Japanese makers, in contrast to the traditional mass-production system (Womack *et al.* 1990). While this research project covered not only product development but also almost every aspect of business and other transactions in the auto industry, the researchers, relying partly on the work by Clark and Fujimoto, also attempted to understand differences in the performance of design methods employed by mass-production and 'lean' producers.

The major finding on the relationship between product development organization and performance, due to Clark and Fujimoto, is that what they call the 'heavyweight product manager system' attains superior performance on speed, productivity, and product quality. Clark and Fujimoto define four modes of development organization based on the differences in the degree of specialization and the power of product managers.

(1) In the traditional *functional structure*, engineers are relatively specialized and no individual has overall responsibility for the total product; instead, the heads of functional divisions are responsible for the performance of their own functions.

(2) In the *lightweight product manager system*, work is still organized into functional divisions, and hence engineers belong to their functional groups and may work on other projects at a time. Their degree of specialization is similar to that found in the functional structure. The difference is that a product manager is in charge of co-ordinating activities among participating engineers. However, product managers are 'lightweight' in several respects: compared with functional managers, they have relatively low status within the firm; they have no direct access to working-level engineers on the project and hence only limited influence over them; they are in charge of co-ordination only within the engineering function and possibly product planning, and have neither direct market contact nor concept responsibility.

(3) In the *heavyweight product manager system*, the organization is again largely functional, and hence the product manager has no formal authority. However, the heavyweight product manager has strong direct and indirect influence across all functions and activities in the project, works directly with engineers, and has a status in the firm the same as or higher than the heads of the functional divisions. Furthermore, the product manager in this system has direct responsibility not only for engineering co-ordination, but also for product planning and concept creation. Participating engineers work within their functional areas as in the lightweight product manager system, but they are now more strongly oriented towards the product, and their task assignments are broader than under the first two systems.

(4) The fourth and final mode, called the *project execution team structure* (although no manufacturer has adopted this structure), has a group of engineers who devote all their time to the project. They leave their functional departments, and the product manager now has formal authority over them. The engineers will have broader responsibilities in their functional tasks and as members of the team than under any other system.

Clark and Fujimoto measure the degree of specialization by the total number of engineers and technical support personnel who were involved with the project on a more than short-term basis, and find that the relationship between the degree of specialization and performance is negative: projects with lower degrees of specialization are faster and more efficient. They also find that the heavyweight product manager system has the lower degree of specialization, although it is regarded as the one with the higher degree of integrity and co-ordination, than the functional structure and the lightweight product manager systems. In particular, task assignments among engineers in Japanese projects tend to be broader both in breadth of activities (e.g., an engineer does both design and testing) and in range of components (e.g., an engineer does the entire door lock mechanism rather than only the door hatch).[1]

Clark and Fujimoto further argue that the worldwide trend of organizational change is away from a purely functional structure with no product manager, towards a product manager system, and from lighter to heavier managers. Although many of the best performing projects were Japanese, regional differences do not seem to be the whole story. Even within each region, the same relationships as those reported above can be observed. Although they have not controlled for a size effect in comparison, 'there is at least a hint in the data that the more effective projects are likely to be smaller than average, with broader assignments for participating engineers' (Clark *et al.* 1987: 756).

Womack *et al.* (1990) attribute the Japanese advantages mainly to the following four organizational factors: (1) leadership of the heavyweight product manager; (2) a tightly knit team; (3) highest efforts at the outset of product development; and (4) the pursuit of multiple development activities simultaneously. By (2) they imply that those involved in the project are much better motivated for the success of the project, compared with American style organization, where a project is moved from department to department along with personnel changes at each step. In a US project, the number of people involved is very small at first but grows towards the time of product launch in order to resolve problems that should have been cleared up in the beginning. The manager in the Japanese project resolves conflicts about objectives and roles at the outset. Once consensus is reached, subsequent progress is very rapid. In particular, various aspects of the project progress simultaneously, e.g. body design and die production, with an immense amount of information flow. This factor is also supported by a finding by Clark and Fujimoto (1991). The Japanese projects showed a high degree of overlap of development activities in time, and intensive transfer of preliminary design information from upstream to downstream. The relation between the degree of overlapping and lead time was significantly negative only in the Japanese data; little relation was found in the rest of the sample.

Although little comparative research exists outside the auto industry, the implications from these findings would seem to apply to today's other manufacturing industries with complex products. On the basis of detailed research of several industries, the report by the MIT Commission on Industrial Productivity identifies emerging patterns of best industrial practice, which are largely consistent with the results shown above (Dertouzos *et al.* 1989).

It is not easy to explain these findings from a co-ordination point of view, particularly the better performance of both more centralized (stronger product managers) and simultaneously more decentralized (functionally less specialized) systems. In Sections 4 and 5, I will focus on two distinguished roles of the heavyweight product managers—concept creation and incentive supply—in order to explain these interesting observations. Before doing so, in the next section, I will examine informally the effects of different specialization levels of engineers in a project, because little economic analysis on the extent of division of labour has been done so far. The analysis offers an important basis for my explanation of the optimal form of development organization.

3. SPECIALIZATION AND JOB DESIGN IN A PROJECT

According to Clark and Fujimoto, the degree of specialization in a project is smaller under one system than under another if the total number of engineers is smaller. This implies two possibilities. First, on average, an engineer in the former system performs more tasks. For example, suppose that there are four divisible tasks in a project. If firm A uses four engineers, each of which performs one of the tasks with no duplication, and firm B uses two engineers' one of which works on two of the tasks and the other on the other two tasks, then the degree of specialization is smaller in firm B than in firm A. Note that in these firms each task is performed by only one engineer: there is no joint responsibility. However, there is also a possibility of job duplication. Suppose that in firm C two engineers jointly perform all the four tasks. Firm C has a lower level of specialization than firm A, while the more important difference may be that in firm C each task is performed jointly by two engineers.

These two features of lowering the level of specialization in a project have sometimes similar and sometimes different effects on the performance of the project. In the first subsection, I focus on technological issues such as co-ordination and economies of specialization. I rule out incentive problems by assuming that all the participating engineers are interested only in the success of the project. The second subsection focuses on incentive issues—how the costs of providing engineers with strong incentives to co-operate for the success of the project vary with the degree of specialization.

3.1 Co-ordination and Specialization

Co-ordination advantages If an engineer performs more tasks, co-ordination is likely to be easier. For example, suppose that, in the example given above, activities in the four tasks are interrelated and hence must be arranged properly. In firm A, specialized, independent activities at each of the four tasks may not be optimal for the project as a whole, and hence co-ordination among four engineers by some centralized unit will be necessary. In firm B, centralized co-ordination is required between the two engineers, as long as each of them understands how his two tasks should relate to one another. In firm C, co-ordination among engineers is still needed. However, because they work jointly on all the tasks, they will be able, to some degree, to share knowledge and information and to adjust their activities without a centralized unit. Such lateral co-ordination is difficult in firm A because the engineers there are isolated and specialized. If lateral co-ordination has some advantages over centralized, hierarchical co-ordination, one can conclude that firm C has co-ordination advantages over firm A. For example, because engineers tend to have better information about their tasks, lateral co-ordination may have an advantage of utilizing such information, provided that communication is costly. (See Bolton and Farrell (1990) for an economic analysis.) Or in some situations lateral co-ordination may be fast and flexible (see Aoki 1986; 1988: ch. 2).

Loss in economies of specialization The productivity of each engineer may be higher in firm A than in firms B or C, because in firm A the engineer can concentrate on one task. If each task requires intensive attention and highly distinctive expertise, higher levels of specialization will utilize the talents and efforts of engineers more effectively. Specialization may also result in learning by doing, and can increase the engineers' productivity. Note, however, that if two tasks are interrelated such that performing one task increases the returns from the other task (the two tasks are *complementary*), and this effect dominates the economies of specialization, then these tasks should be performed by one engineer: firm B may be superior to firm A.

Substituting centralized co-ordination The discussion above implies that the centralized co-ordination among specialized members and the decentralized co-ordination with a small degree of specialization are substitutes: *ceteris paribus*, decreasing inputs from a centralized unit for co-ordination purposes increases the need for lateral co-ordination, and hence reduces the degree of specialization. Similarly, if the input by the product manager for co-ordinating the details of the plans increases, the degree of specialization will rise in order to pursue economies of specialization more extensively.[2] This reasoning being accepted, the empirical findings are puzzling. One needs to look at the roles of the heavyweight product manager in more detail.

3.2 Incentive Effects of Job Design

I now consider the effects of task assignments on the engineers' incentives to perform their tasks. Suppose for the time being that the four tasks are technologically independent: activities at one task have no effect on the other tasks. This assumption excludes the technological considerations given in the preceding subsection.

Incentives and measurement   I first assume that performance in each of the four tasks can be measured separately (possibly with noise). Then, in firm A and firm B the performance measure of each task provides information about the effort of the engineer who is assigned to that task. However, in firm C all the performance measures reflect the efforts of the two engineers: sole responsibility has an advantage in supplying more informative performance measures than joint responsibility. Next, suppose that the four tasks differ in terms of measurability. Suppose further that performance at two of the tasks is substantially easier to measure than at the others, while the former tasks are not as important as the latter in terms of their impact on the project outcome. Then, if in firm B each engineer is assigned an easy-to-measure task and a hard-to-measure task, a problem will arise: the engineer may choose to expend too much effort on the less significant but more visible task. Thus, firm B cannot provide strong incentives via the performance measure at the easier-to-measure task. This problem does not occur in firm A. Of course, firm B can remedy the problem by assigning one engineer to the two easy-to-measure tasks and the other to the two hard-to-measure tasks. (See Holmström and Milgrom (1991) for the formal analysis.)

The second case to be analysed is where there are two identical signals, one of which measures the joint performance at two of the tasks and the other, the performance at the other two tasks. Now the task assignment in firm A has a measurability problem. Each performance measure reflects efforts from two engineers, and they may reduce their efforts by attempting to free-ride on each other. In firm B this problem can be avoided by assigning one engineer to the first two tasks and the other to the remaining two. In firm C, all of the four tasks are performed by two engineers, and hence the measurability problem continues to exist. However, it is still possible that the task assignment in firm C, which is broader than that in firm B, can keep the effort incentives high, even without complementarities, by reducing monotonicity or the boredom of performing a few tasks. (See Itoh (1991; 1992) for the formal derivation of this result.)

Finally, consider the most realistic situation, where task-specific performance measures are not at all available: the only measure is the total performance of the project. Assume also that firms can nevertheless impose the task assignments on engineers; for example, assume that firm A can still make each agent work on just one task. Then the degree of specialization does not affect performance measurement, while the three task assignment patterns will have different results in performance, depending on how tasks and engineers interrelate with each other. Obviously, the technological considerations in the previous section are important. Many engineering tasks are likely to be mutually complementary: doing more of any one task increases the marginal profitability of each of the other activities. The existence of complementarities will favour a small degree of specialization because there will be more co-ordination advantages, and fewer disadvantages will arise from the loss of specialization economies. However, there are some other considerations.

Co-operation and incentives Broader task assignments with job duplication as in firm C can not only facilitate lateral co-ordination but also reduce incentive costs. Because the engineers work jointly on the tasks, it is easy for them to monitor each other's activities mutually. Suppose that, as a result of peer monitoring, the engineers jointly make decisions concerning how to perform the tasks together. Such co-operation may be beneficial to the firm, compared with the case in which the engineers behave independently, in the sense that they can be induced to work appropriately while less responsibility needs to be imposed on each engineer. (See Itoh (1992; 1993) for the formal analysis.)

Interpersonal complementarities and incentives In product development organization, not only complementarities among *tasks* but also complementarities among *engineers* at each task may exist. Any one engineer's productivity at a task increases as the other engineers put more work into that same task. This feature mitigates the measurement problem under joint responsibility, and provides job duplication with another advantage over highly specialized task assignments (Itoh 1991).

Changing the level of specialization in a product development project has several effects. The main conclusion is that, in the environment facing the automobile industry today, broadening task assignments and creating job duplication in the project have several advantages. The next two sections relate these results to the heavyweight product manager.

4. CONCEPT CREATION AND CO-ORDINATION

One distinct aspect of the successful product development organization is that the product manager has broader responsibilities—not only co-ordination within engineering, but also product planning and marketing. (See the findings summarized in Section 2.) In particular, he is responsible for creating the concept of the new product and communicating it to designers and engineers in their language.

The importance of product concept appears to be growing. Customers today demand not only a high level of functional performance such as fuel efficiency, noise, handling, etc., but also 'product integrity', such as reliability, product image, total driving experience, etc., which must closely match ambiguous and rapidly changing consumer expectations.

However, the expertise and information necessary for concept creation are not easily available in engineering groups. To improve decision-making in a project, a huge amount of information must be gathered and processed. As Simon (1976) eloquently stated, even though information sources abound, the capacity to process information is a scarce resource, and each member must allocate his limited attention/time to various information sources. Geanakoplos and Milgrom (1991) show formally that in such circumstances asymmetric information is unavoidable in an optimal organization: each member should have better information about some aspect/s of problem-solving than any other member. In some cases, each member will optimally limit his attention to information sources that affect his immediate operating decisions, even if members share the goal of the project. Engineers thus specialize in gathering technological information that is relevant to their own local activities, and are not likely to acquire important information about the product concept of satisfying consumer demand. The point is that engineers do not seem to have advantages in gathering the information needed for creating a product concept that fulfils customer expectations.

In the heavyweight product manager system, top management delegates the task of concept creation to a product manager who optimally specializes in relevant information-processing. According to Clark and Fujimoto, the heavyweight product manager spends considerable time and resources on market information-gathering, often not through the marketing unit but through his own staff or by direct contract with consumers (e.g. dealers). In the functional structure and the lightweight product manager systems, top management may develop product concepts based on information from the marketing division, or may delegate the decision to marketing managers.

What are the advantages of delegating concept development to a product manager? First, every firm has a range of models, and hence it is too costly for top management to allocate its precious time to the concept development of many products; some degree of delegation will be inevitable. The major problem of delegating it to the market division is communication with engineers. It is not easy for marketing people to translate their concept decision into engineers' language. But most heavyweight product managers have a background in engineering; furthermore, they can learn the languages of customers through more direct information-gathering than the mere use of data from the marketing division.

By realizing the role of the heavyweight product manager as a concept creator as well as co-ordinator, the optimality of a project organization with a small degree of specialization and a strong manager can be determined. Although I do not have a specific model, it is possible to construct a model consistent with the theory given here, which features limited managerial attention (as in Geanakoplos and Milgrom 1991). Suppose that, when product integrity becomes more important and customer expectations become more uncertain and volatile, reallocating more attention to the information sources relevant to concept creation leads to higher returns to the project. The product manager then rationally increases his attention to such data and attends less to information pertaining to detailed engineering co-ordination. Then, the return to lateral co-ordination among engineers increases, and they optimally reduce their degree of specialization in order to facilitate such co-ordination, as argued in the previous section. Note that many problems may have been resolved by the manager at the outset of the project, as Womack *et al.* (1990) point out. However, later there could arise many unforeseen problems in implementing the details, and the less specialized structure has advantages of solving the problems more quickly and flexibly. The result is that, as product integrity becomes more important, more centralized (in terms of concept creation and its related information-gathering), and more decentralized (in terms of engineering co-ordination, and hence less specialized), product organization improves.

This simple explanation depends on several assumptions. First of all, each party has only limited attention and hence must decide how to allocate it to various activities. This assumption is what Simon (1976) has emphasized. Second, the marginal returns to the product manager's input into concept creation increases as the understanding of the product integrity and its match with consumer expectations become more critical. To grasp this relationship, it is important to realize that designing a new car is a task with design attributes and innovative attributes (see Milgrom and Roberts 1992: ch. 4). Diverse activities by engineers are likely to exhibit mutual complementarities: doing more of any one activity increases the marginal profitability of each other activity in the engineering group. Then the product development project has *design attributes*: (1) the cost of failing to fit the details together is very high, and hence reaching an internally consistent combination of decisions is very crucial; (2) it is not difficult for engineers to predict how the activities relate with each other. Usually there are many possible combinations of activities that are internally coherent, and each engineer will be able to opt for one of them by making decisions based on history, customs, or what others are doing. However, there is in general only one best combination, which not only is consistent internally but also matches customer expectations well. This information concerning the globally optimal combination is not available to the engineers, as mentioned above. Furthermore, environments surrounding the automobile industry are now very volatile: consumer expectations are changing and ambiguous. These features, which can result in missing information that is useful for reaching the solution, are called *innovative attributes*. In addition, because of complementarities among activities, a small change in each activity could shift the globally optimal combination discontinuously from one combination to another. This is why the importance of the product manager's role as a concept-infuser increases as integration with consumer expectations becomes more critical.

Note that according to this theory, the effort that the product manager puts into engineering co-ordination itself is smaller under the heavyweight system than under the lightweight system. The role of the heavyweight product manager is not to co-ordinate engineers' activities directly, but to ensure that autonomous engineering co-ordination reaches the right combination of activities in the set of internally coherent combinations. The lightweight product manager does not play this role, and hence more attention is allocated to internal co-ordination *per se*. The result is more specialization by engineers under the lightweight product manager system. As for the functional structure, co-ordination under that system is through rules and procedures, detailed specifications, shared traditions among engineers, occasional direct contacts, and meetings (Clark and Fujimoto 1991). Adaptation of product integrity to changing external environments appears to be nil. Therefore, flexible co-ordination across functional areas is not significant, and hence the highest degree of specialization emerges.

In this section, I have taken the so-called team-theoretic approach, where all the members of the organization are assumed to share its common goal. The main theme was the choice of organizational form in order to improve organizational decision-making, from the perspective of limited rationality (imperfect communication and limited attention). Incentive issues were ignored in order to simplify the analysis. These are discussed in detail in the following section.

5. INCENTIVES IN PRODUCT DEVELOPMENT ORGANIZATION

Womack *et al.* (1990) distinguish the best project, with heavyweight managers from other projects in terms of the strength of control exercised over the participants by the managers. In the former,

[the project members] retain ties to their functional department ... but for the life of the program they are clearly under the control of the *shusa* [a typical Japanese word for product managers]. How they perform in the team, as judged by the *shusa*, will control their next assignment, which will probably be another development team ... By contrast, in most Western companies a development project consists of individuals, including the team leader, who are on short-term loan from a functional department. ... Key evaluations will come from the head of the employee's functional division ... (Womack *et al.* 1990: 114).

The role of the heavyweight product manager appears to be not only gathering information to create the product concept and facilitate coordination, but also, providing the members with strong incentives to cooperate for the success of the project.

Note that even the heavyweight product manager has no formal authority over participants. The formal boss of an engineer is the head of the functional department to which he belongs. Formal merit assessments are also conducted on a functional basis. It is thus not clear how heavyweight product managers can motivate project participants. This paper does not offer any answer to the question. However, several case studies indicate that heavyweight product managers can in fact motivate participating engineers to work for the project. The above citation from Womack *et al.* (1990) contains an example: performance of the participating engineers in the project team affects their career. Or, a good product manager can direct the project toward his goal simply by persuading and convincing the participants and functional managers. Hence I assume that top management *can* design product development organization in such a way that the product manager has strong influence over members. I also assume, as in the previous section, that top management itself cannot perform the role of the motivator, owing to the limited amount of attention that it can give to such a task.

Without a centralized incentive system for a project, incentives are provided largely through functional divisions. The degree of specialization in the project will then increase, because project engineers have little incentive to work with those from other divisions, and functional managers would like to limit the time they spend for the project so as to leave much time for functionally oriented tasks. The other direction is similar. If each engineer's activities are restricted to his narrow speciality area in a project, strong, product-oriented incentives will be unnecessary; incentives through functional division will suffice.

Although such a decentralized approach to incentives might be good in motivating each engineer to pursue a high level of functionality with regard to the cars within his speciality field, the priority of well-matched product integrity over specialized functionality in the today's auto industry will drastically diminish the returns from such decentralized incentives. Centralized incentives are crucial.

5.1 Centralized Incentives and Broad Task Assignments

Once the product manager acquires control over the project team members, the discussion in Section 3 offers several reasons why he may seek to induce the project engineers to engage in multiple activities possibly with job duplication. For example, design and testing of a door lock system may be carried out by a group of engineers rather than having each engineer specialize in a narrow sub-task of a small part of the system, and hence more engineers overall would perform the same set of tasks. The major factors are complementarities both across tasks and across engineers: an engineer's marginal productivity at one task increases as he does more at any other task or as the other engineers work more on the same task. Under this condition, a relatively low level of specialization saves incentive costs, and its relative benefits tend to dominate the costs, compared with highly specialized task assignments (see Section 3). Furthermore, the growing importance of product integrity reinforces the advantages of broad task assignments.

A perspective completely different from the argument given above and in Section 3 provides another explanation of the relationship between the heavyweight product manager and a small degree of specialization. Note that the product manager does not have formal authority, and hence must spend a considerable amount of time and energy getting engineer to work on the project. Then, if and when he finds engineers who are eager to exert effort for the project, assigning them with broad responsibilities, rather than keeping them perform narrow tasks and attempting to find other like-minded engineers, will save the product manager time and energy, and thus will be more efficient for the project as well.

The upshot is that the existence of the product manager as a strong motivator induces low levels of specialization in engineers. Without the centralized motivation mechanism, broad task assignments are not likely to emerge.

5.2 The Product Manager's Incentives

I next turn to the product manager's incentives. The job of product manager appears to be a very demanding position. It may bring extraordinary satisfaction, in particular for those who love to make cars, but it is a position that requires personal sacrifices. What makes the product manager work so hard? I argue that the heavyweight product manager system itself provides the product manager with stronger incentives to invest in the project than the lightweight product manager system.

To this end, I interpret the heavyweight product manager system as the one in which top management delegates the control rights of the project as a whole to one product manager. In the lightweight product manager system, most of the control rights are left to top management and/or functional managers. In the functional structure system, the control rights are dispersed among functional managers. Which distribution pattern of the control rights lead to more efficient decisions?

This modelling has been adopted by several economists in the context of integration versus non-integration. They emphasize the concept of *incomplete contracts* (see Williamson 1985; Grossman and Hart 1986; Holmström and Tirole 1989). If parties can write comprehensive contracts, which specify each side's responsibilities in all future contingencies, the organization structure, e.g. whether the project manager is heavyweight or lightweight, does not matter. If contracts are incomplete, on the other hand, responses to some future contingencies will be left unspecified because they are unforeseen or because it is too costly to prespecify what to do. Then, if such an *ex ante* unforeseen event actually occurs, the parties must negotiate. Bargaining is often costly, and hence the parties may want to specify how to resolve bargaining, e.g. who make decisions under unforeseen contingencies. Specifying the allocation of residual control rights (which cannot be contracted explicitly) is one such example. Those who own the control rights can make decisions about unforseen events. However, different allocation patterns of control rights lead to different *ex post* returns, and hence can affect the parties' *ex ante* incentives, in particular, to invest in relation-specific assets.

Human assets appear to be the most important relation-specific assets in product development. Managers should work hard to understand new product concepts and problem-solving. If all the control rights of the project are allocated to a product manager, as in the heavyweight product manager system, then the returns from investment will be fully appropriated by him, and hence his incentives to invest are very high. This explains why the product manager's investment will be higher under the heavyweight product manager system than under the lightweight system.

On the other hand, the heavyweight product manager system will attenuate the incentives of functional managers to work for the project, compared with the functional structure, in which some of the control rights are allocated to the heads of functional departments. However, I can still argue that the system that realizes concentration of the control rights to the product manager will be superior from this viewpoint. The heavyweight product manager system has an advantage of providing strong incentives for the product manager. And because of the importance of product integrity, the product manager's incentives to invest in the project are crucial to the success of the project. Furthermore, the diluted incentives of functional managers under the heavyweight system may not be really a problem, since the heavyweight product manager has direct contact with the engineers in each functional unit who participate in the project, and can obtain control over the engineers' investment decisions by some sort of indirect incentive mechanism.

5.3 Heavier Product Managers?

Although the heavyweight product manager has strong control over the behaviour of participating engineers, the organization is still functional, and the engineers often work for other projects within their functional areas at the same time. How can we understand this phenomenon? One obvious reason comes from technological considerations. If capable engineers are scarce resources, the firm will hesitate to disperse them to different projects on a full-time basis. Such a project assignment will lose a lot of benefits from complementarities.

The incentives viewpoint offers another explanation. Engineers who are assigned to several projects are evaluated by different managers. Because projects are inherently a matter of team production, subjective evaluation by a manager is an important information source about the engineer's effort and ability. However, accompanying the use of subjective information is two kinds of costs: *influence costs*, since the engineers will rationally spend unproductive resources to attempt to influence a manager's decisions to their favour, e.g. better task assignment, higher wages, higher status, and so on (see Milgrom 1988 and Milgrom and Roberts 1988 for formal analyses of influence activities); and costs from *collusion* and *hidden gaming*, since a manager may find it privately beneficial to treat some of his subordinates favourably or to demand some favour from each of them by threatening to favour others. Such behaviour is costly to the organization as a whole (see Tirole 1986 and Laffont 1990 for the formal models).

It is argued that these costs restrict the use of subjective monitoring and that hierarchical organizations inevitably acquire rule-oriented, bureaucratic features. However, the multi-project system can mitigate these problems. 'Influence' activities will lose their effectiveness when there are several targets for such activities, since influencing just one manager now has less return and influencing several managers is costly. Collusion can be less costly because distorted monitoring information from a manager who colludes with an engineer can be checked by information supplied by other managers, and a larger coalition involving several managers is much harder to sustain.

Considering the careers of engineers and product managers offers yet other possible explanations. The firm will want to learn about the engineers' abilities in order to improve task assignments and future promotion decisions. Suppose that an engineer performs several projects simultaneously. Some of them are research activities in the functional departments, others are product development projects of different kinds of cars. He may also perform different tasks in different projects. His performance in each project will then supply valuable information about various aspects of his potential ability. If assigning him to more than one project at a time is better for the learning perspective, then the firm will not select the project execution team structure.[3] In addition, performing multiple projects with great variety will offer important training opportunities to the engineers who may be promoted to product manager.

6. CONCLUDING REMARKS

The development of sophisticated new products such as cars requires large-scale co-ordination among a number of functions and components. It is natural to expect that an effective project organization will have a central unit, such as a product manager, co-ordinating development activities across functional units. But the best performing organization has more than that. The product manager there is 'heavyweight', in that he has wider responsibilities; in particular, he is responsible for concept creation and for communicating this concept; he has direct access to the project members in each functional unit; and he has strong control over their decisions through some indirect incentive mechanism/s.

Given the growing importance of product integrity relative to functionality in a few dimensions, the centralization of concept creation and its direct communication with engineers has come to be more effective. Centralization of the control of project members' decisions provides stronger incentives to work for the success of the project, both for the team members and for the manager himself. And, given such a more centralized structure, members are induced to be less specialized in their task assignments; the product manager can then delegate co-ordination tasks to those engaged in productive interaction more effectively but with less incentive costs.

The paper has exclusively focused on the organization of product development of just one project. However, it is, typical for several projects in the firm to be in progress simultaneously. The analysis of multi-project organizations is an important future research topic. For example, the discussion in Section 5.3 suggests that one examine more carefully the possibility of an engineer engaging in multiple projects in order to understand the optimality of the heavyweight product manager system.

The paper closes with a final but important remark. The high performance of such a product development organization would not appear to be region-specific. However, it is also true that most such organizations are Japanese. Can the 'Japanese-style' system be easily adopted by Western projects? Or should they not attempt to take it on? Those who have studied product development in the auto industry, as well as the MIT Commission on Industrial Productivity (Dertouzos *et al.* 1989), think that they should. However, it is also thought that it may not be easy to adopt the product development system alone: it is a part of a larger system, and there could not exist one aspect without all the rest of it (Aoki, Chapter 1 above). I am of the same opinion, and would like to point out a few aspects about Western economies that might mitigate against the introduction of the product development organization analysed in this paper.

First, it is said that, particularly in the United States, an engineer's career is narrower and his success depends mainly on his moving up through his functional speciality.[4] Under this career pattern, decision-making by engineers participating in a project will be strongly biased towards the interest of their functional divisions, because they will have a much longer relationship with their functional manager than with the product manager. Furthermore, functional managers themselves may not have the interest in cooperating on product development projects under such a specialized career pattern.

This implies that the need for strong product managers is higher in the United States than in Japan. However, simply introducing the same heavyweight product manager system as that of Japanese auto makers may not work, because the product manager there has no formal authority to direct participating engineers. More explicit matrix organization, or even a project execution team structure, may be inevitable.

Second, more competitive labour markets in the West than in Japan may be relevant. The analysis of Prendergast (1991) suggests that, when the labour market is competitive, senior managers may be reluctant to delegate much responsibility to a product manager because exerting more authority may improve their career prospects. For example, by carrying out many tasks, a senior manager may accumulate skills or discover his *forté*.[5] Similarly, the competitive labour market may bias engineers' investment towards specialization, because specialization in narrow tasks is likely to increase their visibility from the labour market.

Because of these elements, the optimal organizational form may not be the same in the West as in Japan. The data in Clark and Fujimoto (1991) seem to show that the trend is in the same *direction* in both areas, however. Although the extent to which this change occurs may differ in the United States and Europe from what has taken place in Japan, their data suggest that the analysis in the current paper be not far wrong.

NOTES TO CHAPTER 10

1. One might argue that the number of participants in the average Japanese project is smaller because Japanese auto makers rely more on their major suppliers for designs and drawings for parts than the Western makers (Asanuma, 1989, 1992). Fujimoto (personal communication) told me that he and Clark adjusted this possible bias to obtain their result.
2. See Itoh (1988) for an attempt to formalize this relationship between specialization and co-ordination systems.
3. However, this conclusion is tentative. Recently Meyer (1991) analyses a learning model of project assignments with team production. In her model, the multi-project engineer system is worse in terms of learning the engineer's ability, while it is better in terms of learning the product manager's ability.
4. See e.g. Sakakibara and Westney (1985), who compare engineers' careers in the computer industry in the USA and Japan and obtain some supporting evidence.
5. Womack *et al.* (1990) report: 'It's common in Detroit, Wolfsburg, and Paris for top management to override the team leader about the specifications and feel of the product—often repeatedly during the course of development' (p. 113).

REFERENCES

Aoki, M. (1986), 'Horizontal vs Vertical Information Structure of the Firm', *American Economic Review*, 76: 971–83.
——(1988), *Information, Incentives, and Bargaining in the Japanese Economy*, Cambridge University Press.
Asanuma, B. (1992), 'Japanese Manufacturer–Supplier Relationships in International Perspective: The Automobile Case', in P. Sheard (ed.), *International Adjustment and the Japanese Firm*, Allen & Unwin, Sydney.
——(1989), 'Manufacturer–Supplier Relationships in Japan and the Concept of Relation-Specific Skill', *Journal of the Japanese and International Economies*, 3: 1–30.
Bolton, P., and Farrell, J. (1990), 'Decentralization, Duplication, and Delay', *Journal of Political Economy*, 98: 803–26.
Clark, K. B., and Fujimoto, T. (1991), *Product Development Performance: Strategy, Organization, and Management in the World Auto Industry*, Harvard Business School Press, Boston.
——Chew, W. B., and Fujimoto, T. (1987), 'Product Development in the World Auto Industry', *Brookings Papers on Economic Activity*, 3: 729–71.
Dertouzos, M. L., Lester, R. K., Solow, R. M., and the MIT Commission on Industrial Productivity (1989), *Made in America: Regaining the Productive Edge*, MIT Press, Cambridge, Mass.

Geanakoplos, J., and Milgrom, P. (1991), 'A Theory of Hierarchies Based on Limited Managerial Attention', *Journal of the Japanese and International Economies*, 5: 205–25.

Grossman, S. J., and Hart, O. D. (1986), 'The Costs and Benefits of Ownership: A Theory of Vertical and Lateral Integration', *Journal of Political Economy*, 94: 691–719.

Holmström, B., and Milgrom, P. (1990), 'Regulating Trade among Agents', *Journal of Institutional and Theoretical Economics*, 146: 85–105.

——— (1991), 'Multitask Principal–Agent Analyses: Incentive Contracts, Asset Ownership and Job Design', *Journal of Law, Economics, and Organization*, 7 (Special Issue): 24–52.

—— and Tirole, J. (1989), 'The Theory of the Firm', in R. Schmalensee and R. D. Willig (eds.), *Handbook of Industrial Organization*, North-Holland, Amsterdam.

Itoh, H. (1988), 'Information Structures, Task Structures, and Coordination Systems', Working Paper no. 4, Faculty of Economics, Kyoto University.

—— (1991), 'Incentives to Help in Multi-Agent Situations', *Econometrica*, 59: 611–36.

—— (1992), 'Cooperation in Hierarchical Organizations: An Incentive Perspective', *Journal of Law, Economics, and Organization*, 8: 321–45.

—— (1993), 'Coalitions, Incentives, and Risk Sharing', *Journal of Economic Theory*, 60: 410–27.

Laffont, J.-J. (1990), 'Analysis of Hidden Gaming in a Three-Level Hierarchy', *Journal of Law, Economics, and Organization*, 6: 301–24.

Lincoln, J. R., and McBride, K. (1987), 'Japanese Industrial Organization in Comparative Perspective', *Annual Review of Sociology*, 13: 289–312.

Meyer, M. A. (1991), 'The Dynamics of Learning with Team Production: Implications for Task Assignment', mimeo, Nuffield College, Oxford.

Milgrom, P. R. (1988), 'Employment Contracts, Influence Activities and Efficient Organization Design', *Journal of Political Economy*, 96: 42–60.

—— and Roberts, J. (1988), 'An Economic Approach to Influence Activities in Organizations', *American Journal of Sociology*, 94 (suppl.): S154–79.

——— (1992), *Economics, Organization and Management*, Prentice-Hall, Englewood Cliffs, NJ.

Monden, Y. (1983), *Toyota Production System: Practical Approach to Production Management*, Industrial Engineering and Management Press, Norcross, GA.

Prendergast, C. (1991), 'A Theory of Worker Responsibility', mimeo, Graduate School of Business, University of Chicago.

Sakakibara, K., and Westney, D. E. (1985), 'Comparative Study of the Training, Careers, and Organization of Engineers in the Computer Industry in the United States and Japan', *Hitotsubashi Journal of Commerce and Management*, 20: 1–20.

Simon, H. (1976), 'Applying Information Technology to Organization Design', reprinted in *Administrative Behavior*, 3rd edn., Free Press, New York.

Tirole, J. (1986), 'Hierarchies and Bureaucracies: On the Role of Collusion in Organizations', *Journal of Law, Economics, and Organization*, 2: 181–214.

Williamson, O. E. (1985), *The Economic Institutions of Capitalism: Firms, Markets, Relational Contracting*, Free Press, New York.

Womack, J. P., Jones, D. T., and Roos, D. (1990), *The Machine that Changed the World*, Rawson Associates, New York.

11

The Economic Role of Corporate Grouping and the Main Bank System

TAKEO HOSHI

1. INTRODUCTION

Miyaji Iron Works, listed in the first section of the Tokyo Stock Exchange, is a leading builder of bridges and steel structures.[1] According to the accounting report of March 1990, Miyaji had assets of ¥36 billion and 750 employees. In that accounting year, Miyaji borrowed ¥11 billion in the form of bank loans, of which ¥3.5 billion (or 32 per cent of the total loan) came from one lender, Mitsubishi Bank. Mitsubishi Bank is not only the largest lender but also the largest shareholder of Miyaji, and holds 5 per cent of total shares outstanding, the maximum allowable holdings by a bank in an industrial firm. Moreover, one of its fourteen board members is a former employee of Mitsubishi Bank. These close ties between Miyaji Iron Works and Mitsubishi Bank are longstanding. For example, in the accounting year 1978, Mitsubishi Bank provided 34 per cent of Miyaji's total bank loans, was the fifth largest shareholder, holding 3.33 per cent of the total shares outstanding, and had one of its former employees as a board member.

This example clearly demonstrates a distinguishing characteristic of Japanese financial system: the close relationship between firms and banks. A firm usually has a bank that is its largest lender, one of its largest shareholders, and sometimes supplies one or two board members. The bank in this case is called the 'main bank' of the firm, and such a relation is often referred to as 'the main bank system'. For large firms, the main bank system is often an important part of a broader alliance of many firms called *kigyo shudan*, or corporate groups. In the above example, Mitsubishi Bank is considered to be the main bank of Miyaji Iron Works, and Miyaji is considered to be a member of a *kigyo shudan*, Mitsubishi group. Miyaji Iron works may also have close ties with other firms in the Mitsubishi group. Indeed, Mitsubishi Trust Bank, another member of the Mitsubishi group, was Miyaji's largest shareholder in 1978, holding 6.36 per cent of the total shares, and the second largest shareholder in 1990, holding 4.6 per cent.

Although close bank–firm relationships and the existence of corporate groups are well known, the economic role of these arrangements is far from clear. Caves and Uekusa (1976) is the earliest attempt to find empirical economic implications of a corporate grouping. The authors failed to find any benefit of group membership in the profits of industrial firms, and concluded that any possible benefit is captured by non-industrial firms, i.e. banks. Nakatani (1984) followed up the Caves–Uekusa study using more recent data and found that the performance of group firms tends to be smoother than that of non-group firms. This finding led him to conclude that corporate grouping serves as an implicit insurance mechanism, where the group banks adjust the interest payment to smooth the profits for industrial firms. The industrial firms pay a premium for the insurance to the group banks by paying, on average, above-market interest rates. Though the implicit insurance hypothesis is consistent with the stability of group firms' performances, empirical tests of the exact mechanism of the insurance produced mixed results. The implicit insurance hypothesis implies that the interest payment is high when the operating income is high and low when the operating income is low, so that the profit is smoothed over time. Horiuchi *et al.* (1988), however, failed to find any significant evidence of such intertemporal adjustment of interest payment according to business condition. Hirota (1990) finds that such profit-smoothing is observed only for some firms and under very severe business conditions.

This chapter also examines the economic role of corporate grouping and the main bank system, but presents a new way of looking at such relations. Relying on the series of empirical studies by Hoshi *et al.* (1990*a*, 1990*b*, 1991, 1993), this paper argues that corporate grouping and the main bank system mitigate some informational and incentive problems in financial markets. The literature in financial economics pointed out a number of problems inherent in arms-length financial contracts. For example, Jensen and Meckling (1976) argue that outside financing is costly because it raises the incentive problem by diluting the original owner–manager's stake. Myers and Majluf (1984) point out another problem with outside financing: if the firms know better about their own prospects than the potential lenders, then good firms may find their securities underpriced, raising the cost of outside financing. This chapter argues that the corporate grouping can reduce these incentive and informational problems and reports the empirical results by Hoshi *et al.* (1991), which are consistent with the assertion.

The informational problem is likely to be especially acute for firms in financial distress. A manager may have trouble convincing creditors that the firm is just temporarily short of cash but is actually economically viable. Moreover, if the firm's debt is diffusely held, then collective action problems among creditors may prohibit co-ordinated refinancing. Citing the results by Hoshi *et al.* (1990*b*), this chapter shows that close bank–firm relations observed in corporate grouping reduces these costs of financial distress.

Although a close relationship with the main bank brings substantial benefit to firms, some Japanese firms seem to have weakened their bank ties during the 1980s as the regulations on financial markets have been gradually lifted. If they have in fact loosened their bank ties intentionally, this suggests the existence of some costs of having close bank ties. Following Hoshi *et al.* (1990*a*, 1993), this chapter describes this recent change in bank–firm relations and discusses possible economic implications.

2. CORPORATE GROUPING AND THE MAIN BANK SYSTEM

Although economists often talk about the main bank 'system', it is not an explicit organizational form, nor is it a legal contract between a firm and a bank. The bank–firm relations in Japan are subtle and the arrangements are implicit. Similarly, the boundary of a 'corporate group' is ambiguous: it is often hard to decide whether a firm belongs to a group or not. The existence of several types of corporate groupings in Japan further complicates the discussion. The word *keiretsu* is often used to refer to corporate groups in Japan; but *keiretsu* sometimes means a series of subcontractors organized under a principal manufacturer (vertical *keiretsu*), and at other times refers to a group of large firms in diverse industries (horizontal *keiretsu*).

This chapter focuses on the economic role of horizontal corporate grouping, and this section briefly explains the defining characteristics of horizontal groups that we call *kigyo shudan*: this literally means 'firm group' and allows us to avoid the more ambiguous word, *keiretsu*. I focus on the six largest *kigyo shudan* in Japan (Mitsubishi, Mitsui, Sumitomo, Fuyo, Sanwa, and Daiichi Kangyo Bank) and identify six types of ties among banks and industrial firms that are observed in those groups: (1) presidents' council meetings, (2) bank borrowings, (3) cross-shareholdings, (4) board members' exchange, (5) transactions in intermediate product markets, and (6) joint projects.[2] This section also defines the 'main bank system' as the close relationship between a firm and a specific bank that is characterized by (2), (3), and (4) of the above ties: i.e. bank borrowings, cross-share-holdings, and board members' exchange.[3]

Presidents' Council Meetings

A presidents' council (*Shacho-kai* in Japanese) is formed by the presidents of the core companies in a *kigyo shudan*. Every one of the six largest *kigyo shudan* has its own presidents' council, and a lunch meeting is held every month. These informal meetings have no agenda, and rarely decide anything important. A presidents' council by no means has control over the member companies, which are separately listed large companies.

The membership of the presidents' councils for the six largest *kigyo shudan* covers broad industries, and all the groups have financial institutions as their members. A presidents' council typically includes one city bank (*toshi ginko*), one trust bank (*shintaku ginko*), one life insurance company, one casualty insurance company, and one or more trading companies (*sogo shosha*). These financial institutions are instrumental in keeping the group members together, as we will see below.

Membership in a presidents' council is well known, so that membership gives one tangible definition of a corporate group. The problem with this definition is that a presidents' council covers only the core companies in a group and does not include some firms that have close ties to the group. For example, Miyaji Iron Works, which we discussed at the beginning of this chapter, is not a member of Kinyo-kai, Mitsubishi's presidents' club, although Miyaji is closely tied to Mitsubishi Bank through borrowings, shareholdings, and board members' exchange and would generally be considered a member of the Mitsubishi group. Thus, membership in a presidents' council is not a necessary condition for a group firm, although it is usually sufficient. We have to look beyond presidents' councils to determine the membership of a *kigyo shudan*.

Bank Borrowing

Group financial institutions (typically, a city bank, a trust bank, a life insurance company, and a casualty insurance company) are important debt-holders of industrial companies in a *kigyo shudan*. A group financial institution (especially the city bank) is most likely to be the largest lender to an industrial firm in a *kigyo shudan*. Although firms also borrow from financial institutions from outside the group, a substantial proportion of bank borrowing comes from group financial institutions. According to data for the 1980s compiled by Kosei Torihiki Iinkai (1992), of the total bank loans received by all the presidents' council members of the six largest *kigyo shudan*, about 17 per cent came from group financial institutions (p. 87).

Cross-Shareholdings

Group financial institutions are also important shareholders of other firms in the group. Thus, debt-holders are often shareholders at the same time. In 1990, group financial institutions held 15–20 per cent of total shares outstanding for group firms. The non-financial members of the group also hold shares of other firms in the same group, so shareholding is mutual. For example, in the fiscal year 1988, Mitsubishi Bank held 3.65 per cent of Mitsubishi Heavy Industries, 4.84 per cent of Asahi Glass, and 4.15 per cent of Mitsubishi Auto; in turn, Mitsubishi Heavy Industries, Asahi Glass, and Mitsubishi Auto held 3.09, 1.48, and 0.40 per cent respectively of Mitsubishi Bank. Moreover, Mitsubishi Heavy Industries held 1.04 per cent of Asahi Glass and 28.50 per cent of Mitsubishi Auto; Asahi Glass held 0.36 per cent of Mitsubishi Heavy Industries and 0.90 per cent Mitsubishi Auto; and Mitsubishi Auto held 0.15 per cent of Asahi Glass.[4] This network of mutual shareholding is often called 'cross-shareholding', which constitutes another defining characteristic of *kigyo shudan*. According to Kosei Torihiki Iinkai (1992), on average, the presidents' council firms of one of the six largest *kigyo shudan* collectively held about 20–25 per cent of themselves through cross-shareholdings (p. 17).

Board Members' Exchange

As we saw in the case of Miyaji Iron Works, the group bank often sends an employee to become a board member of a group firm. When a bank employee is sent to a group firm in this way, he usually leaves the bank, becomes a permanent employee of the industrial firm, and serves as a board member for more than ten years. Thus, he is not an outside director, but can become an important source of information for the bank in critical times. When a firm is in serious financial trouble, the group bank sometimes sends current employees to act as directors and thereby intervenes in the management of the firm in order to rescue it.[5] Firms other than the financial institutions also send their employees to other firms, but rarely to the financial institutions. Thus, the relation between banks and non-financial firms in board member exchange is typically unidirectional: the banks send their employees as a board members to the industrial firms, but the firms seldom send theirs to the bank.

Transactions in Intermediate Product Markets

Some group firms are also linked through the intermediate product markets. They often buy from and sell to other group firms, especially the group trading company. For example, in 1977 Mitsubishi Heavy Industries made 27 per cent of its total purchases and 55 per cent of its total sales with Mitsubishi Corporation (the group trading company). In the same year, Mitsubishi Corporation served as a middleman in 41 per cent of Mitsubishi Chemical's purchases and in 26 per cent of its sales. Some firms, especially those in consumer industries, depend less on the group trading companies. Although Kirin Brewery made 23 per cent of its purchases from Mitsubishi Corporation, it sold only 0.3 per cent of its total sales to the group trading company. Kosei Torihiki Iinkai (1992) calculated the intra-group trade ratio, which is defined to be the proportion of purchases from and sales to the firms in the same group. In 1981, the average intra-group trade ratio for the six largest *kigyo shudan* was 11.7 per cent for purchases and 10.8 per cent sales; by 1989, the ratios have declined to 8.1 per cent for purchases and 7.3 per cent for sales.[6]

Joint Projects

Core companies of *kigyo shudan* sometimes jointly set up a company to start a new line of business. For example, in 1957 the Sumitomo group established Sumitomo Atomic Power Industries, which is closely held by presidents' council members of the Sumitomo group: 80.8 per cent of the total shares were held by presidents' council member companies (Futatsugi 1976: 64). Mitsui and Mitsubishi followed in 1958 when they founded Nihon Atomic Power Projects and Mitsubishi Atomic Power Projects, respectively; Mitsui presidents' council companies held 72.4 per cent of Nihon Atomic Power Projects, and Mitsubishi presidents' council companies held 97.9 per cent of Mitsubishi Atomic Power Projects. Three groups have other group-owned joint ventures in industries such as petroleum, information and research, and urban development.[7]

Of the six defining characteristics of *kigyo shudan* discussed above, (2), (3), and (4) point to especially important roles of financial institutions: they provide debt financing, hold shares, and supply board members. We should note that even a firm outside of a major *kigyo shudan* may establish a close relationship with a specific bank through these three channels. Many companies in Japan in fact develop such ties with their main banks, which are often their largest lenders. The close bank–firm relation established in this way is called the 'main bank system'. This paper defines the main bank relationship as a subset of the inter-firm relationship that is observed in *kigyo shudan*. An industrial firm may develop a main bank relationship without being involved in a *kigyo shudan*.

Even after going through the list of characteristics that we observe in a typical corporate group, deciding whether or not a specific firm belongs to a group is a difficult task. Membership of presidents' councils is clear, but they include only the core companies. Beyond the core companies, one has to determine the membership of a company by looking at its relation to a group in bank borrowings, cross-shareholdings, board member exchange, and so on. Thus, the border of a corporate group is fuzzy.

One attempt along these lines is done annually in the publication *Keiretsu no Kenkyu* (Analysis of Keiretsu), which tries to determine the membership of all the companies in Japan. Many researchers use this publication to identify the memberships of *kigyo shudan*. Empirical studies by Hoshi *et al.*, surveyed in the following sections in this paper, use Nakatani's (1984) refinement of the *Keiretsu no Kenkyu* definition to achieve chronological stability of the membership.[8] Another publication, *Industrial Groupings in Japan*, has the same purpose and is published biannually by Dodwell Marketing Consultants. An annual publication from Toyo Keizai, *Kigyo Keiretsu Soran* (Kigyo Keiretsu Handbook), is also useful in identifying *kigyo shudan* membership. This publication does not try to classify all the firms into corporate groups, but instead presents such key information as borrowings from each bank, major shareholders, and lists of board members sent from other companies.

3. CORPORATE GROUPING, LIQUIDITY, AND INVESTMENT

The corporate grouping described in the last section brings certain benefits to the member firms; the groups are not merely clubs of friendly firms but have important economic implications. This and the next section describe some benefits of group membership, relying on the empirical studies by Hoshi *et al.* First, this section shows the benefit of corporate grouping in mitigating informational and incentive problems in financial markets. This benefit applies to all the firms that may face informational and incentive problems in arms-length financial contracts. The next section demonstrates the benefit to those firms that are experiencing financial distress. Such firms tend to face different but serious informational and incentive problems, and corporate grouping and the main bank system can also help in reducing these problems.

The finance literature has identified certain incentive and information problems in the financial markets that increase the cost of external funds and may prohibit socially efficient financial contracts. For example, Jensen and Meckling (1976) point out several incentive problems between the original owner–manager and outside shareholders and debt-holders of the firm, and argue that those problems increase the cost of external funds. As the firm issues more shares to outsiders, the stake of the original owner–manager shrinks, thereby encouraging the manager to spend the firm's resources for his own purposes. Outside shareholders recognize that they will have to spend more effort monitoring the manager's behaviour, and demand compensation for the monitoring costs through lower share prices. Thus, the lower share price makes financing by new share issues costly for the firm. Similarly, external debt also becomes costly because of this incentive problem. As the firm takes on more debt, the incentive for the manager to choose a risky project increases, because the liability of the owner–manager is limited. If the project succeeds, the manager captures the gain; if the project fails, the debt-holders pay most of the costs. Understanding the incentive problem, and expecting higher monitoring cost, debt-holders will require a higher interest rate and the external debt becomes costly for the firm.

Myers and Majluf (1984) discuss an informational problem that also raises the cost of external funds. This problem arises because a firm has information that potential buyers of the firm's shares do not have. A firm with a project that promises better-than-average returns will find its shares underpriced by the stock market, which does not know that the firm has a very good project. Thus, asymmetric information between a firm and potential lenders increases the cost of external funds.

The corporate grouping and the main bank system are likely to mitigate those informational and incentive problems in the financial markets. Close bank–firm relations through borrowings, shareholdings, and board-members' exchange undoubtedly increase informational flows between group banks and firms. Even informal lunch meetings of the presidents' council may be useful in reducing the informational problem, providing a forum for information exchange. Shareholding and the supply of board members by group banks facilitate the bank's monitoring of the member firms, thereby reducing incentive problems. As the banks hold both debt and equity of the companies, other incentive problems between shareholders and debt-holders are also likely to be mitigated.

Since we cannot easily observe the extent of incentive and informational problems that a firm faces, testing whether corporate grouping in fact reduces those problems is not straightforward. Fortunately, there is a variable that is closely related to the extent of those problems and can be estimated from the data. Note that incentive and informational problems end up increasing the cost of external funds. In an extreme case, the cost of external funds may be so high that a firm will decide to pass up a valuable investment opportunity, even though it would be undertaken if the firm had sufficient internal funds. Thus, there exists a certain class of projects that will be financed only by internal funds: firms with enough internal funds will invest in those projects, but firms with insufficient internal funds will not. This suggests that, when a firm faces incentive and informational problems, the amount of investment becomes sensitive to the availability of internal funds, and we can infer the extent of incentive and informational problems by estimating the sensitivity of investment to internal funds.

There is a problem in this strategy. Although the existence of incentive and informational problems suggests that there should be some correlation between investment and a measure of internal funds such as cash flow, a high cash flow sensitivity of investment does not necessarily imply the existence of serious incentive and informational problems. For instance, this correlation may just signal that both investment and cash flow are correlated with a third factor such as profitability. One way to control for the effect of profitability is to estimate cash flow sensitivity of investment in a regression that includes Tobin's q, which is the ratio of the firm's market value to its replacement cost. Under some assumptions, including the absence of the problems in financial markets, one can show that Tobin's q captures all the profitability information relevant for investment decisions and becomes the sole determinant of investment (see e.g. Hayashi 1982). By including q in an investment equation with cash flow, we can estimate the effect of cash flow on investment net of the effect through profitability.

This strategy leads to another problem, because estimates of q often involve noise: estimated q may substantially differ from true q, and cash flow may contain some additional information for true q. Fortunately, we are interested not so much in the extent of cash flow sensitivity of investment *per se*, as in the extent that corporate groupings reduce this sensitivity. Thus, by comparing the cash flow sensitivity of investment for group firms with that for non-group firms, we can test whether corporate grouping can mitigate the incentive and informational problems, assuming that q estimates for group firms are as noisy as those for non-group firms.

Hoshi *et al.* (1991) followed this approach using panel data of 121 group firms and 24 independent firms for the fiscal years 1977–82 (Table 2).[9] 'Group firms' here are those that are members of the six largest *kigyo shudan* according to Nakatani's refinement of the *Keiretsu no Kenkyu* definition. 'Independent firms' are those for which *Keiretsu no Kenkyu* could not find close ties to any group. This sample selection excludes those firms that (1) are members of a small corporate group, (2) have switched group affiliation, or (3) are subsidiaries of other firms.

TABLE 1 Group Membership and the Cash-Flow Sensitivity of Investment

Independent variable	Group firms	Independent firms
Cash flow	0.041	0.501
	(1.24)	(5.96)
Short-term securities	0.061	0.512
	(2.54)	(6.02)
Tobin's q	0.007	0.007
	(2.33)	(1.75)
Production	0.022	− 0.022
	(7.33)	(− 2.44)
Adjusted R^2	0.432	0.458
Number of firms	121	24

Notes
The numbers reported in the parentheses are t-statistics. The dependent variable is investment divided by the capital stock at the beginning of the period. Production, cash flow, and short-term securities are also normalized by the capital stock. The regressions include yearly dummies and firm dummies and cover the fiscal years 1977–82.
Source: Hoshi *et al.* (1991: 46).

The regression results in Table 1 show that the sensitivity of investment to internal funds is much smaller for group firms, suggesting that they face fewer information and incentive problems than independent firms. The dependent variable in these regressions is the amount of investment in depreciable assets divided by the beginning-of-the-period level of its stock. Hoshi *et al.* (1991) consider both flow and stock measures of internal funds: cash flow and the amount of short-term securities holding. Cash flow is calculated as income after tax plus accounting depreciation less dividend payments. Short-term securities are those securities that the firm describes as readily convertible into cash. The regressions also include Tobin's q, calculated by Hoshi and Kashyap (1990), to control for profitability and the level of production in the last period to capture the accelerator effect, which is often empirically important.[10]

For both measures of internal funds, the estimated sensitivity of investment is much higher for independent firms than for group firms. The difference of the coefficient estimates for cash flow between the two samples is 0.460 with a standard error of 0.0902, implying a t-statistic of 5.10; the difference for short-term securities coefficients is 0.451 with standard error of 0.0883, implying a t-statistic of 5.11.[11] Both differences are statistically significant at the 1 per cent confidence level, and we can conclude that the sensitivity of investment to internal funds is higher for the independent firms. Hoshi *et al.* (1991) report that these results hold across a variety of alternative specifications. Thus, the independent firms face more serious incentive and information problems than the group firms. Corporate grouping mitigates the incentive and information problems in financial markets.

4.   THE MAIN BANK SYSTEM AND THE FINANCIALLY DISTRESSED FIRM

The last section showed that corporate grouping reduces incentive and informational problems and that the investment by a group firm is less sensitive to the availability of internal funds. This benefit of corporate grouping is enjoyed by all the group firms that have to depend on external funds for their investment. Hoshi *et al.* (1990*b*) argue that there is another benefit to corporate grouping that applies to group firms in financial distress. This section reviews that study and shows that corporate grouping and the main bank system can reduce the cost of financial distress.

Financial distress may be costly for at least three reasons. The first is the classical collective action problem among creditors: if there are many creditors, then each creditor has an incentive to refuse debt renegotiation and to free-ride on the other creditors as they bail out the troubled firm. Even if it is collectively efficient for the creditors to forgive some of the debt, the collective action problem may prohibit renegotiation, forcing the firm to be inefficiently liquidated. The second factor is the informational problem discussed in the last section. This problem is likely to be more serious for a firm in financial distress than it is for a financially healthy firm: asymmetric information may make it difficult for the financially distressed firm to convince the creditors that it is economically viable in the long run. The third factor is loss of confidence by suppliers and buyers, who may expect that the financially distressed firm will not stay in business for long. The suppliers may become reluctant to extend trade credit; the buyers may start looking for alternative suppliers, reducing demand for the financially distressed firm. Thus, the suppliers' and buyers' lack of confidence may become self-fulfilling: the financially distressed firm may be forced out of business because the suppliers and buyers believe that it cannot survive.

The main bank system and corporate grouping are likely to help with all three problems. As we saw in the last section, smooth information flow among group firms lessens the extent of the asymmetric information problem. Because the main bank often provides a substantial proportion of the firm's debt and is one of the largest shareholders, the collective action problem is mitigated. Repeated participation in *de facto* lending consortia by major banks is another reason why the main bank system reduces the collective action problem. For example, Mitsubishi Bank may be the main bank of a firm in the Mitsubishi group, but the firm borrows also from banks outside the group. Mitsubishi in turn lends to firms outside the Mitsubishi group as a non-main-bank lender. In this way, major banks form a *de facto* lending consortium for major firms. It is clear to all members in a consortium which bank is the main bank of the firm, and the main bank is expected to be responsible for helping out if the firm gets into financial distress. Repeated participation in these consortia and the gains reaped from its non-main-bank lending may deter the main bank from reneging on its expected role even when it has to pay a disproportional cost in the short run.

Finally, because a financially distressed firm in a corporate group is tied to its suppliers and its buyers in numerous ways, the lack of confidence is not likely to be a serious issue. Through the intermediate product markets, the firm has long-lasting ties with its suppliers and buyers, which may also be important shareholders of the firm. Moreover, the firm's main bank may also be the main bank for the suppliers and buyers.

There are numerous anecdotes that describe rescues of troubled firms by their main bank. One well-known example is the rescue operation of Mazda organized by its main bank, Sumitomo Bank. The first oil crisis of 1973 hurt the profitability of Japanese auto makers, among which Mazda was especially hard hit because its new rotary engine was not as fuel-efficient as traditional engines. Sumitomo Bank implemented a rescue operation: it provided new (inexpensive) loans, sent several executives to improve the management, and encouraged Mazda to sell its shares in the bank. Other Sumitomo group firms joined the effort: Sumitomo Trust Bank sent its employees as part of a new management team, and Sumitomo Corporation, which is the group trading company, helped to market the vehicles. Eventually Mazda recovered and became a profitable company. (See Pascale and Rohlen (1983) for more details.)

Sumitomo's rescue of Mazda is one of many cases where the main bank and the corporate group helped a firm in financial distress. Sheard (1985, 1992) gives an extensive analysis of some other cases of main bank rescue operations. Although anecdotes abound, however, there was little systematic statistical evidence on the role of the main bank for firms in financial distress. As Ramseyer (1991) noted, 'scholars have collected little beyond anecdotes' (p. 113). Other than Hoshi *et al.*, (1990*b*), the only other systematic study that I have seen is by Suzuki and Wright (1985); they find that group firms with close ties to the banks are more likely to file for reorganization than liquidation.

At first, it may seem straightforward to check whether the main bank helps its client firms in financial distress by looking statistically at its lending behaviour. But this runs into a problem: a main bank rescue might mean new lending, but, alternatively, it might come about through reduction in the amount of existing debt; in some cases the rescue operation may require fresh loans, but in others writing off some existing debt may be more helpful. As a result, we may not find any significant changes on average in the main bank's lending behaviour during periods of financial distress. Indeed, Miwa (1985), who studied the lending behaviour of the main banks for 134 financially distressed firms in Japan, failed to find any significant changes in lending behaviour during periods of distress.

Instead of looking at the lending behaviour of banks, Hoshi *et al.* (1990*b*) focus on the performance of financially distressed firms after the onset of distress. If the main bank system and corporate grouping help in reducing the cost of financial distress, then we would expect to find that group firms and the firms with close ties to banks recover more quickly from financial distress than other firms.

Hoshi *et al.* (1990*b*) use the yearly interest coverage ratio (ICR), defined as the ratio of operating income to interest payment, to identify financially troubled firms. A firm is classified as in financially distress if (1) the ICR was greater than 1 for one year, *and* (2) the ICR dropped below 1 for the following two consecutive years. Thus, a financially distressed firm must have had trouble meeting its interest payments for two consecutive years. The first condition makes it possible to track the firms from the start of their financial troubles. It also helps to eliminate those firms that have been chronically in financial distress (and perhaps in economic distress). Hoshi *et al.* (1990*b*) adopt the following timing convention to simplify the data description. The second year in which ICR falls below 1 is called period t. Thus, $t-2$ refers to the last year of healthy performance before the distress, and $t+3$ refers to the third year after the second year of the distress.

For the sample period of the fiscal years 1978–84, 168 manufacturing firms were identified as having experienced at least one incidence of financial distress. Because of data shortages, 43 firms were excluded from the regression analysis.[12] Using these firms as the sample, Hoshi *et al.* (1990*b*) tested whether the post-distress performance is affected by group membership, and the intensity of the main bank relationship. The measure of post-distress performance is the investment during the period from $t+1$ to $t+3$. Again, Nakatani's definition is used to identify group firms, and the strength of the main bank relationship is measured by the firm's dependence on the largest lender in borrowings and shareholdings.

TABLE 2 Group Membership and Investment after Financial Distress

Independent variables	Model 1	Model 2
Constant	−0.138	−0.309
	(−1.10)	(−1.89)
Industry mean cumulative investment	0.687	0.674
	(3.27)	(3.19)
Depressed industry dummy	−0.076	−0.111
	(−1.12)	(−1.56)
GROUP	0.131	0.404
	(2.28)	(2.62)
TOPLEND	0.378	1.284
	(1.35)	(2.42)
SHARE	−0.312	3.591
	(−0.25)	(1.29)
GROUP*TOPLEND		−1.390
		(−2.07)
GROUP*SHARE		−0.332
		(−0.14)
SHARE*TOPLEND		−17.267
		(−2.02)
Adjusted R^2	0.114	0.145

Notes
White's (1980) heteroskedasticity-consistent standard errors are used to calculate *t*-statistics, which are reported in parentheses. The dependent variable is the sum of investment (normalized by the amount of capital at the beginning of period) in years $t+1$ to $t+3$.
Source: Hoshi *et al.* (1990*b*: 81).

Table 2 reports the main result of Hoshi *et al.* (1990*b*). The table shows the result of a couple of regressions in which the dependent variable is the sum of the investment rates in the years from $t+1$ to $t+3$, that is, cumulative investment in the post-distress periods. Model 1 includes five independent variables. It includes the mean cumulative investment in the firm's industry during the same period to control for any industry-specific and time-specific effects. It also has a dummy variable that takes 1 if the firm's industry was designated as one of the 'structurally depressed' industry by Ministry of International Trade and Industry (MITI) and received some governmental assistance during the period of distress.[13] The other three independent variables in model 1 measure the firm's relation to a corporate group and its main bank: *GROUP* is a dummy variable for the membership in one of the six largest *kigyo shudan*; *TOPLEND* is the fraction of bank loans from the largest lender; and *SHARE* is the fraction of shares owned by the largest lender. Model 2 includes three interaction terms between *GROUP, TOPLEND*, and *SHARE* in addition to the five independent variables in model 1.

The main findings in the table are the positive coefficients on *GROUP* and *TOPLEND*, although the coefficient estimate on *TOPLEND* is not significantly different from 0. These coefficient estimates suggest that post-distress investment is likely to be high for the firms that belong to *kigyo shudan* and have close ties with their main banks. The results are also economically significant. Consider a group firm and a non-group firm that have got into financial distress at the same time in the same industry with the same amount of dependence on their largest lenders. Suppose that the mean cumulative investment of the industry is 0.528 (sample mean) and that *SHARE* and *TOPLEND* are also equal to sample means of 0.041 and 0.219. The regression result suggests that the cumulative investment for the non-group firm over the next three years will be 0.282. If the capital stock depreciates at the rate of 10 per cent, which is a reasonable estimate according to Hoshi and Kashyap (1990), the firm's capital stock will have depreciated by about 2 per cent by the end of third year after the distress. By contrast, the cumulative investment for the group firm will be 0.413, implying 11 per cent growth of its capital stock over the three years.

Model 2 includes *GROUP*TOPLEND* and *GROUP*SHARE* to see whether close ties to the largest lender are more or less important for group firms than for non-group firms. The negative coefficients on those interaction terms suggest that strong main bank ties are less important for group firms. This could occur because group membership already captures some benefits of close ties to the group bank. Model 2 also includes *TOPLEND*SHARE* to see whether lending and shareholding are substitutes or complements. The negative coefficient suggests they are likely to be substitutes: if a firm depends heavily on the main bank in its borrowing, then the bank does not need to hold substantial shares to help the firm in financial distress.

Thus, Hoshi *et al.* (1990*b*) give statistical evidence to support the idea suggested by numerous anecdotes that troubled firms are rescued by their main banks. The post-distress performance of group firms and those firms with strong main bank relations is much better than that of the other firms. Thus, corporate grouping and the main bank system reduce the cost of financial distress.

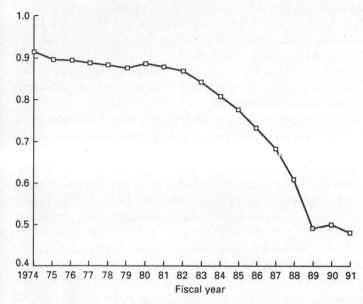

FIG. 1 Bank Debt–Total Debt Ratio for TSE Manufacturing Firms

5. FINANCIAL DEREGULATIONS AND CHANGING BANK–FIRM RELATIONS

Although the evidence in the last two sections suggests that corporate grouping and the main bank system bring substantial benefits to industrial firms, recent data seem to suggest that the ties between firms and banks are weakening. Fig. 1 shows the (weighted) average of the ratios of bank loans to total debt (defined as the sum of bank loans and the corporate bonds including convertible bonds and warrant bonds) for all the manufacturing firms listed on the Tokyo Stock Exchange for the fiscal years from 1974–91. In 1980 these firms had close to 90 per cent of their debt in the form of bank borrowings; the ratio had dropped to less than 50 per cent by the year 1991.

The gradual deregulation of the corporate bond market, which took place in the late 1970s and especially in the 1980s, has been responsible for this dramatic change in debt financing. Before the deregulation, corporate bonds could be issued only if government permission was granted or if significant collateral was posted. As a result, bond markets in Japan were close to non-existent. The first important deregulation was the Reform of Foreign Exchange Law in 1980, which allowed firms to issue unsecured bonds in foreign markets without prior governmental approval. Following this, restrictions in the domestic bond markets were also relaxed during the

1980s. Some statistics are useful for illustrating the gradual deregulation of domestic markets. In 1979, only 2 companies (Toyota and Matsushita) were eligible to issue straight bonds or CBs (convertible bonds) without any collaterals; by 1987, the numbers rose to about 120 companies for straight bonds and 240 companies for CBs; by the end of 1988, further deregulation made about 300 firms eligible to issue straight bonds without collaterals and 500 firms, CBs without collateral.[14]

A result of the deregulations was a dramatic shift from bank borrowing to corporate bonds, as shown in Fig. 1. The aggregate picture, however, hides some important cross-firm heterogeneity. Looking at firm-level data, it becomes clear that firms' reactions to the deregulations were diverse. Some firms aggressively reduced their reliance on bank financing, while others maintained close ties to banks throughout the 1980s. What explains the different reactions to deregulations by Japanese firms? This question is addressed by Hoshi *et al.* (1993).

Using panel data of Japanese manufacturing firms, Hoshi *et al.* (1993) try to discover what determines a firm's choice between bank borrowing and corporate bonds. One problem in carrying out an empirical analysis on this question is that not all Japanese firms really had a choice between bank borrowing and corporate bonds even in the late 1980s. It is true that restrictions on bond issues were substantially relaxed during the 1980s, but some regulations were still in effect in the late 1980s, and the firms still needed to fulfil certain conditions in order to be able to issue certain types of bond. In addition, some firms are qualified to issue only bonds with bank guarantees in foreign markets. Although these bonds with bank guarantees are classified as bonds for accounting purpose, they are not really public debt and are probably closer to being bank debt. Finally, firms differ in when they cleared the restrictions to issue a certain type of bond.

Thus, if one studies all the firms in the sample, ignoring the importance of bond issue regulations that existed even in the late 1980s, one may find that the firms that have aggressively reduced their dependence on bank borrowing are those that are more likely to have satisfied the bond issue criteria. In other words, the result may simply confirm the importance of regulations in bond markets.

To get around this problem, Hoshi *et al.* (1993) focused on a sample of relatively homogeneous firms in their clearance of bond issue criteria. They chose 112 firms that were qualified to issue convertible bonds (CBs) in both domestic and foreign markets in every fiscal year from 1982 to 1989.[15] Since convertible bonds do not come with bank guarantees, these firms could issue true non-bank debts. A series of regressions to explain the bank debt–total debt ratio in the fiscal year 1991 was run in Hoshi *et al.* (1993). The main results are reproduced in Table 3.

The specifications of these regressions are motivated by a simple model based on a moral hazard problem on the part of the firm. The firm chooses

TABLE 3   Determinants of Bank Dependence

Independent variable	Model 1	Model 2
$\dfrac{\text{Bank debt}}{\text{Total debt}}$ in 1981	0.315 (2.78)	0.325 (2.96)
Tobin's q in 1981	−0.003 (−0.05)	
$\dfrac{\text{Financial assets}}{\text{Total assets}}$ in 1981	−1.84 (−2.33)	−1.57 (−2.04)
$\dfrac{\text{Total debt}}{\text{Total assets}}$ in 1981	0.807 (2.52)	0.743 (2.34)
Group		0.240 (1.36)
Tobin's q for non-group firms		0.074 (1.11)
Tobin's q for group firms		−0.146 (−1.86)
Adjusted R^2	0.17	0.22

Notes
The t-statistics are reported in the parentheses. The dependent variable is the bank borrowing–total debt ratio in the fiscal year 1991. The regressions include a constant term, but the coefficient estimate is not reported in the table.
Source: Hoshi *et al.* (1993).

between two projects, and bond-holders cannot observe the firm's choice. Two projects differ in their expected profits and private benefits to the manager of the firm: one project has higher expected profits but the other has higher private managerial benefits. Thus, the firm may choose to take the project with lower expected profits but higher managerial benefits, which is a moral hazard situation.

According to the model, bank borrowing differs from bond financing in the extent of monitoring: banks monitor, and bond-holders do not. Thus, bank borrowing serves as a solution to the moral hazard problem: banks can force firms to choose the project with high expected profits. Since monitoring is costly, the bank will charge a higher interest rate than what would be required by bond-holders.

The model suggests two reasons why a firm may choose bond financing over bank borrowing. First, the firm's moral hazard problem may be so small that it has an incentive to take the project with high expected profits even in the absence of bank monitoring. The moral hazard problem is not serious for those firms that have (1) high profitability, (2) large amount of collateralizable assets, and (3) a small amount of existing debt. High profitability makes it unlikely that the manager will abandon the project for an alternative, less profitable, project with managerial benefits. In addition, a large amount of collateralizable assets that will be forfeited in the case of default will prevent the firm from taking the less profitable project, because to do so would increase the probability of default. Finally, a low level of existing debt implies a large amount of collateral for new bond-holders in case of bankruptcy and again discourages the firm from taking the less profitable project. Thus, a firm with high profitability, a large amount of collateralizable assets, and low level of existing debt may not need bank monitoring, because it may not face a moral hazard problem. Such a firm will choose to issue bonds and enjoy a lower interest rate.

Another type of firm that chooses bond financing over bank financing is the one with a very low level of profitability. The manager of such a firm may find it better to pursue the project with high private benefits rather than being forced by banks to take the more profitable project. Thus, such firms may avoid bank monitoring by issuing corporate bonds and investing in the project with low profits but high managerial benefits.

In summary, the model suggests two reasons why a firm may choose bond financing over bank borrowing. First, a high-profitability firm may decide to issue bonds in order to save the monitoring cost. Second, a low profitability firm may decide to issue bonds to avoid bank monitoring and pursue the project with managerial benefits.

The model's empirical implication is that the choice between bank borrowing and corporate bonds depends on the firm's profitability, the amount of the assets that can be used as collateral, and the level of existing debt. The relation between the firm's profitability and its choice between bank borrowing and public debt is complicated, because both high-profitability and low-profitability firms are likely to choose bond financing, although for different reasons. Thus, a non-monotonic relation between the profitability and the use of bank borrowing may be observed. The effects of more collateral and less existing debt on the firm's choice on debt structure is clear. If the firm has a large amount of collateralizable assets and a low level of existing debt, then it issues bonds and avoids paying the monitoring cost.

In the regressions, Tobin's q is used as the proxy for profitability. The amount of long-term security holdings that are normalized by the total value of assets is used as the proxy for collateralizable assets. The total debt–total assets ratio is included to estimate the influence of the level of outstanding debt. All the independent variables are lagged ten years to eliminate a possible simultaneity problem. Finally, the regressions include lagged dependent variables to control for any adjustment lags and firm-specific effects.

Model 1 gives the basic specification. The moral hazard theory predicts a negative coefficient on financial assets and a positive coefficient on the total debt–total asset ratio. Both estimates have the expected signs and are statistically significant at the 5 per cent level. Thus, the results suggest that firms with more collateral and lower leverage have been more likely to reduce their dependence on bank borrowing.

The coefficient estimate of Tobin's q is essentially zero: high-q firms are not more or less likely to depend on bank borrowings. Although Hoshi *et al.* (1993) report some attempts to find a non-monotonic relation between Tobin's q and the bank debt–total debt ratio, the study fails to find any reliable non-monotonic relationship.

Model 2 checks the effect of group membership on the choice between bank borrowing and bond issues. Given the benefits of membership described in the last two sections, we may expect that group firms might be reluctant to weaken bank ties. But a result in the last section suggests that strong bank ties are *less* important for group firms than for non-group firms. Thus, group firms may be more willing to reduce their dependence on bank borrowing, because the potential benefit of having a strong main bank relationship through borrowing is smaller for group firms.

There is also reason to believe that the relationship between Tobin's q and the choice of bank borrowing for group firms may differ from that for non-group firms. Because of mutual monitoring among member firms, the managers of group firms may put more weight on profits than on their private benefits from a project. In addition, close ties may reduce a group bank's monitoring costs for group firm. Assigning a high weight to profits and low monitoring cost in the model Hoshi *et al.* (1993) implies that it is unlikely for a firm to issue bonds to avoid bank monitoring and pursue the low-profits project.[16] In other words, for group firms, the second reason to choose bond financing may be irrelevant. If this is the case, then the relationship between the profitability of the firm and its dependence on the bank borrowing becomes clear: high-profitability firms depend more on bond financing, and low-profitability firms depend more on bank financing.

Model 2 studies such effects of corporate groups on the choice between bank borrowing and bond financing by introducing three new regressors. *GROUP* is the dummy variable that takes 1 when the firm is in one of the six largest *kigyo shudan*. The coefficient on Tobin's q is now allowed to take different values for group firms and non-group firms.

Of the newly added three variables, Tobin's q for group firms is the only one that enters the regression significantly. The coefficient estimate is negative and is statistically significant at the 10 per cent level. The result is consistent with the conjecture that group firms may value profits and have small monitoring costs. The point estimates of the coefficient on Tobin's q for non-group firms is positive, but it is not statistically significant. The coefficient on the group dummy is also positive but insignificant.[17]

Even though the result from model 2 is consistent with the interpretation that argues that group firms assign a higher weight to profits and are less costly to monitor, there is another interpretation that is also consistent with the result. As the last section showed, corporate grouping reduces the cost of financial distress. This implies that the benefit of group membership is high for those firms that are likely to get into financial distress and low for those firms that rarely experience financial distress. Then group firms with good performance may have more reason to weaken the bank ties than non-group firms with good performance, because they feel that their benefits from group membership are small. This conjecture is also consistent with the result from model 2. Thus, in order to find exact reasons why high-q group firms were more likely to reduce bank borrowing, we need further research.

The findings in Hoshi *et al.* (1993) seem to have some important implications for the future of corporate grouping and the main bank system in Japan. Firms' dependence on bank borrowing has undergone significant changes during the 1980s. Even group firms reduced their dependence on bank debt, and the group firms with high Tobin's q were more aggressive in doing so.

Does the change in the dependence on bank borrowing mean that the main bank system in Japan is crumbling? Or, as Aoki and Sheard (1992) argue, have high-performance firms just shifted to a new stage of the main bank relations, which focus more on cross-shareholding, bond issue services, and other fee businesses than bank loans? As profitable group firms weaken their ties with group banks, will *kigyo shudan* lose the ability to help those firms in financial distress? Or, as Gerlach (1991) suggests, does the change just mean that bank borrowing became less important in corporate grouping and that *kigyo shudan* firms will continue to be closely tied through other channels such as cross-shareholdings? These are interesting empirical questions that cannot be answered until we accumulate more data.

For now, there is an empirical study by Hoshi *et al.* (1990*a*) that suggests that the weakening of ties through bank loans may in fact have serious economic implications. The study investigated the sensitivity of investment to measures of internal funds for group firms in the period 1983–5. During this period, some group firms had already started to reduce their dependence on bank borrowing. Hoshi *et al.* split the group firms into two according to whether the ratio of the borrowings from group financial institutions to total debt fell or rose between 1977 and 1986.[18] Of 109 group firms that were investigated, 69 reduced the ratio of group borrowings between 1977 and 1986, and the other 40 increased it.[19] Hoshi *et al.* (1990*a*) estimated the sensitivity of investment to internal funds for these two groups by running regressions similar to those in Hoshi *et al.* (1991).

Table 4 reports the estimates of sensitivities of investment to internal funds measures. The first and second columns show the estimates for the groups for the fiscal years 1978–82, which is the period examined by Hoshi *et al.* (1991). In both cases, large amounts of internal funds did not induce more investment, which is consistent with the result of Hoshi *et al.*: the investment of group firms is not sensitive to the availability of internal

TABLE 4   Changing Bank Dependence and Cash-Flow Sensitivity of Investment

	GB/D down, 1978–82	GB/D up, 1978–82	GB/D down, 1983–5	GB/D up, 1983–5
Cash flow	0.082	−0.064	0.479	−0.049
	(0.82)	(−1.83)	(3.42)	(−0.50)
Short-term securities	0.044	0.139	0.049	−0.187
	(1.52)	(1.07)	(1.81)	(−1.83)

Notes
The dependent variable is the investment in depreciable assets normalized by the capital stock at the beginning of period. The regressions also include Tobin's *q* (both the beginning-of-period and end-of-period), lagged production, and yearly dummies and are done using first-differenced data. *t* statistics are reported in parentheses. The standard errors used for the *t*-statistics are corrected for serial correlation introduced by the first differencing, following White (1984). GB/D stands for the ratio of group borrowing to total debt. Cash flow and short-term securities are normalized by the capital stock.
Source: Hoshi *et al.* (1990a: 119).

funds. The result is quite different for the fiscal years 1983–5 for those group firms that reduced the dependence on bank borrowing by 1986, as the third column of the table shows. The investments of these firms are now sensitive to both cash flow and (to a less degree) short-term securities. In other words, they look more like independent companies during the fiscal years 1983–5. The last column shows that the amount of internal funds continued to be unimportant for investments by those group firms that maintained close bank ties. Thus, the results of Hoshi *et al.* (1990a) suggest that less dependence on bank borrowing may indeed mean a weakening of bank ties and may make incentive and informational problems for the firm more serious.

6.   CONCLUDING REMARKS

Relying on the recent empirical studies by Hoshi *et al.*, this paper examined the economic role of corporate grouping and the main bank system. These studies found that the corporate grouping and the main bank system are useful in (1) mitigating incentive and informational problems in financial markets and (2) reducing the cost of financial distress. Thus, corporate groups bring certain benefits to their member companies. Following the deregulations in bond markets, however, many firms seem to have weakened bank ties, which play a central role in corporate groupings. A detailed analysis of this change by Hoshi *et al.* (1993) revealed that firms with large amounts of collateral have reduced their dependence on bank borrowing to a greater extent than firms with less collateral. This weakening of bank–firm relations through bank loans is observed among group firms as well; and, among group firms, more profitable firms have more aggressively reduced the dependence on banks.

Studying the economic implications of weakening bank ties is an important topic for future research. But note that, even if it turns out that those firms that reduce their dependence on bank loans indeed leave a corporate group and become rather more independent, it does not necessarily mean that the corporate groups will eventually break down.

As we saw at the beginning of this paper, Miyaji Iron Works continues to be a member of Mitsubishi group even after the financial deregulations in the 1980s. Its dependence on·bank borrowing was rather high, at 0.63, even in March 1992. It is interesting to note that Miyaji Iron Works in fact had a choice between bank debt and public debt during the 1980s. Although it could not issue convertible bonds in every year from 1982 to 1989, and failed to be one of the sample firms in the Hoshi *et al.* (1993) regressions, it could issue convertibles from 1988 on. Thus, Miyaji already had at least four years to adjust its bank dependence by 1992, but it had not reduced its dependence very much. Miyaji seems to have found the ties with Mitsubishi Bank important, and kept them.

Another interesting example is Bunka Shutter, the second largest manufacturer of shutters in Japan and especially lightweight shutters. The company actually strengthened its ties to the DKB (Daiichi Kangyo Bank) during the 1980s. Even though Bunka Shutter was not in the sample of Hoshi *et al.* (1993), it could issue convertible bonds in every year except 1985. Bunka Shutter certainly had a choice between bank debt and public debt. In the 1970s, Bunka Shutter was floating between the DKB group and the Mitsubishi group. For the fiscal year 1973, *Keiretsu no Kenkyu* classified the firm as a marginal member of the DKB group, then in 1977 classified it as a marginal member of Mitsubishi group. In the fiscal year 1978, Mitsubishi Bank was the largest lender, providing 18.5 per cent of the total loans; DKB was the close second, providing 17.7 per cent. Mitsubishi Bank was the seventh largest shareholder, holding 2.14 per cent of the total shares outstanding; DKB was the third largest, holding 2.75 per cent. Neither bank had any of its employees acting as board members. During the 1980s, Bunka Shutter strengthened its ties to DKB, and in the fiscal year 1988 DKB provided 19.9 per cent of the total loans, held 4.07 per cent of the total shares as the third largest shareholder, and had a former employee as a board member. *Keiretsu no Kenkyu* for the fiscal year 1985 classified Bunka Shutter as a solid member of DKB group.

In this way, *kigyo shudan* may continue by strengthening the ties with those firms that previously had only weak relations with the group. Thus, a weakening of existing bank ties does not necessarily mean the decline of corporate groupings in Japan.

NOTES TO CHAPTER 11

I thank Anil Kashyap for helpful comments and Anne Craib for editorial assistance.

1. At the end of 1989, the first section of the Tokyo Stock Exchange listed 1,159 large companies in Japan.
2. See Gerlach (1992) and Okumura (1983) for more detailed description of these defining characteristics of *kigyo shudan*.
3. Aoki and Sheard (1992) adds the ties through (*a*) payment settlement accounts and (*b*) bond issue related services to these three. They argue that the financial state of a firm determines which aspects of the main bank relations become more important than the others.
4. The data are from *Kigyo Keiretsu Soran '90*, pp. 50–1.
5. See Pascale and Rohlen (1983) and Sheard (1985) for more details.
6. The intra-group trade ratios were calculated for all the non-financial presidents' council members. They also report the ratios calculated for the manufacturing firms only. Those numbers are a bit larger: 12.4 in purchases and 20.4 in sales in 1981, and 9.0 in purchases and 16.4 in sales in 1989.
7. See Futatsugi (1976: 61–5) and Gerlach (1992) for more details.
8. Nakatani (1984) used *Keiretsu no Kenkyu* for the fiscal years 1972, 1976, and 1982. A group firm is a firm that was classified as a member of a particular group in all of these three years. An independent firm is a firm whose membership was 'unclear' in all three of the years.
9. The number of independent firms is small because there are not many firms classified as independent according to *Keiretsu no Kenkyu*. 'According to *Keiretsu no Kenkyu*, as of 1981, only 83 of the 859 non-financial firms listed on the Tokyo Stock Exchange were completely independent of an industrial group' (Hashi *et al.* 1991: 41).
10. Significance of production may suggest another failure of q theory, which has nothing to do with the incentive and informational problem. For example, if the firm has some monopoly power, the investment can depend not only on (average) q but also on a measure of monopoly power, which may be correlated with output (see Schiantarelli and Georgoutsos 1987).
11. Since the two samples do not overlap, we can calculate the standard error of difference by taking the square root of the sum of the squared standard errors.
12. Hoshi *et al.* (1990*b*) discuss the possibility of selection bias introduced by the exclusion of 43 firms. More detailed analysis of those firms using available data shows that selection bias is not likely to be serious.
13. During the period of 1978–83, the designation was made by the Law on Temporary Measures for the Stabilization of Specified Structurally Depressed Industries, and during the period of 1983–8, through the Law on Temporary Measures for Structural Reform of Specified Industries (see Uekusa 1987).
14. For more detailed account of deregulations, see Hoshi *et al.* (1990*a*, 1993).
15. All firms in this sample were eligible to issue *unsecured* CBs in foreign markets and *secured* CBs in the domestic market. Hoshi *et al.* (1993) report another set of regressions for a more restricted sample of firms that could issue *unsecured*

CBs in the domestic markets. The results are qualitatively similar to those reported in this section.

16. See Hoshi *et al.* (1993) for a detailed discussion using an explicit model.

17. A positive coefficient on the group dummy, even if it were significant, would not mean that group firms borrow more from banks. We must also allow for differences in the coefficients on Tobin's q between group and non-group firms. When we take the differences into account, the bank debt–total debt ratio for the group firm with the average level of q is similar to that of the non-group firm with the average level of q. See Hoshi *et al.* (1993) for details.

18. Hoshi *et al.* (1990*a*) also experimented with the total bank borrowing to total debt ratio as an alternative criterion and got similar results.

19. Although Hoshi *et al.* (1991) examined 121 group firms far the fiscal years 1978–82, Hoshi *et al.* (1990*a*) excluded 12 firms that either changed their main bank during 1983–6 or for which there were insufficient data for 1986.

REFERENCES

Aoki, Masahiko (1988), *Information, Incentives, and Bargaining in the Japanese Economy*, Cambridge University Press.

—— and Sheard, Paul (1992), 'The Role of the Main Bank in the Corporate Governance Structure in Japan', manuscript, Stanford University.

Caves, Richard, and Uekusa, Masu (1976), *Industrial Organization in Japan*, Brookings Institution, Washington, DC.

Futatsugi, Yusaku (1976), *Gendai Nihon no Kigyo Shudan*. (*Kigyo Shudan* in Contemporary Japan), Toyo Keizai Shinpo-sha, Tokyo.

Gerlach, Michael (1991), 'Twilight of the *Keiretsu*? A Critical Assessment', manuscript, University of California at Berkeley.

—— (1992), *Alliance Capitalism: The Social Organization of Japanese Business*, University of California Press, Berkeley, Calif.

Hayashi, Fumio (1982), 'Tobin's Marginal q and Average q: A Neoclassical Interpretation', *Econometrica*, 50: 213–24.

Hirota, Shin'ichi (1990), 'Nihon ni okeru Mein Banku no Hoken Teikyo Kino ni tsuite,' (On the Insurance Provision Mechanism by Main Banks in Japan), *Doshisha Daigaku Keizai Ronso*, 41: 329–52.

Horiuchi, Akiyoshi, Packer, Frank, and Fukuda, Shin'ichi (1988), 'What Role Has the "Main Bank" Played in Japan?' *Journal of the Japanese and International Economies*, 2: 159–80.

Hoshi, Takeo, and Kashyap, Anil (1990), 'Evidence on q and Investment for Japanese Firms', *Journal of the Japanese and International Economies*, 4: 371–400.

—— —— and Scharfstein, David (1990*a*), 'Bank Monitoring and Investment: Evidence from the Changing Structure of Japanese Corporate Banking Relationships', in R. Glenn Hubbard (ed.), *Asymmetric Information, Corporate Finance, and Investment*, University of Chicago Press, 105–26.

————— (1990*b*), 'The Role of Banks in Reducing the Costs of Financial Distress in Japan', *Journal of Financial Economics*, 27: 67–88.

————— (1991), 'Corporate Structure, Liquidity, and Investment: Evidence from Japanese Industrial Groups', *Quarterly Journal of Economics*, 106: 33–60.

————— (1993), 'On the Choice Between Public and Private Debt: An Examination of Post-Deregulation Corporate Financing in Japan', unpublished paper.

Jensen, Michael C., and Meckling, William H. (1976), 'Theory of the Firm: Managerial Behavior, Agency Costs and Ownership Structure', *Journal of Financial Economics*, 3: 305–60.

Kosei Torihiki Iinkai (1992), *Nihon no Rokudai Kigyo Shudan* (Six Largest Kigyo Shudan in Japan), Toyo Keizai Shinpo-sha, Tokyo

Miwa, Yoshiro (1985), 'Mein Banku to Sono Kinoh' (Main Bank and its Role), in Takafusa Nakamura, Shunsaku Nishikawa, and Yutaka Kosai (eds.), *Gendai Nihon Keizai Shisutemu*, (Contemporary Japanese Economic System), University of Tokyo Press, 170–99.

Myers, Stewart C., and Majluf, Nicholas S. (1984), 'Corporate Financing and Investment Decisions when Firms have Information that Investors Do Not Have', *Journal of Financial Economics*, 13: 187–221.

Nakatani, Iwao (1984), 'The Economic Role of Financial Corporate Grouping', in Masahiko Aoki (ed.), *The Economic Analysis of the Japanese Firm*, North-Holland/Elsevier, Amsterdam, 227–58.

Okumura, Hiroshi (1983), *Shin Nihon no Rokudai Kigyo Shudan* (Six Largest *Kigyo Shudan*), new edn., Diamond-sha, Tokyo.

Pascale, Richard, and Rohlen, Thomas P. (1983), 'The Mazda Turnaround', *Journal of Japanese Studies*, 9: 219–263.

Ramseyer, J. Mark (1991), 'Legal Rules in Repeated Deals: Banking in the Shadow of Defection in Japan', *Journal of Legal Studies*, 20: 91–117.

Schiantarelli, Fabio, and Georgoutsos, D. (1987), 'Monopolistic Competition and the *q* Theory of Investment', Working Paper no. 87/11, Institute for Fiscal Studies, London.

Sheard, Paul (1985), 'Main Banks and Structural Adjustment in Japan', *Pacific Economic Papers* no. 129 (Australian National University).

——— (1992), 'The Role of the Main Bank when Borrowing Firms are in Financial Distress', manuscript, Australian National University.

Suzuki, Sadahiko, and Wright, Richard (1985), 'Financial Structure and Bankruptcy Risk in Japanese Companies', *Journal of International Business Studies*, 16: 97–110.

Uekusa, Masu (1987), 'Industrial Organization: The 1970s to the Present', in Kozo Yamamura and Yasukichi Yasuba (eds.), *The Political Economy of Japan, The Domestic Transformation*, Stanford University Press, 469–515.

White, Halbert (1980), 'Heteroskedasticity-Consistent Covariance Matrix Estimator and a Direct Test for Heteroskedasticity', *Econometrica*, 48: 817–38.

——— (1984), *Asymptotic Theory for Econometricians*, Academic Press, Orlando, Fla.

12

Interlocking Shareholdings and Corporate Governance

PAUL SHEARD

1. INTRODUCTION

The prevalence of interlocking shareholding is one of the most striking features of the large Japanese firm. A typical listed firm in Japan has extensive interlocking shareholdings with transaction partners (banks, insurance companies, suppliers, customers, trading companies) and affiliated firms. The firm both owns shares in these firms and has a significant fraction of its shares held by these firms.[1] The parcels of shares held may be quite small, typically around 1 per cent or less for non-financial firms and up to several per cent for financial institutions; but taken together, shares held in this way usually constitute a majority of the firm's issued shares. In the aggregate, this shows up in the fact that less than a quarter (23 per cent) of listed shares are held by individuals, whereas more than two-thirds (72 per cent) are held by domestic corporations.

This chapter examines the role of interlocking shareholdings in the Japanese system of corporate governance. It has been observed that the take-over mechanism, commonly viewed as an integral aspect of the Anglo-American system of corporate governance, hardly operates in Japan, and

This chapter is a substantially revised and extended version of Sheard (1991a). It was written while I was Visiting Scholar at the Institute for Monetary and Economic Studies, Bank of Japan, and is based on work undertaken as Visiting Scholar in the Department of Economics, Stanford University, Foreign Visiting Scholar at the Institute of Social and Economic Research, Osaka University, and Visiting Scholar with the Foundation for Advanced Information Research, Japan. The support of these organizations, and the financial support of the Daiwa Bank Foundation for Asia and Oceania, and of the Program on the Economy of Japan, Center for Economic Policy Research, Stanford University, is gratefully acknowledged. I would like to thank Takashi Katsumi and Hajimu Tsumoto for kindly arranging interviews and the Japanese businessmen and officials who generously gave their time and views. I benefited from discussions with Masahiko Aoki, Kenn Ariga, Jim Hodder, Hajime Miyazaki, and Ken Scott, and from the comments of participants in seminars at Kyoto University, Osaka University, Stanford University, the Tokyo Center for Economic Research, University of California at San Diego, and the University of Venice. Any deficiencies, however, are my sole responsibility.

that interlocking shareholdings among firms insulate management from external 'hostile' take-over threats. Interlocking shareholdings are typically associated with 'stable shareholding arrangements' (*antei kabunushi kosaku*), agreements to hold the stock on a 'friendly' basis. Controversy has surrounded the interpretation of these arrangements. Some authors argue that they have contributed to the competitive strength of the Japanese firm by enabling management to take a long-term view of investments and decision-making without being subject to short-term stock market pressures (Abegglen and Stalk 1985: chs. 7–8; Dore 1986: 67–72; 1987: ch. 6). Others identify them as a factor behind the alleged closedness of Japanese markets (Johnson 1990; Okumura 1990). The failure of the American investor T. Boone Pickens to secure a seat on the board of Toyota supplier Koito Manufacturing after obtaining a 26 per cent shareholding served as a catalyst for this kind of international criticism. One aim of this chapter is to provide a more solid analytical foundation on which to assess the role that 'stable shareholding arrangements' play in the corporate governance of the Japanese firm.

Why corporate governance in Japan takes on the form that it does is an intriguing issue. One answer is that the insider-based system of corporate governance is complementary to the way that the employment system in Japanese firms operates.[2] In particular, the chapter explores the idea that some degree of endogenous insulation from competition in the market for corporate control may be conducive to the operation of a managerial and employment system based on 'lifetime' employment, that is, a system involving mutually held expectations of continuing associations between employees and firms and imperfect secondary managerial and other labour markets. Commitment problems arising from the existence of quasi-rents and contractual incompleteness play a key role in the analysis.

An argument commonly encountered in discussions of the Japanese firm is that individual shareholders—considered the ultimate owners in neoclassical theory—are excluded from having an effective voice in corporate governance.[3] Some writers cite the structure of intercorporate shareholding as evidence that the Japanese firm and Japanese system of capitalism are fundamentally different from prevailing forms elsewhere. According to the analysis that follows, this critique may reflect an overly 'Anglo-American'-centric assessment of corporate governance in Japan, and one too captive to a traditional view of the firm in economics, a view that has been enriched and superseded in recent years by contractual theories stressing information and incentive issues. In particular, it presupposes that individual investors would want to play an active role in corporate governance, and that it would be desirable for them to do so. Recent literature in economics suggests that it may not be feasible, or even desirable, for small, well diversified individual investors to play a central role in corporate governance, given the strong (local) public-good nature of corporate governance activities

(Stiglitz 1985). It is not feasible because of the well-known free-rider problem (Grossman and Hart 1980), and not desirable because of the duplication of costs that monitoring by a large number of small investors would entail (Diamond 1984). Such institutional devices as stable shareholdings, by giving more discretionary power to managers, may appear detrimental to outside investor interests; however, in a dynamic framework these can be interpreted as being a kind of investor commitment device facilitating efficiency-enhancing intertemporal investments and actions in the firm.[4]

2. STRUCTURE OF CORPORATE SHAREHOLDINGS

It is fair to say that competition through the stock market, *à la* the take-over mechanism or the 'competitive market for corporate control', does not play a large part in corporate governance in Japan. It appears that, by engaging in extensive share interlocks, the managements of Japanese firms are effectively able to insulate themselves against the threat of external takeover (Aoki 1987; Nakatani 1984; Sheard 1986*b*).

The following 'stylized facts' are noteworthy in this regard:

1. A typical Japanese firm has about 70 per cent of its shares held by other corporations.
2. The shares are held by a large number of firms in relatively small fractional parcels.
3. The firm has some kind of transactional relationship with these corporate shareholders (banking, insurance, lending, supply of inputs, purchase of outputs).
4. The firm holds shares in many of these firms: the shareholdings are reciprocal.
5. Firms hold each other's shares as 'stable shareholders' (*antei kabunushi*).

In 1990, the distribution of share ownership of listed Japanese corporations was as follows: financial institutions held 45.2 per cent (4.5 per cent as investment or pension trusts), domestic non-financial corporations (including securities companies) held 26.9 per cent; domestic individuals held 23.1 per cent; and foreign individuals and corporations held 4.2 per cent (Zenkoku Shoken Torihikijo Kyogikai 1991:16).

Top shareholder positions are of interest as these are the shareholders that are most likely to be able to exercise influence in corporate governance either directly or in a coalition with other shareholders. Some aggregate figures can be used to gain an insight into the structure of top shareholding positions.

Almost half (46.3 per cent) of the shares of listed firms in Japan are held in parcels of 5 million shares or more; 5 million shares represents on average a holding of 2.63 per cent. Almost two-thirds (64.1 per cent) is held in parcels of 1 million shares or more. Averaging the number of large-parcel shareholders over all listed firms, there are about five shareholders per firm holding parcels of 5 million shares or more and about twenty-one per firm holding parcels of 1 million shares or more. Roughly speaking, this means that in principle a coalition of the largest twenty or so shareholders could exercise control over a firm, 'control' defined as being in a position to replace incumbent directors [5] On the other hand, 98.6 per cent of all shareholders hold parcels of less than 50,000 shares (50,000 shares on average represents a shareholding of 0.026 per cent); shares held in this way represent 20.6 per cent of total shares. While a minority of listed firms have among their top twenty shareholders one or more individuals, typically the founder or a member of the founder's family, most of the top shareholder positions are occupied by corporate shareholders.[6] In particular, financial institutions (banks and insurance companies) monopolize the top share-holder positions. An analysis of firms listed on the first section of the Tokyo Stock Exchange in 1980 showed that for 78 per cent of firms at least six of the top ten shareholders were financial institutions and for 42 per cent at least eight were (Sheard 1986*b*: 14).

The picture that emerges from the aggregate data is of individual investors (directly) holding a minority of shares and of these being held in a highly dispersed manner, and of corporate shareholders holding a majority of shares and of a relatively small number of shareholders being in a position to exercise joint control over any given firm. Ownership is both dispersed and concentrated: a listed firm has on average 12,910 shareholders, but between ten and twenty of these could exercise joint control.

Much Japanese corporate shareholding involves interlocks. A share interlock occurs when two firms own shares in each other. A feature of interlocking shareholdings in Japan is that a firm typically has a large number of interlocks, each of which individually represents a minor parcel of shares (frequently, a fraction of 1 per cent), but which, taken collectively, as seen, may constitute a majority of the firm's voting shares: firm A is interlocked with firms B, C, D, and E; B with A, C, D, and E; and so on. The phenomenon of multilateral, fractional share interlocks centring on the top shareholder positions has been discussed most often in the context of the six main financial corporate groupings (*rokudai kigyo shudan*), where the level of intra-group intercorporate shareholding ranges from 12.1 per cent for the Daiichi Kangyo group to 26.9 per cent for the Mitsubishi group in the case of presidents' club members (Toyo Keizai Shinposha 1991: 40–9) and from 10.9 per cent for the Sanwa group to 25.3 per cent for the Mitsubishi group in the case of the more extensive Keizai Chosa Kyokai (1989: 4) classification. Interlocking shareholding is not confined to group-related firms, however; interlocks also occur between firms associated with different groups and between long-term transaction partners.

Table 1 analyses interlocking shareholding for five listed firms. Although the sample is small, the firms represent a variety of types and industries. Mazda, an auto-maker, is 24 per cent owned by a foreign firm, Ford, but has close links to the Sumitomo group. Mitsubishi Corporation, a leading general trading company, is a core member of the Mitsubishi group. Nihon Housing Loan is a leading finance company, founded in 1971. Nintendo, a computer game maker, has been one of the most successful postwar firms; it is a typical 'non-group' firm, having no bank borrowings and being 11.5 per cent owned by its founder-president. Tobishima Corporation is a family-controlled construction company with strong links to the Fuji Bank group. The table reveals the state of share interlocks between each firm and the listed corporate shareholders among its top twenty shareholders.[7]

A number of points can be made. First, interlocks centring on the top shareholder positions seem to be pervasive: in 61 of 73 relevant cases there is an interlock. Second, the most prominent interlock, in terms of both number of shares and value, is with the bank that would be recognized as the firm's 'main bank': in three of the five cases the value of the firm's shareholding in the bank exceeds that in the reverse direction, even though the bank ranks much higher as a shareholder in the firm than vice versa. Third, interlocking extends across group lines, although the holdings in both directions tend to be smaller. Fourth, in most cases the firms' holding in their top shareholders are fractions of 1 per cent, much too small to exert a control influence in isolation but, because of the value of bank shares, often representing a sizeable asset, ranging from several million dollars in minor cases to US $897 million in the case of Mitsubishi Corporation's 1.7 per cent holding in Mitsubishi Bank.[8] Finally, interlocking is less pronounced for Nintendo, typically regarded as an 'independent' firm, although there is a significant interlock with its 'main bank', Kyoto Bank, Nintendo ranking seventeenth as a shareholder.

3. STABLE SHAREHOLDINGS AND CORPORATE GOVERNANCE

Most corporate shareholding in Japan is based on what Japanese businessmen term 'stable shareholding arrangements'. 'Stable shareholding' is a colloquial term used in Japanese capital markets; it appears to imply the following behaviour. A stable shareholder:

- holds the shares as a 'friendly' insider sympathetic to incumbent management;

TABLE 1 Interlocking Shareholding between Selected Japanese Corporations and their Top Shareholders, 1991[a]

Shareholder	Shares held (%)	Market value (¥ million)	Shares held by corporation in shareholder-firms (%)[b]	Market value (¥ million)	(2) − (4) (¥ million)
	(1)	(2)	(3)	(4)	(5)
(a) Mazda					
Sumitomo Trust	39,820 (3.70)	25,066.7	10,453.3 (0.84)	18,345.5	6,721.1
Sumitomo Bank	37,624 (3.49)	23,684.3	17,971.3 (0.57)	39,626.7	−15,942.4
Mitsubishi Trust	33,228 (3.08)	20,917.0	9,094.4 (0.70)	16,415.4	4,501.6
Sumitomo Marine	25,415 (2.36)	15,998.7	1,125.6 (0.18)	1,085.1	14,913.7
Yasuda Marine	25,223 (2.34)	15,877.9	1,107.0 (0.12)	1,057.2	14,820.7
Tokio Marine	25,210 (2.34)	15,869.7	1,680.2 (0.11)	2,301.9	13,567.8
Nichido Marine	19,550 (1.81)	12,306.7	912.1 (0.21)	835.5	11,471.2
Dai-Tokyo Marine	19,435 (1.80)	12,234.3	761.3 (0.19)	687.1	11,547.3
Mitsui Trust	13,442 (1.24)	8,461.7	3,351.3 (0.28)	4,859.4	3,602.4
Industrial Bank of Japan	13,038 (1.21)	8,207.4	5,470.4 (0.23)	19,146.4	−10,939.0
Toyo Trust	12,634 (1.17)	7,953.1	3,351.3 (0.43)	5,881.5	2,071.6
Yasuda Trust	10,707 (0.99)	6,740.1	1,178.8 (0.11)	1,962.7	4,777.4
Mitsui Marine	9,255 (0.86)	5,826.0	—	—	5,826.0
Hiroshima Bank	9,245 (0.85)	5,819.7	5,735.6 (0.93)	5,276.8	543.0
Nippon Credit Bank	9,242 (0.85)	5,817.8	6,083.7[c] (0.35)	6,965.8	−1,148.0
(b) Mitsubishi Corporation					
Tokio Marine	95,257 (6.09)	130,025.8	36,107.5 (2.34)	49,467.3	80,558.5
Mitsubishi Trust	85,913 (5.49)	117,271.2	40,568.9 (3.12)	73,226.9	44,044.4
Mitsubishi Bank	77,200 (4.93)	105,378.0	49,726.5 (1.73)	120,089.5	−14,711.5
Tokyo Bank	76,128 (4.87)	103,914.7	41,172.0 (2.05)	55,993.9	47,920.8
Daiichi Kangyo Bank	54,738 (3.50)	74,717.4	32,088.4 (1.03)	73,001.1	1,716.3
Mitsubishi Heavy Industries	48,921 (3.12)	66,777.2	53,230.0 (1.58)	42,796.9	23,980.2
Sanwa Bank	37,935 (2.42)	51,781.3	20,542.8 (0.71)	48,481.0	3,300.3
Tokai Bank	33,088 (2.11)	45,165.1	13,303.2 (0.66)	23,014.5	22,150.6

TABLE 1 Interlocking Shareholding between Selected Japanese Corporations and their Top Shareholders, 1991ᵃ—Continued

Shareholder	Shares held (%)	Market value (¥ million)	Shares held by corporation in shareholder-firms (%)ᵇ	Market value (¥ million)	(2) – (4) (¥ million)
	(1)	(2)	(3)	(4)	(5)
Nippon Yusen	26,790 (1.71)	36,568.4	9,999.3 (0.87)	6,759.5	29,808.8
Mitsubishi Electric	22,568 (1.44)	30,805.3	20,000.0 (0.93)	15,460.0	15,345.3
Mitsui Taiyo-Kobe Bank	21,406 (1.38)	29,484.0	6,251.5 (0.19)	12,159.2	17,324.8
Toyo Trust	21,145 (1.35)	28,862.9	3,473.4 (0.44)	6,095.8	22,767.1
Fuji Bank	20,748 (1.32)	28,321.0	13,120.9 (0.45)	34,376.8	−6,055.7
Industrial Bank of Japan	19,703 (1.26)	26,894.6	6,884.2 (0.29)	24,094.7	2,799.9
Sumitomo Bank	19,677 (1.25)	26,859.1	12,005.1 (0.38)	26,471.2	387.9
(c) Nihon Housing Finance					
Mitsui Taiyo-Kobe Bank	7,237 (4.99)	7,779.8	4,947.4 (0.15)	9,622.7	−1,842.9
Sanwa Bank	7,231 (4.99)	7,773.3	3,675.4 (0.13)	8,673.9	−900.6
Toyo Trust	4,904 (3.38)	5,271.8	445.2 (0.06)	781.3	4,490.5
Mitsui Trust	4,661 (3.21)	5,010.6	397.2 (0.03)	575.9	4,434.6
Hokkaido Takushoku	4,461 (3.08)	4,795.6	1,979.8 (0.21)	1,742.2	3,053.4
Kyowa Bank	4,461 (3.08)	4,795.6	2,782.5 (0.21)	3,199.9	1,595.7
Daiwa Bank	4,461 (3.08)	4,795.6	2,086.6 (0.15)	2,754.3	2,041.3
Yokohama Bank	3,802 (2.62)	4,087.2	977.5 (0.09)	1,148.6	2,938.6
Chiba Bank	3,801 (2.62)	4,086.1	394.4 (0.05)	399.7	3,686.4
Tokyo Bank	3,382 (2.33)	3,635.7	2,362.5 (0.12)	3,213.0	422.7
Okasan Securities	1,261 (0.87)	1,355.6	562.8 (0.28)	518.1	837.5
Ikeda Bank	1,192 (0.82)	1,281.4	495.0ᶜ (0.42)	457.9	823.5
Tokyo Tomin Bank	1,011 (0.69)	1,086.8	—	—	1,086.8
(d) Nintendo					
Osaka Securities Finance	9,206 (8.77)	152,359.3	3,285.4 (1.37)	—	152,359.3
Kyoto Bank	5,130 (4.88)	84,901.5	633.0 (0.04)	6,784.4	78,117.1
Daiwa Bank	5,130 (4.88)	84,901.5	847.4 (0.04)	835.6	84,065.9
Tokai Bank	5,130 (4.88)	84,901.5	847.4 (0.04)	1,466.0	83,435.5

Toyo Trust	4,639 (4.42)	76,775.5	405.4 (0.05)	711.5	76,064.0
Mitsubishi Bank	4,618 (4.40)	76,427.9	645.6 (0.02)	−559.1	74,868.8
Chuo Trust	3,853 (3.67)	63,767.2	145.2 (0.06)	388.4	63,378.7
Sumitomo Trust	3,340 (3.18)	55,277.0	—	—	55,277.0
Industrial Bank of Japan	2,129 (2.02)	35,235.0	89.1 (0.00)	311.8	34,923.1
Daiichi Kangyo Bank	2,100 (2.00)	34,755.0	29.8 (0.00)	67.8	34,687.2
Mitsui Taiyo-Kobe Bank	2,097 (1.99)	34,705.4	147.5 (0.00)	286.9	34,418.5
Mitsubishi Trust	1,732 (1.65)	28,664.6	—	—	28,664.6
Tokyo Bank	1,566 (1.49)	25,917.3	262.4 (0.01)	356.9	25,560.4
Sumitomo Marine	900 (0.85)	14,895.0	—	—	14,895.0
Shiga Bank	832 (0.79)	13,769.6	—	—	13,769.6
Mitsui Trust	708 (0.67)	11,717.4	—	—	11,717.4
(e) Tobishima Corporation					
Yasuda Trust	11,569 (4.91)	14,576.9	3,156.7 (0.29)	255.9	9,321.0
Fuji Bank	11,403 (4.84)	14,367.8	5,347.2 (0.18)	1,009.7	358.1
Mitsubishi Bank	8,449 (3.59)	10,645.7	4,650.9 (0.16)	1,231.9	−586.2
Mitsubishi Trust	7,698 (3.27)	9,699.5	1,901.3 (0.15)	431.8	6,267.6
Nippon Credit Bank	5,098 (2.16)	6,423.5	2,471.0[c] (0.14)	829.3	3,594.2
Mitsui Taiyo-Kobe Bank	5,060 (2.15)	6,375.6	1,761.2 (0.05)	425.5	2,950.1
Yasuda Marine	4,418 (1.87)	5,566.7	319.2 (0.04)	304.8	5,261.8
Tokio Marine	4,359 (1.85)	5,492.3	—	—	5,492.3
Sanwa Bank	3,419 (1.45)	4,307.9	510.6 (0.02)	205.0	3,102.9
Mitsubishi Real Estate	2,589 (1.10)	3,262.1	12,955.6 (1.01)	20,210.7	−16,948.6
Hokuriku Bank	2,541 (1.07)	3,201.7	—	—	3,201.7
Mitsui Trust	2,399 (1.01)	3,022.7	—	—	3,022.7
Toyo Trust	2,304 (0.97)	2,903.0	—	—	2,903.0

[a] Unit: thousand shares; market value calculated as number of shares times average of high and low share price in March 1991.

[b] 'Corporation' refers to Mazda, Mitsubishi, Nihon Housing Loan, etc.

[c] Converted to ¥50 equivalent.

Source: compiled from Toyo Keizai Shinposha (1991), *Kigyo keiretsu soran*, (various years).

P. Sheard

- agrees not to sell the shares to third parties unsympathetic to incumbent management, particularly hostile take-over bidders or bidders trying to accumulate strategic parcels of shares;[9]
- agrees, in the event that disposal of shares is necessary, to consult the firm or at least to give notice of its intention to sell.

In economic terms, 'stable shareholding' can be interpreted as implicitly contracting away some of the property rights associated with the shareholding, in particular property rights pertaining to the transfer of the shares or the exercise of corporate control.[10] Compared with an individual investor who can sell his shares when and to whom he likes, a corporate stable shareholder accepts some restrictions or has fewer 'residual rights'. In terms of Hirschman (1970), stable shareholdings imply restrictions on the exercise of 'voice' and 'exit'.

Stable shareholding arrangements need to be viewed in a two-period framework: in the first period, firms enter into stable shareholding arrangements via share interlocks, and in the second period (or subsequent periods) the shareholdings have an effect. This framework helps us to focus on two key points. First, it helps to emphasize the intertemporal aspect of stable shareholdings: they must involve some aspect of (implicit) long-term contract that differs in a non-trivial way from a series of short-term contracts. The 'extra' contracting away of property rights implied by stable shareholding can be viewed as a form of commitment device that induces contractual parties to the firm to take actions in the first period that they would not otherwise find optimal.

Second, it helps to focus on the incentives of individual shareholders. In the second period, effective corporate control may rest with the corporate shareholders or, in effect, with incumbent management. In the second period, individual shareholders may appear to have 'lost' control of the firm or to have been disfranchised from corporate governance. The two-period model, however, makes it clear that this is a choice that investors make in the first period, as they control the firm at that point.[11] It is fallacious to argue that investors are disadvantaged by their, apparently marginal, place in the firm's corporate governance.[12]

Stable shareholdings alter the corporate governance environment faced by Japanese firms in two critical ways. The first is that they make it difficult, if not impossible, for 'hostile take-overs' to take place. However, as is being increasingly realized, hostile take-overs through the stock market—although traditionally conceived as the principal means of capital market disciplining of management—are just one among many possible institutional mechanisms of corporate governance. The parties to stable shareholding arrangements can be thought of as forming a latent corporate control coalition, since a relatively small number of shareholders jointly control a majority of the firm's shares. Stable shareholdings ensure that, if control is to be exercised, it is likely to come from, or be sanctioned by, existing shareholders, rather than from third parties.

Secondly, they imply that the inside corporate control coalition is committed to taking a passive role in corporate governance, thereby delegating considerable discretionary authority to incumbent management. On the other hand, it should be noted that this delegation or commitment to a passive, non-interventionist role—to a voluntary suppression of 'voice' while forgoing the right to 'exit'—is a state-contingent one. It obtains as long as the firm is performing well, but in times of corporate failure intervention by the main bank can be expected (Aoki 1990; Sheard 1989a). It should be noted also that, although hostile take-overs are rare in Japan, the threat is real enough. Share-cornering and take-over attempts by speculator and investment groups are commonplace in the Japanese stock market and have been so for many years (see Sheard 1991: 428–9 for example). The relative importance of the take-over mechanism in Japan today would appear to reflect more the successful operation up to now of stable shareholding arrangements than a lack of external take-over threats.

The reciprocity that goes with interlocking shareholding seems to be a key to understanding how stable shareholding arrangements work, and are self-enforcing. Being a stable shareholder involves an opportunity cost; in particular, it implies that in certain states of nature the firm will behave differently from how it would under 'spot market' conditions. If this were not the case, there would be no need for a stable shareholding commitment in the first place. Inasmuch as stable shareholding implies accepting constraints on behaviour, stable shareholders would require some form of compensation. This could come in the form of a side-payment or, equivalently, a discount in the purchase price of the shares. In the case of purchasing shares at a discount, the investors would face a severe commitment problem, as, having received the compensation from the firm, they could renege on their commitment by selling the shares at the market price and making a profit in the process. Having reciprocal stable shareholding arrangements through share interlocks helps to mitigate the commitment problem by having the compensation take the form of a reciprocal exchange of property rights.[13]

A feature of stable shareholding arrangements is that the firms involved generally have some other form of transactional ties. In the case of banks, it is lending and various forms of banking service transactions; in the case of trading companies, it is intermediation in inter-firm transactions and various forms of trading-related transactions; in the case of supplier or customer firms, it is an input or output transactional relationship; in the case of insurance companies, it is an insurance business relationship; and so on.

There appears to be an economy of scope in transacting and engaging in stable shareholdings. One reason for this may relate to information; it makes sense to bring transaction partners into the stable shareholding coalition, as, compared with a random selection of firms, they can be expected to be relatively well informed about the firm. A second reason is that that transaction partners themselves can be expected to have quasi-rents at stake in the firm in the context of long-term contractual relations; it makes sense to give residual rights of control over quasi-rents to a coalition of the owners of those quasi-rents.[14] A third point relates to trust. Suppose that 'trust' is important as an enforcement mechanism. Trust presumably has somewhat the characteristic of a (local) public good: if it is established in one aspect of a relationship, it can be carried over to other aspects. If trust is established in the context of a long-term trading relationship (perhaps involving mutual specific investments), this may be used in the context of shareholding relations as well.[15]

4.   THE INTERMEDIARY ROLE OF SECURITIES COMPANIES[16]

In practice, a share interlock involves not just the two companies but usually a securities company as well. In Japan, just as a listed firm normally has a 'main bank', with which it has close financial and business ties, it also has a close relationship with one or more of the leading securities houses, known as its [shu-]kanji shoken gaisha or 'lead underwriter' (literally, '[principal] manager securities company'). This kanji gaisha plays a key role in stable shareholding arrangements.

Three main aspects of the kanji's role in facilitating stable shareholding arrangements can be identified. One is its role in helping to arrange suitable firms to act as stable shareholders. In many cases, the candidates may be 'obvious', such as key transaction partners, but even in cases where two firms have long-term transactions the securities company can play a role in arranging an interlock of shares. The actual mechanics vary, and have varied with different historical stages in the development of the Japanese stock market. The firms may subscribe to new share issues, either at par (the traditional method) or at the market price (common since the early 1970s), and either as part of a public offering or as a direct placement; alternatively, they may make a co-ordinated purchase of extant shares, either in the market or in a more negotiated purchase (e.g. taking a portion of another corporate shareholder's holding). Whatever the case, the securities company earns commission income, which is one of the motivations for them to offer this kind of 'service'.

A second role relates to enforcement. The typical arrangement for a stable share interlock is for the two firms and the securities company to have a common (usually word-of-mouth) agreement that the shares are covered by a stable shareholding arrangement. In many cases, the shares are then held in trust by the securities company and placed together in the securities company's vault.[17] The economic significance of this practice is that it is virtually impossible for firm A to sell its shares in firm B without this fact coming to the attention of the securities company and in turn to firm B. Firm B then has a chance to consult with the securities company and arrange for the shares to be placed with another suitable corporate holder. (Depending on the circumstances, it may be happy to see the shares go to the open market.) The arrangement of placing the interlocked shares in custody with the securities company can be seen as a means of making credible the implicit promise that, 'as a stable shareholder, I will not dispose of the shares unilaterally without prior consultation' The arrangement suits the securities company also, because it virtually guarantees that the securities company will get to handle the sale of the shares, and it is a way in which the firms can make a credible commitment to allow it to do so.

A third role relates to liquidity services in the 'market' for stable shareholders. The main economic aspect of stable shareholdings is the commitment not to transfer the shares to third parties not desired as shareholders by incumbent management. Stable shareholders may for various reasons, however, wish to sell their shares, most commonly as a financial measure when in financial distress.[18] In such cases, the securities company frequently provides the service of assisting the firm to place the shares being disposed of in new stable shareholding hands, either by 'recruiting' a new firm to act as a stable shareholder or by asking an existing holder to increase its holding.[19]

More generally, the main or *kanji* securities company seems to perform a kind of 'watchdog' role for the firm in the market for its securities, in particular, by reporting any untoward movements in the market suggestive of possible takeover or share-cornering activity. A typical employee in the corporate operations division (*hojin jigyobu*) of a leading securities company has responsibility for a number of stocks and provides market information on a daily basis to a counterpart in the firm's finance or general affairs department. In particular, the securities company reports each day its share of that day's market trading in the firm's stock. The securities company's 'market share' in the stock is then used by the firm as a benchmark in deciding on the securities company's underwriting share in new securities issues.[20]

What is the explanation for this pattern of behaviour, which would seem to have no rationale in a 'competitive markets' setting? The following tentative set of hypotheses can be suggested. The management of the firm, in trying to minimize the risk of take-over or opportunistic share-cornering, is concerned about two things: that stable shareholding arrangements remain intact, and that the remaining shares remain in the hands of dispersed individual investors in the market, and do not become concentrated in the hands of a take-over agent. The firm cannot prevent individual investors from selling their shares to a third party such as a take-over or speculator group, but it can aim to get advance warning of such a move. If most of the trading in its stock is conducted by two or three securities companies with which it maintains close (i.e. daily) contact, then it can obtain such advance warning and consult with the securities companies about appropriate (i.e. defensive) measures. Tying, in effect, day-to-day market shares to the irregular underwriting of shares is a way of giving incentives to the securities company to supply such information services. A securities company that captures a large market share in a firm's stock is putting itself in a position whereby it can, to a significant extent, in effect guarantee the 'integrity' of that portion of the firm's floating stock. It can be 'rewarded' or given incentives to do this by an increased share of underwriting. On the other hand, if it fails to do this, or does obtain a large market share but does not act as a watchdog for the firm (or, worse still, even assists a raider to build up a strategic parcel), it can be 'punished' by having its share of underwriting business reduced.[21]

5. CORPORATE GOVERNANCE AND THE EMPLOYMENT SYSTEM

The literature approaches the issue of corporate control and managerial incentives from a finance-theoretic viewpoint, through the eyes of the shareholder–investor: the object is to align managerial incentives and curb various forms of managerial moral hazard and opportunism. An issue less studied in the literature is that there may be various forms of opportunism on the investor side *vis-à-vis* management, associated with imperfect contracting.[22] Shareholders, inasmuch as they possess residual control, get to 'fill in' the detail of incomplete contracts, and, positing self-interested behaviour, can be expected to do so in a way that is most favourable to them.

In a world of incomplete contracting, shareholders are likely to face a problem of imperfect commitment or time inconsistency (Mayer 1988). To see this starkly, consider a simple two-period model where quasi-rents are generated in the second period because of first-period actions or investments. Quasi-rents are rents that are created in the course of a relationship. Suppose that a worker's outside opportunity cost is w per period. Then a contract that promised the worker zero in the first period and $2w$ in the second (assuming no discounting) would involve no rents, as the worker's participation constraint is just binding, but involves a quasi-rent of w in the second period. These quasi-rents 'belong' to managers or employees, but shareholders may find it hard to commit themselves in advance to not snatching these quasi-rents in the second period. Suppose that (at least some portion of) the quasi-rents are non-contractible, for whatever reason (transaction costs/incomplete contracts/information asymmetries). If the shareholders are the residual claimants, they may face a 'time inconsistency' problem with respect to the promise not to claim the quasi-rents as residual income (see also Mayer 1988).

In a world of complete contingent contracting, there is no problem of shareholder opportunism even in the presence of quasi-rents. This is because in every state of nature the payments to economic agents are fully specified. But in such a world the notion of a 'residual claimant' is a vacuous one. There is no 'residual', as everything is fully specified in state-contingent terms; it makes no sense to identify any claimant as the residual claimant (Milgrom and Roberts 1992: 291).[23] Residual claimancy in the normal sense commonly used in the theory of the firm has meaning only in a world of incomplete state-contingent contracting. But that is precisely the case in which shareholder opportunism becomes a potential issue.

The imperfect commitment problem may be exacerbated by the liquidity of the stock market.[24] Even if the 'incumbent' shareholders are able to commit themselves to not snatch the rents directly (through the exercise of 'voice') (Hirschman 1970), it may be difficult for them to commit themselves to not transfer the rights to a third party if a very liquid market for the exchange of those claims exists ('exit'). In general, the more liquid the market for the transfer of shares, the less credible will be any commitments that the shareholders enter into that rest on non-contractual means of implementation. The reason is that liquidity, or an active market for trading shares, makes it very easy for shareholders to 'escape' from implicit or non-contractible agreements. It might be thought that shareholders could develop a reputation for 'forbearance' (Williamson 1985), and no doubt this occurs to some extent. Note, however, that for the 'small investor' reputation-building is likely to be neither feasible (because of anonymity) nor profitable (because of its negligible effect, being a small holding); for reputation to work, the investor needs to be a *large* holder, whose actions, by definition, are of consequence. But again, we see a break with the traditional view of the well diversified portfolio investor.

Turning the argument around, making financial and their associated control instruments illiquid may enhance their commitment value. Inter-locking shareholdings based on stable shareholding arrangements are share-holdings that, in a sense, have been made more illiquid. Bank loans, particularly when there exists no secondary market for their trading, are another example of an illiquid instrument. A bank loan can be viewed as an instrument that allows the supplier of funds credibly to commit itself to certain actions, e.g. to not withdraw its funds or (in the case of non-variable interest rates) to not alter the cost of funds, even should new information arrive.

Actions that enhance the credibility of shareholder commitments, by decreasing the risk of opportunistic behaviour, are likely to be of value to shareholders. Shareholders will have to pay for their inability to commit, and will likely do so through monetary compensation to managers for the increased risks that they face. The higher the risk of being subject to 'shareholder opportunism', the greater the up-front payment or directly contractible component of income that managers will require. Where the risks of opportunism are highest, one would expect to observe the greatest efforts to economize on the costs of opportunism through the design of appropriate security structures to limit the scope for such behaviour. It is perhaps not suprising, then, that in the Japanese firm a high level of quasi-rents associated with long-term employment contracts is accompanied by the prevalence of relatively illiquid (i.e. commitment-enhancing) financial instruments on both the equity and the debt sides.

There is a problem, however, only if there are quasi-rents. If there are no quasi-rents in the relationship, shareholders have no scope for renegotiating or driving other contractual parties down to their outside reservation levels. The issue of shareholder opportunism, then, is an interesting one only inasmuch as there are significant quasi-rents and contractual incompleteness. Is it reasonable to think that these are serious problems in the real world? And, if so, is there any reason to think their acuteness varies from one country to another, for example that the problems are more acute in Japan than in the United States?

An exhaustive analysis of this issue cannot be attempted here. Suffice it to note that the Japanese firm does appear to be characterized by the existence of significant quasi-rents. Quasi-rents, by definition, go hand in hand with long-term transactional relationships. Long-term transactions create the scope for quasi-rents to come into play, and it is because quasi-rents are generated that a long-term contract differs from a series of short-term ones.[25] The existence of a 'lifetime employment system' in large Japanese firms seems to imply the existence of significant quasi-rents.

Three specific reasons for expecting quasi-rents in the context of the Japanese large-firm employment system can be cited.[26] One relates to high levels of firm-specific human capital investments, widely thought to characterize the core employee sector of large Japanese firms. If part of the human capital investment is financed by employees, the returns on that investment will accrue in latter periods and create a disparity between the employee's wage and the outside reservation level. A second relates to incentive wages. Firms may use a rising wage schedule ('seniority wages') as a way of preventing shirking or of encouraging employees to stay with the firm (i.e. inducing less labour mobility and encouraging employees to have a long-term horizon). A third reason relates to the outside reservation wage. In an economy marked by internal labour markets—initial port of entry mainly at junior levels and the filling of higher positions by internal promotion—employees who separate later in their careers face relatively poor re-employment prospects, at least in firms of equivalent size and status.

What about the level of contractual incompleteness? Although there is no firm evidence, much of the conventional wisdom about the Japanese firms would point in the direction of there being a high level of contractual incompleteness. Again, the issue is too complex to survey adequately here, but several points can be noted. One is that the degree of contractual completeness is related to the length of the contract: there is more scope for contractual incompleteness to arise and be a problem when the contracts are multi-period, as there are more contingencies to specify. A second relates to the team nature of Japanese work organization, which seems to imply more scope for contractual incompleteness at the individual level. A third, which goes beyond the realm of economics, relates to cultural aspects, such as the pervasiveness of informal channels of communication and means of enforcement in Japan and the correspondingly lower level of reliance on explicit contracts and the legal system.

The potential shareholder opportunism problem can be viewed as an issue of commitment. Shareholders do not benefit from being able to snatch quasi-rents, either because, expecting this to happen, other agents require compensation in some way, or, more likely, because certain efficient transactions are forgone. This suggests that shareholders would like to be able to commit themselves to not behaving in this way.

One way would be to increase the level of contractual completeness. There may be limits to this solution, particularly when the contractual completeness derives from informational asymmetries. A second solution is for shareholders to bind themselves in some way, that is, make it more difficult *ex post* to claim the quasi-rents. By making it more difficult to do so, the *ex ante* promise has more credibility. Stable shareholdings in Japan can be interpreted in this light; by making it harder for individual investors to intervene *ex post*, incentives to take the actions that generate quasi-rents in the context of the firm are preserved. What appears detrimental to shareholder interests in a single period may be beneficial to them when viewed in a dynamic setting. (See Sheard 1991*a*: 442–4 for a simple model illustrating this point).

6. STABLE SHAREHOLDERS AND INDIVIDUAL INVESTORS

The focus on quasi-rents suggests a reason why stable shareholding relations centre on transaction partners. Firms that transact with one another on a long-term basis in product markets, like management, are likely to have quasi-rents at stake in their relationship.[27] If, as appears plausible, these quasi-rents cannot be fully protected by contractual safeguards, they are susceptible to appropriation by an opportunistic residual claimant. Consider the two main motivations that exist for a corporate control transaction such as a take-over: to generate value by improving inefficient management, and to capture quasi-rents. A 'good' corporate governance mechanism would be one that encourages the former kind of take-over and discourages the latter kind. Suppose that a substantial amount of equity is in the hands of agents that have long-term relations with the firm and therefore have quasi-rents at stake. What are the incentives of these agents when faced with a take-over bid from an outside agent? If the take-over is of the former variety, they should not oppose it; but on the other hand, it is unlikely that an outside agent will have superior information to that of the firm's own long-term transaction partners, including banks, about how best to manage the firm's assets. Whatever the outside agent proposes to do, the inside shareholders, who presumably have some form of informational advantage, should be able to do, and perhaps do better. If the outside take-over agent has special skills or knowledge not possessed by inside shareholders, these can be tapped by hiring the take-over agent as an input supplier such as an employee–manager or consultant.

Looking at the issue from a different angle, there is a cost associated with arranging corporate governance in such as way that external agents cannot participate—some fruitful ideas or beneficial improvements may go untapped—but in the Japanese case, because of the organization of firms and markets, those costs are likely to be relatively small. On the other hand, the risk associated with allowing free entry of third parties into corporate governance—they may renege on implicit long-term contracts in order to appropriate quasi-rents—may be quite acute in the Japanese system.

Suppose that the take-over is motivated by quasi-rent-seeking. Inside shareholders face a trade-off. On the one hand, they receive a higher share price when they sell the stock; on the other hand, after the take-over they face the prospect of having their own product market contracts renegotiated. Suppose that the only gain that the take-over agent can obtain is the appropriation of quasi-rents. Then, whatever the inside shareholders gain from selling their shares, they lose in the form of appropriated quasi-rents. Rationally, they will not tender their shares.

It might be felt that, while protecting property rights to quasi-rents associated with the firm, the Japanese system of corporate governance leaves individual investors in a vulnerable position. First, it should be borne in mind that individual investors, at an aggregate level, invest in firms directly as shareholders and indirectly via various financial intermediaries, particularly banks and insurance companies, and via various forms of corporate shareholding. Focusing only on their relationship with firms as direct investors is misleading.

A more important point involves the protection that liquidity in the stock market provides to individual shareholders and the indirect disciplining effect that this has on firms and their managers. At the risk of oversimplification, the system of stable interlocking shareholdings results in two kinds of shareholders: inside shareholders, who accept a restriction in (short-term) liquidity, and individual shareholders, who enjoy the normal liquidity services of the market for risk-bearing in the stock market. Inside shareholders occupy the key positions in corporate governance; individuals have no incentive, because of their small holdings, and no means, because of their aggregate minority share, to participate in active corporate governance.

It is crucial to note, however, that individual shareholders cannot be 'exploited' by firms, as some popular critiques would claim. Individuals as individuals, as opposed to in the aggregate, have miniscule holdings, are price-takers in the stock market, and have no restrictions on when, how, or to whom they sell their shares. Although for most firms individuals form a minority of their shareholders, they are none the less competing with one another to maintain those individuals as shareholders. Individuals can be expected to exercise their exit option if they are dissatisfied with a firm's performance. Listing requirements dictate that firms maintain a certain level of individual holdings and holders; desertion of a firm by its individual shareholders will not only precipitate a share price fall but can also trigger delisting from the stock exchange, not to mention prejudicing the firm's future prospects for raising funds from the capital market.

Liquidity allows individuals, if they so desire, to contract to share in the risks associated with the firm's activities. In the case of Japanese, the 'firm' is largely a collection of parties co-operating under implicit long-term contracts—such long-term contracts giving the incentive and means for agents to engage in intertemporal transfers that have associated with them the generation of substantial quasi-rents. The control structure of the Japanese firm is arranged in such a way that it is difficult, if not impossible, for individual shareholders to claim those quasi-rents as residual income, that is, to renege opportunistically on an implicit bargain with management *ex post* (Ramseyer 1987). Individual shareholders, like other shareholders, face their own hold-up problem (Williamson 1985): *ex ante*, they supply part of the capital to fund the deployment of long-term physical assets, but *ex post*, their hands are tied in terms of exercising control. Individual shareholders hold an asset that allows them to specialize in risk-bearing, and the liquidity that establishes that market also establishes the conditions that protect shareholders from being the victims of opportunism from incumbent management.[28]

The above characterization of Japanese corporate governance highlights an important fact: despite the apparent mechanical or institutional differences, the economics of corporate governance in Japan operates under a remarkably similar principle to that commonly ascribed to the open take-over system in economic thinking. In the traditional view of take-overs, departures from maximizing behaviour by managers would lead to a decline in share prices; this decline would lead shareholders to sell their shares, leading to further declines in price, and making it profitable for a take-over agent to purchase the shares cheaply, displace the management, and implement changes in the firm's management. The mere threat that this would occur was thought to be sufficient to discipline managers and minimize agency costs associated with the separation of ownership and control.[29]

In Japan there is a twist on this scenario. Suppose a firm is performing below the expectations of existing individual shareholders, either because of bad management or because of excessive diversion of funds to quasi-rent-holders. Because individuals on average own only about one-quarter of any firm, their selling of shares cannot result in a take-over agent gaining a sufficiently large stake to gain control (say, 50 per cent). However, this will not prevent them from selling their stock, in order to transfer their claims to other firms. When they sell, either other individuals will buy the stock or existing inside shareholders will. In the former case, share prices will have to fall to induce buyers into the market for the firm's shares, and, given that there is no prospect of an outside take-over agent appearing, this share price fall can be expected to be quite precipitate. If so, existing inside shareholders will suffer large capital losses on their considerable holdings and can be expected to start to exert influence on the firm's management—for quite self-interested reasons.[30] In the latter case—which it is sometimes argued does occur—the shareholding level of inside shareholders will rise and something akin to the transfer of shares under the takeover mechanism will occur, except that the take-over agent is an inside shareholder. Inside shareholders can keep up the share price, and protect the value of their own holdings, only by in effect increasing their holdings.

The analysis above brings out the state-contingent nature of the rescinding of corporate control rights implicit in stable shareholding arrangements. Stable shareholders refrain from intervening, or arranging an intervention, when the firm is performing well, but if the firm is performing badly the top shareholders will have the incentive and means to exert influence on the management.[31] Put differently, the 'commitment' to not interfere with the incumbent management is a credible one only in as much as the firm performs reasonably well. Management performing well and stable shareholders delegating control can be sustained as equilibrium behaviour, but management abusing its discretion and stable shareholders remaining 'loyal' is unlikely to be.

Viewed in this light, a critical difference between the Japanese and Anglo-American systems of corporate governance relates to take-over in good states. In an open market for corporate control, take-over targets can be, and often are, firms that are performing well, as well as firms that are performing badly. The Japanese system is crafted so as to prevent take-overs unless the firm is performing badly, and then to have take-over—bank intervention—occur in a predictable way by an informed party (Sheard 1992*d*). The reason is that good states are the states where there is most scope for appropriating quasi-rents, and where it is most profitable for an external party to do so. On the other hand, bad states threaten the viability of the firm as an ongoing organization and are most indicative in a signal extraction sense of changes being required in the management.

An important aspect of what is achieved by the implementation of stable shareholding arrangements may be the reduction in uncertainty about the identity of shareholders in future periods. The fact that a firm will be transacting with another firm in the future in a product market may enhance the credibility of its promise to maintain a shareholding. Contrast two capital market environments differing in the trading behaviour of investors: in one, investors trade frequently so that who owns the firm may change from period to period; in the other, investors rely mainly on buy-and-hold strategies so that ownership, in the sense of the identity of the investors, remains stable from period to period. These two capital market environments can be said to differ along one key dimension. Suppose that managers in both are hired under long-term employment contracts. In both cases, those long-term contracts will face the prospect of renegotiation each period. In the latter case, managers know who it is that they will be dealing with in future periods when their contracts face renegotiation, whereas in the former case this is not so. In a world of complete contracting, the distinction between the two environments is irrelevant. However, in a world of incomplete contracting, the distinction may be important: the identity of the contracting party may matter, for reasons that are not yet fully understood. One conjecture is that, by imposing more structure on the *ex post* renegotiation environment, the set of *ex ante* feasible contracts may be expanded.[32]

7. INTERLOCKING SHAREHOLDINGS AND RISK-SHARING

This section further explores the argument in Sheard (1991*a*) that share interlocks provide a mechanism for a group of firms to pool their income streams and reduce the risk of low outcomes leading to financial failure.[33] Recall Nakatani's (1984) hypothesis of the financial corporate grouping as an implicit insurance mechanism aimed at stabilising corporate performance, further discussed by Aoki (1988, ch.6) and Sheard (1989*a*, 1989*b*, 1991*b*). The role of interlocking shareholdings, however, does not appear to be to stabilize returns *per se*, but rather to provide the firms involved with a form of 'insurance' against financial failure, that is, to avoid very bad states of nature in which the viability of the firm itself is threatened. Intuitively, share interlocks create a pool of financial reserves upon which firms can 'draw' when their profit realization is particularly low.

There are two reasons why investors might want to have firms diversify risks directly. First, information places severe restrictions on risk-sharing possibilities because of adverse selection and moral hazard. Well diversified investors are able to insure contractible risks, but many risks will be uncontractible because arms-length anonymous investors lack the information to do so. The firm itself may be in a better position to insure risks, particularly those faced by contractual parties to the firm such as managers, employees, suppliers, and customers. A second reason relates to commitment: in order credibly to commit themselves to delegating risk-sharing to firms, investors may need to have committed the funds in some form *ex ante*. Share interlocks is a way of doing this.

A necessary, almost definitional, condition for the lifetime employment system to operate is that the firm must remain in operation as a viable entity. To the extent that employees of the large Japanese firm expect to enjoy a long-term association with the firm, they must entertain the notion that the firm will be in a position to offer ongoing employment. On this basis, it would be hypothesized that the firm will organize itself in such a way that its continued existence is more or less guaranteed. The risk-sharing aspect of interlocking shareholdings can be seen in this light as a device that indirectly enhances the capacity of the firm to offer meaningful lifetime employment guarantees to its employees.

The situation can be contrasted with that in an economy in which employees operated under short-term contracts. Then the event of financial distress or even liquidation of any particular firm would be a matter of little consequence to workers. The external labour market, being well developed, in effect provides a form of insurance to owners of human capital. When substantial investments in firm-specific human capital are involved, however, the employee is looking to recoup the investment at that firm, and so is interested in the issue of whether or not the firm will exist in future periods. Institutional mechanisms that allow the firm to insure itself against future failure can be seen as enhancing the firm's capacity to operate a lifetime employment system.

The risk-sharing role of interlocking shareholdings can also be given an interpretation in terms of commitment in the capital market. Suppose that shareholders wished to guarantee the survival of the firm for n periods in order, for instance, to enable the firm to implement long-term employment contracts. Such a guarantee could take the form of an implicit agreement to inject fresh funds into the firm, should the need arise. A problem is that it would be difficult for shareholders to commit themselves in advance to supplying funds in certain contingencies unless it was optimal at that point in time to actually supply the funds. But if it were optimal to do so, there would be no need to enter into an implicit contract in the first place!

To enter into a credible commitment to meet certain contingencies that may arise in the future, the shareholders may have to supply the requisite funds, or some form of property rights to the funds, in advance. Now recall the interlocking shareholding arrangement. One way to interpret it is precisely in these terms, as a device that places claims on firms' income flows in the hands of the firms themselves. In times of financial crisis, firms have claims on income flows of other firms that they can draw down, without having to turn to the shareholders. The argument here recognizes the fact that, in a world of agency relationships, and where contracts are neither complete nor costlessly enforceable, a dollar that is in the hands of incumbent management is not the same dollar to the firm as a one that is 'promised' to the firm but is in the hands of shareholders. Delegating risk-sharing to the firm via the share interlocks may be the way that shareholders make commitments to engage in intertemporal risk-bearing more credible.

The practice of stable shareholdings may play a role in solving a commitment problem on the firm side. In the analysis above, shareholders want to make funds available to firms in certain contingencies, namely to avoid financial distress. In principle, however, once interlocks were entered into, the firm could sell the shares and generate 'free cash flow' (Jensen 1986) at any time. The practice of stable shareholding, however, means than in normal times firms do not trade their shares. Stable shareholding can be viewed in that light as being a device that firms use to commit themselves to refraining from morally hazardous behaviour with respect to the use of funds 'earmarked' for corporate crises.[34] That is, there may be a complementarity between the corporate governance and the risk diversification roles of interlocking shareholding that attaches to stable shareholding practices.

In fact, share disposals in times of financial distress are a typical feature of Japanese corporate behaviour. Table 2 provides data from a sample of 350–80 large Japanese firms on profits registered from the sale of securities since 1974. During the 1974–90 period, profits realized on the sale of securities was equivalent to 21 per cent of total net (after-tax) profits of the firms.[35] The level of sales rose during economic downturns, particularly 1975–6 and 1986–7; in 1975 and 1986 profits from securities sales more than doubled over the previous year's level, and profits from sales of securities were 70 per cent or more of after-tax profits.

Aggregate figures do not provide information on the kinds of firms engaged in share disposals or the circumstances under which this takes place. However, scrutiny of the financial press and of the securities reports of individual firms confirms that the disposal of shares has been a common response of large firms facing financial distress.[36] There were numerous such reports in the 1970s involving loss-making firms, particularly steel-makers, textile firms, general trading companies, and other firms associated with structurally depressed industries.[37] For example, between 1978 and 1982, the six largest general trading companies registered ¥250 billion in special profits from the sale of shares, offsetting part of the ¥400.3 billion in losses incurred on account of affiliated operations in the same period.[38]

An important aspect of these share disposals is that they appear generally to take place in the context of stable shareholding arrangements. Rarely are shares sold in arms-length market transactions on the stock market; rather, consultations and negotiations usually take place between the firm

TABLE 2   Accounting Profits from the Disposal of Assets and Securities for a Sample of Listed Japanese Manufacturing Firms, 1974–1990 (¥ million)[a]

| | Special profit registered from disposal of: | | Sub-total | Net profits after tax | (3)/(4) (%) | (2)/(4) (%) |
	Fixed assets[b] (1)	Securities (2)	(3)	(4)	(5)	(6)
1974	132,043	138,044	270,087	813,641	33.2	17.0
1975	332,162	377,545	709,707	537,386	132.1	70.3
1976	240,142	201,580	441,722	880,279	50.2	22.9
1977	254,857	316,548	571,405	933,469	61.2	33.9
1978	249,557	179,889	429,446	1,136,307	37.8	15.8
1979	233,438	143,975	377,413	1,719,214	22.0	8.4
1980	178,768	146,490	325,258	1,893,682	17.2	7.7
1981	294,578	215,492	510,070	1,508,320	33.8	14.3
1982	361,819	256,794	618,613	1,795,662	34.5	14.3
1983	309,240	373,644	682,884	1,956,356	34.9	19.1
1984	248,685	260,255	508,940	2,396,359	21.2	10.9
1985	303,282	523,245	826,527	2,373,048	34.8	22.0
1986	483,827	1,194,876	1,678,703	1,642,671	102.2	72.7
1987	380,185	995,296	1,375,481	2,228,453	61.7	44.7
1988	265,040	553,369	818,409	3,116,173	26.3	17.8
1989	289,678	540,158	829,836	3,805,172	21.8	14.2
1990	323,415	438,144	761,559	3,952,996	19.3	11.1

[a]Until 1982, about 350; from 1983, about 380 firms.
[b]Mainly land.

Source: Nihon Ginko (various years); Shuyo kigyo keiei bunseki (Managerial Analysis of Major Firms), Nihon Ginko, Tokyo.

selling the shares, the firm whose shares are being sold, and the buyer-firms. Shares are placed with other firms in direct transactions outside the stock exhange (*shijogai torihiki*) or in 'cross-transactions' (*kurosu torihiki*), a form of transaction within the stock exchange where the terms of the transaction are settled in advance with the buyer firm and a single securities firm executes the transaction.[39]

8 INTERLOCKING SHAREHOLDINGS AND THE MAIN BANK SYSTEM

In Sheard (1991*a*), it was argued that the system of interlocking share-holdings both creates the need for, and facilitates the operation of, a capital market monitoring and control mechanism such as the main bank system. The main bank system fulfils a monitoring and control (intervention) role that closely parallels the more market-oriented mechanisms associated with Anglo-American capital markets. To the extent that the main bank system operates successfully, potential problems associated with stable shareholding arrangements, such as managerial moral hazard and free-rider problems in the provision of capital market monitoring services, are minimized. On the other hand, stable shareholdings may be important in giving the main bank the confidence that: (1) it will be able to enforce implicit contracts with the firm when the time comes (e.g. taking over the running of a firm in financial crisis and reorganizing the management); (2) it will not suffer at the expense of opportunistic behaviour by the firm's shareholders; and (3) it will be able to obtain a commensurate share of quasi-rents that are generated by its own inputs as main bank. This section provides further analysis of the prominent role of main banks in interlocking stable shareholding arrangements.

Not only are financial institutions major corporate shareholders in Japan, they are also among the most tightly cross-held firms, particularly by non-financial firms (Table 3). Whereas, for listed firms as a whole, the level of corporate stockholding is about 72 per cent, in the case of the major financial institutions (the three long-term credit banks, the eleven city banks, and the seven trust banks), the level of corporate holding is on average 92 per cent. 58 per cent of the stock of the major banks is held by non-financial domestic corporations, more than twice the figure of 25 per cent for all listed firms, and only 6 per cent is held by individuals.

As is the case with other firms, corporate shareholders dominate the top shareholder positions of the Japanese banks (Table 4): of the 400 top 20 (or 10) shareholder positions identifiable for the 21 major banks (3 long-term credit banks, 11 city banks, 7 trust banks), almost all (396) are

TABLE 3 Proportional Share Ownership of Principal Japanese Financial
Institutions, 1991

Bank	Type of shareholder			
	Financial institutions[a]	Other corporations	Subtotal	Individual (domestic)
Industrial Bank of Japan	40.1	56.1	96.2	2.2
LTCB of Japan	44.7	51.7	96.4	2.7
Nippon Credit	65.9	30.4	96.3	3.2
Daiichi Kangyo	34.7	55.7	90.3	7.5
Hokkaido Takushoku	40.7	46.0	86.7	12.1
Bank of Tokyo	55.7	37.3	93.0	5.7
Sakura[b]	35.9	54.1	89.9	8.2
Mitsubishi	36.2	55.8	92.0	6.7
Fuji	28.8	63.7	92.5	6.0
Sumitomo	28.3	62.4	90.7	6.2
Daiwa	28.4	62.0	90.4	8.0
Sanwa	32.8	58.9	91.6	6.2
Tokai	28.9	61.0	89.8	8.7
Kyowa-Saitama	35.5	54.0	89.5	7.4
Mitsui Trust	23.1	70.0	93.1	5.5
Mitsubishi Trust	22.5	70.4	92.9	4.2
Sumitomo Trust	17.7	74.8	92.5	4.1
Yasuda Trust	26.8	68.9	95.7	3.0
Nippon Trust	31.6	57.6	89.2	10.2
Toyo Trust	33.3	58.1	91.5	7.7
Chuo Trust	29.5	65.7	95.2	3.9
Average	34.3	57.8	92.2	6.2
Average for all listed firms	46.9	25.2	72.1	23.1

[a]Including securities companies.
[b]Formerly Mitsui Taiyo-Kobe.

Source: Compiled from *Kaisha Nenkan* (company annual), (1991), Nihon Keizai
Shinbunsha, Tokyo; Tokyo Shoken Torihikijo Chosabu (1992).

domestic corporations. On average, 10 of the top 20 shareholders are non-
financial domestic firms, 6 are insurance companies, and 4 are banks or
other financial institutions. The top 20 shareholders collectively account for
an average of 35 per cent of the bank's stock (Toyo Keizai Shinposha
1991).

The role of the main bank in stable shareholding can be explored further
by examining the relationship that the bank has to its main shareholders.
This is done in Table 5 for the case of Daiichi Kangyo Bank (DKB).[40]
Table 5 lists the top twenty shareholders of DKB and also shows whether
DKB owns shares in its corporate shareholders, and its position as a supplier

TABLE 4 Top Twenty Shareholders of Principal Japanese Financial Institutions by Type of Shareholder, 1992

Name of financial institution	Insurance companies	Banks and other financial institutions	Non-financial corporations	Other
Industrial Bank of Japan	6	5	9	
Long-Term Credit Bank of Japan	5	8	7	
Nippon Credit	7	12	1	
Daiichi Kangyo	7	2	11	
Hokkaido Takushoku	7	6	7	
Bank of Tokyo	6	9	5	
Sakura[a]	8	4	7	1[b]
Mitsubishi[c]	5	1	4	
Fuji	5	3	12	
Sumitomo	5	1	14	
Daiwa	4	6	9	1[b]
Sanwa	6	3	11	
Tokai	7	2	10	1[b]
Kyowa-Saitama	8	3	9	
Mitsui Trust	2	2	16	
Mitsubishi Trust[c]	2	2	6	
Sumitomo Trust	2	1	17	
Yasuda Trust	4	3	13	
Nippon Trust	5	4	11	
Toyo Trust	8	4	8	
Chuo Trust	4	5	10	1
Average number[d]	5.6	4.4	9.8	0.2

[a]Formerly Mitsui Taiyo-Kobe.
[b]Employee ownership fund.
[c]Top 10 shareholders only.
[d]Excluding Mitsubishi and Mitsubishi Trust.
Source: Compiled from Toyo Keizai Shinposha (1991: 591–4, 609–11).

of bank loans. All of DKB's top twenty shareholders are corporations, and collectively they hold almost one-third of its shares. Setting aside the insurance companies, which are mutual companies and so do not have shareholders, in every case DKB is a prominent shareholder.[41] That is, in every feasible case, there is a reciprocal shareholding between DKB and its top shareholders. Regarding borrowings, DKB has the largest loan share in almost all of the relevant cases. In other words, the bank is owned in large part by firms to which it acts as main bank. Also shown are the shareholding ranks in 1981, indicating a high level of temporal stability in interlocking shareholdings over the ten-year period.[42]

TABLE 5   Analysis of Corporate Interlocking among Daiichi Kangyo Bank (DKB) and its Top Twenty Shareholders, 1991

DKB's top 20 shareholders[a]	Shareholding (%) (Rank in 1981)	DKB's shareholding in firm (%) (Rank) [Rank in 1981]	DKB's share in firm's borrowings (%) (Rank)
1. Asahi Life	4.46 (1)	—	—
2. Nissay (Life)	3.77 (2)	—	—
3. Daiichi Life	2.90 (3)	—	—
4. Long-Term Credit Bank	2.82 (4)	3.66 (1) [1]	—
5. Meiji Life	1.84 (5)	—	—
6. Nippon Credit Bank	1.37 (7)	3.49 (1) [1]	—
7. Fukoku Life	1.36 (9)	—	—
8. Kawasaki Steel	1.22 (6)	4.32 (1) [1]	13.51 (1)
9. Nisshinbo	1.20 (8)	4.99 (2[b]) [2]	36.75 (1[b])
10. Nippon Tsuun	1.03 (12)	4.67 (2) [2]	16.94 (1)
11. Mitsubishi Corporation	1.02 (15)	3.50 (6) [7]	5.18 (3)
12. Shimizu Construction	0.98 (14)	4.97 (2) [1]	19.44 (1)
13. Ishikawajima Harima	0.92 (10)	3.54 (3) [3]	12.89 (1)
14. Nissan Marine	0.92 (18)	5.00 (7[b]) [3]	—
15. Tokio Marine	0.89 (19)	1.93 (5) [7]	—
16. Hitachi	0.83 (—[c])	1.98 (10) [9]	13.84 (1)
17. Asahi Glass	0.82 (—[c])	3.62 (7) [7]	0.00 (–)
18. Asahi Chemical	0.81 (—[c])	3.45 (6) [3]	10.35 (1[b])
19. Kobe Steel	0.78 (17)	3.68 (3) [2]	12.76 (1)
20. C. Itoh	0.77 (20)	3.74 (1) [1]	7.95 (1)
Total/average	30.71	3.77 (3.8) [3.3]	13.60 (1.2[d])

[a]'Life' in a company name denotes a mutual life insurance company; 'Marine', a property insurance company.
[b]Equal rank with another firm.
[c]Not in top 20.
[d]Excluding Asahi Glass case.

Source: Compiled from Toyo Keizai Shinposha (1981, 1991).

In the case of main bank interventions in distressed firms, the bank plays a key role in assisting with the firm's reorganization, an important element of which is typically a program of negotiated share disposals. As is evident from Tables 1 and 5, the shareholding in the main bank is usually one of the firm's key shareholding assets, and it is not uncommon for the bank to be in the position of arranging for, or assisting with, the disposal and placement with other stable shareholders of its own shares.[43] This pivotal role of the main bank in the process of share disposals during financial reorganization may be quite important in the policing and enforcement of the implicit contracts governing the stable shareholding arrangements.

The reciprocal nature of financial relations between the banks and their corporate shareholders raises a number of interesting issues. It points to the main bank performing a monitoring and control (intervention) role as a kind of delegated 'insider', rather than as the kind of arms-length institutional investor envisaged in US policy discussions of active investors (Black 1992). Put starkly, the banks are 'owned' essentially by the firms that they either lend to (non-financial firms) or lend in concert with (other financial institutions). Banks are not just delegated monitors of depositors or outside investors à la Diamond (1984) but, in principle, are collectively owned and controlled by the main corporate participants in the capital market.

In practice, it appears that non-financial corporations, although in most cases they collectively own more than half of the bank's stock, do not exercise joint control over the banks. They behave as stable shareholders waiving the exercise of control rights. One indicator of this is that, whereas the banks dispatch directors to corporate borrowers, there is almost no flow in the reverse direction.[44] Instead, the function of 'monitoring the monitor' appears to be carried out by the banking authorities (Ministry of Finance and Bank of Japan) as part of their charter to maintain stability in the banking and financial systems.

Table 6 presents evidence on the relationship between main banks and stable shareholdings from a different perspective, namely that of director dispatches. An important aspect of corporate governance in Japan is that major banks frequently arrange for senior executives in late career to enter client firms as senior managerial directors.[45] Table 6 analyses the 247 cases of major financial institutions arranging for executives to enter listed firms in director positions in 1991. In particular, it asks what shareholding and lending relationship the financial institution had with the firm. The results show a close relationship between director dispatches and main bank (lending/shareholding) relationships. The flow of directors from banks to firms occurs primarily between banks and firms with close financial relations. The average shareholding of the banks in the firms to which directors were supplied was 4.6 per cent, and the bank on average was the number 3 or 4 top shareholder. In one-fifth of cases, the firms had few or no borrowings, but in the other cases the bank had an average loan share of 21 per cent and an average lending rank of 2, suggesting that in many if not most cases it was the top lender.

The corporate governance role of the main bank—monitoring and *ex post* intervention—has attracted much attention. Many authors stress the importance of the main bank's equity holding in allowing it to play the active role that it does (e.g. Prowse 1990: 48). This section has presented some evidence on the banks' own equity structure, pointing out that banks are interlocked with borrowing firms and other financial institutions. The implications of this aspect of cross-shareholding for understanding the banks' role in corporate governance are not entirely clear, but deserve further analysis.

TABLE 6 Relationship between Supply of Corporate Directors by Japanese Financial Institutions and Other Financial Ties, 1991

Name of financial institution	Number of directors supplied (No. of firms)	Average shareholding in firm	Average shareholding rank (Average rank among banks[a])	Average loan share[b] (Average loan rank)
Industrial Bank of Japan	25 (22)	4.2	3.0 (1.2)	23.8 (1.7)
Long-Term Credit Bank of Japan	7 (7)	3.9	4.2 (1.1)	25.3 (1.8)
Daiichi Kangyo	32 (26)	5.3	4.4 (1.2)	19.9 (1.9)
Bank of Tokyo	6 (6)	4.8	3.3 (1.7)	21.2 (7.0)
Sakura[c]	27 (26)	4.0	3.6 (1.2)	23.3 (1.3)
Mitsubishi	20 (19)	4.5	4.3 (1.5)	19.0 (1.4)
Fuji	18 (17)	4.5	3.5 (1.3)	17.7 (1.7)
Sumitomo	23 (20)	4.1	2.3 (1.2)	28.7 (1.7)
Daiwa	9 (9)	4.5	1.5 (1.0)	29.1 (1.3)
Sanwa	21 (20)	4.2	3.8 (1.1)	21.7 (1.4)
Tokai	18 (13)	4.5	2.8 (1.2)	36.2 (1.3)
Kyowa-Saitama	8 (7)	4.0	4.0 (1.2)	21.6 (2.3)
Mitsui Trust	7 (7)	4.9	3.6	16.2 (2.6)
Mitsubishi Trust	5 (5)	4.7	4.2	16.6 (2.2)
Sumitomo Trust	7 (7)	4.2	5.6	14.5 (2.2)
Yasuda Trust	6 (6)	3.8	3.8	8.9 (3.3)
Asahi Life	7 (7)	8.3	1.7	3.6 (8.0)
Daiichi Life	14 (14)	5.0	4.7	6.6 (1.2)
Nissay (Life)	9 (9)	6.8	1.9	5.9 (5.1)
Total (weighted) average	14 (13)	4.6	3.5 (1.2)	21.4 (2.0)

[a]City and long-term credit banks.
[b]Excluding (49 out of 247) cases where there were few or no borrowings, or information not available.
[c]Formerly Mitsui Taiyo-Kobe.

Source: Compiled from Toyo Keizai Shinposha (1991).

9. CONCLUSION

This essay has considered two key aspects of the interlocking shareholdings that characterize contemporary Japanese corporate organisation: their role in providing firms with a form of insurance against the risk of financial distress, and their role in insulating incumbent managements from exposure to an unfettered take-over market. Following Aoki (1989), the importance of understanding the relationship between the financial contracts of the firm and the employment contracts of the firm was stressed. Much recent literature on the Japanese firm has focused on the employment and management systems and has examined the implications of long-term firm–employee associations for firm-specific investments, for work incentives, for attitudes to structural change and innovation, and for the planning horizon of managers. A conclusion of this chapter is that the capacity of the firm to implement long-term employment contracts in the first place may have much to do with the financial organization of the firm.

Stable shareholdings influence the way that corporate governance operates in Japan, but it is necessary to analyse and assess the impact of shareholdings in the context of the other key aspect of corporate governance—the main bank system—and in the context of an understanding of the managerial employment system operating in Japanese firms. This paper has explored the idea that stable shareholdings provide insulation for incumbent managers against external take-over, and that this may be necessary in order for the firm to be able to operate the kind of 'lifetime' employment system that it does. The key insight is that having a class of security holder with residual claimancy and residual control rights is not consistent with quasi-rents existing in the firm unless those quasi-rents are protected by complete contracts. The problem is that shareholders then face a time-consistency problem with respect to their promise not to snatch those quasi-rents as 'residual income'—which they have a 'right' to do, by virtue of their residual claimancy status, and the 'means' to do, by virtue of their residual control status. Stable shareholding arrangements make it more difficult *ex post* for shareholders to exercise residual control and can be viewed as, in effect, making credible their *ex ante* promise not to claim the quasi-rents opportunistically. The contracting away *ex ante* of certain property rights implicit in stable shareholding arrangements in this view becomes a way of more clearly protecting the property rights to quasi-rents, and thus of providing the necessary incentives for them to be generated in the first place.

NOTES TO CHAPTER 12

1. The exception to the first part of this sentence is life insurance companies, most of which do not issue shares.
2. This paper is in the spirit of recent analyses that emphasize the interrelatedness of different aspects of the Japanese firm's organization, particularly its capital and employment market attributes. See also Aoki (1989) and Ch. 1 above; Sheard (1992*a*), Williamson (1991). For recent theoretical analyses of the link between corporate governance and the employment system, see Aoki (1992) and Garvey and Swan (1992).

3. See e.g. Johnson (1990*a*: 119), Matsumoto (1991: 10–11), Nakatani (1992), Okumura (1990: 85–6).

4. The idea that individuals can make themselves better off by constraining the scope of their future actions is a familiar one from contract theory in economics. 'Efficiency-enhancing' is a weak criterion: it refers to the feasible choices of the transacting or contracting parties (e.g. investors and managers); it does not mean that the resulting arrangement is Pareto-efficient for the parties (they may be trapped in a low-level equilibrium, but better off than if they had not contracted), or from the viewpoint of third parties (society).

5. Under the Japanese Commercial Code (sec. 257, pt. 2), a director can be dismissed by a special motion at the shareholders' meeting; this requires a two-thirds majority at a shareholders' meeting, at which at least half of the shares are represented.

6. Matsumoto (1991: 2) reports that about 9% of firms listed on the first section of the Tokyo Stock Exchange in 1988 had an individual among the top ten shareholders, but in no cases did the shareholding exceed 40% and in 60% of cases it was less than 10%.

7. Life insurance companies are omitted as these do not issue shares. There are four life insurance companies among Mazda's top twenty shareholders, five among Mitsubishi Corporation's, five among Nihon Housing, none among Nintendo's, and four among Tobishima Loan Corporation.

8. Calculated at the exchange rate of ¥133.85 = US$1.00, current at the time.

9. Although hostile take-overs of listed firms are rare, many firms have become targets of share-cornering by 'hostile' speculator groups, often having underworld connections. See e.g. Kester (1991: ch. 10), Sheard (1986*b*).

10. That stable shareholding arrangements may be based on explicit agreements can be inferred from the following comment by Ishida Taizo, former chairman of Toyota Motor, a company renowned for its 'stable' share register: 'Even financial institutions are not stable shareholders in the strictest sense. So we have an arrangement whereby if for some reason they sell their shareholding they will let us know beforehand. In such a case we want the Toyota group to take over [the shares]. In the last resort, it is only the Toyota group [firms] that you can depend on and for that reason we leave them so that they are always able to hold [our] shares' (Shukan toyo keizai 1967: 107; author's translation).

When General Motors purchased 34.2% of Isuzu's shares in 1971, the Ministry of International Trade and Industry required more than 400 of Isuzu's shareholders to undertake not to dispose of Isuzu's shares, thereby freezing 39% of Isuzu's stock in Japanese corporate hands. Part of the measure entailed the transfer by financial institutions, general trading companies, and other Japanese corporate shareholders of their shares (amounting to 26% of Isuzu's shares) and voting rights to a consortium of the seven trust banks and Daiwa Bank. The explicit agreement was terminated in 1978. See 'Isuzu kabushiki toketsu o kaijo e: GM shusshiritsuage mo kano ni' (Towards the Release of Isuzu's Frozen Shareholdings: Possible for GM to Lift its Holding), *Nikkei*, 23 February 1978, p. 8; Sumitomo Shintaku Ginko gojunenshi henshu iinkai, 1976, p. 1232. When shares are acquired in third-party issues (1% of funds raised in 1989, 10% in 1990), a securities industries agreement requires firms not to sell their stock for a period of two years.

11. As with any model, this is not necessarily a literal description of the historical process, but rather an abstraction aimed at distilling the essential insight. In fact, according to a version of the Coase theorem, it does not matter who controls the firm initially, as all parties who contract to interact in the context of the firm have incentives to organize it in such a way as to maximize expected value (Milgrom and Roberts 1992: ch. 2).

12. Another fallacy is that individuals are disadvantaged by the low rate of dividends that Japanese firms pay. Undistributed income accrues to shareholders as capital gains, and until 1989 these were, in principle, not taxed for individuals. Stock market returns, taking account of capital gains, have been favourable for Japanese investors in the post-war period. See Aoki (1988: 113–16), Hamao (1991).

13. Japanese businessmen frequently make references to the retaliation scenario. For instance, in a recent interview with the Nihon Keizai Shinbun, the president of Kawasaki Steel was quoted as making the following comment regarding the possible disposal of its shareholdings in other firms: 'Up until now the business practice of mutual holding has existed and they [the shares] have not been the kind of thing we could sell in a unilateral fashion. If we sell, the other party will sell Kawasaki's shares and our stable shareholding ratio will fall.' See 'Kabu baikyaku nado fukumi katsuyo mo' (Utilization of Latent Profits through Share Sales), *Nikkei* (American edn.), 19 February 1991, p. 17. See McKenzie (1993) for an analysis of stable shareholdings by mutual life insurance companies where reciprocity cannot take the form of shareholdings.

14. Most listed firms have employee stock ownership plans (92.4% in 1989), typically owning about 1% of the firm's stock and considered the most solid stable shareholder (Tokyo Shoken Torihikijo Chosabu 1991: 262–3).

15. The argument may, of course, run in the reverse direction: the trust that the firm is able to build up as a stable shareholder—which presumably increases with time—may be used to facilitate long-term transactions. In reality, the spillover of trust probably runs in both directions. At the very least, empirical evidence suggests a connection, as firms that enter into long-term trading relations frequently engage in a stable shareholding tie-up.

16. This section draws heavily on information obtained in interviews at a large Japanese securities company and its associated research institute during 1992.

17. As an indication of the extensiveness of this practice, known as *hogo azukari* ('custodianship'), in 1990, 15.1% of all listed shares in Japan were held in trust with the four leading securities companies; a further 11.4% was held with the other 206 securities companies (Okurasho Shokenkyoku 1992: 241, 261).

18. On share disposals in financial distress, see Aoki (1987: 281), Sheard (1986b, 1991b).

19. The main bank also frequently plays a similar role, especially when it is closely involved in the firm's reorganization. See Sheard (1986b; 1991a: 436–8; 1991b) for examples.

20. The share of the four leading securities companies in 1990 in total share transactions was 40.1% and their share of underwriting business was 73.7% (Okurasho Shokenkyoku, 1992: 258, 260). The four companies dominate the lead underwriting positions: Suto (1987: 125) reports that in 1984 the four accounted for 73% of lead underwriting positions of the largest 948 listed firms,

and close to 100% of the (175) cases where the firm engaged a sole lead underwriter.

21. The mechanism described seems to be another example of long-run 'ratings' or the ranking form of competition employed by the Japanese firm, other examples being the labour market (Aoki 1990), bank lending, parts supply systems (Asanuma 1989), and intermediate product market relations, e.g. newsprint supply (Itoh 1992). As pointed out by Itoh (1992), although set in the context of ongoing transactional relations, such long-run 'face-to-face' competition can be quite intense. This may give a clue to understanding the perception gap that seems to exist between outside and inside observers of the Japanese system. Outside observers see the prevalance of long-term relations, and, equating competition with spot-market-like relations, suspect a lack of competition. Inside observers counter that Japanese markets are intensely competitive.

22. But see Shleifer and Summers (1988), and in the Japanese case Ramseyer (1987) and Kester (1991). Mayer (1988) and Bizer and DeMarzo (1992) also focus on the time inconsistency issue.

23. An example can illustrate the point. Consider three states of nature, having payoffs of 10, 15, and 20 respectively. Suppose that the state-contingent contract specifies that agent A receives 10 in each state and agent B receives the 'residual', 0, 5, and 10 respectively. It is conventional to call A a 'fixed claimant' and B the 'residual claimant'. But equivalently, we could just as easily say that B receives 0 in state 1, 5 in state 2, and 10 in state 3, and that A receives the residual, which happens to be 10 in each state. In a complete contracting framework, the only difference between A and B is the distribution of risk that they contract for. There is no residual uncertainty.

24. See Coffee (1991) for further analysis along these lines.

25. The logic is as follows. Imagine a multi-period relationship involving no quasi-rents (realized or expected). Then in each period, in each state of nature, the agents are paid exactly their outside reservation values. But this is equivalent to a series of period-by-period 'spot market' trades, or short-term contracts.

26. The literature on the Japanese employment system is vast. For a survey from the viewpoint of economic theory, see Itoh's Ch. 9 above.

27. See Flath (1992*b*) and Gilson and Roe (1993) for alternative views of the relationship between shareholdings and transactional ties.

28. The point can be made this way. Individual shareholders, like other contractual parties to the firm, have quasi-rents at stake; but, unlike those other parties, they have a means of capitalizing those quasi-rents and taking them out of the firm at short notice. In effect, the market for the asset provides a form of protection that long-term employees and transaction parties do not have.

29. See Manne (1965) and Jensen and Ruback (1983) for important contributions to this line of thinking. Economists are now less sanguine about the efficacy of take-overs, partly because of free-rider problems and strategic behaviour; see Holmström and Tirole (1989), Spatt (1989), and Stiglitz (1985).

30. Empirical studies by Kaplan (1992) and Morck and Nakamura (1992) tend to confirm that poorly performing firms in Japan are subject to capital market (bank) interventions.

31. As noted by Aoki (1990), a useful theoretical analogy is provided by Aghion and Bolton's (1992) analysis.

32. Investors who are known to the management and new investors differ potentially in two aspects, relating to reputation and information. Because management and investors have a history of interaction, investors may have developed some kind of reputation, e.g. for not behaving opportunitically in the past, and this reputation may have value, hence may influence investor behaviour at the time of renegotiation. In a world of asymmetric information, investors will also have different information; in particular, the set of information shared by management and investors may differ between the two environments, with implications for equilibrium behaviour.

33. On the financial and valuation effects of interlocking shareholdings, see also Brioschi and Buzzachi (1989), Ellerman (1991), Fedenia *et al.* (1991), Flath (1992*a*), French and Porterba (1991), Hoshi and Ito (1991), McDonald (1989), and Ueda (1990).

34. It should be noted that shares are frequently used as collateral against loans, partly undoing the commitment effect. On the other hand, funds extended as bank loans are subject to a form of capital market scrutiny and checks that internal free cash flow is not.

35. If firms were actively trading in shares, there would be a considerable degree of double-counting in these figures. As a rule, however, firms sell the shares they hold in other firms only when they face financial difficulties as a so-called 'settlement of accounts measure' (*kessan taisaku*). The figures quoted can be thought reasonably to reflect 'one-off' transactions.

36. A number of Japanese researchers have focused on the use of share disposals to cushion the impact of business losses; see particularly Irie (1979), Kobayashi (1983; 229), Matsui (1977, 1979), and Okumura (1978; 85–8; 1979). See also the discussion by Aoki (1987; 281; 1988; 113, 233) and the case-study evidence presented in Sheard (1986*b*).

37. See e.g.: 'Jigyo kaisha toginkabu o tairyo baikyaku tekko sen'i nado gensho medatsu' (Large-Scale Disposal of City-Bank Shares by Operating Companies: Reduction [in Holdings] by Steel and Textiles [Firms] Conspicuous), *Nikkei*, 15 December 1977, p. 13; Kon shimoki mo yarikuri kuroji koro ote gosha: Shin Nittetsu kabushiki baikyaku 340 oku Sumikin 80 oku Kokan wa 60 oku' (The Big Five Integrated Steel Makers Scrape into the Black in this Second Half: Nippon Steel's Profit on Share Disposals 34 Billion [Yen], Sumitomo Metal's 8 Billion, Nippon Kokan's 6 Billion), *Nikkei*, 19 January 1978, p. 13; 'Kawatetsu keijo akaji chijimaru: kabushiki baikyaku wa issen man kabu kyo' (Operating Loss of Kawasaki Steel Shrinks: Sells More than Ten Million Shares), *Nikkei*, 11 March 1976, p. 13; 'Gosen ote nanasha shimoki mo yarikuri tsuzuku: kabushiki uri akaji shukushu Teijin Kurarei' (Barrel-Scraping of Big Seven Synthetic Fibre Makers Continues in Second Half; Teijin and Kuraray Sell Shareholdings and Reduce Losses), *Nikkei*, 16 February 1978, p. 13.

38. Compiled from the published accounts of the companies (*Yuka shoken hokokusho*). See Sheard (1986*b*: 40–1) for details.

39. There are no published data on direct transactions outside the stock exchange, but press reports and sample surveys suggest that the volume is high, and that this has been the main route via which firms dispose of shares to offset losses. For instance, a survey by a large securities company (of 43 firms known to have disposed of shares on a large scale) revealed that, of about 2 billion shares sold

by these firms in the 12 months to March 1978, only 330–440 million were sold through the stock exchange, including cross-transactions; the remainder were sold in direct transactions outside the stock exchange. One steel maker disposed of 70 million bank shares, with 95% being sold outside the market. See: 'Kabu no jogai oguchi torihiki: Tosho kisei e ugoku' (Large-Scale Share Transactions Outside the Market: Tokyo Stock Exchange Moves to Regulate), *Asahi shinbun*, 25 January 1978, p. 8. A 1978 survey of 22 leading firms by the Tokyo Stock Exchange and the Ministry of Finance revealed substantial dealings outside the market and reported that a principal reason that manufacturers gave for engaging in direct transactions was the necessity to find a buyer acceptable to the firm whose shares were being sold, since a change in shareholding structure was involved; banks and insurance companies stated that they were taking over the shares at the request of the firms concerned. See 'Tosho nado shijogai torihiki no jittai chosa' (Investigations of the State of Transactions Outside the Market at the Tokyo and Other Stock Exchanges), *Nikkei*, 9 September 1978, p. 11.

40. A similar analysis, providing quite similar results, is carried out for the case of Sumitomo Bank (top 30 shareholders) in Sheard (1992*c*: 68–9).

41. See McKenzie (1992) for an analysis of the stable shareholding motivations of insurance companies.

42. See Tachibanaki and Taki (1991) for a quantitative study of the intertemporal stability of financial institutions' lending and shareholding.

43. As just one example, in 1977 Tokyo Bank and Daiichi Kangyo implemented a rescue package as the main banks towards the troubled general trading company Kanematsu-Gosho which included the dispatch of a Tokyo Bank vice-president as chairman of the company, the provision of interest rate reductions on ¥15 billion of loans, and the shelving of interest payments for three to five years on ¥20 billion of real-estate-related loans (*Nikkei*, 28 April 1977, p. 1); it was also reported at the time that Kanematsu-Gosho disposed of 10 million shares in Tokyo Bank and 3.3 million shares in Daiichi Kangyo under the direction of the banks; see 'Ote shosha ginko kabu o tairyo kaikyaku' (Large-Scale Disposal of Banks' Shares by Big Trading Companies), *Nikkei*, 22 November 1977, p. 13. For further details of the Kanematsu-Gosho case, see Sheard (1985; 1986*a*: 43–4).

44. Of the 831 directors of the 21 major financial institutions listed in Table 3, only 4 are former or current executives of non-financial corporations; 11 are former Ministry of Finance officials, 8 are former Bank of Japan officials, and 13 are former or current executives of financial institutions. Overall, 96% of the directors are internally promoted bank managerial employees (compiled from Toyo Keizai Shinposha 1991: 591–4, 609–11).

45. In 1990, 5.3% of total directorship positions of listed Japanese firms were occupied by former (and, in a fraction of cases, concurrent) bank executives (Toyo Keizai Shinposha 1991: 90).

REFERENCES

Abegglen, J. C., and Stalk, G. Jr (1985), *Kaisha: the Japanese Corporation*, Basic Books, New York.

Aghion, P., and Bolton, P. (1992), 'An Incomplete Contracts Approach to Financial Contracting', *Review of Economic Studies*, 59: 473–94.

Aoki, M. (1987), 'The Japanese Firm in Transition', in K. Yamamura and Y. Yasuba (eds.), *The Political Economy of Japan*, Vol. 1, *The Domestic Transformation*, Stanford University Press, 262–88.

——(1988), *Information, Incentives, and Bargaining in the Japanese Economy*, Cambridge University Press.

——(1989), 'The Nature of the Japanese Firm as a Nexus of Employment and Financial Contracts: An Overview', *Journal of the Japanese and International Economies*, 3: 345–66.

——(1990), 'Towards an Economic Model of the Japanese Firm', *Journal of Economic Literature*, 28: 1–27.

——(1992), 'Ex Post Monitoring of Team Production by the Main Bank', mimeo, Stanford University.

Asanuma, B. (1989), 'Manufacturer–Supplier Relationships in Japan and the Concept of Relation-Specific Skill', *Journal of the Japanese and International Economies*, 3(1): 1–30.

Bizer, D. S., and DeMarzo, P. M. (1992), 'Sequential Banking', *Journal of Political Economy*, 100 (1): 41–61.

Black, B. S. (1992), 'Agents Watching Agents: The Promise of Institutional Investor Voice', *UCLA Law Review*, 39: 811–93.

Brioschi, F., and Buzzacchi, L. (1989), 'Risk Capital Financing and the Separation of Ownership and Control in Business Groups', *Journal of Banking and Finance*, 13: 747–72.

Coffee, J. C. Jr. (1991), 'Liquidity versus Control: The Institutional Investor as Corporate Monitor', *Columbia Law Review*, 91: 1277–368.

Diamond, D. (1984), 'Financial Intermediation and Delegated Monitoring', *Review of Economic Studies*, 51: 393–414.

Dore, R. (1986), *Flexible Rigidities: Industrial Policy and Structural Adjustment in the Japanese Economy 1970–80*, Stanford University Press.

——(1987), *Taking Japan Seriously: A Confucian Perspective on Leading Economic Issues*, Athlone Press, London.

Ellerman, D. P. (1991), 'Cross Ownership of Corporations: A New Application of Input–Output Theory', *Metroeconomica*, 42: 33–46.

Fedenia, M., Hodder, J. E., and Triantis, A. J. (1991), 'Cross-Holding and Market Return Measures', *CEPR Discussion Paper No. 28*, Center for Economic Policy Research, Stanford University.

Flath, D. (1992a), 'Indirect Shareholding within Japan's Business Groups', *Economic Letters*, 38: 223–7.

——(1992b), 'The *Keiretsu* Puzzle', mimeo, North Carolina State University.

French, K. R. and Porterba, J. M. (1991), 'Were Japanese Stock Prices Too High?', *Journal of Financial Economics*, 29: 337–63.

Garvey, G. T. and Swan, P. L. (1992), 'The Interaction between Financial and Employment Contracts: A Formal Model of Japanese Corporate Governance', *Journal of the Japanese and International Economies*, 6: 247–74.

Gerlach, M. (1989), '*Keiretsu* Organization in the Japanese Economy: Analysis and Trade Implications', in C. Johnson, L. D.'A. Tyson, and J. Zysman (eds.), *Politics and Productivity: The Real Story of Why Japan Works*, Ballinger Press, Cambridge, Mass., 141–74 174.

Gilson, R. J., and Roe, M. J. (1993), 'Understanding the Japanese Keiretsu: Overlaps Between Corporate Governance and Industrial Organization', *Yale Law Journal*, 102: 871–906.

Grossman, S. J., and Hart, O. D. (1980), 'Takeover Bids, the Free-Rider Problem, and the Theory of the Corporation', *Rand Journal of Economics*, 11: 42–64.

Hamao, Y. (1991), 'Japanese Financial Markets: An Overview', in W. T. Ziemba, W. Bailey, and Y. Hamao (eds.), *Japanese Financial Market Research*, North-Holland, Amsterdam, 3–21.

Hirschman, A. O. (1970), *Exit, Voice and Loyalty*, Harvard University Press, Cambridge, Mass.

Holmström, B. R., and Tirole, J. (1989), 'The Theory of the Firm', in R. Schmalensee and R. D. Willig (eds.), *Handbook of Industrial Organization*, Vol. 1, North-Holland, Amsterdam, 61–133.

Hoshi, T., and Ito, T. (1991), 'Measuring the Coherence of Japanese Enterprise Groups,' paper presented to TCER Finance Conference.

Imai, K. (1990), 'Japanese Business Groups and the Structural Impediments Initiative', in K. Yamamura (ed.), *Japan's Economic Structure: Should It Change?* Society for Japanese Studies, Seattle, 167–202.

Irie, K. (1979), '1970 nendai no Nihon no kigyo kin'yu to kabushiki shijo' (Corporate Finance and the Stock Market in Japan in the 1970s), *Shoken Keizai*, 129: 33–58.

Itoh, M. (1993), 'Organisational Transactions and Access to the Japanese Import Market', in P. Sheard (ed.), *International Adjustment and the Japanese Firm*, Allen & Unwin, Sydney, 50–71.

Jensen, M. C. (1986), 'Agency Costs of Free Cash Flow, Corporate Finance, and Takeovers', *American Economic Review*, 76: 323–9.

—— and Ruback, R. S. (1983), 'The Market for Corporate Control: The Scientific Evidence', *Journal of Financial Economics*, 11: 5–50.

Johnson, C. (1990), 'Trade, Revisionism, and the Future of Japanese–American Relations', in K. Yamamura (ed.), *Japan's Economic Structure: Should It Change?* Society for Japanese Studies, Seattle, 105–36.

Kaplan, S. N. (1992), 'Top Executive Rewards and Firm Performance: A Comparison of Japan and the US', National Bureau of Economic Research Working Paper no. 4065.

Keizai Chosa Kyokai (various years), *Keiretsu no kenkyu: daiichibu jojo kigyohen* (Research on Corporate Affiliations: First-Section Listed Firm Edition), Keizai Chosa Kyokai, Tokyo.

Kester, W. C. (1991), *Japanese Takeovers: The Globel Contest for Corporate Control*, Harvard Business School Press, Boston, Mass.

Kigyo keiretsu soran (various years), *Kigyo keiretsu soran* (Directory of Corporate Affiliations), Toyo Keizai Shinposha, Tokyo.

Kobayashi, J. (1983), 'Jigyo hojin no kabushiki hoyu' (Shareholdings by Operating Companies), *Shoken Kenkyu*, 67: 151–234.

Lincoln, E. (1990), 'US–Japan Trade Talks: Hope for Progress', *The Heritage Lectures*, 234, Heritage Foundation, Washington, DC.

McDonald, J. (1989), 'The *Mochiai* Effect: Japanese Corporate Cross-holdings', *Journal of Portfolio Management*, Fall: 90–4.

McKenzie, C. R. (1992), 'Stable Shareholdings and the Role of Japanese Life Insurance Companies', in P. Sheard (ed.), *International Adjustment and the Japanese Firm*, Allen & Unwin, Sydney., 83–98.

Manne, H. G. (1965), 'Mergers and the Market for Corporate Control', *Journal of Political Economy*, 73: 110–20.

Matsui, K. (1977), 'Nichibei kigyo no zaimu kozo to kabuka keisei' (The Financial Structure and Share-Price Formation of Japanese and US Firms), *Shoken Keizai*, 125: 41–121.

——(1979), 'Nichibei kigyo no kabushiki shoyu kozo to kabuka keisei [jo]' (The Shareholding Structure and Share-Price Formation of Japanese and US Firms, part 1), *Shoken Keizai*, 128: 18–63.

Matsumoto, K. (1991), *The Rise of the Japanese Corporate System: The Inside View of a MITI Official*, Kegan Paul, London.

Mayer, C. (1988), 'New Issues in Corporate Finance', *European Economic Review*, 32: 1167–89.

Milgrom, P., and Roberts, J. (1990), 'Bargaining Costs, Influence Costs, and the Organization of Economic Activity', in J. E. Alt and K. A. Shepsle (eds.), *Perspectives on Political Economy*, Cambridge University Press, 57–89.

————(1992), *Economics, Organization and Management*, Prentice-Hall, Englewood Cliffs, NJ.

Morck, R., and Nakamura, M. (1992), 'Banks and Corporate Control in Japan', mimeo, University of Alberta.

Nakatani, I. (1984), 'The Economic Role of Financial Corporate Grouping', in M. Aoki (ed.), *The Economic Analysis of the Japanese Firm*, North-Holland, Amsterdam, 227–58.

——(1992), 'Reforming Japanese Capitalism', *Journal of Japanese Trade and Industry*, 4: 15–17.

Nikkei (various issues), *Nihon Keizai Shinbun* (Japan Economic Journal), Nihon Keizai Shinbunsha, Tokyo.

Okumura, H. (1978), *Ginko to kigyo sono kiken na kankei* (Banks and Firms: The Dangerous Relationship), Toyo Keizai Shinposha, Tokyo.

——(1979), '"Hojinka gensho" to kabuka' (The "Corporatisation" Phenomenon and Share Prices), *Shoken keizai*, 127: 12–35.

——(1990), 'Seitoka dekinai "Keiretsu" no gorisei' (Rationalization of "Keiretsu" Cannot be Justified), *Ekonomisuto*, 10 July: 78–89.

Okurasho Shokenkyoku (Ministry of Finance) (1992), *Dai29kai Okurasho Shokenkyoku nenpo heisei 3nenban* (29th Ministry of Finance Securities Bureau Annual, 1991 ed.), Kin'yu Zaisei Jijo Kenkyukai, Tokyo.

Prowse, S. D. (1990), 'Institutional Investment Patterns and Corporate Financial Behavior in the United States and Japan', *Journal of Financial Economics*, 27: 43–66.

Ramseyer, J. Mark (1987), 'Takeovers in Japan: Opportunism, Ideology and Corporate Control', *UCLA Law Review*, 35 (1): 1–64.

Sheard, P. (1985), 'Main Banks and Structural Adjustment in Japan', *Pacific Economic Papers*, no. 132, Australia–Japan Research Centre, Australian National University, Canberra.

—— (1986*a*), 'General Trading Companies and Structural Adjustment in Japan', *Pacific Economic Papers*, no. 132, Australia–Japan Research Centre, Australian National University, Canberra.

—— (1986*b*), 'Intercorporate Shareholdings and Structural Adjustment in Japan', *Pacific Economic Papers*, no. 140, Australia–Japan Research Centre, Australian National University, Canberra.

—— (1989*a*), 'The Main Bank System and Corporate Monitoring and Control in Japan', *Journal of Economic Behavior and Organization*, 11: 399–422.

—— (1989*b*), 'The Japanese General Trading Company as an Aspect of Interfirm Risk-Sharing', *Journal of the Japanese and International Economies*, 3: 308–22.

—— (1991*a*), 'The Economics of Interlocking Shareholding in Japan', *Ricerche Economiche*, 45: 421–48.

—— (1991*b*), 'The Role of Firm Organization in the Adjustment of a Declining Industry in Japan: The Case of Aluminum', *Journal of the Japanese and International Economies*, 5: 14–40.

—— (1992*a*), 'Stable Shareholdings, Corporate Governance, and the Japanese Firm', ISER Discussion Paper no. 281, Institute of Social and Economic Research, Osaka University.

—— (1992*b*), 'Long-Term Horizons and the Japanese Firm', ISER Discussion Paper no. 283, Institute of Social and Economic Research, Osaka University.

—— (1992*c*), 'Japanese Corporate Finance and Behaviour: Recent Developments and the Impact of Deregulation', in C. McKenzie and M. Stutchbury (eds.), *Japanese Financial Markets and the Role of the Yen*, Allen & Unwin, Sydney, 55–72.

—— (1992*d*), 'The Role of the Main Bank when Borrowing Firms are in Financial Distress', CEPR Discussion Paper, No. 330 Center for Economic Policy Research, Stanford University.

Shleifer, A., and Summers, L. H. (1988), 'Breach of Trust in Hostile Takeovers', in A. J. Auerbach (ed.), *Corporate Takeovers: Causes and Consequences*, University of Chicago Press, 33–56

Shukan toyo Keizai (1967), ' "Antei kabunushi kosaku" no subete' (All about 'Stable Shareholder Schemes'), *Shukan Toyo Keizai*, no. 3353: 104–31.

Spatt, C. S. (1989), 'Strategic Analyses of Takeover Bids', in S. Bhattacharya and G. M. Constantinides (eds.), *Financial Markets and Incomplete Information: Frontiers of Modern Financial Theory*, Rowman and Littlefield, Totowa, NJ, 106–21.

Suto, M. (1987), *Nihon no shokengyo* (Japan's Securities Industry), Toyo Keizai Shinposha, Tokyo.

Tachibanaki, T., and Taki, A. (1991), 'Shareholding and Lending Activity of Financial Institutions in Japan', *Bank of Japan Monetary and Economic Studies*, 9 (1): 23–60.

Tokyo Shoken Torihikijo Chosabu (various years), *Shoken tokei nenpo* (Annual Securities Statistics), Research Department, Tokyo Stock Exchange.

Toyo Keizai Shinposha (various years), *Kigyo keiretsu soran* (Corporate Affiliations Annual), Toyo Keizai Shinposha, Tokyo.

Ueda, K. (1990), 'Are Japanese Stock Prices Too High?' *Journal of the Japanese and International Economies*, 4: 351–70.
Williamson, O. E. (1985), *The Economic Institutions of Capitalism*, Free Press, New York.
——(1992), 'Strategizing, Economizing and Economic Organization', *Strategic Management Journal*, 12: 75–91.
Yuka shoken hokokusho (Securities Report), financial reports lodged with the Ministry of Finance by Japanese corporations under Clause 1 of Section 24 of the Securities Transactions Act.
Zenkoku Shoken Torihikijo Kyogikai (1991), *Heisei 2nendo kabushiki bunpu jokyo chosa* (1990 Share Distribution Investigation), Zenkoku Shoken Torihikijo Kyogikai, Tokyo.

13

The Japanese Firm under the Wartime Planned Economy

TETSUJI OKAZAKI

1. INTRODUCTION

The Second World War exerted a strong and persistent shock to the demand and supply sides of the Japanese economy. Such an impact was brought about by a number of factors. While the government consumed an enormous volume of military ammunition, the supply capacity was handicapped by the sudden rise in international prices of raw materials, the blockade by the Allied Forces, and the mobilization of labour to the military. In order to carry on the war, the government had to change the resource allocation drastically. To this end, it chose to design a planned economy based on controlled means (Okazaki 1987b, 1988). From 1937–9 onwards, the economy was under the rigid control of the government. This continued for about ten years, until economic control was relaxed through the implementation of the Dodge Plan.[1] The Japanese economy during that period was subject to extensive planning, analogous to the structure of the Soviet economy before the birth of *perestroika*.[2]

From the eruption of the Sino-Japanese War in 1937, the Japanese government dealt with the task of planning the economy by successively establishing mechanisms for formulating and implementing annual plans. The Kikakuin (Planning Board), which corresponded to the Soviet Gosplan, was established, government ministries were expanded, and a Toseikai (Control Association) was created in each industry to bear a part of the burden of planning and implementing measures. These made up the upper and middle strata of the planned economy system, while the firm was given the status of a subordinate organization responsible for production within the system. Needless to say, the function and position of the firm within this context did not conform to its previous capitalistic mode of behaviour. Thus, it came to be of vital importance for the government to introduce policies that would reform the nature of the firm. When the market mechanism of the pre-war economy was transformed into a planning mechanism, what was the impact of this on the firm, the basic unit of the economic system? This chapter attempts to analyse the changes that the firm underwent as the government attempted to transform the economic system.[3]

An emerging view is that one key to understanding the Japanese economy today lies in the structural and behavioural characteristics of the firm. As Aoki (1988) has noted, the Japanese manager is not an agent of stockholders but a *de facto* arbiter between the body of stockholders and the body of quasi-permanent employees. However, scholars have not yet reached a consensus regarding the evolution of the present-day Japanese firm. While economists have focused on the importance of economic reforms and their subsequent post-war progress (Aoki 1988; Imai and Komiya 1989), economic and business historians have placed greater weight on the changes that occurred in the inter-war period and during the Second World War (Nakamura 1989: 37; Morikawa 1981). This difference in focus is due partly to the lack of sufficient substantial data on the issue. In order to obtain a better understanding of which event marked the key point of transition for the firm, it is necessary to examine the characteristics of the pre-war Japanese firm, its transition phase, and, in effect, how it reacted to such transition. We will investigate these various issues by considering the Second World War as the transition point in question, bearing in mind the earlier research that has been conducted on this topic.

A word on the theoretical framework adopted for analysing the firm is in order. Here I adopt the position that the firm is an organizational entity composed of the suppliers of 'productive resources and management resource—managers, labourers, stockholders, and financial agencies' (Aoki and Itami 1985: 1–11). The actions these agents take in the process of decision-making and risk-sharing shape the economic organization of the firm.

2. THE JAPANESE FIRM IN THE PRE-WAR PERIOD

In this section we will compare the firm–factor market relationship in the pre-war period with that of the post-war period. Our main task here is to examine how the basic corporate resources of funds, labour, and managerial ability were related to each other, and how they contributed to the structure of the firm. The main characteristics of the pre-war Japanese firm are summarized in Table 1. First of all, let us look at the relationship between the firm and the capital market.

As in the post-war period, surplus household savings were channelled to firms, but the role of direct finance through the securities market was by far more significant in pre-war than in post-war times (Teranishi 1982: 26–9). There existed in pre-war Japan an affluent class which acquired much property income and accumulated financial assets in the form of securities. In pre-war times, 30–40 per cent of the funds of the firm came from the capital market, compared with a mere 10 per cent in post-war times; and

TABLE 1   Investment–Savings Balance, by Sector, 1931–35 to 1966–70 (% of GNP)

	Government	Enterprises	Households	Overseas
1931–35	− 5.2	− 1.9	8.7	− 0.0
1936–40	− 10.8	− 10.9	15.0	0.4
1941–44	− 22.0	− 10.3	22.3	− 1.4
1946–50	3.6	− 9.9	1.3	− 1.6
1951–55	− 1.6	− 4.5	5.7	0.7
1956–60	− 1.2	− 5.7	7.7	0.2
1961–65	− 1.8	− 6.8	7.1	− 0.3
1966–70	− 2.2	− 3.3	6.4	1.0

Source: Management and Co-ordination Agency (1987).

the degree of dependence of the firm on financial institutions was quite low (Table 2).

TABLE 2   The Supply of Funds to Japanese Industries, 1931–35 to 1966–70 (%)

	Retained earnings and depreciation	Stocks	Bonds	Loans	Others
1931–35	66.5	39.9	1.0	− 8.7	1.3
1936–40	31.4	29.5	4.6	34.1	0.4
1941–45	28.8	19.5	8.6	41.8	1.2
1946–50	28.6	9.3	2.5	51.7	7.9
1951–55	43.0	8.0	2.1	41.0	5.8
1956–60	42.7	8.1	2.7	41.8	4.6
1961–65	41.0	8.2	2.6	44.1	4.1
1966–70	49.2	3.4	1.6	41.3	4.6

Source: Ministry of Finance (1978).

At this point, it is worth mentioning *zaibatsu* (Mitsui, Mitsubishi, and Sumitomo) firms. First note that, of the sixty largest mining and manufacturing firms by asset size only ten were *zaibatsu*-related (Table 3). The *zaibatsu*-related firms were a minority of leading firms in the mining and manufacturing industries. Although *zaibatsu* and non-*zaibatsu* firms hardly differed in terms of their mode of fund-raising, in both cases-equity carried a heavy weight (Table 4), and there was a marked contrast in the composition of suppliers of capital. In the case of the *zaibatsu*, more often than not the holding companies were overwhelmingly the large stockholders, and therefore a concentration of the stock among the top stockholders was very high; whereas in the non-*zaibatsu* firms ownership was more diffuse, with

TABLE 3   The Ranking of Private Companies in the Mining and Manufacturing Industries based on Total Assets, 1935

Rank	Company	Total Assets (¥'000)	Affiliations
1	Oji Paper Co. Ltd	347,976	
2	Nippon Mining Co. Ltd	226,078	
3	Kanegafuchi Spinning Co. Ltd	212,636	
4	Mitsui Mining Co. Ltd	179,389	Mitsui
5	Toyo Spinning Co. Ltd	176,102	
6	Mitsubishi Heavy Industries Co. Ltd	166,775	Mitsubishi
7	Mitsubishi Mining Co. Ltd	160,803	Mitsubishi
8	Kawasaki Shipbuilding Co. Ltd	152,762	
9	Nihon Oil Co. Ltd	141,614	
10	Asano Cement Co. Ltd	137,371	
11	Dainippon Beer Co. Ltd	136,677	
12	Dainippon Spinning Co. Ltd	129,916	
13	Nippon Wool Textile Co. Ltd	115,289	
14	Dainippon Sugar Manufacturing Co. Ltd	115,149	
15	Hokkaido Colliery and Steamship Co. Ltd	102,954	
16	Meiji Sugar Manufactruring Co. Ltd	99,662	
17	Nippon Kokan Kabushiki Gaisha	97,416	
18	Hitachi Co. Ltd	96,803	
19	Asahi Benberg Spinning Co. Ltd	92,867	
20	Katakura Spinning Co. Ltd	83,686	
21	Fuji Gas Spinning Co. Ltd	82,579	
22	Dainippon Synthetic Fertilizer Co. Ltd	78,240	
23	Sumitomo Metal Industries Co. Ltd	75,737	Sumitomo
24	Naigai Cotton Co. Ltd	65,615	
25	Tokyo Electric Co. Ltd	59,165	
26	Teikoku Synthetic Silk Co. Ltd	57,972	
27	Nippon Electric Industries Co. Ltd	57,397	
28	Koga Electric Industries Co. Ltd	54,516	
29	Nisshin Flour Milling Co. Ltd	50,632	
30	Onoda Cement Co. Ltd	48,700	
38	Toyo Rayon Co. Ltd	41,316	Sumitomo
39	Nippon Flour Mills Co. Ltd	40,811	Mitsui
51	Mitsubishi Electric Co. Ltd	32,088	Mitsubishi
52	Sumitomo Chemicals Co. Ltd	31,586	Sumitomo
59	Sumitomo Electric Wire Mfg. Co. Ltd	26,492	Sumitomo
60	Toyo Koatsu Industries Co. Ltd	26,375	Mitsui

Sources: Toyo Keizai Shinposha, *Kabushiki Gaisha Nenkan* (Year Book of Joint Stock Companies), 1936; Ministry of Finance (1982).

middle- and small-scale capitalists supplying funds through external capital markets (Table 5).

This difference exerted an influence on the corporate governance: the *zaibatsu* firms exhibited more 'separation of ownership and management'

TABLE 4 Changes in the Composition of Liabilities of Leading Mining and
Manufacturing Companies, 1935, 1943, and 1950 (%)

Company	(1) Retained earnings	(2) Capital	(3) Bonds	(4) (2) + (3)	(5) Others
Zaibatsu					
1935	19.3	43.9	0.6	44.5	36.2
1943	14.1	24.7	6.4	31.1	54.8
1950	18.0	8.6	4.7	13.3	68.7
Non-zaibatsu					
1935	22.2	37.2	6.8	43.9	33.9
1943	25.3	30.4	7.3	37.7	37.0
1950	32.0	8.7	3.6	12.3	55.7

Note
These figures refer to the first ten *zaibatsu* and non-*zaibatsu* firms in Table 3.
Source: Ministry of Finance (1978).

(Morikawa 1981: 155–6), as is confirmed by the percentage of large stock-holder-directors among the overall number of directors in the two types of firm (Table 6). In the *zaibatsu* firms, the *zaibatsu* families who were overwhelmingly the large stockholders entrusted the management of the firms to professional salaried managers, while in the non-*zaibatsu* companies the large stockholders were in most cases concurrently directors of the companies. In the latter case, the stockholders did not simply assume the posts of director, but it was through this or other means that they exerted influence on the management policies of the firms. Kamekichi Takahashi's *Kabushiki Gaisha Bokokuron* (The Stock Company: A Cause of National Decay), publised in 1930, reveals the tenor of the argument in those days. According to Takahashi, the primary manifestations of 'the degeneration of firm management' were the short-sighted attitude towards business management and the inability of management to aim at the so-called 'business prosperity for 100 years'. Degeneration of company management was largely caused by the 'high-handed and short-sighted selfishness of large stockholders' and the corruption of the board of directors (Takahashi 1930: 4–5).

The 'high-handedness' of large stockholders was manifested in their demand for high dividends and their neglect of long-term considerations such as profit reserves, depreciation charges, research and development, and equipment investment. The 'corruption of the board of directors' referred to the breach of trust, the payment of large bonuses, the manipulation of stock prices, and the lack of management ability. One last point stressed by Takahashi was that: 'it is uncommon to find members of the board of directors who acquired their status and position by virtue of their man-

TABLE 5 The Structure of Stockownership of Leading Mining and Manufacturing Companies, 1935, 1942, and 1960 (%)

	% of stocks owned by the No. 1 stockholder			% of stocks owned by the top 10 stockholders			Share of financial institutions in top 10 stockholders		
	1935	1942	1960	1935	1942	1960	1935	1942	1960
Total	26.8	20.6	6.5	41.2	37.8	25.1	13.4	23.7	83.6
Zaibatsu	47.7	34.6	7.0	62.9	54.1	27.0	13.3	23.9	81.9
Mitsui Mining Co. Ltd	—	—	4.5	—	—	24.0	—	—	22.2
Mitsubishi Heavy Industries Co. Ltd	51.4	43.0	8.9	69.7	64.6	32.6	15.0	22.5	90.2
Mitsubishi Mining Co. Ltd	56.8	42.8	4.8	63.5	59.7	27.5	4.9	22.5	56.4
Sumitomo Metal Industries Co. Ltd	63.8	25.5	5.8	81.0	45.8	25.4	14.0	30.6	85.0
Toyo Rayon Co. Ltd	45.3	35.6	6.9	56.2	59.0	24.9	5.7	11.4	100.0
Nippon Flour Mills Co. Ltd	49.6	49.6	7.4	57.7	60.3	41.8	0.0	8.3	100.0
Mitsubishi Electric Co. Ltd	43.3	43.8	4.0	51.5	55.1	16.6	2.4	5.4	67.2
Sumitomo Chemical Co. Ltd	23.4	22.8	8.3	39.5	41.8	19.1	3.2	19.0	88.4
Sumitomo Electric Wire Mftg. Co. Ltd	20.0	—	12.9	64.5	—	44.3	3.6	—	53.1
Toyo Koatsu Industries Co. Ltd	50.0	34.6	11.0	68.0	58.8	32.5	6.9	34.3	94.0
Non-Zaibatsu	18.2	11.2	5.5	32.3	26.9	21.7	4.3	23.4	87.9
Oji Paper Co. Ltd	5.2	3.6	4.7	23.6	21.9	24.6	15.8	49.8	94.2
Nippon Mining Co. Ltd	56.3	30.5	3.8	72.9	44.5	24.5	5.8	13.8	92.8
Kanebo Spinning Co. Ltd	5.6	6.3	5.0	26.4	20.2	22.7	45.6	35.9	42.8
Toyo Spinning Co. Ltd	1.6	1.6	5.5	10.1	10.6	21.2	36.9	10.3	87.0
Kawasaki Shipbuilding Co. Ltd	27.3	10.0	5.4	36.9	31.6	16.7	81.7	12.8	82.8
Nippon Oil Co. Ltd	5.4	3.8	6.2	16.3	19.7	18.3	0.0	5.7	95.0
Asano Cement Co. Ltd	28.0	15.6	7.3	43.8	39.2	21.2	16.2	15.2	91.6
Dainippon Beer Co. Ltd	2.3	2.8	11.6	10.4	13.6	34.3	26.0	76.5	100.0
Dainippon Spinning Co. Ltd	2.9	3.1	4.8	14.6	12.3	23.3	14.6	16.8	84.0
Nippon Wool Textile Co. Ltd	5.3	3.7	3.6	20.8	18.9	15.7	5.5	17.7	91.8

Note

The figures reflected in the overall total (for zaibatsu and non-zaibatsu) and total for non-zaibatsu do not include that of Kawasaki Shipbuilding Co. Ltd.

Sources: Toyo Keizai Shinposha, *Kabushiki Gaisha Nenkan* (Yearbook of Joint Stock Companies), 1936 and 1937; Yamaichi Shoken, *Kabushiki Gaisha Nenkan*, 1962.

TABLE 6   The Ownership and Management of Leading Mining and Manufacturing Companies, 1935, 1942, and 1960

	No. of stockholders–directors			% of total no. of directors		
	1935	1942	1960	1935	1942	1960
Total	25	22	1	14.5	10.6	0.3
Zaibatsu						
Mitsui Mining Co. Ltd	4	7	0	5.4	7.7	0.0
Mitsubishi Heavy Industries Co. Ltd	1	2	0	—	12.5	0.0
Mitsubishi Mining Co. Ltd	1	2	0	7.1	13.3	0.0
Sumitomo Metal Industries	0	0	0	10.0	0.0	0.0
Toyo Rayon Co. Ltd	0	0	0	0.0	0.0	0.0
Nippon Flour Mills Co. Ltd	2	1	0	28.6	9.1	0.0
Mitsubishi Electric Co. Ltd	0	2	0	0.0	20.0	0.0
Sumitomo Chemicals Co. Ltd	0	0	0	0.0	0.0	0.0
Sumitomo Electric Wire Mfg. Co. Ltd	0	—	0	0.0	—	0.0
Toyo Koatsu Industries Ltd	0	0	0	0.0	0.0	0.0
Non-zaibatsu						
Oji Paper Co. Ltd	21	15	1	21.2	12.9	0.8
Nippon Mining Co. Ltd	2	1	0	15.4	6.3	0.0
Kanebo Spinning Co. Ltd	1	0	0	10.0	0.0	0.0
Toyo Spinning Co. Ltd	0	0	0	0.0	0.0	0.0
Kawasaki Shipbuilding Co. Ltd	2	1	0	18.2	14.3	0.0
Nippon Oil Co. Ltd	1	1	0	11.1	11.1	0.0
Asano Cement Co. Ltd	4	3	0	44.4	23.1	0.0
Dainippon Beer Co. Ltd	5	2	0	50.0	20.0	0.0
Dainippon Spinning Co. Ltd	2	4	0	20.0	30.8	0.0
Nippon Wool Textile Co. Ltd	3	3	1	33.3	33.3	0.0

Sources: Toyo Keizai Shinposha, 1943; *Kabushiki Gaisha Nenkan*, 1936, 1937; Toyo Keizai Shinposha *Kigyo Tokei Soran*, 1943; business reports of each company.

TABLE 7   The Disposal of Profit among Leading
Japanese Companies, 1931–35 to 1966–70 (%)

	Dividends	Directors' bonuses	Reserves
1931–35	68.7	5.9	25.4
1933–35	64.0	6.2	29.9
1936–40	61.3	5.1	33.6
1941–43	60.1	4.9	35.1
1951–55	47.1	4.8	48.1
1956–60	52.7	3.2	44.1
1961–65	65.4	1.9	32.6
1966–70	43.2	2.1	54.7

Sources: Mitsubishi Keizai Kenkyujo, *Honpo Jigyo
Seiseki Bunseki,* each year; Mitsubishi Keizai
Kenkyujo (Mitsubishi Sogo kenkyujo) *Kigyo keiei
no Bunseki,* each year.

agement ability. A large number of directors get their position on the board
only because of being large stockholders of the firm or having special
relations in government circles' (p. 233). He argued that 'the degree of
corruption in firms directly under *zaibatsu* control was noticeably milder,
and therefore invited a higher degree of trust' (p. 5). Among large pre-war
firms, profit disposal took the form of a high propensity for the payment
of dividends and fairly large managerial bonuses, compared with the post-
war period (Table 7). Furthermore, dividends were more sensitive to profits
(Table 8). As Takahashi pointed out, these features were more conspicuous
in the non-*zaibatsu* firms.

Post-war Japanese industrial relations have been characterized by lifetime
employment, a seniority-based wage system, and company unions. During
the pre-war period the lifetime employment system played a less prominent
role in industrial relations. If we check the coefficient of employment
adjustment (annual data, man-base) for all manufacturing industries in the
pre-war (1921–35) and post-war (1956–60) periods, we find that they are
0.98 and 0.38, respectively.[4] These figures imply that before the war it took
only one year to attain virtually the same degree of employment adjustment
as took five years after the war.[5]

It is worth comparing the modes of employment adjustment between the
zaibatsu and the non-*zaibatsu* firms. Taking the coal industry as an example,
from 1929 to 1931 the output elasticity of employment (monthly data, man-
base) in *zaibatsu* firms was 0.069, and in non-*zaibatsu* firms, 0.54 (Table 9).
If taken on a monthly basis and in terms of production, these figures suggest
that in times of depression the *zaibatsu* firms did not adjust the number of
workers, while the non-*zaibatsu* firms adjusted the number of workers at a

TABLE 8   The Dividend Policy of Leading Mining and Manufacturing Companies, 1921–1936, 1937–1943, and 1961–1970

Company	Dividend propensity			Degree of response to profit rate[a,b]		
	1921–36	1937–43	1961–70	1921–36	1937–43	1961–70
Total	0.70	0.55	0.65	0.71 (20.11)	−0.34 (−2.79)	0.17 (7.55)
Zaibatsu						
Total	0.61	0.49	0.67	0.43 (12.61)	−0.08 (−1.26)	0.17 (6.59)
Mitsui Mining Co. Ltd	0.66	0.66	0.00	0.52 (15.31)	0.08 (1.21)	— —
Mitsubishi Heavy Industries Co. Ltd	0.55	0.27	0.66	0.43 (9.68)	0.00 (0.00)	0.33 (5.27)
Mitsubishi Mining Co. Ltd	0.65	0.65	—	0.48 (14.73)	0.27 (5.70)	0.05 (1.25)
Sumitomo Metal Industries Co. Ltd	0.61	0.42	0.81	0.34 (7.86)	0.06 (0.63)	0.24 (31.06)
Toyo Rayon Co. Ltd	0.55	0.75	0.46	0.52 (7.37)	0.65 (9.10)	0.12 (6.50)
Nippon Flour Mills Co. Ltd	0.64	0.55	0.64	0.27 (5.72)	0.08 (1.62)	0.12 (5.39)
Mitsubishi Electric Co. Ltd	0.51	0.48	0.70	0.33 (6.97)	0.11 (2.53)	0.41 (5.57)
Sumitomo Chemical Co. Ltd	0.49	0.72	0.76	0.37 (7.96)	0.31 (3.13)	0.20 (2.64)
Sumitomo Electric Wire Mfg. Co. Ltd	0.50	0.54	0.60	0.23 (10.22)	−0.01 (−0.13)	0.02 (1.63)
Toyo Koatsu Co. Ltd	0.82	0.75	0.90	— —	0.77 (5.61)	0.82 (7.55)
Non-zaibatsu						
Total	0.73	0.60	0.60	0.77 (29.37)	−0.19 (−1.56)	0.15 (5.15)
Oji Paper Co. Ltd	0.68	0.65	0.56	0.66 (8.15)	0.22 (2.49)	0.13 (3.16)
Nippon Mining Co. Ltd	0.74	0.82	0.57	0.64 (8.06)	1.00 (9.20)	0.31 (3.58)
Kanebo Spinning Co. Ltd	0.66	0.53	0.59	0.68 (8.37)	−0.13 (−1.31)	0.05 (2.00)
Toyo Spinning Co. Ltd	0.75	0.73	0.80	0.63 (14.05)	0.02 (0.33)	0.47 (5.07)
Kawasaki Shipbuilding Co. Ltd	0.95	0.76	0.60	0.96 (44.81)	−0.58 (−4.64)	0.02 (0.62)
Nippon Oil Co. Ltd	0.87	0.35	0.49	1.02 (20.65)	0.00 (0.16)	0.03 (1.01)
Asano Cement Co. Ltd	0.85	0.69	0.54	0.76 (22.83)	0.42 (9.60)	0.18 (4.95)
Dainippon Beer Co. Ltd	0.64	0.59	0.57	0.38 (10.66)	−0.04 (−1.47)	0.13 (6.66)
Dainippon Spinning Co. Ltd	0.75	0.42	0.97	0.75 (27.85)	−0.04 (−1.05)	0.21 (4.54)
Nippon Wool Textile Co. Ltd	0.70	0.45	0.49	0.74 (14.37)	0.01 (0.24)	0.08 (1.60)
All industries[c]	0.77	0.63	0.52	0.35 (4.91)	0.44 (4.96)	0.08 (2.73)

[a] The degree of response is the parameter a in the equation:
dividend rate $= a$ (profit rate) $+ b$.
where dividend rate = dividend/paid in capital
profit rate = profit/paid in capital.

[b] The figures enclosed in parentheses in the second column indicate the t-values.

[c] The figures reflected in the first and fourth columns are values for 1928–36.

TABLE 9   The Output Elasticity of
Employment in the Coal Mining
Industries, 1913–15 to 1929–31

	1913–15	1929–31
Total	0.281	0.384
	(3.33)	(2.20)
Zaibatsu	0.235	0.069
	(2.61)	(0.41)
Non-*zaibatsu*	0.298	0.539
	(3.61)	(3.47)

Notes
1. Figures for *zaibatsu* represent the total of
   Yamano, Hojo, and Tadakuma Mines:
   those for *non-zaibatsu* represent the total
   of Otsuji, Onoura, and Toyokuni Mines.
2. Computed disregarding time trend.
3. Figures in parentheses are *t*-values.

Sources: Chikuho Sekitan Kogyo Kumiai,
Chikuho Sekitan Kogyo Kumiai Geppo
(Monthly Report of Coal Mining Associ-
ation of Chikuho Region).

rate of around half of the percentage of production change. Thus, we can
say that the *zaibatsu*-related firms resembled post-war Japanese firms, while
the non-*zaibatsu* firms behaved more like classical capitalist firms. If we
examine the elasticity of employment during the early years of the First
World War, we find that the *zaibatsu* firms also regulated employment in a
relatively elastic manner, suggesting that between the two world wars the
zaibatsu firms adopted a mode of employment adjustment that resembled
that of the post-war era.

It is a well-known fact that, from towards the end of the First World
War, 'factory committees' were created in heavy industries to tackle labour
disputes and work-related matters. The formation of these committees
institutionalized the right of workers to voice their opinions on issues that
concerned them (Nishinarita 1988: 200–14). The establishment of factory
committees was a primary concern of *zaibatsu* firms, whereas in non-
zaibatsu firms workers' participation was slow in coming. It should be noted
that the personnel staffs in *zaibatsu* firms played an important role in
fostering worker participation (Saguchi 1983: 50). However, as stressed
earlier, the *zaibatsu* firms comprised only a minority in the class of large
firms in the mining and manufacturing industries.

3. THE PLANNED ECONOMY DURING THE SECOND WORLD WAR

The degree and extent of economic changes that took place during the war can be seen from an analysis of macro data. In 1944 the composition of private consumption in nominal gross national expenditure (GNE) had fallen to less than 60 per cent of the 1936 level, and the ratios of government operating expenditure centred on the cost of ammunitions and on capital formation increased by 2.5 and 1.4 times, respectively (Table 10). The Japanese wartime economy was simply structured to squeeze consumption and divert those resources to war supplies and capital formation. The changes in the composition of production were accompanied by substantial import substitution. Whereas in pre-war times the import propensity was on average 20 per cent, in 1944 it was less than 6 per cent.

The decision taken by the government in the latter part of 1936 to expand its budget marked the start of the planned economy. The expansion of both military expenditure and production capacity under the market economy was no easy task. In 1937 wholesale prices rose by 25 per cent, and the balance of current account deficit was 2.5 per cent of the GNP (Table 10). (For further details, see Okazaki 1987a: 34–40.) In early 1937 the government introduced trade and price controls, and in July it issued the 'Three Guiding Principles on Finance and Economics' (Zaisei Keizai San Gensoku). This set of guidelines declared the maximizing of production capacity as the prime economic objective, subject to the balance of international payments and an 'adjustment' in the demand and supply of every good (Okazaki 1987b: 77). This system was founded on the premiss of increasing military expenditure, and with the understanding that the term 'adjustment' also implied 'control' (Hara 1977: 225).

A market solution to this objective was not feasible, for two reasons. First, the government and the military came to be influenced by an ideology of planning. For example, behind the government's plan to expand production capacity was the Five Year Plan of the Japan–Manchuria Finance and Economics Research Group (*Nichi-Man Zaisei Keizai Kenkyukai*) in August 1936. This plan was conceived to implement control over finance, labour, and trade so as to concentrate resources for the expansion of the war industries and the production of basic materials (Ito 1989: Nakamura 1989: 9–10). Government and military planners were heavily influenced by the Soviet planning method. Masatoshi Miyazaki, who presided over the Japan–Manchuria Finance and Economics Research Group, had visited Russia and later pursued his studies on Soviet affairs at the South Manchuria Railways (Hara 1971: 52–6). In 1938 one of the staff members of the *Kikakuin* wrote an article in *Kikaku*, the publication of the Planning Agency:

The fact that after the revolution, in a matter of twenty years, the Soviet Union,

TABLE 10 Gross National Expenditure (GNE), 1936–1944

	Total	Private consumption	Government consumption	Gross domestic capital formation	Surplus of nation on current account	Exports and income from overseas	Imports and income to overseas
Real (¥ million)							
1936	17,157	11,003	2,618	3,045	272	4,568	4,296
1937	21,220	11,540	4,247	4,572	259	4,777	4,518
1938	21,935	11,382	5,491	4,745	−98	4,560	4,658
1939	22,117	10,839	4,688	6,007	198	4,949	4,752
1940	20,796	9,723	7,896	5,967	62	5,342	5,280
1941	21,130	9,410	6,134	6,145	−668	4,317	4,985
1942	21,405	8,956	6,460	6,557	−640	6,182	3,823
1943	21,351	8,469	7,445	5,857	−552	2,827	3,380
1944	20,634	7,006	7,301	—	−271	2,198	2,470
% of composition							
1936	100.0	63.8	15.2	20.0	1.0	25.5	24.4
1937	100.0	56.3	20.7	25.5	−2.5	23.7	26.2
1938	100.0	52.8	25.5	24.1	−2.4	20.1	22.5
1939	100.0	50.5	21.9	27.4	0.2	19.1	19.0
1940	100.0	48.8	24.6	26.9	−0.3	17.4	17.8
1941	100.0	46.3	30.2	26.2	−2.6	13.8	15.9
1942	100.0	43.8	31.6	26.9	−2.2	9.1	11.3
1943	100.0	40.9	35.9	25.0	−1.8	7.5	9.2
1944	100.0	35.8	37.3	27.8	−0.8	5.1	5.9

Notes
1. The real figures refer to real GNE; the percentage of composition, to nominal GNE.
2. The overseas accounts were taken from Yamazawa and Yamamoto (1979).
Sources: Management and Co-ordination Agency (1987); Yamazawa and Yamamoto (1979).

while still fresh from a gloomy Czarist past, rose and made a bold leap to become the leader in manufacturing industries in Europe and second to America in the world, is something to marvel at. (Takahashi 1938)

The *Kikakuin* was commissioned to undertake investigations of the Soviet experience with a planned economy,[6] and the journal *Kikaku* contains numerous articles dealing with Soviet-related matters.

The second reason behind the decision of the government to turn to a planned economy was related to the problem of income distribution. Structural changes in the economy involving expenditure and production were inevitably accompanied by structural changes on the distribution side. Inflation and relative price changes can have enormous effects on income distribution. In 1937 a decline in real wages by 5 per cent caused a jump in the number of workers who participated in the labour disputes (Toyo Keizai Shinposha 1991: iii. 99). This made the government aware of the enormous social instability that inflation could create. Thus, during 1937–9 the government undertook successive measures to prepare for the implementation of a planned economy, including those directed at the firm.

4. THE FIRM UNDER THE NEW ECONOMIC SYSTEM

Early Stages of Economic Control

Before the Second World War broke out in 1939, Japanese firms had already experienced difficulties on two occasions in relation to the government's efforts in preparing them for the wartime economic system. These occurred with the establishment of the Sangyo Hokoku Kai (Industrial Patriotic Society), and the implementation of Article 11 of the National Mobilization Act (Kokka Sodoin Ho).

Sangyo Hokoku Kai was based on the 'Industrial Relations Adjustment Measure' (Roshi Kankei Chosei Hosaku), drafted in March 1938 by Kyochokai. This document marked the implementation of a new doctrine on the firm by describing industry as 'an organic organization whereby employers and employees are bound together in their respective functions' (Kanda 1981: 7–15). An important point is that it recognized employees as well as employers as members of the firm, causing strong opposition from entrepreneurs and management groups. A well-known case is the 'Critique on the Industrial Relations Adjustment Measure of the Kyochokai', which the Federation of Industrial Bodies of the Chubu Region raised in June 1938 (Kanda 1981: 22–5). In this Critique the Federation pointed out that, while the Measure promoted the interests of employers (managers) and employees, it ignored the existence and role of stockholders. Moreover, the

Measure was considered an extremely unscientific idea, when compared with the ideology of the British Whittley Committee, which distinguished (a) capital, (b) ability (managerial and technical knowledge and experience), and (c) labour, based on their functions as constituents of a business organization. Thus, the Federation stressed that in this particular aspect the Kyochokai was far more socialist-oriented than the systems of Britain and Nazi Germany.

Meanwhile, the Ministry of Welfare, which had jurisdiction over labour problems, upheld a doctrine that deviated from that held by the Federation of Industrial Bodies of the Chubu Region. One of the staff members of the Ministry of Welfare claimed in an article in April 1938 that 'stockholders sell out and make money when stock prices have risen; sell out and flee when stock prices are falling. Solely seeking to earn large dividends while neglecting personal labour is the common idea shared by a large number of stockholders.' The article pointed out that, 'if stockholders decide on the managerial board and management policies and drag away the profits of the firm, then there is no doubt that the stock corporation system has a flagrant fault'. In addition, it argued that 'what determines the performance of the firm are [low or high] price and [good or bad] quality of products', and that, 'in order to achieve this end, staff members and workers have to contribute in almost all cases a considerable amount of effort to improve the quality of products and to save on production cost'. In this light, therefore 'the white-collar and blue-collar workers carry far more profound interests and a wider range of responsibilities than the stockholders, who do not even call on or show their faces to the firm'. Following the same line of thought, it was recognized that the white-collar and blue-collar workers impart more commitment to the firm than stockholders do (Suzuki 1938). To sum up, the article advocated the need to institutionalize a system of profit-sharing in favour of administrative staff and company employees.

The debate that centred around the Sangyo Hokoku Kai was settled when the Deputy-Ministers of Public Welfare and Domestic Affairs passed the 'Circular Concerning the Implementation of the Industrial Relations Adjustment Policy' in August 1938 (Kanda 1981). Importantly, the Circular formally acknowledged the class of white-collar and blue-collar workers as a component of the firm. This system was embodied in the establishment of the Sangyo Hokoku Kai at the firm level, that is, in the creation of unitary patriotic societies in all business establishments. The Sangyo Hokoku Kai held meetings that were attended by both management and labour. Through these meetings, the Society was able to work on problems involving the enhancement of efficiency, treatment of workers, provision of welfare facilities, and the like. In this way, the right to voice their concerns, which in pre-war times was enjoyed by only a limited number of workers, centring on *zaibatsu* firms, was now systematically diffused to cover workers of almost all firms (Hagiwara 1983).

Article 11 of the National Mobilization Act, which dealt with such matters as dividend limits and loan orders about to be implemented, underwent the same problematic course (Nakamura and Hara 1972: 80). At the Cabinet Meeting in November 1938, the Ministers of both Public Welfare and Domestic Affairs expressed the opinion that, in order to put Article 6 of the National Mobilization Act (which exerted control over labour) into action, it was necessary to invoke Article 11 simultaneously. But the Minister of Finance raised an objection, marking the beginning of another debate. Later, the Chief of the Information Division of the Ministry of Armed Forces joined in the debate, and contented that 'it is necessary for flourishing industries that have been giving out highly-rated dividends to take serious account of those industries caught in a slump, and the bereaved families of the war dead'. Moreover, he stressed that 'from here onwards more effort must be exerted to expand production, and that it was never appropriate to pursue this task solely for the purpose of profit-making' (Bank of Japan 1973: 218–19). Those advocating Article 11 of the National Mobilization Act not only urged that consideration should be given to income distribution, but also advanced an ideological critique against the notion of profits as the sole objective of economic activity (Nakamura and Hara 1972: 80).

In the end, Article 11 was invoked, effective from April 1939, to regulate dividends and loans. The Article required firms with dividend rates of 10 per cent or more to obtain a permit from the Minister of Finance if they wished to increase their dividend rate, and similarly for firms that had already registered a dividend rate of 6 per cent and wished to increase it by a further 2 per cent or more (Bank of Japan 1970: 221–2). In the latter half of 1938, about two-thirds of the large manufacturing firms showed dividend rates over 10 per cent (Mitsubishi Keizai Kenkyujo 1939). Because of this, a relatively efficacious dividend control was imposed on firms in the manufacturing sector. Thus, wartime economic control in its early stages brought about enormous changes to the position in the firm held by both employees and stockholders in pre-war times.

Furthermore, the implementation of the dividend control programme indirectly diminished the role of stockholders. Because of the Sino-Japanese War and expectations of prolonged economic controls, stock prices declined from the beginning of 1938. In November of the same year, at the time of heated debate regarding the invocation of Article 11 of the National Mobilization Act, stock prices, particularly the high-rate dividend stocks, fell sharply (Asahi Shinbun Sha 1939: 338–9). When the dividend control system was implemented in 1939, an upward trend of paid-in capital flow disappeared, and in a single swoop the overall supply of industrial capital tumbled from 35 to 25 per cent. One primary factor given for this situation was the instability of stock prices (Bank of Japan 1970: 221–2).

There were other macro events that ushered in the sluggish performance of the stock market. It should be recalled that during the war the rate of private savings in Japan was tremendously high (Table 1). This, the government realized from the very beginning, was necessary if they were to attain a simultaneous increase in capital formation and military expenditure while maintaining a balance of international payments. At the Cabinet Meeting in April 1938, the government officially decided to implement the National Savings Promotion Campaign, and set a total of ¥8 billion, which was 30 per cent of the GNP, as the savings target for the year 1938. Of the ¥8 billion, ¥5 billion was required from the issuance of national bonds, and ¥3 billion, from the expansion of production capacity (Ministry of Finance 1957: 173–4). It was a plan, under government guidance, to make the surplus in the private sector cover the expected deficit of the government and business sectors. This plan was incorporated into the Financial Control Plan (Shikin Tosei Keikaku) from 1939.

In July 1938 the Savings Promotion Committee reported that the bulk of the population was expected to participate in the movement for more savings (Bank of Japan 1973: 256–7). In line with this effort, savings co-operatives sprouted in government and public offices, in business establishments, in all types of organizations, and in all regions. In the government and public offices, a standard saving rate corresponding to the income level in terms of salary and bonuses was determined (Bank of Japan 1973: 175–8). The government realized that, in order to raise the private saving rate promptly, it had to expand the base of savers, which should include ordinary staff white-collar and blue-collar workers.

In a report drafted by the Savings Promotion Committee the following year, it was pointed out that there was 'a need to strengthen the movement to reform the civilian lives of workers, by relying on the voluntary co-operation of workers and staff members in the flourishing industries' (Bank of Japan 1973: 183). In short, it meant that white-collar and blue-collar workers in the war industries who were enjoying an increase in income were the primary targets of the savings promotion plan. However, the government realized that, in asking the mass of people to save in this manner, it was unrealistic to expect them to purchase securities directly. If we compare the savings target laid down in the Financial Control Plan in 1939 with the actual savings in 1937, we find that the planned purchase of securities by non-financial sectors was in fact very low (Table 11). Thus, the government's move to expand savings suppressed the role of direct finance and lowered the position of stockholders as suppliers of funds.

The New Economic System

The Second World War had a strong impact on the planned economy, which was still at an early operational stage. Owing to the sudden rise in international prices of raw materials and the decision of the government to

TABLE 11 The Financial Control Plan, 1939, 1940, and 1941

	Raw data (¥000)				% of composition			
	1939	1940	1941	1937 actual results	1939	1940	1941	1937 actual results
Total demand	10,525	12,413	16,598	—	100.0	100.0	100.0	100.0
National bonds	6,025	5,660	8,750	—	57.2	45.6	52.7	—
Industry	3,600	5,403	5,364	—	34.2	43.5	32.3	—
Overseas investment	900	1,350	1,560	—	8.6	10.9	9.4	—
Total supply	10,000	12,413	16,598	5,057	100.0	100.0	100.0	100.0
Financial institutions	7,215	10,245	13,688	3,060	72.2	82.5	82.5	60.5
Bank deposits	4,350	5,900	7,284	1,769	43.5	47.5	43.9	35.0
Trust cash fund	250	325	400	24	2.5	2.6	2.4	0.5
Insurance	500	650	1,200	414	5.0	5.2	7.2	8.2
Postal savings	1,000	1,705	2,010	409	10.0	13.7	12.1	8.1
Association savings	500	800	1,500	222	5.0	6.4	9.0	4.4
Securities	2,785	1,776	2,360	1,997	27.9	14.3	14.2	39.5

Sources: Ishikawa (1975); Ministry of Finance (1978).

freeze the prices of all domestic goods, the relative price system underwent a substantial change. The profit rate of manufacturing firms and the production plan performance rate showed ominous signs of decline (Okazaki 1987*b*: 186–7). Confronted by these conditions, the government decided to move towards a new economic system. On 13 September 1940, the Kikakuin laid out a three-tier model of an economic system, composed of the government, sectoral organizations, and the firms, in the original draft of the 'Outline of the Establishment of a New Economic System' (Keizai Shintaisei Kakuritu Yoko). In this rigid imperative planning model, the basis of operation lay not in the price mechanism, but rather in the flow of quantitive orders from the upper to the lower tier.[7] The sectoral organization which constitued the middle layer of the model carried out the role of (*a*) taking part in the formation of the plan, and (*b*) implementing the plans decided by the government by allocating them to the firms involved. As an embodiment of such organization, a *toseikai* (control association) was established in each industry and participated in the iteration process to draw up plans. In addition, the reforms that took place within the firm at the lowest tier of the economic system were viewed as being critical.

The original draft of the 'Outline of the Establishment of a New Economic System' recorded that, 'as a measure of reform', the firm should be 'set free from control of stockholders' pursuit of profit-making. The firm in its reorganized form would have to uphold the national purpose with a management style based on individual creativity, ability, and responsibility, centred on the securing of quality and quantity of production.' It was expected that the operation of the planned economy would be harmonious if the government could successfully institute a system in which the firm's goal was not profit-making, but rather, the execution of the apportioned production plan. An important feature of this policy was its attempt to alter the firm's goal by removing stockholders' control.

The essential points indicated in the draft were: the introduction of reforms in the commercial law, the separation of ownership and management in the firm, and the establishment of a public-spirited orientation of the firm and of the manager's status. The Kikakuin thought that, since the pursuit of profits was premissed on the role and authority of the stockholder, it could eliminate the pursuit of profit as the firm's objective by isolating the influence of stockholders on management.

The separation of ownership and management met wide opposition from business circles, but the debate finally came to a halt when the Cabinet, on 7 December 1940, passed the 'Outline of the Establishment of a New Economic System', which provided that 'the firm is an organic body composed of capital, management and labour' (Nakamura and Hara 1972: 96–105). This corporate doctrine, viewing stockholders, managers, and employees on the same plane, led to a major overhauling of Japanese firms. Although the move to reform the Commercial Law was not realized, stockholders retreated from the management of firms during the war. Statistics reveal that in the non-*zaibatsu* firms the ratio of top ten stockholders who were simultaneously managers to the total number of managers decreased from the pre-war ratio of 21 per cent to 13 per cent by the end of 1942 (Table 6).

The move to free the management of firms from the influence of stockholders, as provided for in the original draft of the 'Outline of the Establishment of a New Economic System', was not only stipulated in legal measures, but also involved more indirect measures. One official document in those days regarded the following points as the reasons for a firm's pursuit of profits: (1) the need to absorb capital; (2) the need to generate income for the managers of the firm; and (3) the need to set up a criterion for judging firm performance (*Minobe Papers*, G-4–20). It was stressed that, setting aside (1), it should be possible to remove the pursuit of profits as an element of firm management by setting up an appropriate standard for determining a compensation scheme for managers. On the other hand, in the case of (1), the establishment of the 'New Financial System' (Kin'yu Shin Taisei) was intended to be the solution. For under this new system the criterion of a loan was supposed to be not the certainty of repayment, but the contribution the project could make to the national purpose. Thus, it was conceived that by strengthening financial regulations the stockholders, who had exerted influence on the firms' management through the financial market in the past, would finally have their control over management removed. On this score, the New Economic System was complementary to the New Financial System.

At about the same time that the Cabinet was preparing the 'Outline of the Establishment of a New Economic System', it was drawing up the original draft of the 'Outline of the New Fiscal Policy' (Zaisei Kin'yu Kihon Hosaku Yoko), decided upon at the Cabinet Meeting in July 1941 (*Minobe Papers*, G-32–1). The government intended to plan the allocation of funds by taking into consideration both macro variables (private consumption, taxes, savings) and micro variables (funds assignment to individual investment projects). According to the draft, the funds would be 'distributed to each firm on a preferential basis, and the firm will have to make the most of such funds to exhibit maximum efficiency in order to attain sufficiency in production'. For that purpose, it was necessary to switch from the existing financial doctrine, based on trust engendered by the certainty of attaining repayment, to one that would aim at securing the quality and quantity of goods necessary for the state. Specific examples of measures instituted by the government to that end were the imposition of control over mergers of financial institutions, the designation of financial institutions to take charge of each industry, and the 'march towards a private-owned and state-managed financial system'.

The realization of the New Financial System was to some degree delayed, but in May 1942 Zenkoku Kin'yu Toseikai (the National Financial Control Association) was formed. Its main role was to help the banks to organize loan consortia under the guidance of Bank of Japan (Bank of Japan 1984: 299–302). Zenkoku Kin'yu Toseikai instructed the 'manager banks' of the consortia to monitor the borrowers. This mode of delegated monitoring was similar to that of the post-war 'main bank system'.[8] In 1942 the ratio of loan by financial institutions to the supply of total funds, and the position of financial institutions in terms of stock possession, rose considerably (Table 5).

On the other hand, the new system placed emphasis on the improvement of the workers' status. This tenet was fully developed in the original draft of the 'Outline of the Establishment of a New Labour System' (*Kinro Shintaisei Kakuritsu Yoko*), which was passed by the Third Division of the Kikakuin on 5 October 1940 (*Minobe Papers*, G-32-1). One of the salient features of this document was its call for 'the establishment of workers' status'. This document laid down that the firm should not be the property of the stockholders but rather, a communal organization composed of managers, engineers, office clerks, and workers—in short, everybody who worked for the firm. According to this document, an actual management body consisting of employees should take the place of the stockholders. It was, then, through the passage of the outline of this draft that the Kikakuin finally instituted in explicit terms the companies doctrine which was criticized in 1938 by the Chubu Federation of Industrial Bodies as 'socialist-oriented'.

According to the draft, employees' organizations should be set up hierarchically with the managers of each firm acting as top leaders. The lowest level of the organization should encompass all the blue-collar employees. The adoption of this stratagem was definitely in line with the reorganization of the Sangyo Hokoku Kai in August 1941 (Kanda 1981: 211–12).

Thus, the new economic, financial, and labour systems conceived in autumn 1940 can be identified as possessing a coherent logic and complementarity. While eliminating the influence of stockholders in the legal system and financial market, the nature of the firm switched to an organizational body of managers, white-collar, and blue-collar workers, by providing a system of workers' participation at the shop-floor level. Through these changes, it was thought that the Japanese firm would be enabled to move away from its zealous pursuit of profits. On this assumption, a planned economy based on quantitative order was effected by the government-control system.

What evolved after 1941 was the separation of ownership and management, the emergence of the use of indirect finance, the imposition of government control on the Japanese financial system, and the penetration of the Sangyo Hokoku Kai to the shop-floor level. In other words, the relationship between suppliers of 'corporate resources' substantially changed, with the status of stockholders declining on the one hand and that of workers and managers rising on the other. However, whether this phenomenon indeed coincided with the expectations of the Kikakuin, which sought to eliminate profits as the primary objective of firm management, is a different question, as the next section will show.

5. THE FIRM UNDER THE REFORMS ON THE WARTIME PLANNED ECONOMY

As early as 1942, the wartime planned economy experienced a crisis. While in 1941 the main industries enjoyed some success in meeting the targets of the production and distribution plans, the success rate fell markedly in the following year (Okazaki, 1988: 99–101). One of the causes was the continuous fall of profit rates. The government was then pressed to reflect on the root cause of this crisis by looking into the behaviour of firms. The debate over the price control system provided the government with the chance to look once again into this urgent matter.[9]

The debate over the price control system actually started with the passage of the 'New Policy on Price Control' by the Kikakuin in July 1942 (*Minobe Papers*, Ca-18–17). This policy called for 'making producers bear sacrifices to cover the rise in production costs', which assumed the same behavioural mode for firms as in the doctirne of the new economic system. This plan, however, was severely criticized by the Ministry of Commerce and Industry, who claimed that 'the kikakuin's policy was based on a wrong perception of the reality of Japanese wartime economy'.[10] Notwithstanding the fact that the influence of stockholders over the management of the firm was indeed falling, the Kikakuin itself recognized that, in reality, 'there were no changes in the convention and fundamental principles that guided the firm in its direct pursuit of profits; that the firm still saw the increases in production primarily as the means to earn profits; and that it was a long way from considering the rise in production as its primary objective'.[11] Thus, the new system failed to eliminate the pursuit of profits as the primary goal of the firm.

The government was compelled to face the facts. In February 1943 it formulated the 'Outline of Emergent Measures for Price Control' (Kinkyu Bukka Taisaku Yoko) (Okazaki 1987*b*: 191–2), which sought to raise producers' prices through subsidized expenditure. From September of the same year, in response to the demand for more aircraft for the war, the government looked still more closely into all aspects of company policies. The move taken by the government was expressed in the 'Measures for Strengthening the Political and Economic System' (Kokunai Taisei Kyoka Hosaku), concluded by the cabinet on 22 September 1943 (Asahi Shinbun Sha 1944: 16–17).

The concrete measures were embodied in the enactment of the Munitions

Corporation Law in October 1943. According to the Ministry of Munitions, the essence of this law could be summarized as follows:

1. to enhance corporate spirit and make clear the nature of the firm as a public organization;
2. to establish a system of taking responsibility for production; and
3. to carry out reforms in the administrative treatment of munitions corporations. (Kitano 1944: 43–4)

In order to create the system called for in (2), the government proposed that a person responsible for the production of each firm (Seisan Sekininsha) had to be selected. While the government reserved the right to approve and recall the 'responsible person', in general the 'responsible person' was to be selected from among incumbent managers, if possible the general manager (Kitano 1944: 64). The 'responsible person' possessed exclusive representative rights, and was accorded exceptional treatment under the Commercial Law. In other words, by dint of the Munitions Corporation Law, (a) special-resolution matters of the general meeting of stockholders in the Commercial Law became ordinary resolution matters, and (b) the 'responsible person' was able to implement the original draft plan without the approval of a general meeting of stockholders (Kitano 1944: 87–94). This reflected the government's policy to 'disengage the responsible person from the cumbersome intervention of the general meeting of stockholders' (p. 49). The legal restriction on the rights of the stockholders, which had not been possible in 1940–1, was finally enforced by this law.

The elimination of the influence and rights of stockholders was taken further by the Designation System of Financial Institutions for Munitions Corporations (Gunju-gaisha Shitei Kin'yukikan Seido). Under this system, the Ministry of Finance designated one or two financial institutions for every munitions corporation, and these designated financial institutions supplied the munitions corporations with the needed funds 'at the opportune time, simply, promptly, and adequately'.[12] Similarly, the designated financial institution acted in accordance with the wishes of the munitions corporations based on the debt assurance of the government (Bank of Japan 1970: 244). In fact, in 1944 the share of lending by financial institutions to industries increased tremendously. Through this measure, the control of financial institutions on munitions corporations was weakened.

While item (2) above meant the liberation of the 'responsible person' or the managers from the restrictions set by the rights of stockholders, the reforms instituted in the management of munitions corporations called for in item (3) marked an easing of government control over the manager and the firm. To wit, the Munitions Corporation Law stipulated that 'all types of control that inhibit the creation of a vigorous production activity in munitions corporations should be removed, or special exemption must be provided' (Kitano 1944: 94). In short, the purpose behind the execution of the Munitions Corporation Law was to guarantee managers a free hand to exercise control over the firm as much as possible. The Minister of State Affairs and Deputy Minister of Commerce and Industry made it clear that 'the cardinal principle behind the [Munitions Corporation] Law was to entrust the responsible person with full authority and freedom so that he can serve the nation, and use all the experience, knowledge, and skills he has gained over the years'.[13]

It is important to note here that in practice managers *were* allowed to pursue profits as a corporate objective under the Munitions Corporation Law. This can be verified from the measures imposed on the price control system. In the Diet, the Minister of State Affairs and Deputy Minister of Commerce and Industry put forward the opinion that 'the price control should by no means interfere with production: instead, it should be practised so as to improve efficiency and encourage people to increase production'.[14] In a commentary on the Munitions Corporation Law, a staff member of the Ministry of Munitions also stated that, 'in order to emancipate the firm from unstable financial conditions that are consequent upon the execution of the task of taking responsibility over production, and to make the responsible person devote himself wholeheartedly to the task of production, it is necessary to set the proper speed for operation of a workable price control' (Kitano 1944: 51). Through experimentation with the new system, the government had learned that eliminating stockholders' influence did not result in the relinquishment of the pursuit of profits as a corporate objective.

Meanwhile, since all workers of munitions corporations were treated as conscripted men, they were strictly obligated to follow the orders of the 'responsible person'. In this sense, the sphere of activity of the Sangyo Hokoku Kai was reduced and the participation of workers in the management process of the firm retrogressed somewhat (Saguchi 1986: 48). The 'free hand' exercised by managers over the firm was guaranteed not only in their relationships with stockholders or financial institutions, but also in their relationships with the workers. However, if viewed in terms of income distribution, this considerably improved the position of workers in the firm. A Cabinet Resolution ('Outline of the Wage Policy') passed in March 1943 reveals that the wage control system was to be operated elastically, and that, when the firm was rewarded for efficiency improvement, it was to pay a special bonus to the workers (Ministry of Labour 1961: 1075–6). This scheme was applicable to all munitions corporations. At this point, the profit-sharing system with workers was implemented.

In sum, the Munitions Corporations Law introduced a corporate system whereby managers guaranteed a free hand by the government in all dealings with stockholders, financial institutions, and workers, were enabled to carry out a management style aimed at the pursuit of profits, with said profits to be shared with the workers. The features of this corporate system became clearer towards the end of the war. In March 1944 the Ministry of Munitions conceived a plan to define clearly the characteristics of the firm ('No. 1 of the Tentative Draft': *Minobe Papers*, Aa-41–38). According to this draft, while the government assured stockholders of a reasonable annual dividend share of around 5 per cent, such stockholders' rights as the disposal of profits, the enlistment of bonds, and the appointment of managers were to be suspended. And the surplus profits after payment of reasonable dividends were to be distributed under fixed government rules and regulations to managers, white-collar, and blue-collar workers as compensation for their contributions to the advancement of technology and improvement in production; after expenditure on the establishment of a welfare scheme for managers and employees, the remainder of this surplus was to be placed with the government. Under this plan, the nature of stocks was substantially changed to that of a fixed-interest-bearing security.[15]

This income distribution mode is reminiscent of that of a labour-managed firm (Imai and Komiya 1989: 12–13), supplemented by strong government control. This plan did not remain tentative. In 1945 a resolution entitled 'On the Establishment of a Decisive Operation System for War Industries', which contained almost all of these items, was passed by the Cabinet (*Minobe Papers*, Ab-8 and *Asahi Shinbun*, 12 February 1945).

6. CONCLUSION

The majority of Japanese firms in pre-war times were largely classical in orientation. This was especially true of a large number of non-*zaibatsu* firms, where the large stockholders not only played an important role in the supply of capital, but assumed executive posts in the firms as well. As a result, the propensity to pay dividends was high, and the dividend rate was elastically adjusted to respond to the profit rate. In terms of industrial relations, the speed of employment adjustment was high and the system was a far cry from that of lifetime employment; workers were regarded simply as suppliers of labour services. Whatever profits were gained were largely shared among the stockholders.

These structural and behavioural features of the pre-war Japanese firm were soon in conflict with the needs of a wartime economy, and thus the firm needed to be reformed drastically. To stabilize industrial relations, the Sangyo Hokoku Kai was established, and to fend off distortions in income distribution brought about by pre-war dividend policies, Article 11 of the National Mobilization Act was enforced. The government not only directly intervened in the management of the firm, but also mobilized a programme of mass saving to raise the saving rate, in effect weakening the role that stockholders played in the flow of funds to the firm.

The idea of introducing reforms to the firm was consistent with the new economic, financial, and labour systems developed by the government immediately after the out-break of the Second World War. These complementary reforms restricted the rights and authority of stockholders, and improved the status of managers and workers. Through these efforts, the government was able to do away with the pre-war structure of authority and power over the firm. It was the government's intention that, through these changes, the pursuit of profits would cease to be the main goal of the firm and the firm would occupy the base of the well-ordered system of a planned economy. In fact, although from 1941 reforms on the rights of the firm were carried out, the results of these reforms did not accord with the government's plan for removing the pursuit of profits from among a firm's goals.

On the basis of these realities, the government sought to correct fundamental aspects of its policies towards firms by the end of the war. The passage of the Munitions Corporation Law drew a clearer definition of the corporate system, whereby the granting of a free hand to managers was fully endorsed. In this corporate system, the firm was also given the freedom to pursue profits and to apportion such profits (except for the fixed dividend percentages that went to stockholders) to all its constituents including employees.

Needless to say, this corporate system was maintained by wartime laws and government control. It would be rather misleading to relate the firm during this particular period in Japan's history directly to its post-war counterpart. When the Second World War ended, the political system and market environment underwent a complete metamorphosis, and the firm faced extreme uncertainty. At that time, the wartime changes and the experiences that economic constituents had acquired up to then must have proved to be very important. It is probable that those changes and experiences complemented each other to some extent; and because of the complementarity many parts of the corporate system designed and introduced during the war remained and worked in the different environment after the war.[16]

NOTES TO CHAPTER 13

1. For details on wartime economic controls and the Dodge Line, see Yoshikawa and Okazaki (1992).
2. A study focusing on the socialist features of the wartime Japanese Economy is Hagiwara (1983).

3. Many parts of the Japanese economic system today have their origin in the wartime economy. On this topic, see Okazaki (1992).
4. On the employment adjustment function, see Kurosaka (1988: 130–2). The data sources are as follows: (*a*) employment: Umemura *et al.* (1988); Ministry of Labour, *Maitsuki Kinro Tokei Chosa*; (*b*) production: Shinohara (1972); T. K. Shinposha (1991); (*c*) wages: Ohkawa *et al.* (1967); Ministry of Labour, *Maitsuki Kinro Tokei Chosa*; (*d*) prices: T. K. Shinposha (1991).
5. A decline in the speed of employment adjustment between the two world wars was also observed in the cotton-spinning industry; see e.g. Okazaki (1990).
6. Kikakuin Sosai Kanbo Bunshoka (Archives Section of Kikakuin), 'Kikakuin Kiko Enkaku Kiroku' (The History of the Planning Board), in Ishikawa (1975: 51).
7. For the following, see Okazaki (1987*b*: 190–3).
8. For the post-war main bank system, see Aoki (1988).
9. 'Shinbukka Seisaku no Kakuritsu ni Kansuru Ken (Kikakuin An Shu Seibun) ni taisuru Iken' (Comments on the Kikakuin's New Price Policy), *Minobe Papers*, Ca-18-18.
10. *Minobe Papers* (Collections of the Tokyo University Library), G-4–6. See also Okazaki (1988: 27–8).
11. 'Sogo Senryoku Zokyo Kinkyu Taisaku Yoko' (Gist of the Emergent Measures for Strengthening War Potential), *Minobe Papers*, Ca-18-8.
12. Chief of the Bank and Insurance Bureau and Chief of the Bureau, 'Gunju Gaisha ni Taisuru Shikin Yuzu ni Kansuru Ken' (Circuration on the Capital Accomodation for Munitions Corporations), in Bank of Japan (1973: 149–50).
13. Kizokuin, 'Gunju Gaisha Hoan Tokubetsu Iinkai Giji Sokkiroku' (Records on the Minutes of Meetings of the Special Committee on the Munitions Corporation Law), no. 1. Thus, there appears to be some problem in the views taken by Nakamura (1989) and Hara (1989), respectively, on the restrictions on the firm's autonomy as defined in the Munitions Corporation Code.
14. Shugiin, 'Gunju Gaisha Hoan Iinkai Gijiroku' (Records of Meetings by the Committee on the Munitions Corporation Law), no. 2.
15. 'Kigyo Kessen Taisaku' (Measures on the Firm), drafted on 20 March 1944 by the Ministry of Army, stated more explicitly: 'It is necessary to transform stocks to interest-bearing securities, and the character of stockholders as recipients of such interest. The profits made by the firm should be distributed appropriately to all staff members and workers, to everybody who has generated such profits. In management, it is essential to consider first and foremost the people who work for the firm. In one way of another, management, technology, and labour all depend on the overall manipulation of people. This aspect of management is invariably more important than capital itself.' (See *Minobe Papers*, Aa–41–40.)
16. For the concept of complementarity and, its relation to path dependence, see Milgrom and Roberts (1992: pt. 2, ch. 4); Milgrom *et al.* (1991).

REFERENCES

Aoki, M (1988), *Information Incentives and Bargaining in the Japanese Economy*, Cambridge University Press.

—— and Itami, H (1985), *Kigyo no Keizaigaku* (Economics of the Firm), Iwanami Shoten, Tokyo.

Asahi Shinbunsha (1939), *Asahi Keizai Nenshi* (Economic Year Book for 1938), Asahi Shinbunsha, Tokyo.

—— (1944), *Asahi Keizai Neshi* (Economic Year Book for 1944), Asahi Shinbunsha, Tokyo.

Bank of Japan (1970), *Nihon Kin'yushi Shiryo* (Materials on the Financial History of Japan), 27, O Kurasho Insatsukyoku, Tokyo.

—— (1973), *Nihon Kin'yushi Shiryo* (Materials on the Financial History of Japan), 34, O Kurasho Insatsukyoku, Tokyo.

—— (1984), *Nihon Ginko Hyakunen Shi* (100 Year History of Bank of Japan), 4, Bank of Japan, Tokyo.

Emi, K., *et al.* (1988), *Chochiku to Tsuka* (Savings and Currency), Toyo Keizai Shinposha, Tokyo.

Hagiwara, S. (1983), 'Sangyo Hokoku Taisei no Ichikousatsu' (Issues on the Industry Patriotism System), in Kindai Nihon Kenkyukai (ed.), *Nenpo Kindai Nihon Kenkyu* (Annual Report of Research on Modern Japan, 5, Yamakawa Shuppansha, Tokyo.

Hara, A. (1971), 'Shikin Tosei to Sangyo Kin'yu' (Financial Control and Industrial Finance), *Tochi Seido Shigaku* (Journal of Agrarian History), 34: 218–68.

—— (1977), 'Senji Keizai Tosei no Kaishi' (Introduction of Wartime Economic Control in Japan), *Iwanami Koza: Nihon Rekishi* (Iwanami Lectures on Japanese History) 20, Iwanami Shoten, Tokyo.

—— (1989), 'Senji Tosei' (Wartime Economic Control), in T. Nakamura (ed.), *Keikakuka to Minshuka* (Planning and Democratization), Iwanami Shoten, Tokyo.

Imai, K., and Komiya, R. (1989), 'Nihon Kigyo no Tokucho' (The Characteristics of the Japanese Firm), in Ken'ichi Imai and Ryutaro Komiya (eds.), *Nihon no Kigyo* (The Japanese Firm), University of Tokyo Press.

Ishikawa, J. (1975), *Kokka Sodoin Shi* (The History of the National Mobilization of Japan), iii, Kokka Sodoin Shi Kankokai, Fujisawa.

Ito, T. (1989), 'Kokuze, Kokusaku, Tosei, Keikaku' (National Purposes, National Policy, Control, and Planning), in Takafusa Nakamura and Konosuke Odaka (eds.), *Niju Kozo* (Dual Structure), Iwanami Shoten, Tokyo.

Iwai, K. (1988), 'Jugyoin Kanri Kigyo toshiteno Nihon Kigyo' (The Japanese Firm as a Labour-Managed Firm), in Kikuo Iwata and Tsuneo Ishikawa (eds.), *Nihon Keizai Kenkyu* (Research on the Japanese Economy), University of Tokyo Press.

Kanda, F. (ed.) (1981), *Shiryo Nihon Gendai Shi* (Material on the Modern History of Japan), vii Otsuki Shoten, Tokyo.

Kitano, S (1944), *Gunjusho oyobi Gunjugaishaho* (Ministry of Munitions and the Munitions Corporation Law), Takayama Shoin, Tokyo.

Kurosaka, Y. (1988), *Makuro Keizaigaku to Nihon no Rodo Shijo* (Macroeconomics and the Japanese Labour Market), Toyo Keizai Shinposha, Tokyo.

Management and Co-ordination Agency (1987), *Nihon Choki Tokei Soran* (Historical Statistics of Japan), Japan Statistical Association, Tokyo.

Milgrom, P., and Roberts, J. (1992), *Economics, Organizations and Management*, Prentice-Hall, Englewood Cliffs, NJ.

——Qian, Y., and Roberts, J. (1991), 'Complementarities, Momentum, and the Evolution of Modern Manufacturing', *Ammerican Economic Review*, 81(2): 84–8.

Minami, R., and Ono, A. (1987), 'Senzen Nihon no Shotoku Bunpu' (The Income Distribution of Pre-war Japan), *Keizai Kenkyu* (Economic Review), 38(4): 333–52

Ministry of Finance (1957), *Showa Zaisei Shi* (Financial History of the Showa Era), xi, Toyo Keizai Shinposha, Tokyo.

——(1982), *Showa Zaiseishi: 1945–1951* (Financial History of Showa Era: 1945–1951), ii, Toyo Keizai Shinposha, Tokyo.

——(1978), *Showa Zaiseishi: 1945–1951* (Financial History of Showa Era), xix, Toyo Keizai Shinposha, Tokyo.

Ministry of Labour (ed.) (1961), *Rodo Gyosei Shi* (History of Labour Administration), i, Rodo Horei Kyokai, Tokyo.

Mitsubishi Keizai Kenkyujo (1939), *Honpo Jigyo Seiseki Bunseki* (Financial Analysis of Major Companies), Mitsubishi Keizai Kenkyujo, Tokyo.

Mizoguchi, T. (1986), 'Nihon no Shotoku Bunpai no Choki Hendo' (The Long-term Changes of Income Distribution in Japan), *Keizai Kenkyu* (Economic Review), 37(2): 152–8.

Morikawa H. (1981), *Nihon Keiei Shi* (Business History of Japan), Nikkei Bunko, Tokyo.

Nakamura, T. (1989), 'Gaisetsu (A Summary)', *Keikakuka to Minshuka* (Planning and Democratization), Iwanami Shoten, Tokyo.

—— –and Hara, A. (1970), 'Kaidai (A Commentary)', in *Nichiman Zaisei Keizai Kenkyukai Shiryo* (Material on the Japan–Manchuria Financial Economic Research Society), i, Nihon Kindaishi Shiryo Kenkyukai, Tokyo.

——————(1972), 'Keizai Shintaisei' (New Economic System), *Nihon Seiji Gakkai Nenpo* (Annual Report of the Political Society of Japan), Iwanami Shoten, Tokyo.

Nishinarita, Y. (1988), *Kindai Nihon Roshi Kankei no Kenkyu* (A Study on Industrial Relations of Modern Japan), University of Tokyo Press.

Ohkawa, K., *et al.* (1967), *Bukka* (Prices), Toyo Keizai Shinposha, Tokyo.

——(1974), *Kokumin Shotoku* (National Income), Toyo Keizai Shinposha, Tokyo.

Okazaki, T. (1987*a*), '1930 Nendai no Nihon ni okeru Keiki Junkan to Shihon Chikuseki' (Business Cycle and Capital Accummulation in Japan in the 1930s), *Shakai Kagaku Kenkyu* (Journal of Social Science), 39(2): 1–42.

——(1987*b*), 'Senji Keikaku Keizai to Kakaku Tosei' (The Wartime Planned Economy and Price Control System), *Nenpo Kindai Nihon Kenkyu* (Annual Report of Research on Modern Japan), 9, Yamakawa Shuppansha, Tokyo. 175–98.

——(1988), 'Dainiji Sekai Taisenki no Nihon niokeru Senji Keikaku Keizai no Kozo to Unko' (The Structure and Working of the Planned Economy in Wartime Japan), *Shakai Kagaku Kenkyu* (Journal of the Social Sciences), 40(4): 1–132.

——(1990), 'Senzenki Nihon no Keiki Junkan to Kakaku Suryo Chosei' (Price and Quantity in the Business Cycle of Prewar Japan, in Hiroshi Yoshikawa and

Tetsuji Okazaki (eds.), *Keizai Riron eno Rekishiteki Pasupakutibu* (Economic Theory in Historical Perspective), University of Tokyo Press.

——(1992), 'Nihon Gata Keizai Shisutemu' (The Japanese Economic System in Historical Perspective), *Nihon Keizai Shinbun*, 2 April.

Saguchi, K. (1983), 'Dai-ichiji Taisengo no Roshi Kankei no Tenkai' (The Development of Industrial Relations after World War I), *Nihon Rodo Kyokai Zasshi* (Monthly Journal of Japan Institute of Labour), 25(3): 49–57.

——(1986), 'Sangyo Hokoku no Rinen to Soshiki' (The Ideology and Organization of the Industrial Patriotic Society), *Keizaigaku Ronshu* (Journal of Economics) 52(2): 26–53.

Shinohara, M. (1972), *Ko-kogyo* (Mining and Manufacturing), Toyo Keizai Shinposha, Tokyo.

Suzuki, M. (1938), 'Kojo no Rijun Bunpai Seido to Kochingin Taisaku' (The Profit-Sharing System and High Wage Policies of the Factory), *Shakai Seisaku Jiho* (Journal of Social Policy), April: 47–62.

Takahashi, K. (1930), *Kabushiki Gaisha Bokokuron* (The Stock Corporation: A Cause of National Decay), Banrikaku Shobo, Tokyo.

Takahashi, Y. (1938), '1938 Nendo Sorenpo Tan'itsu Kokka Yosan' (The Budget of the Unitary Soviet State for 1938), *Kikaku* (Planning), 1(10): 1–42.

Takeoka, K. (1938), 'Sorenpo niokeru Kokumin Keizai Keikaku no Sakusei oyobi Un'ei nitsuite' (On the Operation and Preparation of the Economic Plan in Soviet Union), *Kikaku* (Planning), 1(5): 25–47; 1(6): 47–86.

Teranishi, J. (1982), *Nihon no Keizai Hatten to Kin'yu* (Finance and the Economic Development of Japan), Iwanami Shoten, Tokyo.

Toyo Keizai Shinposha (1991), *Kanketsu: Showa Kokusei Soran* (Historica Statistics of the Showa Era), Toyo Keizai Shinposha, Tokyo

Umemura, M. *et al.* (1988), *Rodoryoku* (Manpower), Toyo Keizai Shinposha, Tokyo.

Yamazawa, I., and Yamamoto, Y. (1979), *Boeki to Kokusai Shushi* (Foreign Trade and the Balance of Payments), Toyo Keizai Shinposha, Tokyo.

Yoshikawa, H., and Okazaki, T. (1992). 'Sengo Inflation to Dodge Line' (Post-war Hyperinflation and the Dodge Plan), *Business Review*, 39(2): 15–25.

14

Equality–Efficiency Trade-offs: Japanese Perceptions and Choices

RONALD DORE

1. INTRODUCTION

I once met a Sri Lankan engineer, who had been abroad—for six months in Japan—for the first time in his life. He found the experience astonishing, coming, as he did, from a society that had had a British-type class system (in the form of rigid officer–men distinctions in army, civil service, railways, port authorities, and eventually state steel, cement, and ceramics companies) grafted on to a traditional caste hierarchy. Until he lived in Japan he had not imagined that such an egalitarian society could exist.

Such evaluations have been fed back to Japan, and nowadays it has become common for patriotic Japanese businessmen, explaining the virtues of their own system, to claim that Japan is the 'most socialist society in the world'. ('Socialism' is not, as in America, treated as a synonym of once-menacing 'communism'.) A Japanese economist more than a decade ago wrote an article claiming that Japan's was the best *real* welfare state in existence (Nakagawa 1979).

This chapter asks: how far *is* Japan (relative to other industrial societies) egalitarian, and in what sense? Given widespread assumptions of a trade-off between equality (of wealth and also of power) and efficiency, does Japan achieve/enjoy/ suffer the degree of equality it has at the cost of sacrificing some potential efficiency? (Please note: we are talking about efficiency and *equality*, not *equity*, a word sometimes used in this context. 'Equality' is a fairly clear concept; 'equity' depends entirely on the subjective criteria of justice the user of the word adheres to.)

2. THE CORPORATION

Certainly, if one looks at the structure of major business and public organizations in Japan, there are some obvious reasons for calling Japan a relatively egalitarian society. Salary differentials are compressed, compared with other societies. The salary of an Iacocca is a three-figure multiple of a

Chrysler shop-floor worker's; in Toyota or Nissan the ratio is not far into two figures.[1]

A 'true believer' economist would presumably conclude that the difference is the result of inefficiency, deriving from market imperfections, on the Japanese side. Iacocca's talents are clearly a scarce resource. While not being quite a perfect market, America's labour market functions reasonably well, as Iacocca's own job mobility attests. Iacocca, being a rational income-maximizer, will offer his talents to the highest bidder. And the boards of companies (being devoted and rational agents of their shareholder principals) will bid only up to the point at which the marginal increment in profits likely to be achieved by the arrival of Iacocca is equal to his salary. Of course, there is always the danger of some *ex ante* misestimation of the marginal productivity of Iacocca, and you cleverly take care of that by making a part—even a large part—of his rewards contingent and *ex post* in the form of profit-related bonuses. (Which also has what is known as an 'incentive effect', keeping this income-maximizing instinct of his always well-honed, and so making sure that what's good for Iacocca is good for Chrysler.) Thus, Iacocca's talents are allocated to that niche in which they can maximize their contribution to the global welfare. That is what 'efficiency' means. All is for the best in the best of all possible worlds.

So what gives with these funny Japanese? The answer is simple. They have got these segmented labour markets—lifetime commitment and all that. It's not just that the labour market for executive talent is imperfect: over large areas of the economy it just does not exist. The eighty-odd head-hunting firms in Tokyo do nearly all their business enticing Japanese working for one American firm to go and work for another, occasionally topping up the supply of sellers in their market by recruiting a few drop-outs or adventurous dissidents from major Japanese firms. So there you are. If you don't have properly functioning markets, of course you are bound to have extreme price distortions. And if you have price distortions, you are bound to have a misallocation of resources—i.e. inefficiency.

Let us leave cloud-cuckoo-land for the moment and think of some of the organizational and cultural differences which explain? are correlated with? this Japanese–American difference in executive compensation.

1. The CEO (*shacho*) slot in a Japanese company (or at least, one that has gone through that second-generation process which turns a founder-managed family firm into a bureaucracy) is at the top of a planned hierarchy of incremental seniority-constrained salary scales. The MD will have got where he is by climbing those scales. Those scales represent conceptions of justice. You can lengthen the ladder by stretching it, but not by suddenly adding an extension for a detached top rung.

2. The CEO will probably have been recognized as having high potential at an early stage of his career. He will probably have climbed up those scales at a rate matched by only a few of his contemporaries. But the odds

are that there *are* a few of his contemporaries who have kept him company, and that the choice of him rather than one of those other few to head the company for the standard five to ten years was a marginal one. It will probably be the general opinion that two or three others of his contemporaries could have done the job just as well, or almost as well. This knowledge, on the part of CEOs, acts as a useful curb on both greed and megalomania.

3. Ask senior Japanese managers whether it matters *who* the CEO is. They will almost certainly answer: yes. Ask them why, and the answer is not likely to be in terms of the ability to take wise decisions on crucial matters—decisiveness, ruthlessness, quickness of understanding, and the intellectual capacity to encompass simultaneously the interaction of a wide range of variables. It is much more likely to be about leadership, about creating the atmosphere within the firm that ensures that all employees work as hard and as conscientiously and as co-operatively as possible so that *all* the decentralized decision-producing structures of the firm produce the best decisions.

4. Ask an American company president if he attaches great importance to maximizing his income and perks, and he will probably say: frankly, yes. Ask a Japanese CEO, and he will probably be embarrassed and consider the question in poor taste. There is a difference in the norms of the two societies concerning the acceptability and worthiness of different kinds of motives. Perhaps there is greater difference in the norms than in actual motivations; people in both societies are probably marginal hypocrites, and Japanese businessmen are perhaps *slightly* more animated by personal greed than they are willing to acknowledge, whereas Americans are perhaps *slightly* more animated by an altruistic sense of obligation to their firm, by loyalty, than they are willing to acknowledge. (Though go to a convention of IBM managers, and reputedly it's the Japanese type of hypocrisy you find.) In any case, if you *are* claiming to be less interested in your own material rewards than in selfless service to your company, the best way of validating that claim is not to have too much in the way of material rewards.

All of that strikes me as a good deal more illuminating as an explanation of the difference in intra-corporation income spans than 'imperfections in the labour market'.

3. IMPLICATIONS FOR PERFORMANCE

And what about the implications of those two alternative explanations for firm performance? It is reasonable to conclude that the features of Japanese firms outlined above lead, in comparison with American firms, to:

- greater stability and predictability in the reward system and less interpersonal friction arising therefrom;
- more resources available for investment, since less has to be spent on the direct motivation of effort;
- more conscientious, hard work, coming both from the sense of a long-term commitment to the firm and identification with its fortunes, and from the fact that, for any given level of 'natural talent', the only way to maximize personal rewards—by a more rapid than average climb up the ladder—is by gaining a reputation for conscientious hard work;
- and also a reputation for co-operative behaviour (sharing of information, shared problem-solving, willingness to share responsibility, etc.)—all of which is in any case promoted by the minimization of occasions for personal rivalry and of the friction that can be generated by individual bargaining over personal emoluments when their discretionary nature is not constrained by the existence of prescribed incremental scales.

The imperfections in the labour market that a neoclassical economist is likely to be concerned about are those that lead to allocative inefficiency. The features listed above may be thought to lead to greater technical efficiency, productive efficiency, X-efficiency; call it what you will. The relative performance of Japanese and American firms in world markets over the last ten years *might* suggest that the latter outweigh the former.[2]

Our 'true believer' economist, of course, is likely to reject any such suggestion, and to claim that the explanation of that difference in performance is the cheap labour of subcontractors, or strategic targeting under the aegis of MITI, or the way big companies can get away with cheap capital and treating their shareholders with contempt, or the way the *keiretsu* flout all the principles of competition policy, or all those other factors that tilt the playing field so decisively against American firms. Who knows? He may have a point. A single factor, such as the effects of organizational structure on incentives and patterns of co-operation, is unlikely to be the sole explanation of anything. But it would be astonishing if it were not an important part of the explanation of the superior performance of Japanese large corporations.

So I would conclude, on this matter of the intra-corporate dispersion of rewards, that there is no equality–efficiency trade-off—though one probably has to add the qualifier: 'over the range of degrees of equality represented by the United States and Japan'. Outside that range the story might change. The highly egalitarian Mondragon co-operatives are still roughly within that range; they still allow a 7 : 1 income span. Firms with absolute equality of rewards seem not, anywhere, to have lasted for long.

4. OTHER DIMENSIONS OF EQUALITY/INEQUALITY

Before we leave corporations, and for future reference, let us note two other dimensions of their reward structure.

First, compared with countries having something closer to a 'hire and fire' labour market, there is much greater equality of job security in Japan. It is normal in capitalist countries for senior managers to be less likely than other workers to suffer summary dismissal—or at least to have the prospect of a golden handshake if it happens. In Japan, too, senior managers are less likely to be pushed into accepting 'voluntary' retirement than senior blue-collar workers, but the difference in treatment is much less.

Secondly, there are symbolic counterparts to the compression of salary structures and greater uniformity of job security in a Japanese firm—everybody wearing the same uniform, using the same canteens and recreation facilities, etc. These are clearly intended to enhance the sense of 'first-class citizen' membership in the firm on the part of the lower and lowest-paid ranks, thereby enhancing their work motivation (what one might call 'membership motivation', as opposed to the motivation derived from individualistic contracts). Salary structures are clearly consciously constrained by the same considerations.

5. THE WIDER SOCIETY

But of course, the left-wing critic of Japanese society will discount the significance of what happens within large corporations as having little relevance to questions of overall equality in Japanese society—a mere matter, he will say, of distribution within a privileged élite. Japan is a dual society. 'As everyone knows, the lifetime employment system only applies to a quarter, or at most a third, of the population.'

Overall measures of income equality, such as Gini coefficients using tax or household income survey data, show Japan to be a society with a much more even distribution of income than the United States or France, though not quite as egalitarian as Sweden (the Gini for pre-tax household income, for instance, falling from 0.267 in 1970 to 0.260 in 1980 and then rising to 0.289 in 1990[3]). Summary figures have notorious pitfalls, but that approximate 'placing' of Japan seems right. More interesting, however, are some of the constituent factors that go into the determination of these overall spreads. The following points are of most interest.

1. 'Dual society' is a mistaken perception. There is not dualism but rather a spectrum, clear enough in salary terms (the gradation in pay for nominally identical skills, though not necessarily identical marginal productivities, by size of firm) and paralleled by a similar gradation in job security.

2. The dispersion of pre-tax labour incomes in Japan (top and bottom

decile as a percentage of the median) approximated, at the beginning of the decade, very closely to the dispersion of, for example, British labour incomes. Lesser, (though growing) inter-size-class differentials in Britain are compensated for by greater inter-occupational differentials. During the 1980s the dispersion grew in both countries—though by much less in Japan than in Britain (see Table 1).

TABLE 1   Wage Dispersion: All Industries: Full-Time Adult Males

	Japan		UK	
	1982	1990	1982	1990
Bottom decile	61.4	60.8	64.5	57.3
Median	100	100	100	100
Top decile	165.8	172.7	168.1	182.2

Source: Department of Employment, *New Earnings Survey,* vol. A of respective years; Rodosho, *Rodo tokei nempo* (Labour Statistics Yearbook), 1982: table 90; 1990: table 101.

3. Post-tax labour incomes show an even closer compression in Japan—more so than in Britain, for example—since income taxation rates are a good deal more progressive at medium to high levels.

4. Moving from labour incomes to the wage share, one has to think in separate terms about (although one cannot easily find the data needed to separate) the large-scale corporate sector and the owner-managed small-firm sector. How valueadded gets distributed in that latter, middle to lower part of the 'spectrum' as between proprietor's profits and workers' wages is hard to determine precisely. Over a large segment of the traditional industries—textiles, ceramics, etc.—owners' and workers' life-styles seem not very different. On the other hand, there seem to be quite large numbers of small-business proprietors in commerce and in more modern branches of manufacture who have a much larger income (also are much less subject to tax) than the presidents of large corporations.

5. The overall declining wage share over the last fifteen years[4] has been accompanied by a rise in investment; it is not clear that there has been a significant increase in the proportion of unearned income in total household income.

6. Except for—until early 1990—capital gains. Manifestly, whatever has happened to *income* distribution, the distribution of *wealth* has become vastly more skewed in recent years, as a result of the bubble—the appreciation of stock market and real estate assets, which continued well into September 1992 was still in the process of being corrected. For subjective *perceptions*, this inequality—especially as it results in an inequality of access to owner-housing, which affects the salaried middle-class as much as blue-collar

workers—is of the greatest importance. It is thought by some that a concern for the social-stability effects of the growth in inequality, as well as the animosity of (low)-salaried officials towards *nouveau riche* speculators, may well be one of the reasons why, despite all the pressure from financial circles, the nation's economic managers have stood by and watched the bankruptcies multiply as falling stock and land prices eroded paper reserves—to the point, indeed, at which the stability of the whole banking system was threatened.

Is there anything to be said about these aspects of income and wealth distribution in relation to 'efficiency'? Here we enter a field in which ideology dominates over empirical evidence. A few empirical observations are, however, in order.

First, the extent to which a rate of income tax progression that is high by international standards acts to blunt incentives, is a subject hardly ever discussed in Japan. Japan may have a few Laffers, or even conscious Laffer disciples, but they hardly get a hearing. The perennially discussed tax question is the discrepancy in taxation rates and the incidence of evasion between salaried workers on the one hand and business-proprietors, self-employed professionals (especially doctors, who enjoy a special dispensation), and farmers on the other.

Secondly, neither poverty, nor the contrast between poverty and riches is at the heart of political debate in Japan. Socialist members of the Diet can get far more excited about sending minesweepers to the Gulf than about the rate of income tax progression. The *ressentiment* that plays such a large part in the politics of many capitalist nations is not of such volume as to affect the stability of the ruling party. And stability and predictability, it might be said, provide an 'efficient' business environment.

6. EQUALITY AND HIERARCHY

'Precisely!' our left-wing critic will say. Your point about *ressentiment* gives the game away. False consciousness! It is not because Japan is a particularly egalitarian society that income distribution is not at the heart of political controversy: it is because egalitarian*ism* is so weak; because the lower orders in Japan are so deferential, because they are so willing to accept hierarchy as part of the order of nature.

There is a good book to be written, sorting out the complexities of this argument. Let me isolate certain important strands.

Hierarchy is particularly respected in Japan *within* organizations. Compared with other societies, there is a much greater difference in the degree of deference accorded by juniors to seniors within the same grade, than in the degree of deference shown by lower to higher grades in general. The two principles partly cancel out. A senior blue-collar worker is not so deferential to a junior manager. Also, the deference of lower to higher grades is affected by the highly institutionalized patterns of recruitment by educational qualification. In comparison with other societies, the deference of subordinates on a lower career track is more likely to be seen as justified by differences in intellectual competence—as those differences have been revealed in performance during schooling. They are less likely to be perceived as the result of social class privilege or luck.

Because hierarchy *is* so well respected, because deference is taken for granted and automatic, there is less need for authority-asserting behaviour. This means that hierarchy can coexist with something that may be seen as distinct from or as an aspect of equality: namely, fraternity—fellow-feeling, mutual respect for others, low levels of reticent reserve in personal inter-action. This is also fostered by the homogeneity of the educational system; the fact that there are few private schools with a distinctive social class colouring, transmitting for an élite a culture differentiated from that of the mass.

The social hierarchy in general is much less clearly delineated than hierarchies within organizations—see all those endless questionnaire surveys which 'prove' that 90 per cent of the Japanese are middle class. In fact, it is probably true that the defence that 'important people' receive (all those politicians addressed as *sensei*—'teacher') is greater than in most industrial societies. A delinquent train passenger who tries to overawe the conductor by letting him know that he is dealing with the managing director of a major company is less likely to be told: 'I don't care if you're the Queen of Sheba; you're sitting in the wrong seat'; but on the other hand, he is no more likely, in the end, to get away with his delinquency.

What this suggests is the following.

There is a difference between Japan and most other industrial societies in:

• the weighting attached to the three different dimensions of inequality:
  of income and wealth;
  of social prestige;
  of power;
• and the 'rates of exchange' as between one dimension and another.

What was said earlier about the motivations of company presidents suggests that social prestige is, for a Japanese, a relatively more important, and income and wealth a relatively less important, dimension of inequality than for an American. One can make the same deduction from the fact that important civil servants, who have higher prestige than important business men—and *a fortiori* than all but the most important politicians—nevertheless have considerably smaller incomes; and also from the fact that the administrative civil service remains a career that can attract the best and brightest from each year's crop of graduates. The low prestige of the stock market, where large sums of money are to be made, is another example. High income and great wealth are less easily and less automatically translated into high social prestige; the dimensions are more independent.

Similarly—think of the example of the train conductor—social prestige is less easily translated into power. Power adheres more specifically to formal organizational positions. Where no one dimension of inequality is overwhelmingly important, and where the dimensions are more independent, there is a greater possibility of more overall equality; more people have a chance of occupying a respected position in at least one dimension of some importance.

Also relevant to the assessment of overall social equality is the notion of a 'social minimum'. This applies both to the minimum income and to the 'dignity minimum', i.e. the minimum level of social respect, guaranteed to the handicapped, the unemployed, and the hard-to-employ. Non-insurance social welfare payments are not generous, but they still allow recipients a life-style that does not mark them off too obviously from their neighbours, and the means tests avoid humiliation. The fact that these welfare payments are made to less than 1 per cent of the population is to be attributed more to low demand, because of family support and stigma effects (perhaps more the loss of self-respect than of explicitly expressed neighbour respect), than to indifference and administrative toughness. When Japan awoke to the problems of disabled people in the UN Year of the Handicapped, it did a quite thorough job of adapting public places, and the famous social consensus took care of the respect aspect. Traditional words like *mekura* (a blind person) almost overnight became taboo; they were deemed to have disparaging connotations. Political correctness required one to say '*me no fujiyu na hito*' ('a person who has trouble with his eyes') instead. Japan's juvenile reformatory and prison system is well known for the fact that the balance between reform and punitive objectives is a good deal more heavily weighted towards the former than in most societies. For the despised second-class citizens of the former outcast *burakumin*, the volume of positive-discrimination expenditure on housing and education has reached sufficient proportions that many *burakumin* leaders associated with the Communist Party are in favour of its discontinuance; they argue that it serves only to keep alive a social segmentation that is on the verge of disappearance, and propagates an unhealthy clientelism (from which, it has to be said, their Socialist Party opponents gain the most benefit, since they control the bulk of the funds to be distributed).

There would seem to be efficiency gains rather than costs in all this; there are very few ghettos breeding sub-cultures hostile to the majority society, and crime rates and policing costs are relatively low.

7. EQUALITY AND EDUCATION

There is, however, something much more problematic—as far as possible equality–efficiency trade-offs are concerned—in the way Japan applies its concern for what one might call the 'dignity minimum' to the education system. One of the striking characteristics of Japanese education over the compulsory (6–15 years) span is the absence—as in the United States, also, but in very few countries in Europe—of any kind of ability-streaming, to use the British term, or ability-tracking to use the American. And the fact that so few of these schools' products fail to aquire a moderate competence in reading and writing a language with as difficult a script as Japanese is testimony to the fact that children of low ability *do* get a good deal of attention (and in extraordinary forty-pupil classes, too). Cummings, an American sufficiently struck by this egalitarian aspect of Japanese primary schooling to give 'equality' prominence in the title of his book (Cummings 1980), has described some of the methods by which this is achieved, particularly in the early primary years.

Does this not mean that the more able pupils are held back, with all the social loss that is entailed by failing to give the right stimulus to the nation's best brains at a crucial stage of their development? That may be so to some extent. But there are several mitigating considerations.

1. First of all, the story given above about state schools is not, in fact, the whole picture. Something over 2 per cent of each age group go to selective, 12–18 middle schools, 320 of them private and 60 state schools, mostly the 'experimental lab schools' of the Education Faculty of a state university. The institutionalization of these schools as important social selection mechanisms is fairly recent. Since the early 1980s it has been marked by the development of a flourishing market for information about the selection mechanisms of these schools. The following information comes from the 1990 edition of the most comprehensive guide.[5] Entrance to ten of these schools, which select almost entirely on grounds of academic ability, has required test scores two standard deviations above average (which in a normal distribution are achieved only by the top 1.25 per cent of performers), and another eighteen require scores more than one-and-a-half standard deviations above average. These twenty-eight schools in 1989 produced one-third of all the successful candidates in the entrance examination for the top university, Tokyo. Of the twenty high schools that produced the most Tokyo University entrants, fifteen were numbered among the twenty-eight. The accelerated and amplified education that these highly selected children receive—not to mention the acquisition of a sense of being marked out for an élite destiny at the age of 12—makes these schools a clearly important mechanism in the reproduction of corporate and governmental élites. Arguably, the 20,000 or so children who annually enter this track is quite enough to supply the nation's needs for those high-level scientific or

administrative talents that can be fostered only by intensive education at an early age.

2. As an outgrowth of the dominance of selective examinations in the educational system—selection for the élite at 11–12 years, as just described, selection for all the rest when they are allocated to ability-streamed high schools at the age of 15, and then, for 40 per cent of the age group, for ability-streamed universities at age 18—there is a wide range of supplementary education available in the private *juku*, to which a large number of pupils go. *Juku* serve multiple purposes. Some aim primarily to help less able children to keep up with the school curriculum. Others, however, more aptly deserving the usual translation 'cram schools', are devoted to honing the achievements of those of higher abilities. They themselves have competitive entrance examinations which serve to homogenize the intake and make the 'education' they purvey—directed towards success in a specific segment of the entrance examination range—more effective.

3. In any case, it is arguable that any loss in the intellectual development of more able children is amply compensated for by the social and economic gains derived from raising the *general* level of intellectual competence in the population, notably of those of below-average ability. It has become a cliché of recent discussions of Britain's education problems that a much greater dispersion of educational achievement levels in Britain than in either Germany or Japan is a major problem. In the international comparisons of achievement in maths, science, or social studies, British children score well enough at the top of the ability distribution; the big difference comes below the median. Many believe that it is here that one important source of the productivity problems of the Anglo-Saxon countries is to be found.

8. IN CONCLUSION

One should beware of overall characterizations of societies as 'egalitarian' or 'hierarchical' or 'authoritarian'. Nevertheless, there are many aspects of Japanese society that can be justly described as promoting more interpersonal equality than most other industrial societies.

Given the common impression that the pursuit of social and economic equality was a major cause for the economic inefficiency of the now collapsed East European regimes, given that Eastern Europe is now flooded with American advisers telling eager listeners that entrepreneurial dynamism requires the acceptance of much greater income inequalities, the question naturally arises: does Japan achieve the level of equality it has at the expense of efficiency? If efficiency is to be understood as having to do with the ratio of outputs to inputs, both being measured at market valuation, the answer would seem to be: 'overall, probably no'.

And why? It would take a book to answer that, but I will risk a short paragraph. The secret ingredient—the common source of both egalitarianism and efficiency—is 'togetherness'. Japanese are bothered about the dignity minimum accorded their fellow-Japanese because 'Japaneseness', and a sense of their membership in the nation, is still an important part of their self-identity. (In the same way, the British cared more about the dignity minimum of fellow-Britons at the time of the Beveridge report—in wartime, when a united nation was fighting first for survival and then for victory— than they do in a far more internationalized Britain at the end of the Thatcher era.) Within the Japanese firm, too, it is a valued sense of togetherness that keeps salary differentials relatively compressed.

And, if togetherness is at the root of egalitarianism, it also promotes efficiency—whether, within the firm, enhancing the level of co-operation between manufacturing and sales or, at the national level, enhancing the effectiveness of pre-competitive research clubs designed to put 'Japan' ahead in biotechnology.

Are these 'eternal' cultural characteristics? Probably not. Japan's competitors—but not those Japanese who are intellectually or physically ill-endowed—can look forward to the erosion of togetherness, just as has occurred in Britain, as Japanese society becomes progressively internationalized.

NOTES TO CHAPTER 14

1. CEO salary figures are hard to come by, except anecdotally. Remuneration of the average company director as a ratio of the average remuneration per employee is available, however, in the *Kigyo tokei nempo tokushu* (Special Annual Report on Incorporated Firms), published annually in the *Zaisei kinyu tokei geppo* (Financial Statistics Monthly Bulletin). They are not altogether reliable figures, because some firms count bonuses and others do not, and some do not include the salary an executive director gets by virtue of his functional job; but the figures are roughly indicative. For firms with more than 1,000 workers, the ratio was 2.72 in 1980 and even less in 1990.
2. A point that Lester Thurow makes well in his recent *Head to Head* (Thurow 1992).
3. Using household savings survey data. Quoted in Sako (1992).
4. From over 55% in 1975–7 to just under 54% in 1989, notwithstanding an increase in the proportion of wage/salary employees in the labour force from 70 to 76%. If the two indices are combined into a single index, the wage share had improved to 118 in the runaway inflation years of 1975–7 (1970 = 100), and thereafter steadily declined to 106 in 1989.
5. As summarized by Amano (1991: 1–4).

REFERENCES

Amano, Ikuo (1991), 'Shiken-shakai no shintenkai' (New Developments in the 'Examination Society'), in Amano Ikuo and Iwaki Hideo (eds.), *Hendo suru shakai no kyoiku-seido* (The Educational System of a Changing Society), Tokyo.

Cummings, W. W. (1980), *Education and Equality in Japan*, Princeton University Press, Princeton, NJ.

Nakagawa, Yatsuhiro (1979), 'Japan, the Welfare Superpower', *Journal of Japanese Studies*, 5(1): 5–51.

Sako, Mari (1992), 'Dualism in the Japanese Economy: Perceptions, Trends, and Mechanisms', draft paper for EC workshop, Paris, June.

Thurow, Lester (1992), *Head to Head*, William Morrow, New York.

INDEX